W9-BEQ-321

"Liberal secularist ideology rests on a mistake, and Nancy Pearcey, in her terrific new book, puts her finger right on it. In embracing abortion, euthanasia, homosexual conduct and relationships, transgenderism, and the like, liberal secularism conceives the body not as an aspect of the personal reality of the human being, fully sharing in his or her intrinsic worth and dignity, but rather as an extrinsic instrument of the mind or psyche or self—which is considered the true 'person.' This instrumentalization of the body underwrites liberal secularist ethics from top to bottom; yet, as Pearcey shows, it is philosophically as well as theologically untenable. The mental-spiritual and bodily aspects of the human person are a unity. The body truly is part of the personal reality of the human being and shares fully in his or her inherent dignity. From that, as Pearcey demonstrates, much follows for the ethics of life and death and sexuality and marriage."

Robert P. George, McCormick Professor of Jurisprudence, Princeton University

"Nancy Pearcey unmasks the far-reaching practical consequences of mind-body dualism better than anyone I have ever seen. This book is not only good reading for all well-informed Christians but it should be used as a textbook for applied philosophy. I heartily recommend it."

Jennifer Roback Morse, founder and president, The Ruth Institute

"Nancy Pearcey models on every page how to understand secular worldviews in order to engage them effectively in post-Christian America. *Love Thy Body* is a must-read book."

Rosaria Butterfield, former professor, Syracuse University; author, *The Secret Thoughts of an Unlikely Convert*

"Nancy Pearcey gets straight to the fundamental issue of our day: What makes humans valuable in the first place? How we answer will do nothing less than determine cultural norms on abortion, doctor-assisted suicide, and sexual ethics. For years, I've warned pro-lifers our primary problem is a destructive worldview that defines humans by function, not nature. If you want to engage the culture, you simply must get this book. Don't just read it. Master it."

Scott Klusendorf, president, Life Training Institute; author, *The Case for Life*

"The group of serious thinkers who speak so clearly and wisely of the application of Christian truth to contemporary society is unfortunately small. Nancy Pearcey is one of the very bright spots in that select group. Each of her books is a gem. *Love Thy Body* richly enhances the treasure box that is her collective work. And we all benefit. I heartily recommend it."

Glenn T. Stanton, director, Global Family Formation Studies, Focus on the Family

"Nancy Pearcey has once again gifted us with a book that will be of great service to many. Writing with both deep compassion and clear thinking, she helps us to better understand the worldview that lies behind the huge cultural shifts we have recently experienced in the West. This book will equip and inspire many. Pearcey is a wonderful guide."

Sam Allberry, The Gospel Coalition; author, *Is God Anti-Gay?*

"In this work Nancy Pearcey provides an astute but accessible analysis of the intellectual roots of the most important moral ills facing us today: abortion, euthanasia, sexual immorality, and redefining the family. Pearcey takes us beyond the 'thou shalt nots' to show why God's ways are best. Highly recommended!"

Richard Weikart, professor of history, California State University, Stanislaus; author, *The Death of Humanity: And the Case for Life* and *Hitler's Religion*

"Nancy Pearcey's characteristic clarity and careful scholarship take the reader through the history of our shifting perceptions on what it means to be human. She unpacks the competing worldviews that undergird central issues of human identity, such as euthanasia, abortion, the hook-up culture, and the like. With a philosopher's mind and the sensitivity of a teacher and parent, Pearcey's scholarship emerges holistically. *Love Thy Body* is highly readable, insightful, and informative."

Mary Poplin, professor of education, Claremont Graduate University; author, *Is Reality Secular? Testing the Assumptions of Four Global Worldviews*

"In an age in which moral discussion is increasingly a shouting match of slogans and monologues, Nancy Pearcey in *Love Thy Body* shares penetrating wisdom regarding the role that fundamentally different understandings of the nature of reality play in our cultural debates about the painful moral choices facing us regarding life and sexuality. This readable book is a treasure trove of critical insights."

Stanton L. Jones, former provost and professor of psychology,
Wheaton College; coauthor, *God's Design for Sex*

"Like her other monumental works, *Total Truth*, *Saving Leonardo*, and *Finding Truth*, Nancy Pearcey's *Love Thy Body* is another brilliant and realistic cultural analysis of the inherent problems and practical consequences that flow from secularization. Pearcey helps us understand not only the current application of secularization to our personhood, family, and society, but also its devastating implications in view of who we are and where we live."

Paul R. Shockley, professor of Bible and Theology,
College of Biblical Studies–Houston

"Future leaders must have answers about the value and worth of every individual life. Nancy Pearcey once again drills down to truth. *Love Thy Body* brings clarity and understanding to the multitude of complex and confusing views in discussions about love and sexuality. This book is essential reading for all!"

Becky Norton Dunlop, Ronald Reagan Distinguished Fellow,
The Heritage Foundation

"Pearcey invites us into Scripture to celebrate the body as a good gift from God. She refutes the idea that Christianity is 'anti-sex' and 'anti-body' with a biblical understanding of the significance of the human being and a high view of the body as God's creation. In the end, only the gospel is actual romance."

Kelly Monroe Kullberg, founder, The Veritas Forum;
author, *Finding God Beyond Harvard*

"Nancy Pearcey's *Love Thy Body* is what you would expect from her—timely, relevant, insightful, superbly documented, and thoroughly Christian. She does her usual great job of critiquing cultural trends through the lens of a Christian worldview. I highly recommend it."

Scott B. Rae, dean of faculty and professor of Christian ethics,
Talbot School of Theology, Biola University

"Nancy has done it again! With her keen mind, depth of analysis, and clear, concise writing, she has provided the best book on the postmodern sexual ideology. She exposes the foundation of this 'new' sexuality and shows how to set forth the beautiful, life-giving truth of human sexuality built into creation. This book is a must-read for any who would engage in the fight to restore the glory and dignity of 'male and female created in God's own image.'"

Darrow L. Miller, cofounder of Disciple Nations Alliance; author, *Nurturing the Nations*

LOVE THY BODY

Answering Hard Questions about Life and Sexuality

NANCY R. PEARCEY

BakerBooks
a division of Baker Publishing Group
Grand Rapids, Michigan

© 2018 by Nancy R. Pearcey

Published by Baker Books
a division of Baker Publishing Group
PO Box 6287, Grand Rapids, MI 49516-6287
www.bakerbooks.com

Printed in the United States of America

All rights reserved. No part of this publication may be reproduced, stored in a retrieval system, or transmitted in any form or by any means—for example, electronic, photocopy, recording—without the prior written permission of the publisher. The only exception is brief quotations in printed reviews.

Library of Congress Cataloging-in-Publication Data
Names: Pearcey, Nancy, author.
Title: Love thy body : answering hard questions about life and sexuality / Nancy Pearcey.
Description: Grand Rapids : Baker Books, 2018. | Includes bibliographical references and index.
Identifiers: LCCN 2017028374 | ISBN 9780801075728 (cloth)
Subjects: LCSH: Human body—Religious aspects—Christianity. | Sex—Religious aspects—Christianity.
Classification: LCC BT741.3 .P43 2018 | DDC 241/.697—dc23
LC record available at https://lccn.loc.gov/2017028374

Unless otherwise indicated, Scripture quotations are from the Holy Bible, New International Version®. NIV®. Copyright © 1973, 1978, 1984, 2011 by Biblica, Inc.™ Used by permission of Zondervan. All rights reserved worldwide. www.zondervan.com

Scripture quotations labeled ESV are from The Holy Bible, English Standard Version® (ESV®), copyright © 2001 by Crossway, a publishing ministry of Good News Publishers. Used by permission. All rights reserved. ESV Text Edition: 2011

Scripture quotations labeled EXB are from The Expanded Bible. Copyright ©2011 by Thomas Nelson. Used by permission. All rights reserved.

Scripture quotations labeled HCSB are from the Holman Christian Standard Bible®, copyright © 1999, 2000, 2002, 2003, 2009 by Holman Bible Publishers. Used by permission. Holman Christian Standard Bible®, Holman CSB®, and HCSB® are federally registered trademarks of Holman Bible Publishers.

Scripture quotations labeled ISV are from *The Holy Bible: International Standard Version*. Release 2.0, Build 2015.02.09. Copyright © 1995–2014 by ISV Foundation. All rights reserved internationally. Used by permission of Davidson Press, LLC.

Scripture quotations labeled KJV are from the King James Version of the Bible.

Scripture quotations labeled NASB are from the New American Standard Bible®, copyright © 1960, 1962, 1963, 1968, 1971, 1972, 1973, 1975, 1977, 1995 by The Lockman Foundation. Used by permission. (www.Lockman.org)

Scripture quotations labeled NLT are from the *Holy Bible*, New Living Translation, copyright © 1996, 2004, 2015 by Tyndale House Foundation. Used by permission of Tyndale House Publishers, Inc., Carol Stream, Illinois 60188. All rights reserved.

Some names and details have been changed to protect the privacy of the individuals involved.

Published in cooperation with The Steve Laube Agency (www.stevelaube.com).

18 19 20 21 22 23 24 7 6 5 4 3

In keeping with biblical principles of creation stewardship, Baker Publishing Group advocates the responsible use of our natural resources. As a member of the Green Press Initiative, our company uses recycled paper when possible. The text paper of this book is composed in part of post-consumer waste.

green press INITIATIVE

Contents

Fate, not God, has given us this flesh.
We have absolute claim to our bodies
and may do with them as we see fit.

Camille Paglia, *Vamps & Tramps*

Christians should confess their faith in the natural order
as the good creation of God. . . .
We must cherish nature,
we must defer to its immanent laws,
and we must plan our activities in cooperation with them.

Oliver O'Donovan, *Begotten or Made?*

Introduction

A Guide to the Wasteland

Human life and sexuality have become *the* watershed moral issues of our age. Every day, the twenty-four-hour news cycle chronicles the advance of a secular moral revolution in areas such as sexuality, abortion, assisted suicide, homosexuality, and transgenderism. The new secular orthodoxy is being imposed through virtually all the major social institutions: academia, media, public schools, Hollywood, private corporations, and the law.

It is easy to get caught up in the latest controversy or breaking news story. But current events are merely surface effects, like waves on the ocean. The real action happens below the surface, at the level of worldviews. These are like the tectonic plates whose movements *cause* the roiling surface waves. In *Love Thy Body*, we will move beyond click-bait headlines and trendy slogans to uncover the worldview that drives the secular ethic. By learning the core principles of this worldview, you will be able to engage intelligently and compassionately on all of today's most controversial moral challenges.

As a former agnostic, I give an insider's road map to postmodern moral theories, showing how they devalue the human being and destroy human rights.

Dissenters to the politically correct orthodoxy are accused of intolerance and discrimination, branded as bigots and misogynists, and targeted for campaigns of shame and intimidation. Want proof? In its 2013 *Windsor* decision, the United States Supreme Court ruling struck down the Defense of Marriage Act (DOMA), a federal law recognizing that marriage is between one man and one woman. The majority opinion accused DOMA supporters of being motivated by "animus" (animosity, hostility, hatred). It claimed that their purpose was to "disparage," "injure," "degrade," "demean," "humiliate," and "harm" people in same-sex unions . . . to brand them as "unworthy," to "impose a disadvantage, a stigma" and to "deny them equal dignity." In short, the Court did not just say people who support man-woman marriage are mistaken. It denounced them as hostile, hateful, and mean-spirited.

Those who disagree with the prevailing secular ethos plead a right to religious liberty. But the chairman of the US Commission on Civil Rights wrote disdainfully that "the phrases 'religious liberty' and 'religious freedom' will stand for nothing except hypocrisy so long as they remain code words for discrimination, intolerance, racism, sexism, homophobia, Islamophobia, Christian supremacy or any other form of intolerance."[1] Notice that the phrase *religious liberty* is put in sneer quotes, as though it were an illegitimate claim instead of a foundational right in a free society.

The next stage will be to deny citizens their religious liberty—and it has already begun. Those who resist the secular moral revolution have lost jobs, businesses, and teaching positions. Others have been kicked out of graduate school programs, lost the right to be foster parents, been forced to shut down adoption centers, lost their status as campus organizations . . . and the list of oppression is likely to grow.[2]

The same politically correct orthodoxy is being aggressively promoted around the globe through the State Department, the United Nations, the European Union, private foundations, and the media. Wealthy nations are pushing poorer nations to change their laws on abortion and sexuality as a prerequisite for aid.[3] The sexual revolution is going global.

Co-Opted Churchgoers

Don't think churchgoers are immune. Many people who identify as religious or Christian are being co-opted by the secular worldview, often without realizing it. The numbers are disturbing:

Pornography: About two-thirds of Christian men watch pornography at least monthly, the same rate as men who do not claim to be Christian.[4] In one survey, 54 percent of pastors said they viewed porn within the past year.[5]

Cohabitation: A Gallup poll found that almost half (49 percent) of teens with religious backgrounds support living together before marriage.[6]

Divorce: Among adults who identify as Christians but rarely attend church, 60 percent have been divorced. Of those who attend church regularly, the number is 38 percent.[7]

Homosexuality and Transgenderism: These issues are dividing even conservative religious groups. In a 2014 Pew Research Center study, 51 percent of evangelical millennials said same-sex behavior is morally acceptable.[8]

Abortion: A LifeWay survey found that about 70 percent of women who had an abortion self-identify as Christians. And 43 percent said they attended a Christian church at least once a month or more at the time they aborted their baby.[9]

The problem is that many people treat morality as a list of rules. But in reality, every moral system rests on a worldview. In every decision we make, we are not just deciding what we want to do. We are expressing our view of the purpose of human life. In the words of theologian Stanley Hauerwas, a moral act "cannot be seen as just an isolated act, but involves fundamental options about the nature and significance of life itself."[10]

To be strategically effective, then, we must address what people believe "about the nature and significance of life itself." We must engage their worldview.

C. S. Lewis put it this way: "The Christian and the Materialist hold different beliefs about the universe. They can't both be right. The one who is wrong will act in a way which simply doesn't fit the real universe."[11] My goal in *Love Thy Body* is to show that a secular morality "doesn't fit the real universe."

True for You, Not for Me?

The first step is to recognize that secular morality rests on a deep division that runs through all of Western thought and culture—one that blows apart the connection between scientific and moral knowledge. In the past, most civilizations held that reality consists of both a natural order and a moral order, integrated into an overall unity. Therefore, our *knowledge* of reality was likewise thought to be a single, unified system of truth.

In the modern age, however, many people came to think that reliable knowledge is possible only of the natural order—of empirically testable scientific facts. What does that imply for moral truths? They cannot be stuffed into a test tube or studied under a microscope. Many people concluded that morality does not qualify as objective truth. It consists of merely personal feelings and preferences.

The unified concept of truth has been exploded, split into two separate domains.

Theologian Francis Schaeffer illustrated the division using the metaphor of two stories in a building. In the lower story is empirical science, which is held to be objectively true and testable. This is the realm of public truths—things that everyone is expected to accept, regardless of their private beliefs. The upper story is the realm of morality and theology, which are treated as private, subjective, and relative. This is where we hear people say, "That can be true for you but not true for me."[12]

The concept of truth has been divided

THEOLOGY, MORALITY
Private, Subjective, Relativistic

SCIENCE
Public, Objective, Valid for Everyone

When Schaeffer's books were first published, most people treated his two-story image as little more than an idiosyncratic metaphor for relativism. But years later, when I was studying what in the academic world is called the fact/value split, it struck me that *this* is what Schaeffer was talking about, although he did not use the phrase.[13] Do you see the parallels?

The fact/value split

VALUES
Private, Subjective, Relativistic

FACTS
Public, Objective, Valid for Everyone

I described the parallels in my earlier book *Total Truth*, and suddenly Schaeffer's two-story analysis became strikingly relevant to our own day. A leading Christian philosopher told me that he had read Schaeffer extensively, and, as a professor, he said, "I have taught about the dangers of the fact/value split all my life . . . but I never made the connection." By making the connection, *Total Truth* helped bring Schaeffer's ideas into fresh and fruitful conversation with secular thought.

A Fragmented Worldview

Still later I realized that the fact/value split is just the tip of the iceberg—that all of modern philosophy has divided into two major streams. One stream began with the scientific revolution. It gave rise to the Enlightenment tradition, composed of philosophers who claimed to build upon science. They proposed philosophies that treat the *fact* realm (lower story) as the primary reality—"isms" such as empiricism, rationalism, materialism, and naturalism.

As you may remember from high school English classes, however, there was a reaction against the Enlightenment called the Romantic movement. It was composed of thinkers who sought to keep alive the *value* realm (upper story). They focused on questions of justice, freedom, morals, and meaning. Thinkers in this tradition proposed "isms" such as idealism, Marxism, existentialism, and postmodernism.

Today these two traditions are loosely summarized under the headings of modernism versus postmodernism, and they remain at loggerheads. The split between them has grown so wide that one philosopher says it's almost as if Western thought has split into "two philosophical worlds." Another worries that "we have reached a point at which it is as if we're working in different subjects" and "shouting across the gulf."[14]

Modernists claim that the lower story is the primary or sole reality—facts and science. Postmodernists claim that the upper story is primary—that even facts and science are merely mental constructs.[15]

The split in Western thought

ROMANTIC TRADITION
Postmodernism

ENLIGHTENMENT TRADITION
Modernism

Because philosophy is so foundational, this divide affects every other subject area, including morality.[16] In moral questions, we are asking: What is the right way to treat people? Our answer depends on what we think people are—on what it means to be human. (Philosophers call this our anthropology.) The key to understanding all the controversial issues of our day is that the concept of the human being has likewise been fragmented into an upper and lower story. Secular thought today assumes a body/person split, with the body defined in the "fact" realm by empirical science (lower story) and the person defined in the "values" realm as the basis for rights (upper story). This dualism has created a fractured, fragmented view of the human being, in which the body is treated as separate from the authentic self.

A New Strategy

This two-story division equips us with a powerful new strategy for helping people see why a secular ethic fails, both personally and publicly. Chapter 1, "I Hate Me," surveys all the most salient issues, highlighting the two-level view of the human being that drives them all. Even if you wish to focus on a later topic, I recommend that you start by reading chapter 1 to become familiar with the overall strategy I will be applying throughout the rest of the book. (Because these are controversial issues, not all objections can be addressed in the text. Please check the endnotes for further discussion.)

Chapter 2, "The Joy of Death," asks how the body/person dualism undergirds secular arguments for abortion and infanticide. Chapter 3, "Dear Valued

Constituent," uncovers the devastating impact of the same dualism in arguments for euthanasia, as well as related issues such as embryonic stem cell research, animal rights, genetic engineering, and transhumanism. Chapter 4, "Schizoid Sex," exposes the lies of the hookup culture. Contrary to its claims to liberate the body, in reality it expresses disdain for the body. Chapter 5, "The Body Impolitic," uncovers how same-sex practice likewise demeans the body. Chapter 6, "Trans*gender*, Trans*reality*," asks how to help people who think their body is at odds with their true, authentic self. The final chapter, "The Goddess of Choice Is Dead," moves from the individual to the social realm: How is the body/person dualism destroying our most intimate relationships, especially marriage and family, leaving people lonely and isolated?

■ ■ ■ ■ ■

We live in a moral wasteland where human beings are desperately seeking answers to hard questions about life and sexuality. But there is hope. In the wasteland we can cultivate a garden. We can discover a reality-based morality that expresses a positive, life-affirming view of the human person—one that is more inspiring, more appealing, and more liberating than the secular worldview. To start learning how, turn to chapter 1.

1

I Hate Me

The Rise and Decline of the Human Body

Zoe seemed to have everything going for her. A brilliant, high-achieving homeschool student, she was offered a full ride by two Ivy League universities when she was only seventeen years old and a junior in high school.

Then, without any warning, Zoe ran away from home.

Frantic with fear and grief, her parents learned that she had been seduced by a twenty-two-year-old college senior—we'll call her Holly—who attended a nearby evangelical Christian university. They had met at a Christian homeschool organization where Holly was teaching. Because the age of consent in the state where they lived is eighteen, their relationship was illegal. Worried about a possible lawsuit, Holly persuaded Zoe to run away to another state with a lower age of consent.

Though Zoe's parents chose not to press charges, sexual assault laws that might have applied include statutory rape, enticement of a minor for sexual activity, abduction of a minor, and sexual assault of a child by a school staff person or a person who works or volunteers with children. (In the law, "child" means a minor.)

To garner sympathy (and get government benefits), Zoe claimed that her parents had kicked her out of the house. Many family friends believed her, with the result that her parents were cut off by friends in addition to the heartache of losing their daughter.

Within months of persuading Zoe to move with her across the country, Holly dropped her to engage in affairs with other women. Today Holly is completing her doctoral degree at a prestigious Ivy League university, studying gender and sexual orientation. Zoe is waiting on tables at a coffee shop—confused and depressed. A victim of the sexual revolution.[1]

In our day, issues of life and sexuality are not merely theoretical; they affect virtually everyone in a personal way. To respond effectively to today's secular moral revolution, we must dig down to the underlying worldview that drives it. In the introduction, we learned that the worldview supporting secular morality is a profoundly fragmenting dualism that separates body and person. If you get a handle on this two-story division, you will have the tools to uncover the deeply dehumanizing worldview at the heart of abortion, assisted suicide, homosexuality, transgenderism, and the sexual chaos of the hookup culture.

In this chapter, I map out the two-story worldview through an overview of the most salient moral issues. Then, in later chapters, I will unpack each one in greater detail and answer the most common objections. By contrast with the secular worldview, it will become clear that a biblical ethic affirms a full-orbed, wholistic view of the person that supports human rights and dignity.

Being Human Is Not Enough

The best way to grasp the body/person dichotomy is through an example. A few years ago, an article appeared by a British broadcaster named Miranda Sawyer, who described herself as a liberal feminist. In the article she said she had always been firmly pro-choice.

Until she became pregnant with her own baby.

Then she began to struggle. "I was calling the life inside me a baby because I wanted it. Yet if I hadn't, I would think of it just as a group of cells that it was OK to kill. . . . That seemed irrational to me. Maybe even immoral."[2] Babies in the womb don't qualify as human only if someone wants them.

Sawyer had run up against the wall of reality—and reality did not fit her ideology. So she began researching the subject, and even produced a documentary. Finally she reached her conclusion: "In the end, I have to agree that life begins at conception. So yes, abortion is ending that life." Then she added, "But perhaps the fact of life isn't what is important. It's whether that life has grown enough . . . to start becoming a person."[3]

What has happened here to the concept of the human being? It has been torn in two. If a baby is *human life* from conception but not a *person* until some later time, then clearly these are two different things.

This is a radically fragmented, fractured, dualistic view of the human being.

In ordinary conversation, of course, we use the phrase *human being* to mean the same thing as *person*. The two terms were ripped apart by the Supreme Court in its 1973 *Roe v. Wade* abortion decision, which ruled that even though the baby in the womb is human, it is not a person under the Fourteenth Amendment.

Thus we have a new category of individual: the human non-person.

To picture this modern dualism, we can apply Schaeffer's image of two stories in a building (see introduction). In the early stages the fetus is in the lower story. Here it is acknowledged to be human from conception, in the sense that it is a biological organism knowable by the empirical methods of science. But it is not thought to have any moral standing, nor does it warrant legal protection. Later, at some undefined point in time, it jumps into the upper story and becomes a person, typically defined in terms of a certain level of cognitive functioning, consciousness, and self-awareness. Only then does it attain moral and legal standing.

This is called personhood theory, and it is an outworking of the fact/value split: To be biologically human is a scientific *fact*. But to be a person is an ethical concept, defined by what we *value*.

Abortion rests on personhood theory

PERSON

Has Moral and Legal Standing

BODY

An Expendable Biological Organism

The implication of this two-story view is that simply being human is not enough to qualify for rights. Recall Sawyer's words: "The *fact of life* isn't what is important." Human life in itself is thought to have no value, and what we do with it has no moral significance.

Of course, an individual making a decision about abortion may not be consciously thinking about these philosophical implications. Some people have told me they can support abortion and still feel that the baby has value. But an action can have a logic of its own, whether we intend it or not.

If you favor abortion, you are implicitly saying that in the early stages of life, an unborn baby has so little value that it can be killed for any reason—or no reason—without any moral consequence. Whatever your feelings, *that* is a very low view of life. Then, by sheer logic, you must say that at some later time the baby becomes a person, at which point it acquires such high value that killing it would be a crime.

The implication is that as long as the pre-born child is deemed to be human but not a person, it is just a disposable piece of matter—a natural resource like timber or corn. It can be used for research and experiments, tinkered with genetically, harvested for organs, and then disposed of with the other medical waste.

The assumption at the heart of abortion, then, is personhood theory, with its two-tiered view of the human being—one that sees no value in the living human body but places all our worth in the mind or consciousness.[4]

Personhood theory thus presumes a very low view of the human body, which ultimately dehumanizes all of us. For if our bodies do not have inherent value, then a key part of our identity is devalued. What we will discover is that this same body/person dichotomy, with its denigration of the body, is the unspoken assumption driving secular views on euthanasia, sexuality, homosexuality, transgenderism, and a host of related ethical issues.

"Reading" Nature

To understand this two-story dualism, we need to ask where it came from and how it developed. To begin with, what does the word *dualism* mean? On the one hand, it is simply the claim that reality consists of two kinds of substances instead of only one. In that traditional sense, Christianity is dualistic because it holds that there exists both body and soul, matter and spirit. These two substances causally interact with one another, but neither one can be reduced to the other. The reality of the spiritual realm is important to defend today because the academic world is dominated by the philosophy of materialism (the claim that nothing exists beyond the material world).[5]

Yet Christianity holds that body and soul together form an integrated unity—that the human being is an embodied soul (as we will see in more detail at the end of this chapter). By contrast, personhood theory entails a two-level dualism that sets the body *against* the person, as though they were two separate things merely stuck together. As a result, it demeans the body as extrinsic to the person—something inferior that can be used for purely pragmatic purposes.

How did such a negative view of the body develop?

Because the body is part of nature, the answer lies in the way people have thought about nature. For centuries, Western culture was permeated by a Christian heritage that regards nature as God's handiwork, reflecting his purposes. As the church fathers put it, God's revelation comes to us in "two books"—the book of God's Word (the Bible) and the book of God's world (creation).[6] Nature is an expression of God's purposes and a revelation of his character. The psalmist writes, "The heavens declare the glory of God; the skies proclaim the work of his hands" (Ps. 19:1). In Romans, the apostle Paul says creation gives evidence for God: "Since the creation of the world God's invisible qualities—his eternal power and divine nature—have been clearly seen, being understood from what has been made" (Rom. 1:20).

In other words, even though the world is fallen and broken by sin, it still speaks of its Creator. We can "read" signs of God's existence and purposes in creation. This is called a teleological view of nature, from the Greek word *telos*, which means purpose or goal. It is evident that living things are structured for a purpose: Eyes are for seeing, ears are for hearing, fins are for swimming, and wings are for flying. Each part of an organ is exquisitely adapted to the others, and all interact in a coordinated, goal-directed fashion to achieve the purpose of the whole. This kind of integrated structure is the hallmark of design—plan, will, intention.

Even today, biologists cannot avoid the language of teleology, though they often substitute phrases like "good engineering design."[7] Scientists say an eye is a good eye when it is fulfilling its purpose. A wing is a good wing when it is functioning the way it was intended.

Yet the most impressive examples of engineering have become visible only with the invention of the electron microscope. Each of the nanomachines within the cell (such as proteins) has its own distinctive function. Researchers conduct experiments they describe as "reverse engineering," as though they had a gadget in hand and were trying to reconstruct the process by which it was designed.

The smoking gun for design, however, is in the cell's nucleus—its command and control center. The DNA molecule stores an immense amount of information. Geneticists talk about DNA as a "database" that stores "libraries" of genetic information. They analyze the way RNA "translates" the four-letter language of the nucleotides into the twenty-letter language of proteins. The search for the origin of life has been reframed as the search for the origin of biological information.

And information implies the existence of a mind—an agent capable of intention, will, plan, or purpose. The latest scientific evidence suggests that the New Testament has it right: "In the beginning was the Word" (John 1:1). In the original Greek, the term translated as "Word" is *logos*, which also means reason, intelligence, or information.

Scientists have discovered evidence for teleology not only in living things, however, but also in the physical universe. They have found that its fundamental physical constants are exquisitely coordinated to support life. Harvard astrophysicist Howard Smith writes, "The laws of the universe include fundamental numbers like the strengths of the four forces, the speed of light, Planck's constant, the masses of electrons or protons, and others. . . . If those values were slightly different, even by a few percent, we would not be here. . . . Life, much less intelligent life, could not exist."

This is called the fine-tuning problem, and what it means is that even the physical world exhibits the hallmark of design. The subtitle of Smith's article states, "Almost in spite of themselves, scientists are driven to a teleological view of the cosmos."[8]

How to Be Human

If nature is teleological, and the human body is part of nature, then it is likewise teleological. It has a built-in purpose, part of which is expressed as the moral law. We are morally obligated to treat people in a way that helps them fulfill their purpose. This explains why biblical morality is not arbitrary. Morality is the guidebook to fulfilling God's original purpose for humanity, the instruction manual for becoming the kind of person God intends us to be, the road map for reaching the human *telos*. This is sometimes called natural law ethics because it tells us how to fulfill our true nature, how to become fully human.

In this purpose-driven view, there is no dichotomy between body and person. The two together form an integrated psycho-physical unity. We respect and honor our bodies as part of the revelation of God's purpose for our lives. It is part of the created order that is "declaring the glory of God."

The implication is that the physical structure of our bodies reveals clues to our personal identity. The way our bodies function provides rational grounds for our moral decisions. That's why, as we will see, a Christian ethic always takes into account the facts of biology, whether addressing abortion (the scientific facts about when life begins) or sexuality (the facts about sexual differentiation and reproduction). A Christian ethic respects the teleology of nature and the body.

Matter without Meaning

What changed this purpose-driven view of nature? How did the West lose its positive view of the body?

In the modern age, the most important turning point was Charles Darwin's theory of evolution, published in 1859. (There were others before him, as we will see, but Darwin has the greatest impact today.) Darwin could not deny that nature appears to be designed. But having embraced the philosophy of materialism, he wanted to reduce that appearance to an illusion. He hoped to show that although living structures *seem* to be teleological, in reality they are the result of blind, undirected forces. Although they *seem* to be products of intention (will, plan, intelligence), in reality they are products of a purposeless material process. The two main elements in his theory—random variations and natural selection—were both proposed expressly to eliminate plan or purpose.

As historian Jacques Barzun notes, "This denial of purpose is Darwin's distinctive contention."[9] Zoologist Richard Dawkins agrees: "Natural selection, the blind, unconscious automatic process which Darwin discovered . . . has no purpose in mind."[10]

On a Richter scale of thinkers, Darwin's theory caused an earthquake that ranks well above 9.0. And its seismic waves were not limited to science. It also caused severe aftershocks in moral thought. For if nature was not the handiwork of God—if it no longer bore signs of God's good purposes—then it no longer provided a basis for moral truths. It was just a machine, churning along by blind, material forces. Catholic philosopher Charles Taylor explains, "The cosmos is no longer seen as the embodiment of meaningful order which can define the good for us."[11]

The next step in the logic is crucial: If nature does not reveal *God's* will, then it is a morally neutral realm where humans may impose *their* will. There is nothing in nature that humans are morally obligated to respect. Nature becomes the realm of value-neutral facts, available to serve whatever values humans may choose.

And because the human body is part of nature, it too is demoted to the level of an amoral mechanism, subject to the will of the autonomous self. If the body has no intrinsic purpose, built in by God, then all that matters are human purposes. The body is reduced to a clump of matter—a collection of atoms and molecules, not essentially different from any other chance configuration of matter. It is raw material to be manipulated and controlled to serve the human agenda, like any other natural resource.[12]

We tend to think of materialism as a philosophy that places high value on the material world, because it claims that matter is all that exists. Yet, ironically, in reality it places a low value on the material world as purely particles in motion with no higher purpose or meaning.

Disposable Humans

Do you see how this explains the logic undergirding abortion? In the past, abortion advocates typically denied that a pre-born baby is human: *It's just a blob of tissue—a potential life—a collection of cells*. As a consequence, many pro-life arguments focused on proving that a fetus is human life. Today, however, due to advances in genetics and DNA, virtually all professional bioethicists agree that life begins at conception. An embryo has a full set of chromosomes and DNA. It is a complete and integral individual capable of internally directed development in a seamless continuum from fertilization.

Why isn't this taken as conclusive evidence that abortion is morally wrong? Because according to personhood theory, when talking about the human as a biological organism we are in the realm of science (the lower story) where life has been reduced to a mere mechanism with no intrinsic purpose or dignity. It has been devalued to raw material that may be deployed for whatever pragmatic benefits we get from it. As a result, even bioethicists who recognize the fetus as biologically human do not necessarily conclude it has moral standing or should be legally protected. Instead the fetus is treated as just a piece of matter, which can be used for research or experiments, then tossed out with the other medical garbage.

In the two-story worldview, simply being a member of the human race is not enough to qualify for personhood. The baby in the womb has to *earn* the status of personhood by achieving a certain level of cognitive functioning—the capacity for consciousness, self-awareness, autonomy, and so on.

Personhood theory is the assumption behind most common arguments for abortion. For example, when John Kerry was running for US president in 2004, he surprised the public by agreeing that "life begins at conception." In that case, how could he support abortion? Because, as he explained in an interview with broadcaster Peter Jennings, the pre-born baby is "not the form of life that takes personhood in the terms that we have judged it to be."[13]

Bioethicists who adopt personhood theory often claim to be scientific, yet the theory has no scientific support. Clearly, it would take a dramatic transformation to turn a mere human organism with no rights into a person with an inviolable right to life. But there is no scientific evidence of such a transformation—no single, dramatic turning point that can be empirically detected. Embryonic development is a continuous process, gradually unfolding the potentials that were built in from the beginning. The two-story concept of personhood is neither empirical nor scientific.

The scientific evidence actually favors a teleological view, which sees the human being as a coherent whole from conception. In a Christian worldview, everyone who is human is also a person. The two cannot be separated. This view avoids the radical devaluation of human life. From its earliest stages, the body participates in the human *telos*, and thus shares in the purpose and dignity of the human person. (We will explore abortion more fully and answer objections in chapter 2.)

Dr. Humane Death

What about euthanasia? How does it express the two-story divided worldview? Many Americans still recall the 2005 Terri Schiavo case. Terri was a young married woman who suffered cardiac arrest and was declared by some doctors to be in a persistent vegetative state. Her husband wanted to discontinue her food and water. But her biological family, who took care of her, disputed the diagnosis. They lined up medical experts who claimed that Terri responded to efforts to communicate. After a series of highly publicized court cases, and even the intervention of the US Congress, her food and water were cut off, leading to her slow death by dehydration and starvation.

Terri's story was presented in the media as a right-to-die case. But Terri was not dying. She was not terminally ill. So that was not actually the heart of the debate. The core issue was personhood theory. In a television debate, Wesley Smith of the Discovery Institute asked a bioethicist from the University of Florida, "Do you think Terri is a person?"

"No, I do not," the bioethicist replied. "I think having awareness is an essential criterion of personhood."[14]

Whatever you think of the politics surrounding Terri's case, that interchange captures its worldview significance. According to personhood theory, if you are mentally disabled, if you no longer have an arbitrarily prescribed level of neocortical functioning, then you are no longer a person—even though you are obviously still human.

Those who argued in favor of cutting off Terri's food and water included a neurologist named Ronald Cranford, who styles himself "Dr. Humane Death." Cranford has a reputation for promoting euthanasia even for disabled people who are conscious and partly mobile. In a California case, a man named Robert

Wendland was brain-damaged in a car accident. He was able to perform logical tests with colored pegs, press buttons to answer yes-and-no questions, and even scoot along hospital hallways in an electric wheelchair (like the famous physicist Stephen Hawking). Yet Cranford argued in court that Wendland was not a person and that his food and water should be cut off.[15]

According to the body/person dichotomy, just being biologically part of the human race (the lower story) is not morally relevant. Individuals must *earn* the status of personhood by meeting an additional set of criteria—the ability to make decisions, exercise self-awareness, plan for the future, and so on (the upper story). Only those who meet these added conditions qualify as persons.

Those who do not make the grade are demoted to non-persons. And a non-person is just a body—a disposable piece of matter, a natural resource that can be used for research or harvesting organs or other purely utilitarian purposes, subject only to a cost-benefit analysis.

Just as with abortion, we are talking about the logic implied by the act itself, no matter how an individual feels about it. You may intend to be compassionate by ending the life of a suffering patient. But your actions imply a two-story worldview that is dehumanizing—one in which humans do not have rights, only persons do. The only way to stand against the culture of death is to accept that all humans are also persons. No one is excluded. (We will explore euthanasia and assisted suicide more deeply in chapter 3.)

Hooking Up, Splitting Apart

What about sexuality? Surprisingly, the secular view on sexuality exhibits the same body/person dualism.

In the two-story worldview, if the *body* is separate from the *person*, as we saw in abortion and euthanasia, then what you do with your body sexually need not have any connection to who you are as a whole person. Sex can be purely physical, separate from love.

Our sexualized culture actually encourages people to keep the two separate. *Seventeen* magazine warns teen girls to "keep your hearts under wraps" or boys may find you "boring and clingy." *Cosmo* advises women that the way to "wow a man after sex" is to ask for a ride home. (Make it clear you have no intention of hanging around hoping for a relationship.)

These examples were collected by Wendy Shalit in her book *Girls Gone Mild*.[16] On her website, Shalit posts letters from readers, some of them heart-rending. The day I checked the site, there was a letter from sixteen-year-old Amanda lamenting that in a typical high school, "the more detached you can be from your sexuality, the cooler you are." She added that even adults—teachers, books, magazines, parents—often urge teens to adopt a No Big Deal attitude toward sexuality.

As though to prove the point, reviews of Shalit's book actually defended loveless physical encounters. The *Washington Post* suggested that it is healthy when teenage girls "refuse to conflate" love and sex: "Sometimes they coexist, sometimes not." The *Nation* asked defiantly, "Why should sex have an everlasting warranty of love attached to it?"[17] Why indeed, if the body is just a piece of matter that can be stimulated for pleasure with no meaning for the whole person?

The same bleak view of sexuality is inculcated in even young children. A video put out by Children's Television Workshop, widely used in sex education classes, defines sexual relations as simply "something done by two adults to give each other pleasure."[18] No mention of marriage or family—or even love or commitment. No hint that sex has a richer purpose than sheer sensual gratification.

This is sex cut off from the whole person—sex as an exchange of physical services between autonomous, disconnected individuals. We tend to think sexual hedonism places too much value on the purely physical dimension. But in reality it places a very low value on the body, draining it of moral and personal significance.

In the hookup culture, partners are referred to as "friends with benefits." But that is a euphemism because they are not really even friends. The unwritten etiquette is that you never meet just to talk or spend time together. A *New York Times* article explains, "You just keep it purely sexual, and that way people don't have mixed expectations, and no one gets hurt."[19]

Except when they do. The same article features a teenager named Melissa who was depressed because her hookup partner had just "broken up" with her. No matter what the current secular philosophy tells them, people cannot disassociate their emotions from what they do with their bodies.

In the biblical worldview, sexuality is integrated into the total person. The most complete and intimate *physical* union is meant to express the most complete and intimate *personal* union of marriage. Biblical morality is teleological: The purpose of sex is to express the one-flesh covenant bond of marriage.

The loving way to treat young people is not to hand out contraceptives, which amounts to collusion in impersonal and ultimately unfulfilling sexual encounters. It is far more loving to inspire them with a higher view of sexuality. In reconnecting body and person, they can experience a deep sense of healing and personal integration. (We will delve more deeply into sexuality in chapter 4.)

Same Sex in Conflict

What about homosexuality? Even in churches, young people often do not understand why the Bible teaches that same-sex relations are morally wrong. It makes more sense when we realize that a secular approach rests on the same divided view of the human being, with its devaluing of the body.

Most people assume that same-sex desire is genetically based. Certainly we do not choose our sexual attractions. They come to us involuntarily and feel natural. Yet despite intensive research, scientists have not turned up clear evidence of a genetic cause.

What studies do show is that sexual desires have physical correlates. For example, when scientists use magnetic resonance imaging (MRIs), they find that some men's brains light up in response to female images, while others' light up in response to male images. But people's brains also light up in response to fear, love, and even religious experiences. This should not be surprising. Humans are unified beings. Knowing that feelings have physical correlates can help us be more compassionate toward people. But it does not tell us what is right or wrong, moral or immoral.

Whatever the cause of homoerotic inclinations, when we act on them we implicitly accept the two-story divide. Think of it this way: Biologically, physiologically, chromosomally, and anatomically, males and females are counterparts to one another. That's how the human sexual and reproductive system is designed. Anglican theologian Oliver O'Donovan writes, "To have a male body is to have a body structurally ordered to loving union with a female body, and *vice versa*."[20] The body has a built-in *telos*, or purpose.

To engage in same-sex behavior, then, is implicitly to say: Why should my body inform my psychological identity? Why should the structural order of my body have anything to say about what I do sexually? Why should my moral choices be directed by its *telos*? The implication is that what counts is not my sexed body (lower story) but solely my mind, feelings, and desires (upper story). The assumption is that the body gives no clue to our identity; it gives no guidance to what our sexual choices should be; it is irrelevant and insignificant.

This is a profoundly disrespectful view of the human body.

Every practice comes with a worldview attached to it—one that many of us might not find true or attractive if we were aware of it. Therefore it is important to *become* aware. Same-sex behavior has a logic of its own, apart from what we subjectively feel or intend. The person who adopts a same-sex identity must disassociate their sexual feelings from their biological identity as male or female—implicitly accepting a two-story dualism that demeans the human body. Thus it has a fragmenting, self-alienating effect on the human personality.

By contrast, biblical morality expresses a high view of the dignity and significance of the body. The biblical view of sexuality is not based on a few scattered Bible verses. It is based on a teleological worldview that encourages us to live in accord with the physical design of our bodies. By respecting the body, the biblical ethic overcomes the dichotomy separating body from person. It heals self-alienation and creates integrity and wholeness. The root of the word *integrity* means whole, integrated, unified—our mind and emotions in tune with our physical body. The biblical view leads to a wholistic integration of personality. It fits who we really are. (We will walk through several real-life examples and answer objections to the biblical view in chapters 5 and 6.)

"I Am Not My Body"

Many people find it easier to recognize the denigration of the body in arguments supporting transsexualism or transgenderism. Transgender people often say they are trapped in the "wrong body."

This sense of a mismatch between physical sex and psychological gender is called gender dysphoria. Most people assume that it must have some biochemical basis, perhaps a hormonal cause. To date, however, no clear scientific evidence has been uncovered. More importantly, transgender advocates themselves argue the opposite: They *deny* that gender identity is rooted in biology. Their argument is that gender is completely independent of the body.

For example, Jessica Savano is a male-to-female transsexual, a 6-foot 4-inch model and actor who created a Kickstarter page for a documentary titled, "I Am Not My Body." That title says it all. Savano posted a promotional video arguing that our core identity is completely disassociated from our bodies: "I know I'm not my body. I'm a spiritual being."[21]

In other words, the authentic self has no connection to the body. The real person resides in the spirit, mind, will, and feelings.

In one segment of the video, Savano is filmed doing an audition for a transsexual movie role, reading from a script that says, "Why are you even looking at my penis anyway? I am a *woman*!" The viewer is viscerally struck by the contradiction as Savano claims an identity as a woman even while talking about having a male body.

The implication is that *the body does not matter*. It is not the site of the authentic self. Matter does not matter. All that matters is a person's inner feelings or sense of self.

This radical dualism accepts a modernist, materialist view of the body in the lower story, and a postmodern view of the self in the upper story. The body is not seen as having any purpose or *telos*. It is merely a collection of physical systems—muscles, bones, organs, and cells—providing no clue to who we are or how we should live. Our physical traits give no signposts for the right way to deploy our sexuality.

And if the meaning of our sexuality is not something we derive *from* the body, then it becomes something we impose *on* the body. It is a social construction. Sexual identity is reduced to a postmodern concept completely disconnected from the body.

There are many misconceptions surrounding transgenderism, which I will address in chapter 6. People often confuse gender dysphoria with intersex. Or they conflate gender identity with social roles. Do girls wear pink while boys wear blue? Do men go to work while women raise children? Practices like these are dependent on historical circumstances, and the church should be the first place where people are encouraged to think critically and creatively about stereotypes.

The question raised by the transgender movement is much more fundamental: Do we accept or reject our basic biological identity as male or female? In the two-story worldview, the body is seen as irrelevant—or even as a constraint to be overcome, a limitation to be liberated from.

By contrast, a biblical worldview leads to a positive view of the body. It says that the biological correspondence between male and female is part of the original creation. Sexual differentiation is part of what God pronounced "very good"—*morally* good—which means it provides a reference point for morality. There is a purpose in the physical structures of our bodies that we are called to respect. A teleological morality creates harmony between biological identity and gender identity. The body/person is an integrated psychosexual unity. Matter does matter.

Body Obsession, Body Rejection

Is it true that Western culture devalues the body? Don't many people place a ridiculously high value on physical appearance and fitness? Consider the widespread obsession with diets, exercise, bodybuilding, cosmetics, plastic surgery, botox, anti-aging treatments, and so on. We are surrounded by Photoshopped images presenting unrealistic ideals of physical beauty. A Christian college professor once told me, "It seems to me that people tend to go in the opposite direction—they make an idol of the body."

But to be obsessed by the body does not mean we accept it. "The cult of the young body, the veneration of the air-brushed, media produced body, conceals a hatred of *real* bodies," writes theologian Beth Felker Jones of Wheaton College. "Cultural practice expresses aversion to the body."[22]

Even the cult of the body can be an expression of the two-story dualism. An obsession with exercising, bodybuilding, and dieting can reveal a mindset akin to that of a luxury car owner polishing and tuning up an expensive automobile. Philosophers call that "instrumentalizing" the body, which means treating it as a tool to be used and controlled instead of valuing it for its own sake.

When we do that, we objectify the body as part of nature to be conquered. Feminist philosopher Susan Bordo writes, "The training, toning, slimming, and sculpting of the body . . . encourage an adversarial relationship to the body."[23] These practices express the will to conquer and subdue the body—and ultimately to be liberated from its constraints.

The radical ethicist Joseph Fletcher declared, "To be a person . . . means to be free of physiology!"[24] Nature is treated as a negative constraint to be overcome.

So we end where we began: Our view of the body depends on our view of nature. Do we see nature as essentially good, a gift from the Creator to be accepted with gratitude? Or do we see nature as a set of negative limitations to be controlled and conquered? Of course, Christians engage in diet and exercise as well, but their actions should be motivated by a conviction that the body is a gift. We have a stewardship responsibility before God to treat it with care and respect.

To make the Bible's positive message credible, it must be communicated not only in words but also in behavior by treating everyone with dignity simply because they are made in God's image. Churches have at times used harsh and demeaning rhetoric to describe positions they disagree with, creating a negative stereotype that the media is happy to broadcast to the world. For several centuries Christianity was the dominant worldview in Western culture, and sadly Christians acquired some of the negative traits typical of dominant groups—for example, not really listening to minority groups or answering their objections but shutting them down with moral condemnation.

Today that response is no longer possible. But it was never right or necessary. Scripture gives the intellectual resources to answer any question with confidence. And those who are the most confident are also free to be the most loving and respectful toward others.

Healing Alienation

What is the biblical response to the secular moral revolution? Let's start by addressing the two-level body/person dualism itself head-on. In later chapters, we will delve into individual issues.

We must start by expressing compassion for people trapped in a dehumanizing and destructive view of the body. The two-story worldview is "above all an attack *on the body*," writes a Catholic theologian.[25] We must therefore respond with a biblical defense of the body. We must find ways to heal the alienation between body and person.

The starting point is a biblical philosophy of nature. The Bible proclaims the profound value and dignity of the material realm—including the human body—as the handiwork of a loving God. That's why biblical morality places great emphasis on the fact of human embodiment. Respect for the person is inseparable from respect for the body.

After all, God could have chosen to make us like the angels—spirits without bodies. He could have created a spiritual realm for us to float around in. Instead he created us with material bodies and a material universe to live in. Why? Clearly God values the material dimension and he wants us to value it as well.

Scripture treats body and soul as two sides of the same coin. The inner life of the soul is expressed through the outer life of the body. This is highlighted through the parallelism characteristic of Hebrew poetry (NASB, italics added):

> "My *soul* thirsts for You, my *flesh* yearns for You." (Ps. 63:1)

> "Our *soul* has sunk down into the dust; our *body* cleaves to the earth." (Ps. 44:25)

> "Keep [my words] in the midst of your *heart*. For they are life to those who find them and health to all their *body*." (Prov. 4:21–22)

> "When I kept silent about [refused to *repent* of] my sin, my *body* wasted away through my groaning all day long." (Ps. 32:3)

In one sense, our bodies even have primacy over our spirits. After all, the body is the only avenue we have for expressing our inner life or for knowing another person's inner life. The body is the means by which the invisible is made visible. "We have no access to the free spirit apart from its incarnation in the body," writes Lutheran theologian Gilbert Meilander. "The living body is therefore the locus of personal presence."[26]

This wholistic biblical view is confirmed by everyday human experience. When you eat food, you do not say, "My mouth is eating." You say, "*I* am eating." When your hand is injured, you say, "*I* am hurt." The two-level division of the human being is not true to our inescapable daily experience.

Philosopher Donn Welton sums up by saying that, in the Bible, the body "is not reducible to a material object or bio-physical entity, for it belongs to the moral and spiritual universe as much as it belongs to the physical world." That is, the Bible does not separate the body off into a lower story, where it is reduced to a biochemical machine. Instead the body is intrinsic to the person. And therefore it will ultimately be redeemed along with the person—a process that begins even in this life. Welton writes, "In the final analysis, the New Testament does not argue for a rejection of the body but for its redemption and its transformation into a site of moral and spiritual disclosure."[27]

A biblical ethic is incarnational. We are made in God's image to reflect God's character, both in our minds and in our bodily actions. There is no division, no alienation. We are embodied beings.

Walking Clay

At the time of the early church, this biblical view was radically countercultural. Ancient pagan culture was permeated by world-denying philosophies such as Manichaeism, Platonism, and Gnosticism, all of which disparaged the material world as the realm of death, decay, and destruction—the source of evil. Gnosticism essentially conflated the two doctrines of creation and fall: It treated creation as a kind of fall of the soul from the higher spiritual realm into the corrupt material realm.

Gnosticism thus trained people to think of the body "as a total other to the self," writes Princeton historian Peter Brown. It was an unruly "piece of matter" that the soul had to struggle to control and manage.[28] The goal of salvation was to escape from the material world—to leave it behind and ascend back to the spiritual realm. A popular pun at the time was that the body (Greek: *soma*) is a tomb (Greek: *sema*).

Gnosticism taught that the world was so evil, it must be the creation of an evil god. In Gnostic cosmology, there existed multiple levels of spiritual beings from the highest deity to the lowest, who was actually an evil sub-deity.

It was this lowest-level deity who created the material world. After all, no self-respecting god would demean himself by mucking about with matter.

In this cultural context, the claims of Christianity were nothing short of revolutionary. For it teaches that matter was not created by an evil sub-deity but by the ultimate deity, the Most High God—and that the material world is therefore intrinsically good. In Genesis, there is no denigration of the material world. Instead it is repeatedly affirmed to be good: "And God saw that it was good" (Gen. 1:10, 12, 18, 21, 25).

Humans are presented as beings whose personhood includes being part of the earth from which they were created. The second chapter of Genesis says God formed Adam "from the dust of the ground" (2:7). The name for humanity, *Adam*, is even a pun in the original Hebrew, meaning "from the earth" (*adamah* = earth).

It was this walking, animated clay that God pronounced "very good" (1:31). It was this embodied, earthly, sexual creature that God described as reflecting his own divine image: "Let us make mankind in our image, in our likeness" (v. 26). Rabbi Lord Jonathan Sacks, former chief rabbi of the United Kingdom, explains: "In the ancient world it was rulers, emperors, and pharaohs who were held to be in the image of God. So what Genesis was saying was that we are all royalty."[29] The early readers of Genesis knew the text was making the astonishing claim that *all* humans, not just rulers, are representatives of God on the earth.

Bethlehem Bombshell

What really set Christianity apart in the ancient world, however, was the incarnation—the claim that the Most High God had himself entered into the realm of matter, taking on a physical body. In Gnosticism, the highest deity would have nothing to do with the material world. By contrast, the Christian message is that the transcendent God has broken into history as a baby born in Bethlehem. The incarnation is genuinely physical, happening at a particular time and in a particular geographical location. "The Word became flesh and made his dwelling among us" (John 1:14).

In the days of the early church, this was Christianity's greatest scandal. That's why the apostles repeatedly stressed Christ's body: that in him "all the fullness of the Deity lives in bodily form" (Col. 2:9), that he "'bore our sins' in his body on the cross" (1 Pet. 2:24), that "we have been made holy through the sacrifice of the body of Jesus Christ" (Heb. 10:10). John even says the crucial test of orthodoxy is to affirm that Jesus has "come in the flesh" (1 John 4:2).

When Jesus was executed on a Roman cross, we might say he "escaped" from the material world, just as the Gnostics taught we should aspire to do. But what did he do next? He *came back*—in a bodily resurrection! To the ancient Greeks, that was not spiritual progress. It was *re*gress. Who would want to come back to the body? The whole idea of a bodily resurrection was utter "foolishness to the Greeks" (see 1 Cor. 1:23).

Even Jesus's disciples thought they were seeing a ghost. He had to assure them he was present bodily: "Look at my hands and my feet. It is I myself! Touch me and see; a ghost does not have flesh and bones as you see I have." He then asked for something to eat: "and he took it and ate it in their presence" to demonstrate that his resurrection body was genuinely physical (Luke 24:39, 43).

Not only did Jesus rise from the dead but he also ascended into heaven. We often think of the ascension as a kind of add-on, with no important theological meaning. What it means, however, is that Christ's taking on of human nature was not a temporary expedient, to be left behind when he finished the work of salvation. Because he was taken bodily into heaven, his human nature is permanently connected to his divine nature.

Death, Be Not Proud

Finally, what will happen at the end of time? God is not going to scrap the idea of a material world in time and space as though he made a mistake the first time. The biblical teaching is that God is going to restore, renew, and re-create it, leading to "a new heaven and a *new earth*" (Isa. 65:17; 66:22; Rev. 21:1, italics added). And God's people will live on that new earth in resurrected bodies. From the time of the early church, the Apostles' Creed has boldly affirmed "the resurrection of the body."

It is true that at death, humans undergo a temporary splitting of body and soul, but that was not God's original intent. Death rips apart what God intended to be unified. A second-century theologian, Melito of Sardis, wrote that when "man was divided by death," then "there was a separation of what once fitted beautifully, and the beautiful body was split apart."[30]

Why did Jesus weep at the tomb of Lazarus even though he knew he was about to raise him from the dead? Because "the beautiful body was split apart." The text says twice that Jesus was "deeply moved in spirit and troubled" (John 11:33, 38). In the original Greek, this phrase actually means furious indignation. It was used, for example, of war horses rearing up just before charging into battle. Os Guinness, formerly at L'Abri, explains: Standing before the tomb of Lazarus, Jesus "is outraged. Why? Evil is not normal." The world was created good and beautiful. But now "he'd entered his Father's world that had become ruined and broken. And his reaction? He was furious."[31] Jesus wept at the pain and sorrow caused by the enemy invasion that had devastated his beautiful creation.

Christians are never admonished to accept death as a natural part of creation. The Gnostics saw death as freedom from the encumbrance of the body. But for the early Christians, says Peter Brown, death "was a rending of the self that left the soul shocked and horrified, like a bereaved spouse or parent, at the prospect of parting from the beloved body."[32] Scripture portrays death as something alien—an enemy that entered creation with the fall.

And yet, it is a conquered enemy. "Death be not proud," wrote the poet John Donne. For in the end, "Death shall be no more. Death, thou shalt die."[33] As Paul writes, death is "the last enemy to be destroyed" (1 Cor. 15:26). In the new creation, body and soul will be reunified, as God meant them to be. Eternally.

When the Bible speaks of redemption, it does not mean only going to heaven when we die. It means the redemption of all creation. Paul writes that the whole creation suffers pain and brokenness but that it will be liberated at the end of time: "The creation itself will be liberated from its bondage to decay and brought into the freedom and glory of the children of God" (Rom. 8:21). The gospel message is that the entire physical world will be transformed. Humans will not be saved *out of* the material creation but will be saved *together with* the material creation.

We cannot know exactly what life will be like in eternity, but the fact that Scripture calls it a new "earth" means it will not be a negation of the life we have known on this earth. Instead it will be an enhancement, an intensification, a glorification of this life. In *The Great Divorce*, C. S. Lewis pictures the afterlife as recognizably similar to this world, yet a place where every blade of grass seems somehow more real, more solid, more substantial than anything we have experienced.[34]

Jesus's resurrection is an eloquent affirmation of creation. It implies that this broken world will be fixed in the end. God's creation will be restored. And you and I will live in that renewed creation in renewed bodies. At the end of the great drama, we will not be floating around in heaven as wispy, filmy, gossamer spirits. We will have physical feet firmly planted on a renewed physical earth. The Bible teaches an astonishingly high view of the physical world.

Revenge of the Body Haters

The New Testament concept of a bodily resurrection was completely novel in the ancient world.[35] In fact, it was so astonishing that many simply denied it. In the second century, many Gnostics claimed to be Christians but they adjusted biblical doctrines to fit their philosophy. Denying the incarnation, they taught that Christ was an avatar from a higher spiritual plane who entered the physical world temporarily to bring enlightenment and then returned to a higher state of being. They insisted that he was not really incarnate in a human body nor did he really die on the cross. Spirituality had nothing to do with *this* world but only with escape to higher realms. As theologian N. T. Wright says, the Gnostics "translated the language of resurrection into a private spirituality and a dualistic cosmology."[36]

Just as today, a privatized, escapist, otherworldly spirituality was far more socially acceptable. As a case in point, the Gnostics were not persecuted by the Roman Empire as the Christians were. Why not? Because a spirituality that applies strictly to the private realm poses no threat to power. As Wright explains, "Death is the last weapon of the tyrant, and the point of the resurrection . . . is that death has been defeated." This explains why "it was those who believed in the bodily resurrection who were burned at the stake and thrown to the lions."[37] They understood that when Jesus was raised from the dead and given a new, resurrection body, God was inaugurating the promised new creation, in which all injustice and corruption would be wiped out—and as a result, they were empowered to take a stand against injustice here and now.

At his ascension, Jesus said, "All authority in heaven *and on earth* has been given to me" (Matt. 28:18, italics added). With those words, he authorized his followers to establish his kingdom on earth by opposing evil and establishing justice. That's what it means to live as a citizen of heaven. When Paul says in his letter to the Philippians that we are citizens of heaven, most Christians interpret that to mean we should look forward to leaving earth and going to heaven, which is our true home. But that is not what the passage meant to first-century readers. The city of Philippi in Greece was a Roman colony, where many had the privilege of Roman citizenship. The citizens of a colony were not supposed to aspire to go back to Rome. Their job was to secure a conquered country by permeating the local culture with Roman culture. By telling Christians they are citizens of heaven, then, Paul was telling them to permeate the world with a heavenly culture.[38]

That's why C. S. Lewis calls Christianity "a fighting religion."[39] He means that disciples of Jesus are not meant to passively allow evil to flourish on earth, while looking forward to escaping someday to a higher realm. Instead they are called to actively fight evil here and now. The doctrine of the resurrection means that the physical world matters. It matters to God and it should matter to God's people.

Today secular culture is falling back into a dualism that denigrates the material realm, just as ancient paganism did. As in the early church, it is orthodox Christians who have a basis for defending a high view of the human body.

Don't Handle! Don't Touch!

But doesn't Christianity itself teach that the body is inferior to the spirit? That the body is a stumbling block and a cause of sin?

It's true that at times negative attitudes toward the body have infiltrated the church. Many people have the idea that Christianity is against any form of pleasure or enjoyment. This is called asceticism, the idea that the path to holiness is severe self-denial. But the source of asceticism was not Scripture; it was Platonic and Gnostic philosophies. Because these philosophies regarded the physical world as inherently evil, they concluded that holiness could be attained by physical deprivation—fasting, poverty, solitude, silence, hard manual labor, drab clothing, the rejection of marriage and family, and other forms of austerity.

The ascetics of the ancient world were looked up to as the "spiritual athletes" of their day (the word *asceticism* is derived from a Greek term for athletic training). As a result, they influenced even Christians. This explains why even today there are strains of Christianity that teach a stern, tight-lipped asceticism—as though holiness consists simply in saying no to fun and pleasure. These versions of Christianity speak of the body as though it were shameful, worthless, or unimportant. They treat sexual sin as the most wicked on the scale of sins. They hold an escapist concept of salvation, as though Jesus died to whisk us away to heaven.

I once visited a Lutheran church where the pastor spoke repeatedly about asking for God's forgiveness "so we can go to heaven," about being confident that "we are going to heaven," about thanking God that "we are going to heaven." I began to wonder, *Does this pastor think Christianity makes any difference in* this *life?* Sermons like this one are more Gnostic than biblical.[40] They give the impression the Bible is concerned only about what happens when we die.

Of course, spiritual disciplines such as fasting can be helpful, but they should not be motivated by the mistaken idea that the body is evil or worthless. The biblical text can be confusing because in some passages Paul uses the word *flesh* to mean the sinful nature (see Rom. 8; Gal. 5.) Just as in English, a word can have different meanings depending on the context.

Yet Paul soundly rejects the notion that holiness can be achieved through deprivation of the body. He describes ascetics as those who "forbid people to marry and order them to abstain from certain foods"—those who say, "Do not handle! Do not taste! Do not touch!" (1 Tim. 4:3; Col. 2:21). Rules like these do not work, he argues. "Such regulations indeed have an appearance of wisdom, with their . . . harsh treatment of the body. But they lack any value in restraining sensual indulgence"(Col. 2:23). Paul even warns that it's a heresy to prohibit marriage: "For everything God created is good, and nothing is to be rejected if it is received with thanksgiving" (1 Tim. 4:4).

Who Invented Matter Anyway?

The influence of asceticism even created a Christian version of the two-story division—today we call it the sacred/secular split. It's a mentality that treats the spiritual realm as good and important while demoting the physical realm to a necessary evil.

Two-story Christianity

SACRED

Spirit, Soul, Church Work

SECULAR

Body, Intellect, Professional Work

The sacred/secular split is a major reason many Christians do not enjoy the power and joy that are promised in Scripture. They go to church on Sunday but do not think Christianity has any relevance to the rest of their lives. As C. S. Lewis writes, they regard the physical world as "crude and unspiritual."

But Lewis offers a snappy rejoinder: "There is no good trying to be more spiritual than God. God never meant man to be a purely spiritual creature. . . . He likes matter. He invented it."[41]

And in the end, he will redeem it. The theological image for the resurrection of the body is the seed: "The body that is sown is perishable, it is raised imperishable. . . . It is sown a natural body, it is raised a spiritual body" (1 Cor. 15:42, 44). The term *spiritual body* is often misunderstood to mean something ghostly and intangible. But the adjective does not tell us what the body is made of, rather what powers it. By analogy, a gasoline engine is not made of gasoline but powered by it. The great church father Augustine explains, "They will be spiritual not because they will cease to be bodies, but because they will be sustained by a quickening Spirit."[42] In the resurrection from the dead, our bodies will be fully powered and sustained by God's Spirit.

At that time, what the ancient prophet Job said will come true: "In my *flesh* I will see God" (Job 19:26, italics added).

Contrary to asceticism, the Bible does not treat the body as the source of moral corruption. Instead it says sin originates in the "heart." In Scripture, the word *heart* does not mean our emotions, as it does today. It means our inner self and deepest motivations, as we see in these passages: "Do not lust in your heart" (Prov. 6:25). "Their hearts are greedy for unjust gain" (Ezek. 33:31). God says, "I gave them over to their stubborn hearts to follow their own devices" (Ps. 81:12).

Jesus himself gave the definitive statement: "The things that come out of a person's mouth come from the heart, and these defile them. For out of the heart come evil thoughts—murder, adultery, sexual immorality, theft, false testimony, slander" (Matt. 15:18–19).

Ezekiel sums up the biblical teaching by saying humans harbor "idols in their hearts" (Ezek. 14:3–7). The mainspring of sin is not that we have bodies but that we put things besides God at the center of our lives and turn them into idols. Paul unpacks the idea by saying those who do not worship the transcendent Creator will worship something in the created world instead: In his words, they "exchanged the truth about God for a lie and worshiped and served the creature rather than the Creator" (Rom. 1:25).

When we put anything in the place of God, that functions as our idol.

That's why the Ten Commandments start with the command to love and worship God above all other things. When our hearts are centered on God, only then are we empowered to fulfill the rest of the commandments that deal with behavior—what we do with our bodies.

Body Positivity

But wait, doesn't Paul also talk about the "body of sin" (Rom. 6:6 KJV)? And doesn't that mean the body is the source of evil? No. The context makes it clear that Paul is saying the body can become an *instrument* of sin—but it can also become an instrument of righteousness: "Do you not know that when you offer yourselves to someone as obedient slaves, you are slaves of the one you obey—whether you are slaves to sin, which leads to death, or to obedience, which leads to righteousness?" (v. 16). The problem is not the body but sin. The body is merely the site where the battle between good and evil is incarnated.

This battle does explain why, at times, we do feel estranged from our bodies. Paul expresses that sense of self-alienation when he writes, "I do not understand what I do. For what I want to do I do not do, but what I hate I do" (7:15). Notice that he experiences sin as an unwanted, unwelcome, alien force within his body: "It is no longer I myself who do it, but it is sin living in me" (v. 17).

We have all had similar experiences of bondage and addiction—of compulsively doing things we do not want to do. In the same breath, however, Paul promises that we can be liberated: "But thanks be to God that, though you used to be slaves to sin, you have come to obey from your heart the pattern of teaching that has now claimed your allegiance" (6:17). It is possible to break the power of bondage to sin: "Therefore do not let sin reign in your mortal body so that you obey its evil desires" (v. 12).

The only appropriate response to such liberating grace is to "honor God with your bodies" (1 Cor. 6:20), or to put it more fully, "to offer your bodies as a living sacrifice, holy and pleasing to God—this is your true and proper worship" (Rom. 12:1). It is exciting to think God actually wants to relate to us in our bodies, loving our idiosyncratic shape and size, our bodily quirks, our physical appearance. God wants to love and interact with us not only spiritually but in our entire being.

Scripture even uses a striking bodily metaphor when speaking of the community of Christians: The church is the body of Christ. And it is sustained by physical eating and drinking, an act of bodily consumption: "Is not the cup of thanksgiving for which we give thanks a participation in the blood of Christ? And is not the bread that we break a participation in the body of Christ? Because there is one loaf, we, who are many, are one body, for we all share the one loaf. (1 Cor. 10:16–17). As Welton observes, "It, no doubt, came as a shock to those working within the framework of Greek thought that what Jesus offered was not his mind or soul but his 'flesh' or body, symbolized in the element of the bread."[43] In a biblical worldview, not only does the body have its own dignity but it also supplies images and analogies, metaphors and symbols for our participation in the spiritual world.

God's Work of Art

But isn't this world fallen, and doesn't that mean it is corrupt? Yes, but there is a danger of overemphasizing the doctrine of the fall, tipping it out of balance with the other doctrines of Scripture.

Biblical theology is woven from three themes: creation, fall, and redemption. All created reality comes from the hand of God and is therefore originally and intrinsically good. Humans are called to be stewards of the physical world—which includes our bodies—responsible to the One who made and owns it.

Yet all created reality is marred and corrupted by sin. Because humans were given responsibility for creation, its destiny is bound up with ours. We see this even in human experience—when a father is abusive, the whole family is likely to be dysfunctional; when a national leader is corrupt, the entire nation suffers. In the same way, when humans sinned, all of creation was put out of joint.

Finally, at the end of time, all creation will be restored and renewed by God's grace. The Bible speaks of salvation using terms like *re*store, *re*new, *re*deem—all of which imply a *re*covery of something that was originally good. If humans were originally and inherently evil, there would be nothing to restore. God would have to destroy humanity and start over. It is only because sin is an alien force in God's good creation that we can be rescued, delivered, freed, and restored. The body can once again become an instrument of godliness, as it was meant to be: "Offer every part of yourself to him as an instrument of righteousness" (Rom. 6:13).

Indeed, the reason the fall is such a tragedy is precisely *because* humans have such high value to begin with. When a cheap trinket is broken, we toss it aside without a second thought. But when a priceless work of art is destroyed, we are heartbroken. The reason sin is so tragic is that it destroys a human being—a priceless masterpiece that reflects the character of the Supreme Artist.

Of course, the Christian knows that the created world is not the ultimate reality. But that does not imply that it is worthless or contemptible. There are times, especially moments of crisis, pain, and suffering, when we are deeply grateful that the physical realm is not the sole reality—that there exists a transcendent, spiritual realm that is equally real. God is the sole self-existing, self-sufficient ultimate reality; the material world is dependent on him. That's why we are called to "set your minds on things above, not on earthly things" (Col. 3:2). These verses are not meant to make us despise God's creation but to intensify our reliance on God.

The church father Justin Martyr, writing in the second century, faced the same objections that we face today. In "The Dignity of the Body," he writes this wonderful passage:

> We must now speak with respect to those who think meanly of the flesh. . . . These persons seem to be ignorant of the whole work of God. . . . For does not the word say, "Let Us make man in our image, and after our likeness"? What kind of man? Manifestly He means fleshly man, for the word says, "And God took dust of the earth, and made man." It is evident, therefore, that man made in the image of God was of flesh. Is it not, then, absurd to say, that the flesh made by God in His own image is contemptible, and worth nothing?[44]

The theological insights of Justin Martyr in the second century are still needed in the twenty-first century. As we face the social ills of our own day, we must move beyond denunciations that can sound harsh, angry, or judgmental and instead work to show that the biblical ethic is based on a positive view of the body as part of the image of God. The goal is not to win a culture war or to impose our views on others but to love our neighbor, which means working for our neighbor's good.

How does this biblical and historical background give us better tools to understand secular morality? Now that we have surveyed the most controversial issues, let's dive into each one in greater detail, answering the most common objections and identifying the dehumanizing worldview at its root, starting with abortion.

2

The Joy of Death

"You Must Be Prepared to Kill"

Antonia Senior, a British journalist, had always firmly supported abortion. "Then came a baby, and everything changed. . . . My moral certainty about abortion is wavering, my absolutist position is under siege." Eventually, the young journalist hardened back to her absolutist support for abortion: Yet, surprisingly, she continued to acknowledge that life begins at conception.

"My daughter was formed at conception," Senior writes. "Any other conclusion is a convenient lie that we on the pro-choice side of the debate tell ourselves to make us feel better about the action of taking a life." She concludes, "Yes, abortion is killing. But it's the lesser evil."

What evil could be greater than taking a human life? In Senior's view, even worse would be putting limits on women's right to control their reproduction: "You cannot separate women's rights from their right to fertility control. The single biggest factor in women's liberation was our newly found ability to impose our will on our biology. . . . The nearly 200,000 aborted babies in the UK each year are the lesser evil, no matter how you define life."

Senior ends her article with this chilling line: To defend women's rights, "You must be prepared to kill."[1]

How have we come to the point where many people are "prepared to kill"? What worldview explains such a drastic devaluation of life? Like Senior, most scientifically informed people know that life begins at conception. When dealing with horses or hummingbirds or any other organism, the accepted science is that a new individual begins at fertilization. From that moment on, the organism merely unfolds the capacities that belong intrinsically to the kind of being it is. The same scientific facts apply to humans.[2] Everything intrinsic to a human being is present from fertilization. No outside force or substance enters into the embryo at any point to transform it from some other creature *into* a human. The entire human being develops in a seamless continuum from conception.[3]

According to personhood theory, however, even though the fetus is human, it can be killed without any moral consequence. We have no moral obligation to protect the fetus until it attains personhood (see chapter 1). To understand the deeper roots of abortion, we must ask: Where did this body/person dichotomy come from, and why does it have such inhumane consequences?

By contrast, as we will see, the biblical worldview is wholistic. It recognizes that body and soul are complementary, forming an integrated psychophysical unity. Everyone who is human is also a person. We are embodied persons. The Christian ethic is based on a rich, multidimensional view that says people have moral worth on all levels, physically and spiritually.

The beauty of the biblical ethic emerges clearly when compared to the cold, callous view of life in today's secular thinking. Yet that positive message will get through to people only if we back it up with acts of grace and mercy to those who have experienced the trauma of abortion—women (and men) who were persuaded by the abortion "script" that the fetus is a mere thing with no moral worth. And we must come alongside those who stand against the pressure to abort and courageously choose to carry their babies to term.

The Court Takes Sides

As we saw in chapter 1, personhood theory, with its dichotomy between body and person, prevails today among secular bioethicists—as well as religious ethicists who take their lead from secularism. Joseph Fletcher, a former Episcopal priest, expresses the two-story divide when he writes, "What is critical is *personal* status, not merely *human* status." In his view, genetically defective fetuses and newborns do not attain the status of personhood: They are "sub-personal" organisms and therefore fail to qualify for the right to life.[4]

Another example comes from Hans Küng, a liberal Catholic theologian, who writes: "a fertilized ovum evidently is *human* life but is not a *person*."[5] Princeton ethicist Peter Singer writes, "the life of a *human* organism begins at conception" but "the life of a *person*—. . . [a] being with some level of self-awareness—does not begin so early."[6] For Singer, simply being human has no moral significance. And if you think it does, you are guilty of speciesism, defined as an immoral prejudice in favor of your own species (parallel to racism).

People often claim that laws legalizing abortion are neutral. The idea is that since no one agrees when life begins, the state should remain neutral by permitting abortion. But laws permitting abortion are not neutral. They express personhood theory, which is a substantive philosophy excluding babies in the womb from constitutional protection. In the Supreme Court's *Roe v. Wade* ruling, Justice Harry Blackmun asserted point-blank that the unborn baby is not a person: "The word 'person,' as used in the Fourteenth Amendment, does not include the unborn." If the fetus *were* recognized as a person, he acknowledged, then abortion would necessarily be illegal: "If the suggestion of personhood is established, . . . the fetus' right to life would then be guaranteed."[7]

By legalizing abortion, then, the Supreme Court did not remain neutral. Instead it established personhood theory, with its two-story body/person dualism, as the law of the land.

The Ghost in the Machine

What are the sources of the body/person dichotomy? Where did it come from and how did it develop? Its deepest roots go back to the dawn of Western philosophy. The ancient Greek thinker Plato said the soul in the body is like the driver of a chariot trying to steer an unruly horse.[8] He treated the body as external to the true self.

Dualism took on a modern form, however, in the work of the seventeenth-century French philosopher René Descartes. Using our two-story metaphor, Descartes placed the body in the lower story, conceiving it as a machine—a robot or automaton, like a clock or a windup toy. In fact, he thought of all nature as a vast machine set in motion by God at creation and ever since moving in fixed patterns, subject to mathematical necessity.[9]

In the upper story Descartes placed the human mind—the realm of thinking, perception, consciousness, emotion, and will. In his words, the mind is a "rational soul united to this machine." Cartesian dualism was irreverently dubbed "the ghost in the machine."[10] If you saw the 2004 movie *I, Robot* starring Will Smith, you might remember that the phrase was used repeatedly to describe an especially capable robot: "There may be a ghost in this machine."

Descartes's two-story dualism

MIND

A Free, Autonomous Self

BODY

A Mechanism Operating by Natural Laws

Descartes is best known for his famous phrase, "I think, therefore I am." In that phrase he located authentic human identity in the mind alone. The implication is that the body is not an aspect of the true self; instead the body is a mechanism that serves the needs and desires of the mind, like the pilot of a ship or the driver of a car. Philosopher Daniel Dennett explains, "Since Descartes in the seventeenth century we have had a vision of the self as a sort of immaterial ghost that owns and controls a body the way you own and control your car."[11]

What the typical philosophy textbook does not mention is that Descartes was a devout Catholic, and his two-story division was actually an attempt to render a mechanistic worldview compatible with church teaching. His strategy for protecting the spiritual realm was to separate it completely from the material realm.[12] As one philosopher explains, Cartesian dualism "appeared to effect a compromise and reconciliation between the Church and the scientists." The rule was "to each its own jurisdiction—to the scientists, matter and its mechanical laws of motion; to the theologians, mental substance, the souls of human beings."[13]

It was a clever strategy, but did it work? No, because it does not hold together logically. How can a free mind influence a body that functions as automatically as a machine or robot? How can a mind control a body whose behavior is determined by mindless mechanical laws? These two concepts are logically contradictory. The term "Cartesian" came to refer to the irreconcilable conflict between a free subject connected somehow to a deterministic machine.

As Catholic philosopher Jacques Maritain explains, "Cartesian dualism breaks man up into two complete substances—on the one hand, the body which is only geometrical extension; on the other, the soul which is only thought." The human being is "split asunder."[14]

Nevertheless, the Cartesian two-story dualism was largely accepted. What was its appeal? For scientists, the appeal was that its mechanistic philosophy seemed to justify human control over nature. If nature is a machine, then we only need to uncover its laws to master and manipulate it.[15] Descartes himself said he hoped to empower humans to become "masters and possessors of nature." The human will was pitted against the blind, mechanical workings of nature to wrest from it what we want. The Cartesian promise was that the mind would become independent of the body and its limitations.

The Logic of Abortion

Do you see how this history explains the arguments for abortion? At least since Descartes, the mind has been regarded as the authentic self. It is the part of us that thinks and can say "therefore, I am." The body has been reduced to the sub-personal, functioning solely on the level of biology and chemistry. On that level, virtually everyone today agrees that the baby in the womb is human—biologically, physiologically, genetically human. When recognizable organs are being harvested and sold by Planned Parenthood—fetal eyes, hearts, lungs, brain tissue—it is no longer feasible to insist that the fetus is "just a collection of cells." Virtually no professional bioethicist denies that life begins at conception.[16]

In the two-story metaphor, however, to talk about the fetus as biologically human is in the lower story, the realm of science—where the body has been reduced to a mindless machine to be used and exploited, like the rest of nature. It is just a disposable piece of matter.

This explains *why* being biologically human is no longer thought to confer any moral status or to warrant legal protection. To be human is no longer equivalent to being a person. Human life has been reduced to raw material with no intrinsic purpose or dignity, subject to whatever purposes we choose to impose.

The core question in abortion, then, is the status of the human body. Is the human body an integral part of the person, sharing in its dignity? Or is it extrinsic to the person—a piece of matter that we can control and manipulate any way we want, like driving a car?

People do not have to adopt personhood theory consciously for it to have an effect. It is implied in the practice of abortion itself. To support abortion, by sheer logic, we must decide that human life in its earliest stages has no real value—so little that it may be killed for any reason. Then we must decide that at some later stage it is transformed into a different kind of being of such high value that killing it is murder.

By sheer logic, then, in accepting abortion, we implicitly adopt some form of body/person dualism, even if we do not use those terms. Our actions can imply ideas that we have not clearly thought through.

Of course, when people are actually making a decision about whether to have an abortion, their choice is often based on personal reasons—fear of losing a job, dropping out of school, financial cost, or social stigma. Christian women have told me their first and greatest fear was, *What will the people in my church think?* These are genuine concerns, and churches ought to be the first to step forward with financial support, child care, job training, counseling—and most of all, with grace and mercy.

In discussing personhood theory, however, we are not talking about people's personal reasons or feelings but about the logic inherent in supporting abortion. As an analogy, imagine a person asks you why someone is a Christian. Then imagine the person asks for a logical argument why Christianity is true. Your answer might be quite different. Personhood theory is the hidden premise in arguments for abortion.

Who Qualifies as a Person?

Once we recognize the dualism inherent in personhood theory, we have new tools to engage with our friends who support abortion. The most obvious problem for the theory is that no one can agree on how to define personhood. If it is not equated with being biologically human, then what *is* it? And when does it begin?

Every bioethicist offers a different answer. Some propose that personhood emerges when the developing organism begins to exhibit neural activity, feel pain, achieve a certain level of cognitive function or consciousness or intelligence, or even have a sense of the future. Fletcher proposes fifteen qualities to define when human life is worthy of respect and protection (such as intelligence, self-awareness, self-control, a sense of time, concern for others, communication, curiosity, and neocortical function). Score too low on any measure and for Fletcher you do not qualify as a person. You are "mere biological life."[17]

But *which* of these cognitive functions are really pivotal for defining human life? And how developed do they have to be? No one agrees. To choose any stage in gestation as the point when a pre-born baby becomes a person is arbitrary and subjective.

The problem is that most of these characteristics emerge gradually. They are not traits that someone either has or does not have. They are matters of degree—*quantitative* differences. What we do not find is a clear *qualitative* transition point for the momentous transformation from a non-person to a person.

For that matter, even fully developed adults have these traits in varying degrees. When I meet someone who is more intelligent than I am, does that mean they are more of a person than I am—and should have more rights than I have? Pro-life apologist Scott Klusendorf says the idea of basing legal protection on traits that vary among the population "relegates the proposition that all men are created equal to the ash heap of history."[18]

The only logical grounds for affirming that "all men are created equal" is an appeal to a Creator. That's why the American founders wrote in the Declaration of Independence that human rights are "endowed by [the] Creator." Though the founders did not always live up to their own highest ideals (some were slave owners), they were correct on this point. Even the arch-atheist Friedrich Nietzsche recognized that the "Christian concept . . . of the 'equality of souls before God' . . . furnishes the prototype of *all* theories of equal rights."[19]

For the founders, that Christian concept was so obvious that they wrote, "We hold these truths to be self-evident." Today, however, those truths are no longer self-evident. We need to frame explicit arguments that the existence of a Creator provides the only logical basis for equal rights.

Who's Really Discriminating?

What about timing? Most people say a baby becomes a person while still in the womb. Miranda Sawyer, the British broadcaster whose story we read in chapter 1, concluded that personhood begins sometime before birth: "Once an embryo has developed enough to feel pain, or begin a personality, then . . . ending that life is wrong."[20]

But bioethicist John Harris scoffs at that idea: "Nine months of development leaves the human embryo far short of the emergence of anything that can be called a person." Harris defines a person as "a creature capable of valuing its own existence." Killing is wrong only in the case of someone who is cognitively developed enough to harbor an explicit, conscious desire to live. "Nonpersons or potential persons cannot be wronged in this way because death does not deprive them of anything they can value," Harris argues. "If they cannot wish to live, they cannot have that wish frustrated by being killed"—as though the worth of life depended on our private will.[21]

James Watson, co-discoverer of the DNA double helix, advocates waiting three days after a baby is born before deciding whether it should be allowed to live. The rationale is that some genetic defects are not detectable until after birth. His colleague Francis Crick agrees: "No newborn infant should be declared human until it has passed certain tests regarding its genetic endowment and if it fails these tests, it forfeits the right to life."[22] Peter Singer says even "a three-year-old is a gray case."[23] After all, how much cognitive functioning does a toddler have?

As we saw earlier, Singer accuses others of discrimination on the basis of species (what he calls speciesism), yet ironically he proposes discrimination on the basis of cortical function. But why should mental function be the basis for moral decisions instead of membership in the human species? Certainly being human is more objective and easier to determine.

A Christian concept of personhood depends not on what I can do but on who I am—that I am created in the image of God, and that God has called me into existence and continues to know and love me. Human beings do not need to earn the right to be treated as creatures of great value. Our dignity is intrinsic, rooted in the fact that God made us, knows us, and loves us.

Scarlett Johansson's Blood-Stained "Human Right"

If doctors deny personhood on the basis of defects, where do they draw the line? What about mild or correctable defects? A news story from England quotes a father named David Wildgrove: "It was strongly suggested that we consider abortion after they found our baby had a club foot." Wildgrove was appalled. He knew that club foot is easily corrected, even without surgery. (Splints and casts are used to set the foot in the correct position.) Famous people born with club foot include poet Lord Byron, actor Dudley Moore, and figure skater Kristi Yamaguchi, winner of a 1992 Olympic gold medal.

Yet a 2006 study found that in England today babies with club foot are frequently aborted. Wildgrove's son was not one of them: "We resisted, the problem was treated, and he now runs around and plays football with everyone else."[24]

Then there are the wrenching cases of babies born alive after an abortion. In the now-infamous case *Floyd v. Anders*, a little boy survived for twenty-one days after an abortion. Yet a federal judge said that because the mother had decided to abort him, "the fetus in this case was not a person whose life state law could protect."[25] So a child who survived an abortion for twenty-one days was "not a person," nor protected by state law.

When police came upon Kermit Gosnell's abortion clinic in Philadelphia, they discovered a horrifying scene of dead babies, many of whom had been born alive and then intentionally killed by "snipping" the spinal cord with a scissors. But the officers were told by their supervisor that the investigation of abortion was not their business. The supervisor apparently felt that even when an attempted abortion yields a live baby, it is not legally protected in any way. (Gosnell was later convicted of first-degree murder.)[26]

As columnist George Will trenchantly observes, by refusing to protect a baby born alive in a botched abortion, the law is essentially saying the goal is not just to end the pregnancy. It is saying, "If you pay for an abortion, you are owed a dead baby."[27]

The lesson is that any definition of personhood not connected to simply being human is subjective and arbitrary. Yet these ungrounded definitions have life-and-death consequences. When ethicists decree that someone is a non-person, then doctors and judges will deny them legal protection. As a result, human life is no longer inviolable.

Actress Scarlett Johansson has stated that abortion is no longer "'a woman's rights issue' but 'a human rights issue.'"[28] Yet it is a strange human right that justifies killing humans.

Arguments defending abortion demean the body to the subpersonal level. They trivialize the body as a form of raw material that can be tinkered with, manipulated, experimented on, or destroyed with no moral consequences. They reduce human life to utilitarian calculations weighing practical costs and benefits. As Klusendorf writes, if the unborn are not persons, then killing them for virtually any reason "requires no more justification than having a tooth pulled."[29] At Planned Parenthood clinics, aborted baby parts are treated as nothing more than tissue for research, or garbage to pick through for sellable bits and then thrown away.[30]

The development of ultrasound has transformed the debate by making the baby visible in the early stages. These images have changed many people's minds. Yet not all. In media interviews I have often been asked how people can look at a baby in the womb, kicking its legs, sucking its thumb, and still say, "No, not a person." My answer is, "You are witnessing the power of a worldview. Once someone has accepted the two-story worldview, they can literally look at a baby as just an organism, a piece of matter, with no value and no right to protection."

Using more academic language, Leon Kass, former chairman of the President's Council on Bioethics, says the two-story view "dualistically sets up the concept of 'personhood' *in opposition* to nature and the body" and thus "it fails to do justice to the concrete reality of our embodied lives."[31] The Christian ethic rejects dualism and recognizes our dignity as embodied beings.

Post-Birth Abortion

In recent years, bioethicists have begun to apply the two-story worldview not only to abortion but also to infanticide. In 2013, two philosophers created a firestorm with an article arguing for what they called "after-birth abortion."[32]

What did they mean by that phrase? Infanticide. The killing of newborn babies.

The two philosophers argued that a baby is human but not a person—and that prior to personhood, human life has no moral claims on us. "Merely being human is not in itself a reason for ascribing [to] someone a right to life," they maintained. Thus "fetuses and newborns are not persons." And "since non-persons have no moral rights to life, there are no reasons for banning after-birth abortions."[33]

Do you recognize the key elements of personhood theory? According to these philosophers, a newborn is "merely human" and thus a "non-person." It exists only in the lower story, which implies that it has no moral value. It is merely a piece of matter that can be used for research and experimentation, harvested for organs, then tossed on the garbage heap.

Pro-life thinkers have long warned that America is heading in the same direction as the Nazis in Germany, and that is not just scaremongering. The Nazis did not begin by killing Jews. They first used their gas chambers to kill the handicapped, and the movement was led by the medical profession. Doctors argued that the lives of disabled people were "not worth living" (the German phrase was "*lebensunwertes Leben*").[34] Disturbingly, the 2013 article uses exactly the same phrase, arguing that after-birth abortion should be permitted for infants whose lives are "not worth living."

■ ■ ■ ■ ■

Science and the Soul

The fact that bioethicists come to such wildly conflicting definitions of personhood shows that the concept is virtually impossible to define once it is cut off from the sheer fact of being biologically human. The central role that biology plays in the debate casts a surprising new light on what both sides are really saying.

For example, it is commonly said that pro-life people are motivated by religious teachings about the soul, while pro-choice people rely strictly on science. Blogger Libby Anne writes, "The vast, vast majority of anti-abortion advocates have a problem with abortion because *they believe the zygote/fetus has a soul.*" She concludes that opposing "abortion based on the ensoulment of the zygote really is about pushing specific religious beliefs on the general public . . . [which is] a blatant violation of the separation of church and state."[35]

But this common objection gets things exactly backward. As a sociological fact, it's true that many pro-lifers are members of religious communities, which teach that humans have (or are) spiritual souls. Yet pro-life *arguments* do not start with the soul; they start with science.[36] No one argues about the moral worth of human life until scientific evidence first establishes that life exists.[37]

In the United States, many laws against abortion were passed in the nineteenth century, when medical knowledge first established that life begins at conception. That's when the genetic die is cast. On purely scientific grounds, older concepts were ruled irrelevant, such as "quickening" (the moment when a mother starts to feel the baby moving) or the moment when the baby takes its first breath. As a result, it was physicians—not churches—who were the leading advocates for laws criminalizing abortion.[38]

After all, governments do not decide whether to give legal protection to thirty-five-year-old adults based on whether they have a soul. The law protects them because they are human beings.

Of course, people are much *more* than biological organisms, and biology is not the most important dimension to life. Yet biology gives a baseline for identifying who is human. It is an objective, empirically testable, universally detectable marker of human status. The body is something we can see and identify scientifically—something we can all agree on. Human beings reproduce "after their kind," just as Genesis 1 says. Thus everyone who is human is also a person; they do not need to meet any additional criteria.

By contrast, personhood theory says some humans do not qualify as persons. In that case, how do we determine which humans *do* qualify? How do we identify the additional criteria they must meet? As we have seen, no two bioethicists agree on what personhood is or when it begins. Their definitions are purely subjective, reflecting their own personal values.

Why do we even need the concept of personhood as distinct from simply being human? As science journalist Dick Teresi points out, when talking about your pet, you do not talk about cat-hood or dog-hood as something distinct from the biological fact of being a cat or dog. No, if your pet is biologically a dog, that's enough. Teresi concludes that the two-story concept of personhood is a "philosophical/religious" concept[39]—not a matter of facts but a statement about values. Each bioethicist proposes a different list of the capacities needed to qualify as a person based on what they value most.

Personhood theory thus reflects the fact/value divide, which says values have no grounding in facts but are subjective choices (see introduction). The lesson is that when you accept a modernist concept of the body in the lower story, inevitably you end up with a postmodern concept of personhood in the upper story, cut off from any objective criteria.

Ultimately, someone will have to draw the line defining who qualifies as a person. But without objective criteria, the concept will be defined by raw power. Whoever has the most power—namely, the state—will decide who qualifies as a person.

In 2016 an international group of bioethicists published a statement calling on state authorities to start making hiring decisions in health care. It urged governments to set up "tribunals" to coerce doctors and other healthcare workers to perform abortion, infanticide, and euthanasia even if they believe those practices are morally wrong. And if doctors continue to protest, the statement said, they should be punished by being required to perform community service and attend re-education sessions.[40]

Infanticide as state policy has been around a long time. Just open your Bible to chapter 1 in the book of Exodus:

> The king of Egypt said to the Hebrew midwives . . . "If you see that the baby is a boy, kill him; but if it is a girl, let her live." The midwives feared God, however, and did not do what the king of Egypt had told them to do; they let the boys live. (Exod. 1:15–17)

When the state decides who qualifies as a person, the door is open to tyranny and oppression. If the state creates rights, the state can also take them away. Anyone at any stage of life could be demoted to the status of non-person and denied the right to live. When America's founders wrote in the Declaration of Independence that humans have unalienable rights "endowed by their Creator," they meant rights must come from a transcendent source—a source higher than the state. Otherwise they are not "unalienable."

Who's Bringing Religion into the Public Square?

Today many people think it is inappropriate to talk about rights endowed by a Creator, at least in the public square. Why? Because in the fact/value split, when a position is labeled *religious*, it is assumed to be private and subjective, not shared by others within the polity. Ironically, however, by that definition it is the *secular* view of personhood that should be barred from the public square. Though it claims to be scientific, in reality it is private and subjective.

Listen to Yale professor Paul Bloom, writing about abortion in the *New York Times*: "The question is not really about life in any biological sense," he writes. "It is instead asking about the magical moment at which a cluster of cells becomes more than a mere physical thing." And what "magical" force has the power to convert a "mere physical thing" into a person with a dignity so profound that it is morally wrong to kill it? That "is not a question that scientists could ever answer," Bloom intones. "*It is a question about the soul.*"[41]

So who's injecting religion into politics?

Put bluntly, abortion supporters have lost the argument on the scientific level. They can no longer deny that an embryo is biologically human. As a result, they have switched tactics to an argument based on personhood, defined ultimately by their own personal views and values. And when their view is codified into law, their private values are imposed on everyone else.

This switch in tactics was evident in a fascinating debate a few years ago. It began when professor Stanley Fish wrote in the journal *First Things* that pro-lifers have no right to bring their views into the public arena. Why not? Because their views are based on faith, he claimed, while abortion advocates base their views on science.[42] Robert George of Princeton challenged Fish to a debate at a meeting of the American Political Science Association. In his paper, George argued that in reality it is the pro-life position that is based on science.

As is customary, the two scholars exchanged their papers ahead of time. When the meeting opened, Fish threw George's paper on the table and announced, "Professor George is right, and he is right to correct me." The admission was met by stunned silence.

Fish later explained his startling turnaround. Supporters of abortion have typically cast themselves as "defenders of rational science against the forces of ignorance and superstition," he said. But when science began inexorably pushing back the moment when life begins, "they shifted tactics. . . . Nowadays, it is pro-lifers who make the scientific question of when the beginning of life occurs the key one . . . while pro-choicers want to transform the question into a 'metaphysical' or 'religious' one by distinguishing between mere biological life and 'moral life.'"[43]

The phrasing "mere biological life" versus "moral life" is Fish's way of saying body versus person. His point is that when pro-choicers lost the argument on the scientific level, they "shifted tactics" by adopting the two-story dualism and appealing to a non-scientific, non-empirical concept of personhood.

It's time to turn the tables on the old stereotypes.

With every advance of science, it becomes more evident that to be pro-life is to be on the side of science and reason. Scientists recently discovered that when a sperm meets an egg, an explosion of tiny sparks erupts from the egg at the exact moment of conception. Scientists have even captured these astonishing fireworks on film. "To see the zinc radiate out in a burst from each human egg was breathtaking," researchers said.[44] Human life literally begins in a bright flash of light.

Why Abortion Is Anti-Science

The only strategy left to those who support abortion is to dismiss the evidence from science. Jennie Bristow, editor of *Abortion Review*, wrote an article titled, "Abortion: Stop Hiding behind the Science." The article starts, "With anti-abortionists pushing 'scientific evidence' on fetal viability, it is time to restate the *moral* case for a woman's right to choose." Notice the scare quotes around the phrase "scientific evidence" as though to discredit the very idea. Repeatedly Bristow insists that "the question of abortion cannot be resolved at a scientific level . . . it is a political issue about women's need for abortion in a society committed to women's equality and individual autonomy."[45]

Translation: Who cares about scientific facts?

Personhood theory, with its dismissal of biological facts, is the unspoken assumption even in arguments that do not state it directly. Consider the claim that a fetus's right to life depends on whether or not it is wanted. A few years ago, MSNBC host Melissa Harris-Perry said, "When does life begin? I submit the answer depends an awful lot on the feelings of the parents." She added, "An unwanted pregnancy can be *biologically* the same as a wanted one. But the *experience* can be entirely different."[46]

So biological facts matter less than the "feelings of the parents."[47]

A *Salon* article asks defiantly, "So What If Abortion Ends Life?" The author, Mary Elizabeth Williams, starts by acknowledging the scientific facts: "I believe that life starts at conception. . . . Throughout my own pregnancies, I never wavered for a moment in the belief that I was carrying a human life inside of me."

Williams even castigates her fellow liberals for denying this obvious fact: "When we try to act like a pregnancy doesn't involve human life, we wind up drawing stupid semantic lines in the sand: first trimester abortion vs. second trimester vs. late term, dancing around the issue trying to decide if there's a single magic moment when a fetus becomes a person." Obviously there *is* no "magic moment," no sharp disjunction, no sudden transformation. Human development is a gradual, continuous process.

Yet because Williams supports abortion, she herself is logically required to select some "magic moment." For her, the deciding factor is autonomy. Whoever has autonomy wins. Here's how she puts it: "A fetus can be a human life without having the same rights as the woman in whose body it resides. She's the boss. Her life and what is right for her circumstances and her health should automatically trump the rights of the non-autonomous entity inside of her. Always."

Williams ends her article with these heart-wrenching words: "The fetus is indeed a life. A life worth sacrificing."[48]

Those who support abortion are not relying on science. They have taken a *moral* stance that the Declaration of Independence is wrong in pronouncing that all people are created equal. Williams states it bluntly: "All life is not equal." To borrow a line from George Orwell's *Animal Farm*, some lives are more equal than others.

Who's Imposing Their Beliefs?

The debate on abortion is often portrayed as a conflict pitting those who think the state should remain neutral on moral issues against those who want to "impose" their beliefs on others. Yet, as we have seen, personhood theory is far from neutral.

A few years ago I was invited to speak at a Christian worldview conference hosted by an Ivy League university, and I quickly noticed a pattern emerging. After each speaker, invariably some student would raise the same question, phrased in different words: If we talk about a Christian worldview, aren't we imposing our views on others? Clearly, even well-educated, Ivy League students have absorbed the secular doctrine that it is illegitimate to speak from a Christian perspective in the public arena—that doing so violates ideals of neutrality and objectivity.

When the same question came up after my lecture, as it inevitably did, I was ready with a counter-question: Is the *secular* position neutral? Is *it* unbiased and objective? Of course not. It rests on a highly contentious, two-level view of human nature that involves a crassly utilitarian view of the body (lower story) along with a subjective, arbitrary definition of the person (upper story). Nothing neutral about any of that.

And when the government mandates policies based on that worldview, it is imposing a secular ideology on an entire society.

The problem is that worldviews do not come neatly labeled. No one says that bioethical controversies involve two conflicting views of human nature. Instead people fall back on stereotypical phrases—science versus religion, facts versus faith. When we hear that kind of language, we should press everyone to put their worldview cards on the table. Only then will there be genuinely free and open debate.

What NPR Doesn't Get

I was once invited to be a guest on a National Public Radio program in San Francisco. Before the show, the producer interviewed me about my views on various subjects, including abortion. He commented that most people think abortion is acceptable "until the fetus becomes a person."

"That phrase carries enormous philosophical baggage," I pointed out. "It assumes a fragmented, fractured view of the human being that treats the body as extrinsic to the person, and therefore expendable. By contrast, those who oppose abortion hold a wholistic view of human nature as an integrated unity—which means the body has intrinsic value and worth."

The producer seemed surprised by this argument and had no answer. So I went on. "The pro-choice position is exclusive. It says that some people don't measure up. They don't make the cut. They don't qualify for the rights of personhood."

By contrast, I said, "the pro-life position is inclusive. If you are a member of the human race, you're 'in.' You have the dignity and status of a full member of the moral community."

A few days later the producer contacted me to say my interview had been canceled. It can be difficult for secular people to accept the dehumanizing implications of their own views. I had used venerated liberal buzzwords (*inclusive*, *wholistic*) to demonstrate that a biblical worldview actually fulfills the highest ideals of liberalism better than any secular worldview.

Young people seem to grasp this better than their Baby Boomer parents. Studies consistently find that voters under thirty are more pro-life than their parents. Among millennials, 51 percent believe abortion is morally wrong, compared to 37 percent who say it is morally acceptable.[49] The reason is not that millennials have grown more conservative generally. It's that they understand abortion as a human rights issue. Having grown up in a world surrounded by ultrasound images, they have greater empathy for the child now visible in the womb. And having grown up in a scientific culture, they have witnessed the miracle of neonatal medicine that makes it possible even for babies born extremely prematurely to survive and flourish—babies the same age as those being aborted down the street at the abortion clinic.

As one columnist writes, for many millennials, "the willful destruction of life in the womb seems less an act of 'reproductive freedom' than an act of violence against an innocent victim."[50]

Are Human Rights a "Christian Myth"?

The only worldview with the intellectual resources to protect those innocent victims is Christianity. Even secular thinkers often admit as much. Yuval Harrari, author of the international bestseller *Sapiens: A Brief History of Humankind*, argues that if you accept that life evolved by material processes (which he does), there is no logical basis for human rights.

Consider the Declaration of Independence and its concept of "unalienable rights . . . endowed by [the] Creator." Harrari argues that natural selection is a process for culling the most viable variations among living things. Thus the key to evolutionary advance is not equality but difference: "'Created equal' should therefore be translated into 'evolved differently.'"

In a materialist worldview, of course, there is no Creator to "endow" humans with rights. "There is only a blind evolutionary process, devoid of any purpose," Harrari writes. Organisms simply do whatever their evolved capacities enable them to do: "Birds do not fly because they have a right to fly, but because they have wings." And those evolved capacities are not "unalienable." They are constantly mutating and changing. So much for unalienable rights.

Phrase by phrase, Harrari picks apart the key claims in the Declaration. According to evolutionary materialism, he says, humans are merely biological organisms driven by instinct to seek pleasure. He concludes that the concept of equal rights is nothing but a "Christian myth."[51]

As the implications of evolutionary materialism filter down through the public mind, the rights enjoyed in free societies will be demoted to the status of "myth." And then who will defend those rights?

Wife Tells Husband: Man Up

We should not forget that half the population is effectively disenfranchised when it comes to abortion. Men are repeatedly told that they have no right to hold a position on the subject because they will never get pregnant themselves. On my Facebook page, a lively discussion on the topic ended when one woman snapped angrily, "I do not discuss abortion with men."

And many men are happy to duck the issue. "I lined up on the pro-choice side," writes Ruben Navarrette Jr.

> I arrived there for a simple reason: Because I'm a man. Many will say that this is not a very good reason, but it is my reason. Lacking the ability to get pregnant, and thus spared what has been for women friends of mine the anguishing decision of whether to stay pregnant, I've remained on the sidelines and deferred to the other half of the population.[52]

This attitude may sound humble. But Navarrette says he came to see that in reality his attempt to be neutral was "another name for 'wimping out.'"

It was his wife who challenged him to change his mind. "She's pro-life. . . . She's not buying my argument that, as a man, I have to defer to women to make their own choices about what to do with their bodies. To her, that's cowardly." It's time to man up, Navarrette's wife said to him. "These are babies that are being killed. Millions of them. And you need to use your voice to protect them. That's what a man does. He protects children—his own children, and other children. That's what it means to be a man.[53]

Being a man also means protecting women. Many women are pressured by parents, husbands, or boyfriends into abortions they do not want. In a *Medical Science Monitor* study, 64 percent of post-abortive women in America said they "felt pressured by others" to have the abortion. For themselves, 54 percent said they "were not sure about the decision at the time," and 50 percent actually "felt abortion was morally wrong."[54]

A full half of women having abortions believe it is morally wrong.

No wonder that, in the same study, 78 percent of women checked off that they felt "guilt" afterward and 56 percent reported "feeling sadness and loss." In one of my classes, a student named Christopher said, "I was pro-choice until I saw what abortion was doing to *women*. I have several friends who have had abortions. Every one of them wanted the abortion beforehand. And every one of them regretted it afterward. They were convinced they had taken a human life. When I saw how they struggled with guilt and depression, that's when I began to rethink the issue."

Being a man means protecting the vulnerable, the disenfranchised, and the disadvantaged.

More importantly, that is what it means to be Christian. They oppose abortion because of the biblical admonition to protect those who are weak, powerless, dependent, and needy. As Jesus told his followers, whatever we do to "the least of these," we do to him (Matt. 25:40).

■ ■ ■ ■ ■

Justice for the Unborn

"From ancient times," writes Timothy Keller, "the God of the Bible stood out from the gods of all other religions as a God on the side of the powerless, and of justice for the poor."[55] The Bible is clear that God's love extends to all humans, including those not yet born. The most eloquent expression is by the poet and prophet King David:

> You created my inmost being;
> you knit me together in my mother's womb. . . .
> My frame was not hidden from you
> when I was made in the secret place,
> when I was woven together in the depths of the earth.
> Your eyes saw my unformed body. (Ps. 139:13, 15–16)[56]

Similarly, Job says God created him at the beginning of his life: "Did you not . . . clothe me with skin and flesh and knit me together with bones and sinews" (Job 10:8, 11)? Jeremiah reports that God called him to be a prophet even before birth: "The word of the Lord came to me, saying, 'Before I formed you in the womb I knew you, before you were born I set you apart'" (Jer. 1:4–5). These verses make it clear that God is intimately involved in people's lives before they are born.

In the New Testament, Luke gives a startling account of a child who was even filled with the Holy Spirit before birth. John the Baptist was specially commissioned to proclaim the arrival of the Messiah. For that prophetic task, he received God's Spirit (together with his mother) while in the womb: "When Elizabeth heard Mary's greeting, the baby leaped in her womb, and Elizabeth was filled with the Holy Spirit." That infilling empowered her to recognize the newly pregnant Mary as "the mother of my Lord" (Luke 1:41–43). The tiny embryo in the womb was already "my Lord."

Columnist Matt Walsh writes, "*Jesus was Himself at one point an unborn child.* If there were any questions before His arrival about the sanctity of human life, those questions were answered 2,000 years ago."[57]

How to Be Countercultural

Theologically liberal organizations like the Religious Coalition for Abortion Rights argue that the Bible does not forbid abortion. And it is true that there are no explicit verses against it. That's because during the biblical era, the Jews did not think abortion was acceptable and therefore there was no need to outlaw it. They regarded abortion as a form of murder; thus laws against murder were sufficient.

By the time of the early church, however, Christians did have to take a stand. As we will see in the next section, in Greco-Roman culture both abortion and infanticide were widely accepted and practiced. Thus it is remarkable how strongly and uniformly the church fathers stood against both practices. The *Didache*, an early Christian text (AD 50–120), says, "Do not murder a child by abortion, nor kill it at birth." The second-century *Epistle of Barnabas* says, "You shall not slay a child by abortion." Justin Martyr wrote, "We have been taught that it is wicked to expose even newly born children . . . [for] we would then be murderers." Athenagoras wrote, "We say that women who use drugs to bring on an abortion commit murder . . . [for we] regard the very foetus in the womb as a created being, and therefore an object of God's care."

In the early third century, Tertullian wrote, "It does not matter whether you take away a life that is born, or destroy one that is coming to the birth. In both instances, destruction is murder." In the fourth century, Basil of Caesarea wrote, "A woman who deliberately destroys a fetus is answerable for murder." John Chrysostom asked, "Why do you abuse the gift of God . . . and make the chamber of procreation a chamber for murder?" Jerome called abortion "the murder of an unborn child." Augustine warned against the terrible crime of "the murder of an unborn child."[58]

The historical record of Christianity is impressive for its uniform opposition to abortion. The early Christians were not being "conservative" in the sense of following the lead of their culture. Instead they were radical, even countercultural.

Even if we are not certain that the child in the womb is fully a person, when in doubt a "generous justice" would counsel us to err on the side of protecting life. That is what we would do in any other situation. If we witnessed an auto accident and we were uncertain whether the victim was still alive, we would *not* say, "Since we're not quite sure, let's kill him." No, we would try to save his life. The same principle applies to abortion.

Why Women Love Christianity

The early church would not have been successful in overcoming abortion, however, if it had not at the same time promoted a high view of women. This is an important lesson for churches today. Because of Christianity's opposition to abortion, critics today portray it as hostile to women's rights. But surprisingly, in the early church it was the church's opposition to abortion and infanticide that made it especially *attractive* to women.

Here's why: A culture that practices abortion and infanticide is a culture that demeans women and disrespects their unique contribution to the task of reproduction. It does not treat women's ability to gestate and bear children as a wondrous and awesome capacity but as a liability, a disadvantage, a disability. It does not value and protect women in their childbearing capacity but seeks to suppress women's bodily functions, using toxic chemicals and deadly devices to violently destroy the life inside her.

Up until now, we have talked about how abortion expresses a low view of the body in relation to the fetus. But there are two bodies at stake—and abortion expresses a disrespect for women's bodies as well.

That disrespect was common in Roman society at the time of the early Christian church. Rodney Stark, a sociologist of religion, writes, "The Greco-Roman world was a male culture that held marriage in low esteem."[59] It also held women in low esteem, expressed partly through a high rate of abortion, which was a huge killer not only of children but also of women in this period. Infanticide was widely practiced as well. In fact, leading thinkers of the ancient world—Plato, Aristotle, Cicero—recommended infanticide as legitimate state policy.[60]

Archaeologists have discovered sewers clogged with the tiny bones of newborn babies dumped down the drain. A news article explains, "During Roman times, it was not uncommon for infants to be killed as a form of birth control. It was not a crime, as newborn infants were viewed as being 'not fully human.'"[61] Most of those babies were girls. In fact, it was rare for a Roman family to have more than one daughter. Historians have uncovered a letter written in the first century BC by a Roman soldier to his pregnant wife back home, saying, "If it is a boy, let it live; if it is a girl, expose it"[62] (leave it to die).

In this context, the Christian church stood out for its high view of women. By prohibiting abortion and infanticide, it showed that it cherished the female contribution in bringing new life into the world, treating it as something worthy of respect and protection. Little girls were not to be thrown down the sewer but loved and cared for as much as boys. The early Christians went beyond simply condemning abortion to providing alternatives—rescuing and adopting children who had been abandoned.

We should never defend Christianity by saying it is traditional. From the beginning, it has stood *against* the traditions of its day. Today, as in ancient times, abortion and infanticide are practiced primarily against baby girls. Sex-selection abortion has created a surplus of men in several nations, from China to India. Girls are also more likely to die from malnutrition and neglect. Adult women are subject to violence and death at the hands of husbands and other family members. The United Nations estimates that 200 million women are demographically missing.

Some have labeled it "gendercide."[63]

A documentary on the issue says, "The three deadliest words in the world are, 'It's a girl.'"[64] The world desperately needs the biblical view of a woman's worth.

How Ancient Culture "Humiliated" Women

In the early church, women were also drawn to Christianity because of the biblical sex ethic. It is no secret that the major factor driving the demand for abortion and infanticide is sexual immorality. Sex outside of marriage produces children who are unexpected and unwanted. Historian Michael Gorman writes, in the Greco-Roman world, "by far the most frequent reason [for abortion] was to conceal illicit sexual activity."[65] There is a direct and obvious relationship between sexual hedonism and abortion.

And sexual hedonism is another expression of a low view of women. In ancient Greek and Roman culture, it was widely accepted that husbands would have sex with mistresses, concubines, slaves, and prostitutes (both male and female). An ancient Athenian saying was, "Wives are for legal heirs, prostitutes are for pleasure." In Rome, the taxes collected from prostitution constituted a significant portion of the royal treasury.[66] (This may be one reason Jesus hung out with prostitutes: There were so many of them!)

Promiscuity was even held to be divinely sanctioned. The Roman gods practiced both adultery and rape. In Homer's *Iliad*, Hera, the wife of Zeus, decks herself out to seduce him away from the Trojan battlefield. She is so successful that, to compliment her, Zeus runs through a list of other women, goddesses, and nymphs he has bedded (he ignores the men he has bedded), insisting that none of them attracted him as much as she does at that moment. Touching.

By contrast, the church fathers wrote sermons urging husbands not to have sex with slaves or prostitutes. These practices were not easy to eradicate. In the fourth century, John Chrysostom was still preaching on why it was not okay for married men to have sex with their slaves. An ancient Christian treatise on the sufferings endured by married women included the "humiliation" of being replaced by servants in their husbands' affections.[67]

And what about the humiliation of those female servants who were coerced into sexual slavery? In Roman culture, sexual violence against poor and powerless women was widely accepted. Because they were regarded as social non-persons, they were not thought to have any legal rights that could be violated. Beginning in the fifth century, Christian leaders finally began to wield enough political influence to pass laws against sexual slavery. The church fathers called it "coerced sin." How could the church preach against sexual sin when many women (and men) had no choice? For a slave to resist the sexual advances of her or his master meant death. One historian notes that the most reliable index of the Christianization of an ancient society was the recognition of the injustice of sexual slavery. "Because prostitution was at the center of an ancient sexual culture . . . the progressive realization of its injustice is a privileged index of Christianization."[68]

Let that historical fact sink in: *The* most reliable index of how deeply Christianity had permeated a society was whether it outlawed sexual slavery. Today, as sex slavery and sex trafficking are again becoming widespread, modern Christians must recover their rich moral and humanitarian heritage. As the Western world sinks back into pre-Christian morality, followers of Jesus must once again become countercultural.

"A Common Table, but Not a Common Bed"

In what other ways was Christianity attractive to women? In ancient culture, many marriages were not love based. Spouses were selected with an eye to things like social status, property rights, and legal heirs. In sharp contrast, the New Testament taught men to "love their wives as their own bodies." The husband's "headship" was redefined as self-sacrifice, modeled on Christ's sacrificial love (Eph. 5:25–33). Men were not to abandon their wives through divorce. They were not to abuse their wives physically or emotionally: "Husbands, love your wives and do not be harsh with them" (Col. 3:19).

Husbands were positively commanded not to seek out slaves and prostitutes for sex but instead to keep up regular sexual relations with their wives: "Do not deprive each other except perhaps by mutual consent and for a time, so that you may devote yourselves to prayer. Then come together again" (1 Cor. 7:5).

To the shock of the ancient world, the New Testament taught that men (not just women) were to be faithful to their spouse. Christianity stood out as radically different because it taught that a husband actually *wrongs* his wife by his adultery. Jesus said, "Anyone who divorces his wife and marries another woman commits adultery against her. And if she divorces her husband and marries another man, she commits adultery" (Mark 10:11–12). Such even-handed treatment was revolutionary. At the time, "people thought men couldn't commit adultery," explains Beth Felker Jones. It was "women's bodies [that] were property and could be 'stolen' or 'damaged.'" Jesus "challenges the whole market economy that would buy and sell bodies, especially women's bodies. Adultery isn't a property crime. Adultery is a violation of God's intention for humanity. . . . Jesus radically equalizes the man and the woman in the one-flesh union."[69]

Likewise, Paul enjoined a symmetry unheard of in pagan culture: "The husband should fulfill his marital duty to his wife, and likewise the wife to her husband. The wife does not have authority over her own body but yields it to her husband. In the same way, the husband does not have authority over his own body but yields it to his wife" (1 Cor. 7:3–4). Nothing like this had ever been said before.

To stress that he was describing an obligation, not an option, in this passage Paul borrows legal language. The word used for marital "duty" normally refers to a debt of money. The word used for "authority" included state authority. The word for "deprive" normally meant to "defraud" or "refuse payment."[70] Paul did not care that in the ancient world men's sexual freedom was considered completely acceptable. In the church there was a new law: Men were called to sexual fidelity and exclusivity just as much as women were. Note that a woman was even given "authority" over her husband's body, an idea so radical that even today there are probably few who fully practice it.

Paul describes the mutuality of marriage again in these words: "A married man is concerned about . . . how he can please his wife . . . a married woman is concerned about . . . how she can please her husband" (vv. 33–34). This mutuality is so complete that some church fathers even treated the first part with incredulity—surely Paul was joking when he said a married man should care about pleasing his wife.

At a time when wives were considered legally the possession of their husbands, Paul's writings were radical. By elevating the status of women, they delivered a severe blow to the double standard that was the pre-Christian norm. And by keeping sex within marriage, the biblical ethic drove down the demand for abortion and infanticide. Children were born into families committed to loving and caring for them.

A second-century document called "The Epistle of Mathetes to Diognetus" sums up the surprising behaviors that set Christians apart from the pagan world: "They beget children; but they do not destroy their offspring. They have a common table, but not a common bed."[71]

Radical indeed.

No wonder women flocked to Christianity. As Stark writes, "The Christian woman enjoyed far greater marital security and equality than did her pagan neighbor." He adds, "Christianity was unusually appealing because within the Christian subculture women enjoyed far higher status than did women in the Greco-Roman world at large."[72]

Then, as now, what Christians do with their sexuality is one of the most important testimonies they give to the surrounding world. They are called to build a community of families that respects women and cares for the young and vulnerable.

■ ■ ■ ■ ■

The Real War against Women

From ancient times, the principle is that a culture that engages in abortion, infanticide, and sexual license is a culture that disrespects women. At first sight, modern societies may seem to contradict that principle. After all, Western culture accepts these practices yet women there have greater rights and opportunities than anywhere else in the world.

Yes, but at a price. "Here is the bargain we professional women have been making," writes economist Jennifer Roback Morse.[73] To achieve higher levels of education and professionalism, women are required to suppress their fertility with birth control—to neuter themselves with toxic chemicals during their peak childbearing years. (The World Health Organization classifies hormonal contraceptives as a "class one carcinogenic," that is, a substance known to cause cancer in humans.) Since all contraceptives have a failure rate, women then resort to abortion as a backup. (According to statistics from the Guttmacher Institute, about half of women getting abortions claim they were using contraception during the month they got pregnant.)[74]

To avoid being derailed from their education or career path, women are urged to "meet their sexual needs" through casual affairs without emotional commitment. Reporter Hanna Rosin writes (approvingly) that during college, "women benefit greatly from living in a world where they can have sexual adventure without commitment . . . and where they can enter into temporary relationships that don't get in the way of future success."[75]

The problem is that when women are finally established in their careers, many are finding that their fertility has declined—sometimes damaged by sexually transmitted diseases—and they are no longer able to have the families they want. At that point, they are subjecting themselves to invasive, expensive, and often disappointing fertility treatments, or turning to morally problematic practices such as surrogacy. When they do get pregnant, women who have had abortions are more likely to suffer complications such as very premature birth, so that their babies spend months in the neonatal intensive care unit.[76]

Is *this* pro-woman?

Morse is writing from her own experience. She put off marriage and family to get ahead professionally, then found that she could not have children when she wanted to. She and her husband suffered through years of infertility before finally adopting a child from overseas. She concludes that young women "are being sold a cynical lie." They have accepted the cultural imperative that they must get established in their careers before they can think seriously about marriage and motherhood. "They do not realize that they are giving themselves over to careers during their peak fertility years, with the expectation that somehow, someday, they can 'have it all.'"[77]

The ideal worker standard in American business was set in an earlier age, when men could function in the workplace essentially as though they were single because their wives were home full-time to cook, shop, maintain the home, and raise the children. Today the same standard still prevails in the corporate world, with the result that women are also required to function essentially like single men if they want professional careers. Many young women are petrified of getting pregnant and falling off the career track.

This issue is personal for me because I got pregnant with my first child when I was in seminary. The only way I knew to fulfill my deepest aspirations was in the academic world, so dropping out of school to raise a child felt akin to falling into a black hole. Later I discovered that I loved being a mother, but at the time I felt deeply ambivalent about becoming pregnant. It seemed to me distinctly unfair that my husband, for his part, did *not* face the possible loss of his professional life. The sacrifices women are required to make in industrialized societies by giving up their public life and career is a major reason many hold a negative view of pregnancy and childrearing and then resort to abortion.[78]

A better solution would be for universities and workplaces to be responsive to both mothers and fathers looking for a better work/family balance. There is nothing sacrosanct about the 1950s ideal worker standards, and we should not feel compelled to abide by them when they no longer work. (They were not particularly healthy at the time either, because children rarely had close relationships with their fathers. There was a lot of "father hunger" even when fathers were technically in the home.)

Morse sums up: "Until now, we [women] have been adapting our bodies to the university and the market. I say, we should respect our bodies enough to demand that the university and the market adapt to us and our bodies."[79] That is, instead of asking women to bully their bodies with toxic chemicals (contraceptives), violent acts (abortion), and invasive laboratory-based fertility treatments so they fit into a career path designed essentially for single men, we should design career paths that are supportive for parents—both mothers and fathers.

A culture that respects women's bodies will create more flexible career trajectories that allow women to have their families at the time that is biologically optimal. It will create education and work patterns that fit around family responsibilities. When we do that, we will reduce a major motive for abortion.

Welcoming the Wounded

It is also crucial that the church once again becomes known as a place that values women. Rejecting abortion is a way of expressing respect not only for the child but also for the mother.

The link between the two was clear to me even before I converted to Christianity. In my teens and young adulthood, I identified with the hippie movement—natural food, natural childbirth, natural fiber clothing. I was not morally opposed to abortion. (Even after I became a Christian, it took several years before I understood why abortion is morally wrong.) Yet I did not consider it an option because I saw it as a violent intrusion into the natural processes of the body. I believed in working *with*, not against, the natural functions of a woman's body. Childbearing is a healthy biological function, not a disease to be attacked with sharp instruments and life-destroying chemicals. Eventually I joined an organization called Pro-Life Feminists, because it seemed to me that a genuine feminism should support, affirm, and respect a woman's body and her distinctive role in reproduction.

The church should also strive to be known as a sanctuary for those wounded by the callous cynicism of the abortion culture. Women who have had abortions are often afraid to even talk to Christians about it. One of my students, Nicole, was attending a Christian college when she was raped in her dorm room by an angry former boyfriend. When she realized she was pregnant, her first thoughts were, *What will my church think? Will my family be shunned?* Panicked, she set up an appointment for an abortion at the first available date. Even today, she has not told anyone in her church about it.

"Christians are more likely to accept a convicted criminal than a woman who has had an abortion," Nicole told me. "That may sound like an exaggeration, but think about it: Many churches have prison ministries. But how many have ministries to women who have had an abortion?"

Ironically, Nicole was pro-life at the time of her abortion—and she still is. How tragic that she was so certain she would be rejected by her church that she overrode her own moral convictions. What message is the church sending women that many are afraid of reaching out to those most equipped to help them?

Lecrae: "A Part of Us Died"

And what about men who are wounded by abortion? One of my students, Hannah Zarr, used to work at a pregnancy center, and she recalls the despair of the fathers who accompanied their wives or girlfriends. One man put his head in his hands, then paced the floor, and finally confided to Hannah that he wanted to keep the baby but his girlfriend did not. "He kept asking me, if his girlfriend decided to go through with the abortion, what could he do?" Hannah told me. The answer is that legally there is nothing a father can do. The Supreme Court rejected spousal consent in *Planned Parenthood v. Danforth* (1976) and rejected even spousal notification in *Planned Parenthood v. Casey* (1992).

Hannah said, "As I looked into the man's eyes—filled with such desperation—I realized how unfair it is that legally he had no say whatsoever regarding the life of his child. It was his child too. But he had no way to protect his baby."[80]

Even men who push their wives or girlfriends into getting abortions may regret it later. Lecrae Moore, a Grammy Award–winning hip-hop artist, has publicly admitted the role he played in persuading his girlfriend to abort their child in 2002. At the time, he had converted to Christianity but was still living a lifestyle of drugs and sex. As he dropped off his girlfriend at the abortion clinic, he knew his action was—in his words—an expression of "me choosing my life over yours." In his song "Good, Bad, Ugly," he says, "I was too selfish with my time / Scared my dreams were not gonna survive / So I dropped her off at that clinic / That day, a part of us died."[81]

Lecrae did not confront his sense of guilt until years later, when he was preparing to marry the woman who is now his wife. "I literally broke down over the guilt and the remorse and the shame of it all," he says. "That was the beginning of the healing process for me."[82] Abortion is the number one cause of death for African Americans today.[83]

The next time you are in a church service, look around at the pews and consider the sheer number of people who have been affected by abortion—both women and men. How can you bring a biblical message of hope and healing? As John Piper says, "The gospel teaches us how to live, but it also rescues us when we fail to live the way we are supposed to live."[84]

Fortunately, creative Christians are breaking the mold by starting recovery programs for those who regret their abortions, such as Rachel's Vineyard and Surrendering the Secret. Yet the number of people affected by abortion far exceeds those who are currently getting help.[85]

"You Have No Right to Talk"

Another creative response to abortion is the work of pregnancy centers that give support to people who experience a problem pregnancy. These centers offer practical help, social support, financial assistance, clothing, and child care for pregnant women and their children.

A secular friend of mine once said angrily, "You pro-life people have no right to talk about abortion until you are willing to stand alongside pregnant women and give them support." But his demand has already been granted. In the United States there are roughly twice as many pro-life pregnancy centers as abortion clinics.[86] These centers are all or mostly operated by Christians. Secular people who claim to care about women are missing in action when it comes to giving practical help to women facing a difficult pregnancy.

In 2016 Stephanie Chatfield, the wife of Michigan state representative Lee Chatfield, publicly revealed that she had an abortion. Her husband had been tipped off that an unnamed source planned to go public with the information in an attempt to discredit him. So Stephanie decided to get out in front with her own confession.

In a Facebook post, she shared that as a teenager in high school she attended a party where she drank too much alcohol. "I have no memory of the majority of that night, but judging by my appearance and physical condition the next morning, I knew I had been taken advantage of," she wrote. "Three weeks later, I found out I was pregnant." She did not tell anyone. "I was ashamed and I was scared." A week later, she had an abortion.

Today she calls that decision "the worst one of my life." She writes, "It was my easy way out, but little did I know that I would be stricken with an unbearable guilt for the months and even years to follow. . . . It's haunted me. It's made me weep. It's made it difficult to look in the mirror at times."

Finally she confided in her parents and in Lee, who at the time was her ex-boyfriend. They embraced her with the good news of "the full forgiveness and grace that God freely offers through His Son Jesus Christ. . . . Christ took my place on the cross and bore the weight of my sin, so that I could have eternal life."[87]

In her Facebook post, Stephanie addresses young women who are facing an unplanned pregnancy:

> There are crisis pregnancy centers in our area that exist for the sole purpose of helping girls like you. The support is there. You will not be judged, but rather you will be loved and forgiven. Be courageous. Reach out and look for support![88]

Imagine the healing potential if churches were to become widely known as places of transparency and healing. Too many people have the impression that Christians are people who claim to be holy while looking down on others. We should strive to make our churches places where people like Stephanie feel safe to share their stories and to encourage others.

Love in Action: Baby Boxes

Meanwhile, across the globe, a pastor has discovered a creative way to help save abandoned babies. In a ragged working-class neighborhood in Seoul, South Korea, one house has a small drop box built into the wall. A hand-scrawled sign outside the drop box says, "If you can't take care of your disabled babies, don't throw them away or leave them on the street. Bring them here." The box is lined with a soft pink and blue blanket and has a bell that rings when the little door is opened.

The drop box is in the home of Presbyterian pastor Lee Jong-rak, and since 2009 Lee has saved the lives of more than six hundred children. He and his wife adopted ten (the maximum number allowed in South Korea), then arranged for the adoption of others.

Inscribed along the top of the drop box is Psalm 27:10, "For my father and my mother have forsaken me, but the Lord will take me in" (ESV).

Pastor Lee's concern for the disabled started when he and his wife gave birth to a baby who was severely brain damaged. The tragedy sparked a cascade of questions that even caused him to rethink his Christian convictions: "I asked God, 'Why would you give me a handicapped child?'"

As he cared for his helpless son, however, Lee began to be convinced of the preciousness of life. At the hospital where his son spent most of his early years, he began to encourage other families with disabled children. In South Korea, Lee says, babies with deformities are seen as a national shame. It is a culture addicted to perfection, where cosmetic surgeries have become as common as haircuts.[89]

The abandonment of babies is not a problem only in South Korea, however. In 2016 the first baby box in the United States was installed at the Woodburn Fire Department in Woodburn, Indiana. Under Indiana's Safe Haven Law, a mother has thirty days after the birth of her baby to decide if she wants to keep the child or turn it over to authorities with no questions asked.

When a mother places her baby inside the baby box, it locks automatically and authorities are alerted. Within three minutes of the call, emergency personnel arrive to take care of the baby.

Appropriately enough, it was a woman who was herself abandoned as an infant who founded the Safe Haven Baby Boxes organization, which is now sponsoring additional depositories in other states for mothers in crisis. "As a child who was abandoned by my birth mother two hours after I was born," Monica Kelsey says, "I am honored that Christ has me spearheading a program that will save the lives of abandoned children."[90]

The best scenario, of course, is that someday drop boxes will no longer be needed. In the meantime, they are one way for Christians to show the world that even those who have been rejected as unwanted have great value in God's eyes.

In the ancient world, Christians were distinctive for their humanitarian efforts—taking care of babies and slaves, of widows and orphans, of the sick and elderly, of the unwanted and abandoned. Today, as the West sinks back into pre-Christian practices, we must once again be ready to stand with courage and conviction. We need to confront the underlying worldview of personhood theory, with its dehumanizing impact, and then find practical ways to express the Bible's high view of human life.

As the population ages, the question of personhood is also coming to the fore in a new and troubling way as we care for a growing population of the elderly. In addition, new ethical challenges are being raised by technology. In the next chapter we will analyze practices such as euthanasia and eugenics, stem cell research, and the sale of fetal tissue—while offering life-giving Christian alternatives.

3

Dear Valued Constituent

You No Longer Qualify as a Person

Science fiction writer Philip K. Dick is highly respected for his many short stories that have been turned into movies, including "Blade Runner," "Minority Report," and "Total Recall." But one story exposed him to intense public criticism and controversy.

It was titled "The Pre-Persons."[1]

Dick composed the story shortly after the Supreme Court's 1973 *Roe v. Wade* decision, and his purpose was to highlight the difficulty of defining personhood. As we saw in chapter 2, once the concept of personhood is detached from biology, there is no objective way to draw the line—no point at which we can logically say, "Up to this point, there was merely a human, but now it has been magically transformed into a person."

In Dick's fictionalized America, the age at which a child could legally be aborted had been relentlessly pushed forward. First, abortion was legal only in the early months of pregnancy. Then the later months. Then the abortion lobby argued that even newborns were just expelled fetuses.

"Where was the line to be drawn finally?" muses a character in the story. "When the baby smiled its first smile? When it spoke its first word or reached for its initial time for a toy it enjoyed?"

Lawmakers kept moving the line from one arbitrary stopping point to the next, until finally they decided the right age was . . . twelve years old. The age when you can do algebra. That's when you have the cognitive capacity to qualify as a person. "Up to then, it was only body, animal instincts and body, animal reflexes and responses to stimuli. Like Pavlov's dogs."

Up to the age of twelve, then, children were pre-persons and could be killed for any reason. If parents decided they did not want their child any more, they called the local abortion center. It would send a van to collect the child, like a dogcatcher, and take him or her to be euthanized. The procedure was called a postpartum abortion. The van was even equipped with a Good Humor–style jingle, playing nursery school songs. Read the first few lines of the story:

> Past the grove of cypress trees . . . Walter saw the white truck, and he knew it for what it was. He thought, That's the abortion truck. Come to take some kid in for a postpartum down at the abortion place.
>
> And he thought, Maybe *my* folks called it. For *me*.
>
> He ran and hid among the blackberries, feeling the scratching of the thorns but thinking, It's better than having the air sucked out of your lungs. That's how they do it. . . . They have a big room for it.
>
> For the kids nobody wants.[2]

The point is that when the concept of personhood is detached from biology, it becomes arbitrary, with no objective criteria. Eventually, the definition of a person will be enforced by whichever group has the most power, using the instrumentalities of the state. If an unborn baby is not a person, what about children already born? What about people with disabilities? People who are terminally ill? The mentally ill? The elderly?

Ultimately, we are all at risk. The main character in the story reflects, "What was so sad was the sight now of the small child playing bravely in his yard day by day, trying to hope, trying to pretend a security he did not have."[3] Once human status is not enough to guarantee rights, we are all like those little children, pretending to have a security none of us has.

When Christians argue ethical issues in the public square, they are not seeking to impose their values on everyone else, as they are often accused of doing. They are not seeking power and control for themselves. Instead they are working to protect human rights in ways that benefit everyone. In this chapter we will see how personhood theory, which was first applied to abortion, is now being applied to a host of other issues, from euthanasia to selling fetal tissue, from stem cell research to animal rights, from genetic engineering to eugenics. Personhood theory is *the* concept driving threats to the dignity of human life today.

Euthanasia Vans

No doubt, Philip Dick intended "The Pre-Persons" as dystopian fiction. But life often imitates art. In 2015 British columnist Katie Hopkins began to call literally for euthanasia vans. "We just have far too many old people," Hopkins said in an interview. "It's ridiculous to be living in a country where we can put dogs to sleep but not people." Her proposed solution? "Easy. Euthanasia vans—just like ice-cream vans—that would come to your home."

Hopkins is being deliberately provocative, but she is also serious. "It would all be perfectly charming," she said. "They might even have a nice little tune they'd play. I mean this genuinely. I'm super-keen on euthanasia vans."[4]

I'm sure she is . . . until one comes for her.

Hopkins's reference to ice-cream vans playing tunes makes me think she may have read "The Pre-Persons." Or perhaps she just read the newspapers. For the past few years, the country of Holland has already had euthanasia vans. A Dutch right-to-die organization offers a mobile euthanasia service, with teams traveling around the country to deliver lethal drugs or injections to patients whose own doctors have ethical objections to helping them die. Critics have dubbed them "mobile death squads."

Once a society accepts a worldview, it tends to work out the logical consequences. The process may proceed quickly or slowly, but because we are rational beings made in God's image, we tend to live out the implications of our convictions. As we saw in chapter 2, the two-story dualistic worldview was applied first to babies in the womb. The fetus was declared a non-person—expendable, disposable, and fair game for research and experimentation. But today bioethicists have begun to apply the same dehumanizing logic to those already born.

According to personhood theory, human dignity consists in the ability to exercise conscious, deliberate control over our lives (upper story). If a disabled patient loses that mental control due to disease or injury, then personhood itself is lost—even though the patient is still alive and human (lower story).

For example, bioethicist Daniel Callahan says once a patient has lost "the capacity to reason, to have emotions, and to enter into relationships," they cannot "be called a 'person' any longer. . . . It is a mere body only." At that point, Callahan concludes, the principle of the "sanctity of life" no longer applies.[5] You can be unplugged, your treatment withheld, your food and water discontinued, your organs harvested.[6]

Personhood theory applied to euthanasia

PERSON

Exercises Autonomy and Control

BODY

Is a Disposable Piece of Matter

Of course, medical professionals have always had to make difficult practical decisions when treating severely ill patients. The best principle is always to err on the side of life. But it can be a judgment call whether a particular medical procedure is saving life or merely prolonging death. When a patient's organ systems are all shutting down despite the best medical treatment, then intervention may merely prolong the dying process. In that case, ending invasive and painful forms of medical intervention may allow for more humane care of the patient.

As Hauerwas notes, there is "a distinction between putting to death and letting die."[7]

Yet bioethics is not driven only by such practical considerations. It is also driven by worldviews. Peter Singer expresses the dualistic worldview when he insists "that the concept of a person is distinct from that of a member of the species Homo sapiens, and that it is personhood, not species membership, that is most significant in determining when it is wrong to end a life."[8] In other words, being a member of the human species is not enough to qualify as a person with the right to life. You must also meet some additional standard, some level of mental functioning. If you fail to meet that standard, you are just a piece of matter, and your body can be used in experiments, harvested for organs, subject only to a cost-benefit analysis. As bioethicist

Tom Beauchamp writes, "Because many humans lack properties of personhood or are less than full persons . . . they might be aggressively used as human research subjects or sources of organs."[9]

In our day, it is secular bioethicists like Singer and Beauchamp who influence the doctors who set hospital policy, the legislators who write laws, the judges who rule in court cases, and the healthcare workers who make decisions about our parents and relatives—and eventually about ourselves. That's why it is critical that we delve more deeply into the personhood theory that lies at the heart of secular bioethics.

Darwinian Path to Death

In chapter 2, we learned that a key turning point in the development of the two-story worldview was Darwin's theory of evolution. So it is not surprising that many of the leading figures who first called for abortion and euthanasia were supporters of Darwinism. Many of them advocated eugenics, the attempt to improve humanity by eliminating people with disabilities and genetic defects, as well as people deemed to be of "lower" races. In the public mind, eugenics is linked to the Nazis, but in reality it was practiced and promoted throughout much of the Western world even before the rise of Nazism.

In the nineteenth century, German biologist Ernst Haeckel gained fame as an outspoken promoter of Darwin's theory. In his opinion, modern civilizations that care for the disabled are interfering with the evolutionary principle of survival of the fittest. He urged them to follow "the example of the Spartans and Redskins" who killed disabled infants immediately after birth. He favored euthanasia for disabled adults as well.[10]

On this side of the Atlantic as well, Darwinism led many prominent thinkers to accept abortion and euthanasia. One historian writes, "The most pivotal turning point in the early history of the euthanasia movement was the coming of Darwinism to America."[11]

For example, most people are familiar with Jack London's famous novels, such as *The Call of the Wild*. But what they don't know is that London was an enthusiastic supporter of both euthanasia and eugenics. As a young man, London underwent what one historian calls "a conversion experience"[12] to radical materialism by reading the works of Charles Darwin. He memorized long passages from Darwin and could quote them by heart, the way Christians memorize Scripture.

In his short story "The Law of Life," written in 1901, London portrays an old Eskimo left behind by his nomadic tribe to die in the snow. As the wolves close in to devour him, the old man ponders that, after all, evolution assigns the organism only one task: to reproduce so the species will survive. After that, if the individual dies, "What did it matter after all? Was it not the law of life?"[13]

The story pounds home the theme that humans have no higher purpose beyond sheer biological survival—that those who have outlived their biological usefulness should be willing to die.[14]

Margaret Sanger, who founded Planned Parenthood in 1921, was another disciple of Darwin. Modern feminists honor her as an early promoter of birth control, but many do not know that she also promoted death control (euthanasia)—the "one being to bring *entrance* into life under control of reason, and the other to bring the *exit* of life under that control." She wrote, "The most merciful thing that the large family does to one of its infant members is to kill it."[15]

Oliver Wendell Holmes Jr. was one of the most revered Supreme Court justices in American history. Many are surprised to learn that he, too, was an avid Darwinian who supported euthanasia and eugenics. He penned the infamous *Buck v. Bell* decision (1927) supporting compulsory sterilization laws, which many states had enacted to promote eugenics. In private correspondence he also advocated "putting to death infants that didn't pass the examination." Holmes expressed his "contempt" for anyone "not prepared . . . to kill anyone below standard."[16]

Another supporter of euthanasia was Clarence Darrow, a trial lawyer best known for arguing in favor of Darwinism in the Scopes trial of 1925. Many people know his name from the famous movie *Inherit the Wind*. Darrow favored infanticide, urging people to "chloroform unfit children. Show them the same mercy that is shown beasts that are no longer fit to live."[17]

Why Christianity Is "Evil"

Why did Darwinism lead so many leading thinkers to support eugenics? Darwin's theory is often regarded as crucial scientific support for the philosophy of materialism, which reduces humans to material organisms, motivated by physical pain and pleasure. As journalist John Zmirak explains, according to materialism, humans are "merely potential sites for either suffering or pleasure. If we cannot guarantee their pleasure, we at least can end their suffering."[18] Even if the only way to end their suffering is to end their life.

The corollary is that any morality that forbids taking life in such circumstances must be suppressed—especially Christian morality. After all, moral principles are not material. They cannot be seen, heard, weighed, or measured. Consequently, materialist philosophy concludes that morality is not real. It is an illusion—window dressing to disguise what is *really* nothing but the human organism's drive to avoid pain and enhance pleasure.

The irony is that, in practice, even committed materialists end up with a form of dualism. To use our two-story metaphor, materialists try to "live" in the lower story, defining reality strictly in terms of material objects knowable by science. But logically, they must decide there is some dividing line that distinguishes those who are sub-personal, who may be killed with impunity, from those who are full persons deserving legal protection. Otherwise they would think it was okay to kill everyone.

Thus even the most rigorous materialists are logically required to operate with an implicit personhood dualism. They are compelled to draw a distinction between the human as a biological organism (lower story) who is expendable and the person (upper story) who has rights and liberties.

An act has an intrinsic logic of its own, and the logic of euthanasia is the two-story division of the human being.

Who Deserves to Live?

The concept of personhood was first explicitly proposed in 1968 by a group of thirteen medical doctors and professors who met at Harvard Medical School. They offered what came to be called "the Harvard criteria" for establishing when a patient has died. In the process, says science journalist Dick Teresi, "the Harvard criteria switched the debate from biology to philosophy. You are dead not when your heart cannot be restarted, you can no longer breathe, or your cells die, but when you suffer a 'loss of personhood.'"[19]

The problem is that the concept of personhood is not based on any objective reality. Most people think brain death is established by an EEG. Not so. Back in 1971, it was discovered that some patients diagnosed as brain dead still had brain waves, so the requirement of an EEG was eliminated. The measures that doctors now use to determine death vary widely.[20] As we saw in chapter 1, some doctors like Ronald Cranford have argued that even patients who are conscious—who can answer questions and scoot around the hospital in an electric wheelchair—are not "persons" and should have their food and water discontinued.

Teresi concludes that death has become "a social construct. We write people off as dead when it is convenient to do so. . . . Doctors are not making medical judgments but rather moral judgments about who deserves to live or die."[21]

Essentially a patient is no longer a person when the attending physician says so.

When Death Is Cheaper

Polls reveal that many ordinary people are accepting personhood theory, even if they are not familiar with the term. That is, they are accepting the idea that the value of their lives depends on their ability to exercise autonomy and control. Advocates for assisted suicide typically use scare tactics that tap into our fear of intense pain. But in jurisdictions that have legalized assisted suicide, surprisingly, most people who choose to die are *not* experiencing pain or suffering. One study found they are most afraid of the "impending loss of self, abilities, and quality of life"—and when that happens, "they fear being a burden to others."[22]

Similarly, another study found that the majority of those who seek out a doctor to give them a lethal prescription fear losing control. They check off reasons like "losing autonomy" (91 percent) and "less able to engage in activities" (89 percent). Only a minority check off reasons we might normally expect, such as debilitating pain (24 percent) or worry about the cost of medical treatment (3 percent).[23]

These polls show that secular society has successfully drilled into people's minds the idea that when we lose control and autonomy, our lives lose their value.

In 2015, a seventy-five-year-old woman named Gill Pharaoh ended her life in an assisted suicide clinic, abandoning her children and a life partner who loved her. Her reason? "I do not think old age is fun." The woman suffered no serious health issues. She even stated, "I am enjoying my life." But she worried that at some later time, she might deteriorate to a "stage when I may be requiring a lot of help."[24]

It is outrageous that people today are terrified of one day requiring "help." We must stand by people struggling with their fears and let them know that even when they become less independent and productive, they are worthwhile persons deserving of care and respect. A student of mine named Alison DeLong, who works for a suicide hotline, told me, "I spend hours every week persuading people not to end their lives, telling them that their lives still have value. It breaks my heart that people think they must be able to function in a certain way to be considered significant."

In the future, the decision may be taken out of our hands. In states where assisted suicide (also called voluntary euthanasia) is legal, some patients report being pressured to end their lives to avoid costly medical treatment. In Oregon, there have been several reports of cancer patients being pushed toward assisted suicide because it is cheaper than the medical treatment they need. Cancer drugs can cost anywhere from $3,000 to $6,000 a month, while the cost of lethal medication is about $35 to $50.[25]

It doesn't take a genius to see that the easiest way to reduce healthcare costs is physician-assisted suicide. When human life is no longer seen to have inherent value, it will be subject to purely utilitarian calculation of costs and benefits.

Voluntary euthanasia may not remain voluntary.

It is a tragedy to see the medical profession move from suicide prevention to suicide facilitation. The right-to-die movement presents euthanasia as compassionate. But disparaging human life as expendable is not compassionate. The term *compassion* literally means to "suffer with" (*com* = with, *passion* = suffer). True compassion means being willing to suffer on behalf of others, loving them enough to bear the burden of caring for them.

If Humans Are Machines, Why Not Pull the Plug?

What about *in*voluntary euthanasia, when individuals are not capable of giving informed consent? If they are not lucid enough to make decisions for themselves, that in itself is taken to mean that they are no longer persons. Peter Singer insists that the severely mentally incapacitated are candidates for euthanasia because they "were once persons" but no longer. "Their lives have no intrinsic value. . . . They are *biologically* alive, but not *biographically*."[26]

Joseph Fletcher even manages to turn an ethic of life into a form of cruelty: "To prolong life uselessly, while the personal qualities of freedom, knowledge, self-possession and control, and responsibility are sacrificed, is to attack the moral status of a person."[27]

The arts are addressing the issue as well. An opera by minimalist composer Steve Reich explores various threats to human life, with a libretto that juxtaposes recordings from scientists. The well-known atheist Richard Dawkins is heard saying that humans "are machines created by our genes." Immediately biologist Robert Pollack draws the logical conclusion: "I have no sense of guilt pulling the plug on any machine."[28]

If humans are reduced to machines, why should anyone object to pulling the plug?

These are not merely abstract moral issues to debate. I am often invited to lecture on the topics in this book, and when I get to euthanasia almost invariably someone in the room starts weeping. Talking to them afterward, I learn that they have gone through the experience of making a difficult life-and-death decision about a father or mother or grandparent.

During one lecture, I noticed that a stately older black woman had tears in her eyes. Introducing herself as Evelyn, she explained that her father had been in the hospital for heart problems but was not dying. Nevertheless, the doctors decided his time had come. Unfortunately, Evelyn was out of town, and the doctors persuaded the rest of the family to say yes to a lethal injection. In urgent phone calls, Evelyn begged them not to decide until she could get back home, but she was too late. By the time she got off the plane, her father's life had been ended.

The only reliable support for human rights is the conviction enshrined in the Declaration of Independence that "all men are created equal," even if they are disabled or elderly. A biblical worldview says a disabled person is just that—a disabled *person*. Its view of the human being is wholistic and incarnational, treating the body as the embodiment of the person. As Meilander puts it, in bioethics we must constantly remind ourselves that in dealing with the human body, we are dealing with "the place where we come to know a person."[29]

Euthanasia advocates are essentially saying that our personhood consists solely in the higher mental functions. The implication is that our bodies are not part of our identity as persons. But the idea of personhood based on cerebral function is very fragile. My personhood might end the moment my cortex starts to malfunction. By contrast, the biblical view is much more resilient and enduring. "In Christian thinking," writes physician John Wyatt, "whatever happens to you in the future, whatever disease or accident may befall your central nervous system, even if you are struck down by dementia or enter a persistent vegetative state, you will still be you: a unique and wonderful person known and loved by God."[30] The pressure is off to prove our worth or persuade people that our lives have value.

At the end of time, with the redemption of the body, we will finally recognize the beauty and grandeur in each human being. We can start even now to train ourselves to see people within that eschatological perspective. In the words of theologian David Hart, we can learn to recognize that there is "a glory hidden in the depths of every person, even the least of us—even 'defectives' and 'morons' and 'genetic inferiors,' if you will—waiting to be revealed, a beauty and dignity and power of such magnificence and splendor that, could we see it now, it would move us either to worship or to terror."[31]

Don't Impose Your Views

Liberals often say, "If you're against abortion, don't have one. If you're against assisted suicide, don't do it. But don't impose your views on others." At first, that might sound fair. But what progressives fail to understand is that every social practice rests on certain assumptions of what the world is like—a worldview. When a society accepts the practice, it absorbs the worldview that justifies it.

That's why issues like abortion and euthanasia are not matters of purely private individuals making personal choices. They involve deciding which worldview will shape our communal life.

We grasp the connection more clearly when considering other issues: "Don't like murder? Then don't kill anyone. Don't like slavery? Then don't own slaves. But don't tell me I don't have that choice." No one makes those arguments. We understand that granting private individuals the right to murder and enslave people inescapably implies a worldview—one that says some people's lives are expendable, not worthy of legal protection.

In the same way, accepting abortion or euthanasia inescapably implies personhood theory—one that says some people's lives are expendable, not worthy of legal protection. And when that worldview is absorbed, it has life-and-death consequences ultimately for everyone. Any cutoff point becomes arbitrary. The dehumanizing effects put all of us at risk. When Christians argue for the truth of the biblical worldview, they are seeking to protect human rights and dignity for everyone.

■ ■ ■ ■ ■

Harvesting Humans

To get a clearer sense of the central role played by the two-story dichotomy in secular ethics, let's run through several additional issues that appear regularly in news headlines, starting with research on human embryos. In two-story thinking, human embryos are merely biological entities, not persons. Therefore they may be destroyed without moral significance, if a utilitarian calculation suggests some practical benefit to society. Many people have come to accept the idea that in the search for new medical cures, human embryos may be sown, harvested, patented, and sold—as though they were just another natural resource.

If we reject the two-story dualism, however, then personhood is inextricably linked to being biologically human at every stage of development. Destroying an embryo is morally akin to killing an adult. All the arguments in chapter 2 against abortion apply equally to destroying embryos in the lab.

Even more problematic, embryo research typically involves creating human life with the direct intention of destroying it. Even those who are uncertain whether the embryo is fully a person often find this troubling. A fundamental principle of ethics is that people should be treated as intrinsically valuable, not valuable only as a means to some extrinsic end. Or as we say in ordinary conversation, it is wrong to *use* people.

For example, columnist Charles Krauthammer writes, "I am not religious. I do not believe that personhood is conferred upon conception. But I also do not believe that a human embryo is the moral equivalent of a hangnail and deserves no more respect than an appendix." So where do we draw the line? Krauthammer suggests that we draw a "bright line prohibiting the deliberate creation of human embryos solely for the instrumental purpose of research—a clear violation of the categorical imperative not to make a human life (even if only a potential human life) a means rather than an end."[32]

Wesley Smith puts the objection more succinctly: There is something deeply dehumanizing about "treating human life—no matter how nascent—as a mere natural resource to be harvested like a soy bean crop."[33]

Even our language reflects a shift in worldview. Ancient Israel, stressing the transmission of life from father to child, used a verb translated as "to beget." The Christian world, impressed with primacy of the Creator in the generation of life, used the verb "to procreate." And moderns? We use the language of the machine and the factory—"to reproduce." When we move the process to the laboratory and talk about "reproductive technologies," the emphasis is on treating life as a product that we are free to master and reshape. And those who *make* human beings in vitro feel entitled to *unmake* them—to treat them as products of technology, objects at our disposal. Life is being reduced to a marketable commodity.[34]

The irony is that embryonic stem cell research is not even necessary. Adult stem cell research often produces better outcomes. For example, a 2016 *Washington Post* article describes a study that stunned researchers. They injected adult stem cells, harvested from bone marrow, into the brains of stroke patients. "Their recovery was not just a minimal recovery like someone who couldn't move a thumb now being able to wiggle it. It was much more meaningful. One 71-year-old wheelchair-bound patient was walking again," said Gary Steinberg, chair of neurosurgery at Stanford. The study's positive outcome challenges "a core belief about brain damage—that it is permanent and irreversible."[35] Using adult stem cells avoids the ethical issues involved with destroying embryos while producing better results.[36]

Baby Farming for Body Parts

What about harvesting aborted babies for their body parts? Once we have dehumanized fetuses as objects, it is natural to ask: Why not get some benefit from them, just as we recycle plastic bags and glass bottles to gain benefit from other waste products? Comedian Sarah Silverman has argued that since "abortion is legal" in America, "it would be insane not to use fetal tissue for science and education." (Critics responded that since gas chambers were legal in Nazi Germany, it would have been insane not to use human skin for lamp shades.)[37]

Once the idea of human strip-mining is accepted, the next step is the outright sale of fetal organs. Bioethicist Jacob Appel argues, "If a woman has the fundamental right to terminate a pregnancy, why not the right to use the products of that terminated pregnancy as she sees fit?" Why not allow her to gain some economic benefit? "Many women would likely use the proceeds of such sales to finance college educations or to help raise their children."

Appel ends by predicting, "Someday, if we are fortunate, scientific research may make possible farms of artificial 'wombs' breeding fetuses for their organs."[38]

It is worth reminding ourselves *why* our law does not allow the sale of human beings or human body parts. "There are, in a civilized society, some things that money cannot buy," wrote the New Jersey Supreme Court in 1988. "There are . . . values that society deems more important than granting to wealth whatever it can buy, be it labor, love, or life."[39] The New Jersey case involved surrogate motherhood, and the court ruled that it is a form of baby selling, hence illegal. The sale of children is morally problematic in the same way that slavery is problematic: Human beings are not objects that should ever be for sale.

There is also the problem of the status of the surrogate mothers, who are reduced to rent-a-wombs. "The accelerating boom in surrogacy for gay couples . . . represents a disturbing slide into the brutal exploitation of women who usually come from the developing world and are often bullied or pimped into selling their wombs to satisfy the selfish whims of wealthy gay or lesbian westerners," writes journalist Julie Bindel, who herself identifies as a lesbian. "This cruelty is accompanied by epic hypocrisy. People from Europe and the USA who would shudder at the idea of involvement in human or sex trafficking have ended up indulging in a grotesque form of 'reproductive trafficking.'"[40]

A member of the European Parliament says surrogacy "reduces the woman to a reproductive machine and the child to an asset in a business transaction."[41]

The ethical principle here is that some things should be immune from commercial transactions—that some social spheres lie outside the range of the market. The most fundamental is the right of the human being not to be bought and sold. In the words of Christian ethicist Scott Rae, the reason we do not allow the sale of human beings "is that there are things that are so close to one's personhood and individual self-fulfillment that they cannot be objects of barter without denigrating personhood."

The underlying problem, Rae explains, is that "when a monetary price is put on a human being or an attribute of personhood, this creates an alienation by separating the person from the thing that has been commodified."[42] Whatever is monetizable—including the body—is thereby treated as alienable from the self instead of integral to the self.

The heart of the issue is a dualism that alienates the body from the self.

Transhumanism: Creating Supermen

A relatively new movement that adopts the two-story secular ethic is transhumanism. The logic goes like this: Since humans are nothing special, why not use technology to create a new stage of life *beyond* humanity? Transhumanists say it's time to take charge of evolution through genetic engineering. They argue that human life as it exists today is merely one step in an endless evolutionary chain, a chance configuration of cells that will be surpassed in the next stage of evolution. Waxing poetic, philosopher John Gray writes that humans are "only currents in the drift of genes."[43]

Transhumanism zealously promotes the vision of a bioengineered utopia in which we will be liberated from our human limitations. It promises that we are moving toward a "post-human" future, when wealthy parents will be able to afford genetic improvements so extensive that they will literally create a new race.

The human body has been reduced to a mechanism on the level of gizmos and gadgets, which clears the decks for unbridled experimentation with genes and DNA.

But wait a moment: Isn't this eugenics? And didn't we witness the tragic results of eugenics under the Nazis? To avoid any unsavory association with Nazism, transhumanists stress that the new eugenics will be consumer based. Parents will be empowered by technology to choose their offspring's genetic traits. Choice, the key tenet of modern liberalism, magically makes everything morally acceptable.

In reality, however, the new eugenics will be as dangerous to liberty as the old eugenics was. Nick Bostrom, a leading transhumanist at Oxford, says human nature is "a work-in-progress, a half-baked beginning that we can learn to remold in desirable ways."[44] But who will have the power to decide which ways are desirable? Is it reasonable to expect power of that magnitude to remain in the hands of parents? Hardly.

If it becomes possible to remold human nature itself, in reality that will lead to the worst forms of tyranny.

One of the most prominent advocates of transhumanism is geneticist Lee Silver of Princeton University. In *Remaking Eden: Cloning and Beyond in a Brave New World*, Silver spins out a scenario in which humanity will bifurcate into two separate races—genetic übermenschen (super-persons) who rule over untermenschen (sub-persons). The first group will become the controllers of society. The second group will become the low-paid laborers and service-providers.[45]

Silver is clearly inspired by Nietzsche's concept of the übermensch as the next stage in evolution. Though he projects this bioengineered society as a utopia, it is far more likely to become a coercive *dys*topia. Once we deny that humans have unique dignity just for being human, we have opened the door to tyranny. As philosopher Mortimer Adler warns, "Groups of superior men [will] be able to justify their enslavement, exploitation, or even genocide of inferior human groups, on factual and moral grounds akin to those that we now rely on to justify our treatment of the animals we harness as beasts of burden."[46]

The Cartesian dualism of the mind as a separate entity controlling the body will be worked out socially as a class of mental workers controlling a class of manual laborers.

This prediction calls to mind the plotline of countless dystopian novels and movies. C. S. Lewis, in *The Abolition of Man*, sums up the problem in one of his most unforgettable lines: "What we call Man's power over Nature turns out to be a power exercised by some men over other men with Nature as its instrument."[47]

Finally, there are transhumanists who hope to transcend the body altogether. Ray Kurzweil, Google's director of engineering, hopes that advances in artificial intelligence will enable us to download the brain to a computer, making possible a kind of digital immortality. "The whole idea of a 'species' is a biological concept," he says. "What we are doing is transcending biology."[48]

A similar anti-body ideology animates the work of influential futurist Martine Rothblatt, who is a transgender woman (born male). Rothblatt's book *Virtually Human* proposes that a digital database of your life and personality can be used to create a "mindclone," a kind of digital consciousness that will survive the death of your body. Do you prefer a flesh-and-blood body? Then in Rothblatt's view, you are guilty of "fleshism."[49]

And people say *Christianity* is anti-body!

In a culture that demeans and disparages the flesh-and-blood body, the Bible's high view of the material world is one reason it is "good news." The message of Christianity does not start with salvation but with creation. What God created has intrinsic value and worth.

The Biological Book of Life

If humans are just a chance collection of cells, as personhood theory claims, why not mix in cells from other species, creating human-animal hybrids? Transhumanists argue there is no ethical barrier to splicing animal DNA into human DNA. These transgenic technologies (*transgenic* means "across species") are being proposed as a means to enhance human capabilities and create a post-human race.

The same technologies could also be used to enhance animals' capabilities. Futurist James Hughes advocates what he calls "uplifting" chimpanzees genetically to give them human intellectual capacities—not because that would be good for chimps but because it would prove that they deserve the legal status of persons. Hughes says, "Persons don't have to be human, and not all humans are persons"[50]—which reveals how undefined and open-ended the secular concept of personhood has become.

Using a literary metaphor, biologist Thomas Eisner says a species is not "a hard-bound volume of the library of nature" but instead "a loose-leaf book, whose individual pages, the genes, might be available for selective transfer and modification of other species."[51]

This is a highly revealing metaphor. It suggests that if there is no author of the book of life, then there is no basis for regarding organisms as integrated wholes. When an author tells a story, all the segments are held together by a unifying theme. But if life is an accident produced by blind, material forces, organisms can be treated as random collections of genes and other spare parts to be mixed and matched at will. If there is nothing special about humans, why *not* splice together animal and human genes to create a post-human race?

The assumption that drives all these futurist scenarios, explains embryologist Brian Goodwin, is the Darwinian claim that there is no such thing as species. Most people do not realize that, technically, Darwinism denies that species are real. The theory proposes that evolution proceeds through minor changes in an ever-continuous chain of individuals. What appear to be species are merely temporary groupings in the ever-shifting populations of evolving organisms, eddies in the genetic stream. (It is ironic that Darwin's major work is called *On the Origin of Species* when in fact he denied the reality of species.)

What are the implications? Because of the assumption that there are no species, explains Goodwin, "we've lost even the concept of human nature." No special status is assigned to being human—because there *is* no human species. As a result, "life becomes a set of parts, commodities that can be shifted around" to suit some geneticists' vision of progress.[52] The floodgates have been flung open for unfettered refashioning of human nature itself.

As former pope John Paul II writes, for secularists there is no "truth of creation which must be acknowledged, or a plan of God for life which must be respected." As a result, "everything is negotiable, everything is open to bargaining."[53] Humanity itself is up for grabs.

When the plan of God *is* respected, genetic research can be a tool for great good. Within a Christian worldview, it can be pursued with the same motives we pursue other forms of scientific research. Science is a means of fulfilling the cultural mandate given to our first parents to "subdue the earth" by discovering nature's laws and developing its potential. We have freedom to be creative and inventive as long as we do not violate human dignity. Many historians say it was Christianity that sparked the scientific revolution in the first place. For example, science required the conviction that nature has a rational order because it was created by a rational Mind.[54]

Science can also be a means of overcoming the effects of the fall, repairing its brokenness and recovering our original condition. Genetic medicine, like other forms of medicine, aims at alleviating the suffering caused by the fall and recovering the whole and healthy life that God originally intended when he created the human race.[55]

Bloodsuckers, Vampires, and Cockroaches

Transhumanists often speak in euphoric tones, as though a technology-created utopia is just around the corner. We are on "the cusp of a new enlightenment," enthuses Adrian Woolfson of Cambridge University. We can finally "entertain the possibility of modifying our own nature and creating artificial life."[56] But this utopian vision is an illusion. What counts most in producing a truly humane society is not the level of technology but the prevailing worldview. And a worldview that says human life has no inherent value or dignity will never lead to utopia, no matter how advanced the tools and technology.

Philosopher Luc Ferry—surprisingly, in a book promoting atheism—says it was Christianity that introduced the concept of equal rights. It overthrew ancient social hierarchies between rich and poor, master and slave. "According to Christianity, we were all 'brothers,' on the same level as creatures of God," Ferry writes. "Christianity is the first *universalist* ethos."[57]

Another atheist, Richard Rorty, agrees. In a lecture to UNESCO, he noted that throughout history, societies have come up with various ways to exclude certain groups from the human family. Those who belonged to a different tribe, clan, race, or religion were labeled *subhuman*. By contrast, Rorty notes, Christianity gave rise to the concept of universal rights, derived from the conviction "that all human beings are created in the image of God."

In the modern age, however, Rorty says, due to Darwin we no longer accept the idea of creation. Therefore we are no longer morally bound to maintain that everyone who is biologically human has equal dignity.[58]

The implication is clear: Once a culture abandons the conviction that all humans are created in God's image, human rights are up for grabs. Any category of humans is fair game to be excluded or even eliminated. That's why the stakes in this debate are so high. As Wesley Smith writes, "If human life does not matter simply and merely because it is human, this means that moral worth becomes subjective and a matter of who has the power to decide." And we already know what happens then: "History shows that once we create categories of differing worth, those humans denigrated by the political power structure as having less value are exploited, oppressed, and killed."[59]

The history of chattel slavery in America and the totalitarian systems of the twentieth century give stark evidence of the morally horrific consequences of treating humans as mere things. The slaveholders argued that Africans were less than fully human, then sold, whipped, hunted, raped, and killed them. Nazi propaganda dehumanized Jews, calling them "rats" and "the vermin of mankind," then murdered six million of them. In the Red Terror, Lenin called whole categories of people "former persons," or more colorfully "bloodsuckers," "vampires," "parasites," and "class enemies." That made it easier to ship them off to concentration camps or simply shoot them. In the 1994 Rwandan massacre, the Hutus were incited to violence by government radio addresses calling the Tutsis "cockroaches" that must be "exterminated."

In addition to the testimony of history, the impact of personhood theory has been tested experimentally. In an ingenious sociological study, John H. Evans measured the moral views of Christians against those who accept personhood theory. The experiment found that personhood theory is indeed associated with lower support for human rights. Members of the public who agree with personhood theory are more supportive of buying organs from poor people, of experimenting on prisoners against their will, of torturing people to potentially save lives—and are less willing to sacrifice to stop genocide.[60]

We tend to work out the logic of our basic convictions. Because of Darwin, many people no longer have a moral basis for universal human rights. We should expect to see the logical consequences played out in the denial of human rights to those deemed to be non-persons.

Animal Rights and Wrongs

People often ask me if the concept of animal rights contradicts personhood theory. Doesn't it express respect for biological, organic life? Not at all. Arguments for animal rights are just another example of weighing the value of life by instrumental measures, such as cognitive ability, instead of intrinsic value.

Animal rights activists say they want to elevate animal rights to the same level as human rights, and no doubt they are sincere. But what is the logic of their argument? How do they support giving rights to animals? By arguing that certain animals—such as pigs, dogs, chimps, dolphins—have higher cognitive abilities than some humans. Therefore, those animals qualify as persons, while "inferior" humans do not.

By this reasoning, not all people are persons, but some animals are persons. Peter Singer states that a newborn baby is not a person but the more intelligent animals are: "The life of a newborn baby is of less value to it than the life of a pig, a dog, or a chimpanzee is to the nonhuman animal."[61] He recommends using humans in medical experiments instead of animals, if the animals have higher cognitive capacities.

Thus the value of any living thing is measured by its mental function. The animal rights movement does not contradict personhood theory. It relies on it.

Genuine respect for animals and the rest of nature does not rest on an ideology that disparages biology in favor of mental skills. It derives from the conviction that all creation comes from the hand of God and therefore has intrinsic dignity and value. Scripture teaches that humans are stewards of creation, responsible to a higher authority for the way we care for the world around us (Gen. 1:28). Proverbs 12:10 says, "The righteous care for the needs of their animals." Humanity is not the highest rung of an evolutionary ladder, free to use nature any way we want for our own benefit. Instead we will answer to the Creator for the way we treat his creation.

■ ■ ■ ■ ■

How Children Became Persons

The public still largely takes for granted that infanticide and euthanasia are morally wrong, but they have forgotten where that idea came from. Historian O. M. Bakke argues that it was Christianity that made these moral views nearly universal in the West.

In his book *When Children Became People*, Bakke explains that in ancient Greece and Rome, children were considered non-persons. Ancient society was organized in what we can visualize as concentric circles: At the center was the freeborn, adult male. They had the most value. Other people were valued depending on how similar they were to that model: women, foreigners, slaves, and children. Literature from the classical world describes children in tones of contempt, using adjectives like *weak*, *fearful*, and *irrational*.

This demeaning of children had concrete consequences. Not surprisingly, it led to a cold and callous view of children. Abortion was widespread. Unwanted children were abandoned or exposed, left outside to die of hunger or to be devoured by wild animals. Children were treated roughly; it was considered normal to beat them. In Rome, fathers even had the legal right to kill their children for any reason.

A negative view of children also contributed to a low view of women. The very fact that women were more involved in childrearing and more likely to develop emotional attachments to children was taken as a sign of weakness and vulgarity on their part. Bakke sums up: "Children and slaves were the father's property, just material objects. To a very large extent, he could treat his wife, his children, and other household members as he pleased, without any fear of legal consequences."[62]

That included the legal right to sexually abuse their slaves—both male and female, adult and children. Brothels specializing in sex slaves, including children, were legal and thriving businesses. Abandoned babies were often rescued then forced into sexual slavery. Romans who owned young slaves even hired them out to brothels.[63]

Today we often hear it said that the ancient world was more "tolerant" in sexual matters, but tolerance had nothing to do with it. It was an expression of social status: Most sexual acts were considered permissible as long as they involved a person of higher status dominating a person of lower status. In the ancient world, explains philosopher Martha Nussbaum,

> The gender of the object . . . is not in itself morally problematic. Boys and women are very often treated interchangeably as objects of [male] desire. What is socially important is to penetrate rather than to be penetrated. Sex is understood fundamentally not as interaction, but as a doing of some thing to someone; and the passive recipient is marked by that fact as of lower social status.[64]

This is the culture in which the Christian church was born. This is the culture in which Jesus shocked his contemporaries by treating children not as contemptible but as valuable: "See that you do not look down on one of these little ones. . . . Whoever welcomes one child like this in my name welcomes me" (Matt. 18:10, 5 HCSB). Jesus even held up children as a positive paradigm for adults to emulate: "Unless you are converted and become like little children, you will never enter the kingdom of heaven" (v. 3). "Let the little children come to me . . . for the kingdom of heaven belongs to such as these" (19:14). No one before had set up children as a positive model for adults. The church fathers wrote extensively on Jesus's words, puzzling over what they meant in a culture where a high view of children was a complete novelty.

Eventually, as Christians gained political influence in the Roman empire, they succeeded in getting laws passed outlawing infanticide (in AD 374). They also passed laws granting government aid to poor families who did not have the means to raise their children, so they would not be tempted to abandon or expose them. Yet the custom of exposure was not ended just by passing laws. It continued to be practiced until the clergy finally persuaded parents to give up their babies at the door of the church instead, which gave rise to the first orphanages.

Jesus's Appalling Scandal

Modern Christians need to recover an appreciation of the uniqueness of the Christian worldview. Since we were toddlers in Sunday school, we have sung "Jesus Loves the Little Children." We no longer realize how radical Christianity was when it first taught the value of children.

Ultimately it was Jesus's own life and death that destroyed the underlying notion that the value of life depends on social status. After all, the God who made heaven and earth humbled himself to become a child. He lived a life of poverty and weakness, then submitted to death, even death on a cross. We are used to seeing the cross surrounded by flowers and stained glass windows, or worn as a shiny piece of jewelry. Most of us no longer realize that in ancient Rome, crucifixion was considered a barbaric form of execution reserved for the lowest, most reviled criminals—mostly slaves and political rebels. It was the ultimate form of shame and humiliation, something not even to be mentioned in polite company. The execution of Jesus was therefore considered an appalling scandal.

And by submitting to such hideous humiliation, he utterly destroyed differences in social status. Christians began to proclaim the radical message that basic human rights do not depend on status or power or stage of life. At the foot of the cross, the poor, the slave, the oppressed, the young, and the weak are all equal to the rich and powerful. Christians are forbidden to show favoritism (James 2:1–9; 5:1–6).

Right from the start, then, the early Christians viewed children as complete and valuable human beings. One result, says Bakke, was that Christian parents practiced a much "greater involvement in upbringing than was generally the case in pagan families."[65] In contrast to wealthy Romans, who often turned the care of their children over to servants and nurses, the church fathers urged parents to raise their own children. In the fourth century, John Chrysostom wrote, "Let everything take second place to care for our children, our bringing them up in the discipline and instruction of the Lord."[66] After all, what is at stake is a human being's eternal destiny.

In all these ways, Christianity invented a novel concept of childhood, a new mindset that regarded children as persons to be valued, cherished, and cared for.

The practices of a *pre*-Christian society signal the direction that our *post*-Christian society is likely to take. As the world rejects the biblical ethic, it loses not only the basis for human rights generally, as we saw earlier, but also the basis for the humane care of children. Social critics note that practices like contraception, abortion, and artificial reproduction are already creating an attitude that having a child is merely a lifestyle choice, an accessory to enrich adult lives and meet adult needs. Take away a Christian view of childhood, and there is no guarantee that our society will continue to offer special protections to children.

Hate Thy Neighbor

We live in a time of propaganda and sales pitches, where words are used to manipulate. For example, a Gallup poll shows a 20 percent increase in support for assisted suicide if it is described using euphemisms. A full 70 percent of Americans are in favor of allowing doctors to hasten a terminally ill patient's death when it is described as allowing doctors to "end the patient's life by some painless means." But only 51 percent support euthanasia when it is described as doctors helping a patient "commit suicide."[67] Clearly, there is still moral opposition to suicide.

What this means is that social evils like infanticide, euthanasia, and assisted suicide will likely become enshrined in the law in a manner very different from history's previous great evils, such as slavery or the Holocaust. These practices will most likely be imposed in the name of reducing suffering and enhancing choice, under the heading of bioethics.

They may even come with a Christian veneer. A few years ago, Anne Lamott, a favorite writer among Christian young adults, helped a man kill himself. "The man I killed did not want to die, but he no longer felt he had much of a choice," Lamott writes in the *Los Angeles Times*. With his body wasting away from cancer and his mind beginning to waver, the man was open to Lamott's offer to acquire the lethal drugs needed to commit suicide.

The friend "was sort of surprised that as a Christian I so staunchly agreed with him about assisted suicide," Lamott notes. To justify her stance, she does not reflect deeply on the data of Scripture or the history of Christian moral thought. In fact, she does not reflect on those things at all. Instead she compares life to a school, assuring her friend that it's okay to drop out early and get an Incomplete.[68] Though in her writings Lamott positions herself as a Christian, she essentially jettisons scriptural principles regarding life as a gift from God. There is nothing distinctively Christian in her essay, even though it deals with an issue as serious as ending a person's life.

Lamott shows no interest in Scripture on the issue of abortion either. In an earlier *Los Angeles Times* piece, she describes a conference where she unleashed an angry tirade against the pro-life position. "As a Christian and a feminist," she writes, she felt compelled to speak out for "women whose lives had been righted and redeemed by *Roe v. Wade*."[69]

"Righted and redeemed" by abortion? This is putting a veneer of biblical language over a secular ethic. It illustrates how even those who identify as Christian can get taken in by a secular worldview. Too often, they fail to recognize it because they know Christianity only as a spiritual experience, not as an alternative worldview. They do not realize that the Bible provides not only a message of salvation but also a lens through which we view all of life—the human person, history, nature, and society.

To be strategically effective in protecting human dignity, we need to get beyond the slogans and placards, helping others recognize the secular worldviews that shape people's thinking. We must stand against those who enable death and despair, while making a positive case for "loving thy neighbor."

A Body of Broken Bones

One reason issues like euthanasia are so salient today is that people no longer have positive ways to respond to suffering. The biblical answer to the problem of suffering and death is that they were not part of God's original plan. Evil entered into creation at a particular time in history—which caused a cataclysmic change, distorting and disfiguring the original creation. That's why evil is so hateful, repulsive, and tragic. When we recoil from sickness and death, our response is entirely appropriate. It's important to remember that *God is on our side*. He did not create evil. And he hates it even more than we do.

But Christianity also teaches that, amazingly, God himself entered into the human condition and experienced suffering and death by execution on a Roman cross. In doing so, God inverted death into a means of achieving new life. "By his wounds we are healed" (Isa. 53:5).

As a result, God can use difficult and painful events in a redemptive way to deepen our character and reconcile our relationships. My favorite analogy is a broken bone that has healed wrong. The surgeon has to break the bone again, which is painful, to get it to grow straight and strong. Spiritually speaking, we are full of broken bones. Our character is wounded by sinful patterns that have hardened. That's why it often takes crises and difficulties to "break" our destructive life patterns, so we can grow straight and strong.[70]

Though evil is still evil, the wonder is that God is greater and can turn it to good.

Even secular psychologists note that suffering can be transformative, and they have coined a term for it: "post-traumatic growth." An article in *Psychology Today* reports that many people who have suffered traumatic life-events such as bereavement, divorce, serious illness, job loss, or combat actually grew through the experience: "They became more compassionate for the sufferings of others . . . so that they had deeper and more satisfying relationships. One of the most common changes was that they developed a more philosophical or spiritual attitude to life."[71]

That is, the crisis spurred a spiritual search. Psychologist Judith Neal studied forty people who went through post-traumatic growth, and describes the process in these words:

> Initially, most of them experienced a "dark night of the soul," where their previous values were thrown into question, and life ceased to have any meaning. After this, they went through a phase of spiritual searching, trying to make sense of what had happened to them, and find new values. And finally, once they had found new spiritual principles to live by, they entered a phase of "spiritual integration," when they applied these new principles. At this point they found new meaning and purpose in life, together with a gratitude for being alive, and even for having been through so much turmoil.[72]

Most amazing is that last phrase: They came to be thankful even for the turmoil itself because it was the spur to inner growth. The conclusion is that we should not assume a person is a candidate for euthanasia just because they are suffering.

Of course, there is nothing automatic about such a positive outcome. Suffering can deepen us but it can also make us angry, bitter, and resentful.

The key is whether we respond by turning to God in our suffering. Then it becomes possible to follow in the path of Jesus, who "learned obedience from what he suffered" (Heb. 5:8).

■ ■ ■ ■ ■

Ella: Wheelchair Hero

Sometimes the best argument against practices like assisted suicide is a striking example. Ella Frech is a spunky, homeschooled eleven-year-old who is currently the number-two ranked professional female wheelchair skater (WCMX) in the world. She regularly practices drop-ins, wheelies, and ride-the-rail at the skate park. (Did you even know that people can use wheelchairs like skateboards, performing hair-raising tricks?)

Ella wrote an article protesting the movie *Me Before You*, which is about a young man in a wheelchair who commits assisted suicide. She subtitled her article, "Dear Hollywood, Why Do You Want Me Dead?"

"Please don't deny it," she starts out. "The movies you make tell me the truth about what you really think about me." She references an earlier pro-euthanasia film, *Million Dollar Baby*, then continues:

> "Me Before You" [is] the story of a guy who gets in an accident, and has a spinal cord injury, and has to spend the rest of his life in a wheelchair. A guy you think should want to die because he has to live a life that looks like mine.
>
> Well, what's wrong with a life that looks like mine?[73]

Hollywood is promoting a worldview that says if your body is not perfect, you should stop being a burden to yourself and society and just kill yourself, Ella writes. She concludes,

> You may not believe in God. . . . But I do, and because of that I believe in the value of all people. I believe we are all made in His image and likeness. That's why I believe all people are worth something. If you believe that people only get their value from each other, then people can take that away. But if our

value comes from God, then nobody has the right to say someone who walks is worth more than someone who doesn't.[74]

Most people do not realize that the disability rights movement is almost unified in opposing assisted suicide—precisely because disabled people know they are the prime targets of the death movement.

Ghost Boy: "I Hated Barney"

For another inspiring example, meet a man who spent twelve years trapped inside his body, with no way of communicating with the outside world. After suffering an illness at age twelve, Martin Pistorius fell into a coma. When he regained consciousness a few years later, he was unable to speak or move his limbs. Everyone thought he was still a vegetable. This nightmarish condition is known as total locked-in syndrome. Doctors said Martin should just be kept comfortable until he died. Every day his parents dropped him off at a day care, where the staff parked him in front of a television for hours to watch reruns of children's cartoons.

"I cannot even express to you how much I hated *Barney*," Martin says today, referring to a children's TV show featuring a purple dinosaur, which he was forced to watch day in and day out. Worse, he was abused mentally, physically, and even sexually by various caregivers. Without a voice, he could not tell anyone about it. He even overheard his mother say, in a moment of extreme frustration, "I wish you would die."

But Martin's father never gave up. Daily he washed and fed Martin, dressed him, and took him to the care center. His father's persistence finally paid off. When Martin was twenty-five, an empathetic therapist noticed that he was able to make nearly imperceptible smiles and nods. She persuaded his parents to have him tested. To everyone's shock, his brain was fully functioning. In the following years, he learned to use a computer to communicate, taught himself to read and write, graduated from college, trained as a web designer, and got married.

In his book *Ghost Boy*, Martin says that all along he had a strong sense of God's presence. Because his family never attended church, he knew nothing of Christian doctrine. "I had no idea why I felt His presence so strongly. . . .Yet somehow I instinctively knew that He was with me. . . . My faith didn't waver. He was as present to me as air, as constant as breathing."[75] When Martin met the beautiful Christian woman who would later become his wife, he finally learned about the God whose presence he had sensed all his life.

Making the Womb a "Safe Place"

Of course, the majority of brain-damaged people do not wake up. But a 1996 study found that close to half—43 percent—of patients thought to be in persistent vegetative states had been misdiagnosed.[76] The difficulty with making life-and-death decisions is that human knowledge is never completely certain. (The Hebrews knew that people sometimes revive after they appear to be dead, so their tradition was to wait three days after death to make sure the person was dead—which may explain why Jesus was in the tomb for three days.)[77]

Even in cases when the outcome is more predictable, how should we respond—by ending life or by loving life as long as God gives it?

Joseph and Janelle Banks learned through an ultrasound that their twins were conjoined (they shared a heart and liver) and most likely would not survive birth. As predicted, the two little boys, Josiah and Josias, were stillborn. During the pregnancy, abortion was presented as an option more than once, but Janelle says, "I was thankful for the opportunity to enjoy my babies as long as God gave them to us." The couple also welcomed the chance to explain profound issues of life and death to their older children.[78]

Betsey and her husband knew that their pre-born son Jacen suffered from anencephaly (a major part of his brain and skull was missing), which meant he would likely live only a matter of days. Despite pressure to abort, they chose to carry Jacen to term and love him as long as God gave him life.[79]

Through an ultrasound, Marshall and Susan's son Toby was diagnosed with Trisomy 13, which meant he would not survive long outside the womb. Asked if they wanted to abort, Susan answered, "We believe God is the giver and taker of life. If the only opportunity I have to know this child is in my womb, I don't want to cut that time short. If the only world he is to know is the womb, I want that world to be as safe as I can make it."[80]

In these and many other cases, parents are choosing life over death.

Snowflake Babies

Christians are also coming up with ingenious solutions to the moral issues posed by modern technology. Consider embryo adoption. Research that destroys embryos is often justified by the fact that in vitro fertilization (IVF) produces excess embryos. IVF is a process in which eggs are extracted from the wife and fertilized by her husband's sperm in a Petri dish. The resulting embryos are then implanted in the wife. Typically many more embryos are created than are actually implanted, and the surplus embryos are either used for research or simply dumped down the drain as medical waste products.

Couples with strong moral principles often request that the clinic fertilize only the number of embryos that will actually be implanted. But that still leaves the question of what to do about the extra embryos that IVF clinics are creating for other couples. In some cases, the extra embryos are frozen and preserved in case the couple wants more children. Amazingly, when these frozen embryos are thawed and implanted in the mother's womb, they gestate and develop exactly as in a normal pregnancy. These tiny persons have been dubbed "snowflake" babies.

If frozen embryos can be implanted, why not offer them for adoption? Organizations such as Nightlight Christian Adoptions and the National Embryo Donation Center bring couples and clinics together to facilitate frozen embryo adoption. A friend and colleague of mine at Houston Baptist University, Bruce Gordon, discovered that he and his wife were unable to have children. Across the country, another Christian couple suffering fertility issues had undergone in vitro fertilization and had two extra frozen embryos. Bruce and his wife adopted them and were happy to have their own family that way.

What are the advantages of embryo adoption? "It's much cheaper than ordinary adoption," Bruce said. "And it gives parents the opportunity to be in control of prenatal care to ensure a healthy baby—no smoking or drinking."

"Babies also bond with their parents while still in the womb," added his wife Mari-Anne. According to one report, "Fetuses can hear in the womb, and, as a result, newborn babies are already familiar with their mothers' voices. In experiments using playbacks of recorded voices, newborns prefer their mothers' voices to the voices of other women."[81]

I read the Gordons' contract drawn up by the fertility clinic, and it was almost comical to see the complex verbal gymnastics employed to avoid acknowledging that the frozen embryo is a human person. The procedure was not described as an embryo adoption but as a "tissue transplant." The embryo itself was a "cryopreserved specimen" consisting of "biological materials" intended to "achieve a pregnancy." What could possibly "achieve a pregnancy" except a living human embryo?

Embryo adoption is proving to be an innovative and humane strategy to preserve the lives of already living tiny humans and give them the chance to be raised by loving parents.

Total Care for the Total Person

Another example of practical solutions is the rise of hospice care. Most people do not know that the hospice movement has Christian roots. It was the brainchild of an English medical humanitarian, Dame Cecily Saunders, in the 1960s, and it arose directly from her deep Anglican faith. After years of working with dying patients as a hospital social worker, she longed to come up with a better strategy.

Physicians trained solely in a scientific outlook tend to see the body as little more than systems of cells and organs. In recent decades, as medical technology advanced, patients were dying shut up in isolated, sterile, institutional settings, surrounded by strangers, hooked up to machines, and often subject to painful and invasive treatments. That form of medical treatment might prolong their physical life, but it did not address the needs of the whole person. In fact, much of the push for euthanasia and assisted suicide is a reaction against such a cold, inhumane approach—one that treats patients as merely physical systems whose physical life must be prolonged at all costs.

The concept behind the hospice movement is that patients are whole persons, not just physical organisms. Saunders said, "I coined the term 'total pain,' from my understanding that dying people have physical, spiritual, psychological, and social pain that must be treated."[82] For many people, the greatest pain in dying is the emotional isolation.

Saunders argued that medical care should be balanced by other forms of care: palliative care to manage pain, psychological counseling for emotional support, and practical aid for the caregiving family. In hospice care, everything is aimed at allowing the patient to live as fully as possible in the final months, with a clear mind, surrounded by family and friends. Often patients find that this becomes a time to resolve conflicts in relationships, strengthen bonds with those they love, and work through the spiritual challenge of facing their mortality. It can be a profoundly meaningful stage of their lives.

Hospice care has even changed the minds of some non-Christians. Ian Haines, an oncologist who describes himself as a secular humanist, used to believe "that euthanasia was the only humane solution. I no longer believe that." What changed his mind? As Haines explains, pain management techniques have advanced to the point where most patients no longer suffer excruciating pain but are able to engage in meaningful activities. There are "opportunities for patients and families to share deep and poignant moments of bonding and reflection, or nurse a new-born grandchild, or attend a wedding or a graduation." Pro-death advocates defend euthanasia as "death with dignity." But Haines concludes, "I have seen palliative care reach the point where the terminally ill can die with equal or more dignity than euthanasia will provide."[83]

Sadly, this is becoming a minority view in bioethics today, even in the hospice movement. Many hospice professionals are accepting the two-story worldview that justifies euthanasia and assisted suicide. As one euthanasia advocate put it, they are transforming "hospice into hemlock."[84]

No Dissent in the Culture of Death

What bioethicists debate eventually becomes law, enforced through the courts. This is already happening in countries that have legalized assisted suicide. In Holland in 2015, a doctor was sued for refusing to sign off on a request by a patient for the drugs to commit suicide. In Belgium in 2016, a Catholic nursing home was sued for refusing to allow a doctor to give a woman a lethal injection on church-run premises.[85]

In the culture of death, no dissent is allowed.

What this means is that eventually Christian medical professionals around the globe may be forced by law to act against their biblical convictions—or lose their jobs and shut down their healthcare facilities. It is imperative to act now to persuade our colleagues, neighbors, students, and children of a more humane view of life.

A biblical view is desperately needed in the realm of sex ethics as well. As we move to the next chapter, we will discover that, surprisingly, secular sex ethics is based on the same two-story body/person dualism that drives abortion and euthanasia. When we grasp how the divided view of the human being shapes the hookup culture, we will be better equipped to speak healing truth into today's sexual chaos.

4

Schizoid Sex

Hijacked by the Hookup Culture

After giving a presentation on apologetics recently at a local church, I was surrounded by several twentysomething young men. "Now we need a talk on how to get a date," one said with a wry smile. "Maybe you can give us some tips." As the comments flew back and forth, I discovered that none of these half-dozen young men had ever gone on a date.

Today's hookup culture glamorizes impersonal sex but gives no clue how to start a real relationship. An evening when you just go out for dinner and have a conversation? None of these young men had ever done it.

At Boston College, professor Kerry Cronin was shocked to learn that none of the students in her senior seminar had ever gone on a date either. So Cronin started including how-to lessons on dating. The final assignment: You must ask someone out on a date. Over the years, Cronin's "Go On a Date" assignment has achieved considerable notoriety on campus. She has been dubbed the "dating doctor."[1]

What is the doctor's diagnosis? Why have so many young adults lost the ability to form relationships? Because the "social script" they hear most often tells them that having fun means engaging in physical relationships without emotional attachment.

If you have not talked with young people lately, you may not realize how soulless the hookup culture is. A hookup can be any level of physical involvement, from kissing to sexual intercourse. According to the rules of the game, you are not to become emotionally attached. No relationship, no commitment, no exclusivity. The script is that you are supposed to be able to walk away from the experience as if it did not happen.

Researcher Donna Freitas, after interviewing hundreds of students, concluded that the hookup culture "creates a drastic divide between *physical* intimacy and *emotional* intimacy." It teaches young people not to "reckon with someone's personhood."[2]

Does the hookup culture reflect the same personhood concept that underlies arguments for abortion, infanticide, and euthanasia? Surprising as it may seem, the answer is yes. The same Cartesian dualism is responsible for the "drastic divide" that Freitas observed between physical and emotional intimacy. The dualistic mentality encourages young people to disassociate their bodies sexually from who they are as whole persons. It devalues the body and drains relationships of their moral and emotional depth.

Young people desperately need to hear the biblical ethic framed in positive terms showing that it overcomes the two-story divide—that it reintegrates body and person. When young people learn how to "reckon with someone's personhood," the result is sexual relationships that are far healthier and more fulfilling.

What *Rolling Stone* Says

What does it mean to say the hookup culture is based on Cartesian dualism? Most college students have probably never read Descartes. But they can describe the split mindset perfectly. In an interview in *Rolling Stone* magazine, a student named Naomi said hooking up has made "people assume that there are two very distinct elements in a relationship, one emotional and one sexual, and they pretend like there are clean lines between them."[3]

Do you recognize the language of dualism? Young people assume that sexual relationships can be solely physical (lower story), disconnected from the mind and emotions (upper story)—with "clean lines" between them. This is Descartes's ghost in the machine in a new guise. You might picture the division like this:

The hookup culture: "clean lines between them"

PERSONAL
Mental and Emotional Relationship

PHYSICAL
Sexual Relationship

Sexual intercourse, the most intimate of *bodily* relations, has been disconnected from *personal* relations. Sex is cast as a purely recreational activity that can be enjoyed apart from any hint of love or commitment. All that matters is consent (as though agreeing to perform an act makes it right).

Young people can recite the script by heart, even if they don't like it much. A college student named Alicia says, "Hookups are very scripted. . . . You learn to turn everything off except your body and make yourself emotionally invulnerable."[4] Another student, Fallon, laments, "Sex should stem from emotional intimacy, and it's the opposite with us right now." A senior named Stephanie chimes in: "It's body first, personality second."[5]

Sexuality is treated not as the embodied expression of our selfhood but merely as an instrument for physical release and recreation.

What Miley Cyrus Finds Hard to Do

Living out the hookup script is not easy, however. In her interviews, Freitas learned that students have to work hard to disassociate their feelings from their sexual encounters. They find their meaningless sexual encounters disappointing. They feel hurt and lonely. Privately they admit they wish they knew how to do more—how to create a genuine relationship in which they are known and appreciated for who they are as a whole person. Even Miley Cyrus says, "F—ing is easy. You can find someone to f— in five seconds. We want to find someone we can talk to. And be ourselves with. That's fairly slim pickings."[6]

At the same time, students feel intense pressure not to admit their dissatisfaction with the hookup scene. If you admit that you want more than sex, students told Freitas, you will be labeled needy, clingy, and dependent. A student named Amanda said, "It's a contest to see who cares less. . . . But if you say any of this out loud, it's like you're weak, you're not independent, you somehow missed the whole memo about third-wave feminism."[7]

To suppress their emotions, students often turn to alcohol. Many admit that getting drunk is the only way they can go through with having sex with people they do not like or even know. One student was particularly candid: Though she had a regular hookup partner, she admitted that without alcohol, the two of them could not even sustain a conversation. "We don't really like each other in person, sober," she told the *New York Times*. "We literally can't sit down and have coffee."[8]

George Bernard Shaw highlighted the same problem in his 1932 play *Too True to Be Good*, even using the image of an upper and lower story. A character says, "When men and women pick one another up just for a bit of fun, they find they've picked up more than they bargained for, because men and women have a top story as well as a ground floor." He adds, "You can't have the one without the other. They're always trying to; but it doesn't work."[9]

Today's young people are still desperately "trying to," but it still doesn't work. Freitas writes, "Regardless of what students brag about or tell their friends, most are terrible at shutting out the emotional dimensions of sexual intimacy."[10]

The fact that it does not work ought to tell us something. It means the hookup culture rests on an inadequate conception of human nature. People are trying to live out a worldview that does not fit who they really are. Because humans are created in God's image, the secular view will never quite match their actual experience. The square peg of their convictions will never fit the round hole of reality. As a result, in practice, non-Christians will always run into some point of contradiction between their secular worldview and their real-life experience.

That contradiction provides an opening to make the case that the secular view is flawed. It does not fit reality. Young people are trying to live out a worldview that does not match their true nature, and it is tearing them apart with its pain and heartache.

■ ■ ■ ■ ■

The Ghost in the Sex Machine

The key to understanding the secular ethic is that it is based on a materialist view of nature. It tells us that our bodies are products of purposeless, amoral Darwinian forces and therefore they are morally neutral. The implication is that what we do with our bodies has no moral significance. The self is free to use the body any way it chooses, without moral consequences.

"Sex raises no unique moral issues at all," says Peter Singer of Princeton. "Decisions about sex may involve considerations of honesty, concern for others, prudence, and so on, but there is nothing special about sex in this respect, for the same could be said of decisions about driving a car."[11] For Singer, the act of sex itself is amoral. It has no moral significance. The only moral dimension comes from accompanying attitudes like honesty and prudence. Like driving a car.

What does this amoral view look like in practice? Feminist author Naomi Wolf found out in extensive interviews with students. One young woman said, "We are so tightly scheduled. Why get to know someone first? It is a waste of time. If you hook-up you can just get your needs met and get on your way."[12] This bleak, one-dimensional view of sexuality assumes that sex is just a physical urge—that there is no deeper, more wholistic yearning to connect with another person. Anonymous perfunctory encounters are enough to "get your needs met."

We might call this the Proverbs 30 picture of sexuality, with its portrayal of someone who has committed adultery: "She eats and wipes her mouth and says, 'I've done nothing wrong'" (Prov. 30:20). In other words, sex is just a natural appetite, like eating. When you feel a sexual hunger, you satisfy it. No big deal. It is a dishearteningly low view of sexuality.

Some may think sexual hedonism gives sex *too much* importance, but in reality it gives sex *too little* importance. It treats the body as nothing more than a physical organism driven by physical urges. It treats sex as a strictly physical act isolated from the rich inner life of the whole person. Thus it deprives sex of its depth by detaching it from its meaning as self-giving between a man and a woman committed to building an entire life together.

Under all the hype about sex as fun and games is actually "a fundamental despair" about the body, explains Catholic writer (and former lesbian) Melinda Selmys. "Beneath all the pageantry of free sex and self-love, there is a fundamental belief that the body doesn't *mean* anything, that it is insignificant in a literal sense: signifying nothing." Therefore what you do with the body has no moral consequence. "You can do anything that you like with it," Selmys says. "You can pleasure it with a vacuum cleaner or . . . you can give it away to anyone for any reason. It's just a sort of wet machine, a tool that you can use and exchange for whatever purpose suits your fancy."

When scientists and philosophers decide that nature is just a vast machine, that has implications for morality. The human body becomes a "wet machine." As Selmys concludes, you must implicitly accept that "your body is not you, it is just a shell, or a juicy robot, that the real you—the disembodied ghost—controls."[13]

The ghost in the sex machine.

In literature on the ecology movement, it is often asserted that Cartesian dualism has alienated us from nature, leading us to mistreat and pollute our environment. Yet we rarely make the connection to morality: The same dualism has alienated many people from their bodies, leading them to mistreat their bodies sexually. As Meilander says, the environmental movement has taught us that we should "not treat nature as simply an object over which we exercise dominion." Yet many people are "strangely unconcerned when we objectify and instrumentalize the body."[14]

Feminists complain that sexual hedonism objectifies women, but the problem runs much deeper: It objectifies the human body itself.

"Be Like Porn Stars"

Unfortunately, adult culture is not helping. Sex education courses typically focus solely on the physical dimension: on body parts, health risks, avoiding pregnancy, and the mechanics of sex. Universities invite sex toy companies on campus to display their wares. At Yale University's Sex Week, porn stars have been invited as speakers, and students are invited to attend workshops on topics such as sadomasochism, incest, and bestiality. "The message: Don't be boring. Be like porn stars."[15] But sex education programs do not teach how to form and maintain a relationship.

Adult culture is essentially telling young people that they are mature, they are ready for sex, if they can be uncommitted and emotionally detached. The message in this kind of literature, says Shalit, is that those who can separate sex from love are sophisticated. "They are ready to embark on a lifetime of meaningless encounters. Conversely, those who still dream of love are immature, and should return to playing with dolls and trucks until they can be callous enough to seek sexual non-intimacy."[16]

Educators are so afraid of being "moralistic" that they submit to a strict code of political correctness governing what they say to students. A UCLA psychiatrist named Miriam Grossman reveals that she was not permitted to counsel students in moral terms of right and wrong—or even to discourage harmful behavior. She grew so frustrated about the limitations placed on her counseling that she wrote a book titled *Unprotected: A Campus Psychiatrist Reveals How Political Correctness in Her Profession Endangers Every Student*.

For example, Grossman describes a freshman named Olivia who came to see her, in deep depression over her first sexual encounter with a boy who dropped her soon afterward. "Why, Doctor," she asked, "why do they tell you how to protect your body—from herpes and pregnancy—but they don't tell you what it does to your *heart*?"

Why indeed? Grossman asks. "Why are students inundated with information about contraception, a healthy diet, sleep hygiene, coping with stress and pressure—but not a word about the havoc that casual sex plays on young women's emotions?"[17] Despite extensive research, Grossman found virtually no educational materials designed to take young people beyond the sheer physical dimension.

Sex education reduces the meaning of sex to a how-to manual.

It is demoralizing to young people to suggest that the only protection they need is instruction in how to use drugs and devices for safe sex. It infantilizes them by denying them any moral agency in a context where they desperately need to be empowered to act as moral agents—in matters that affect their physical, psychological, and spiritual health. A male student named Vu Le writes in a student newspaper, "I am amazed that there is no academic course or guidance in that all-important area, the Romantic Relationship."[18]

And let's not forget the other segments of adult culture that push young people into early sexual experimentation. Businesses and corporations are complicit in the sexualizing of ever-younger children, producing "slut" style fashions for little girls—all the way down to infant clothing that says "I'm

Too Sexy for My Diaper." Dolls have morphed into "tramps" wearing fishnet stockings, red-hot lingerie, and heavy makeup. Advertisers use sex to sell, filmmakers use sex to entice viewers, musicians incorporate sexualized lyrics into their songs and music videos.

The irony is that when young people experiment sexually, they typically think they are rebelling against adult culture. But in reality they are following a script that adult culture is giving them. They are falling for a sales pitch. The real rebellion in our day is to practice chastity. *That* requires genuine courage.

"No Names, Just Sex"

Why does secular sexual morality place such a strong emphasis on emotional detachment? Because if the main goal is pleasure, then taking account of the partner as a whole person gets in the way. "When sex is reduced to an exchange of pleasures, the other person's personality becomes a burden," explains Selmys.

> If the purpose of sexuality is mere pleasure, sooner or later the other person, with all of their personality and their own, separate desires, is going to become burdensome. The ideal, then, becomes "no names, just sex"; the partners use each other to gain a particular pleasure, trying as much as possible, to remain totally separated in their own realms of subjective experience.[19]

Recognizing the other individual's personhood is "a burden" to impersonal sex.

The irony is that impersonal sex is rarely satisfying, even to the person who seeks it out. The pleasure of sexual activity is not just physical. When we reach out for another person, we are not driven by a desire for sheer physical pleasure but by a hope for at least some level of personal contact.

William Beardslee, psychiatry professor at Harvard University, says young people are trying to persuade themselves that "true *sexual* intimacy is unconnected from *personal* intimacy." But they are fooling themselves.[20] Humans can't help functioning as a body-person unit—which is just what the biblical worldview says we are.

Christianity is often accused of being negative because of its teaching on sin and guilt. But in reality it has a much more positive view of sexuality than the secular view. As Juli Slattery and Dannah Gresh write in *Pulling Back the Shades*, "The truth is that you were created for something more! Your sexuality was never meant to be separate from your deepest spiritual and relational longings but to be an expression of them."[21]

Porn vs. Intimacy

The most extreme example of depersonalized sex is pornography. The viewer disconnects the woman's body from any interest in who she is as a person. Pornography tears apart what is meant to be integrated, treating the body as an object or instrument for one's own purposes.

Tragically, porn is where many young people are getting their sex education today. Naomi Wolf describes students she interviewed at a large university: "It became clear that after a decade of having access to the internet they were intimately familiar with porn, but intimacy—and the hearts of the opposite sex—were more of an elusive mystery than ever."[22]

From childhood, young people are awash in sexual *imagery*, but sexual *intimacy* is increasingly difficult to achieve.

Even secular researchers are growing alarmed about porn's harmful consequences. Porn is "a public health crisis," blared a *Washington Post* article. "The science is now beyond dispute." For example, "In a content analysis of best-selling and most-rented porn films, researchers found that 88 percent of analyzed scenes contained physical aggression." Most of the victims were women. As a result, those who watched mainstream pornography "were more likely to say they would commit rape or sexual assault (if they knew they wouldn't be caught)."[23]

Today, the average age that a boy first encounters pornography is nine years old. By the time he is an adult, he has been consuming porn for more than a decade. How does that affect his relationships with real women? *Time* magazine reports, "Many of them are simply unable to experience a sexual response with a real live woman. They are only able to respond to pornography. In fact, they prefer pornography."[24] In other words, they prefer not going to the trouble of dealing with a real person.

When these men marry, they are shocked—shocked—to discover that porn has destroyed their ability to relate to their spouse. It has trained them to objectify the opposite sex. They literally don't know how to relate to a woman as a full person.

The first longitudinal study on porn found that men who start watching porn after they marry are twice as likely to divorce.[25] Other studies found that watching porn actually shrinks the brain and reduces neural activity.[26] There is now firm data showing that porn is addictive, it leads to violence, it destroys relationships, it feeds sex trafficking and prostitution.

Yet, surprisingly, teens and young adults tend to shrug off porn as unimportant. In a Barna survey, they rated it as less morally objectionable than "overeating" or "not recycling."[27] As a result, an organization called Fight the New Drug addresses especially young people with the message that "Porn Kills Love." For example, one survey found that porn puts enormous pressure on women:

> Girls and young women are under a lot of pressure to give boys and men what they want, to become a real life embodiment of what the boys have watched in porn, adopting exaggerated roles and behaviors and providing their bodies as mere sex aids. Growing up in today's porn culture, girls quickly learn that they are service stations for male gratification and pleasure.[28]

There's a reason Jesus said sin gets its hold on us first in our hearts: "Anyone who looks at a woman lustfully has already committed adultery with her in his heart" (Matt. 5:28). We could translate that into a modern idiom by saying, "Don't objectify women. Don't strip them of their identity as full persons by reducing them to objects of your sexual lust." Pornography is literally training a generation of young people to violate Jesus's proscription by engaging in depersonalized sex. And the mental habits taught by porn bleed into real relationships.

The next step, some say, is robotic sex (with sex dolls). Futurists predict that in ten years sex robots will become more popular than porn. The first sex doll brothel has already opened in Barcelona, Spain.[29] A materialist philosophy has been teaching people that they are merely complex mechanisms, and now we are seeing the logical outcome—the substitution of machines for real persons. The ultimate depersonalization.

The Science of Sex

The irony is that science is constantly uncovering new evidence of the profound interconnection between body and person. Pick up any recent book on sexuality and you will read about the role played by hormones such as oxytocin and vasopressin. Scientists first learned about oxytocin because of its role in childbirth and breastfeeding. The chemical is released when a mother nurses her baby, and it stimulates an instinct for caring and nurturing. It is often called the attachment hormone.

Imagine the surprise when scientists discovered that oxytocin is also released during sexual intercourse, especially (but not exclusively) in women. Consequently, the desire to attach to the other person when we have sex is not only an emotion but also part of our chemistry. Oxytocin has been shown to create a sense of trust. As one sex therapist puts it, when we have intercourse, we create "an involuntary chemical commitment."[30]

The upshot is that even if you *think* you are having a no-strings-attached hookup, you are in reality creating a chemical bond—whether you mean to or not. An advice columnist for *Glamour* magazine warns that because of hormones, "we often get prematurely attached." Even when you intend to just have casual sex, "biology might trump your intentions."[31]

That may be why Paul said, "Whoever sins sexually, sins against their own body" (1 Cor. 6:18). Sex involves our bodies down to the level of our biochemistry.

The same holds true for men. The main neurochemical responsible for the male response in intimate sexual contact is vasopressin. It is structurally similar to oxytocin and has a similar emotional effect. Scientists believe it stimulates bonding with a woman and with offspring. Vasopressin has been dubbed the monogamy molecule.[32]

As Grossman observes, "You might say we are designed to bond."[33]

Paul's words ring even more true today than in his own time: "Do you not know that he who unites himself with a prostitute is one with her in body? For it is said, 'The two will become one flesh'" (v. 16). Lauren Winner at Duke University translates Paul's words like this: "Don't you know that when you sleep with someone, your body makes a promise, whether you do or not?"[34]

The implication is that repeatedly hooking up involves repeatedly breaking that bodily "promise." No wonder breakups are so painful that many young adults cultivate a cynical attitude just to overcome the pain. In many cases, their emotional detachment is a form of what psychologists call defensive detachment: *I'm afraid you will hurt me, so I will build an emotional wall to avoid being vulnerable to you*. As a result, however, deep attachment becomes ever more difficult. Even when young adults want to marry, they have a harder time making a lasting commitment. A YouGov poll found that almost half of millennials have given up the hope—or even desire—for a monogamous relationship.[35]

The hookup culture is unraveling the social fabric. It produces isolated, alienated adults who come together temporarily for physiological release. By repeatedly breaking up (or never connecting in the first place), many people fail to learn how to form the strong, resilient bonds needed to create happy, fulfilling, long-term marriages and families.

Even pornography has the addictive power it does because it literally changes the chemistry of our brains. Like other addictive triggers, pornography floods the brain with dopamine. That rush of brain chemicals, when it happens repeatedly, rewires the brain's reward pathway and can become a default setting.

Brain scientists refer to this as neuroplasticity: Neurons that fire together, wire together.

Eventually the brain is overwhelmed by the chemical overload and shuts down some of its dopamine receptors—which means the porn viewer does not get the same "high" and has to seek out more hardcore porn to feel the same dopamine effect. That's why porn is addictive.[36]

The latest science is confirming that the human being is a unified whole. The body/personhood divide is not true to who we are. In fact, the reason all the sex education and deprogramming aimed at young people is necessary is precisely *because* they do not, by nature, thrive on casual, meaningless sexual encounters. They crave emotional intimacy and fidelity.

No Prozac for the Heart

When they fail to find intimacy and fidelity, many people turn to psychotherapy for help. Psychiatrist Dr. Paul McHugh says vast numbers of young women consult him because they keep getting sexually involved with men who don't want to get married. "There must be something the matter with me," these women say. "Dr. McHugh, give me a pill." They're asking for Prozac to help them get over their hurt and disappointment. "There's nothing the matter with you," McHugh tells them. The problem is that the world is pressuring you into "immediately hopping into bed with all these guys."[37]

Philosophy professor Anne Maloney reports the same distress among her students: "It is no coincidence that the top two prescribed drugs at our state university's health center are anti-depressants and the birth-control pill."[38]

Yet no amount of Prozac or Zoloft will solve this form of depression.

Young men often feel greater pressure not to admit their dissatisfaction with the hookup culture, but many are growing cynical. A *Vanity Fair* reporter interviewed several young men who use dating apps like *Tinder*. Some one hundred million people are using their phones as a sort of all-day, every-day, handheld singles club. "It's like ordering Seamless," says Dan, an investment banker, referring to the online food-delivery service. "But you're ordering a person."

Are the men happy with the "delivery service"? No. They complain that the apps make hookups so accessible that they reduce all incentive to form relationships. "When asked if there was anything about dating apps they didn't like," the reporter writes, again and again the young men said, "'Too easy,' 'Too easy,' 'Too easy.'" Alex, a twenty-five-year-old New Yorker, lamented, "Romance is completely dead."[39]

A young man quoted in *Verily* says, "I can't stand how ads and TV shows and pop culture portray the idea that men just want casual relationships. . . . Who has ever been satisfied by that? We all want something that lasts, someone we can lean on and trust. We want authentic relationships that are grounded in sacrifice and not on fleeting feelings and pleasure alone."[40]

■ ■ ■ ■ ■

What the Sex Therapist Prescribes

Roger Libby is a sex therapist who has made the rounds on all the big talk shows like *Oprah*, *Donahue*, and *Geraldo*. His much-touted contribution is to urge couples to engage in a PSD: a Pre-Sex Discussion to get to know one another. With all the flourish of announcing a breakthrough discovery, Libby says sexual relations are more fulfilling when a couple actually *talks* first. "A PSD is an intimate and entertaining conversation that informs prospective lovers about each other's feelings, desires, expectations. . . . A PSD encourages mutual honesty; sex without honesty is not meaningful, long lasting, or fun." Libby concludes that "a properly conducted PSD minimizes dangers and maximizes pleasures."[41]

Who would have guessed? If people get to know one another as *persons*, even a little, they actually experience greater sexual pleasure. That may be why studies consistently show that the people who are happiest sexually are married, middle-aged, conservative Christians.[42]

How did so many Westerners lose sight of such a commonsense truth? What are the deeper roots of the hookup culture? We can help people gain a truer idea of sexuality if we know where false ideas came from and how they developed. As we learned in chapter 3, after the Enlightenment many leading thinkers began to adopt a materialist worldview, which sees humans as nothing but complex physical organisms. The logical conclusion is that the goal of life is to avoid physical pain and maximize physical pleasure.

What does a materialist worldview do with *non*material realities such as moral ideals and principles? Ideals cannot be observed, weighed, or measured in a laboratory. As a result, strict materialists dismiss them as unreal. They endorse a utilitarian ethic in which the only good is pleasure. "The Enlightenment's great historical watershed lay in the validation of pleasure," says historian Roy Porter. "The new science promoted mechanical models of man essentially as a machine motivated to pursue pleasure and avoid pain."[43]

I was once asked on a radio show, "Why is America moving toward such moral debauchery?" I responded, "It proves the power that worldviews have on our minds. If it is true that humans are just complex machines, operating by stimulus-response mechanisms, the logical conclusion is that they are driven solely by pleasure and pain. Their bodies are pleasure machines. And they may use their bodies any way they want as long as it maximizes physical pleasure."[44]

The Religion of Sex

Who are the key thinkers who forged the modern sexual ethos—whose ideas shape what is taught in today's textbooks, from college down to kindergarten?

When we look at the history of these ideas, we find that, ironically, even those who adopt a purely materialist worldview often end up turning sex into a substitute religion. If you picture matter in the lower story, even materialists keep climbing up into the upper story and claiming religious significance for sexuality.

And when sex becomes a religion, then nothing is allowed to stand in its way—especially not Christian morality. All the most prominent sexual theorists have been "morality critics" (to borrow a phrase from philosopher Brian Leiter). They treat morality as an obstacle to human happiness, an evil force from which we must be liberated.[45] Let's meet a few of the most influential, and learn how they shaped today's politically correct sexual orthodoxy.[46]

Sigmund Freud: Sex as Instinct

Sigmund Freud fit the stereotype of the German scientist, with his round lenses and pointed white beard, a fat cigar propped between his fingers. Freud was a committed Darwinian, treating sexuality solely as a biological drive. He wrote that pleasure is "the main purpose" of our entire "mental apparatus." Jonathan Ned Katz, a historian of sexuality, says Freud conceived of a person as "a machine with satisfaction as its mission."[47]

Freud conceded that sexual restraint is necessary for civilization, but he taught that for the individual it is harmful and unhealthy, leading to neurosis. He had nothing but contempt for people who kept sex within the covenant bond of marriage: "Only the weaklings have acquiesced in such a gross invasion of their sexual freedom."[48] Freud had an enormous influence in persuading the modern world that sexual liberation is the path to mental and sexual health.

Margaret Sanger: Sex as Salvation

Margaret Sanger, founder of Planned Parenthood, was another morality critic. She described the great drama of history as a struggle to free our bodies and minds from the constraints of morality—"the cruel morality of self-denial and 'sin.'" In her view, sexual liberation was "the only method" by which a person could find "inner peace and security and beauty."[49] It was also the means to advance to the next level of evolution—to "remodel the race" and create "a real civilization."

Sanger even resorted to explicitly religious language: "Through sex, mankind may attain the great spiritual illumination which will transform the world, which will light up the only path to an earthly paradise."[50]

If this isn't a religious vision, I don't know what is. For materialist thinkers, immersion in the biological instincts became nothing less than a means of salvation.

Alfred Kinsey: The Pseudoscience of Sex

The 2004 movie *Kinsey* portrayed him as a heroic pioneer. But Alfred Kinsey was likewise a morality critic. He emphasized repeatedly that sex is "a normal biologic function, *acceptable in whatever form it is manifested.*"[51]

To liberate sex from morality, Kinsey reduced it to the sheer act of physical orgasm. He then claimed that all orgasms are morally equivalent, whether between married persons or unmarried persons, between people of the opposite sex or the same sex, between adults and children, between strangers or with prostitutes, even between humans and animals. He ignored the fact that these situations involve vastly different relational, emotional, social, moral, and spiritual dimensions. All of them he labeled simply "sexual outlets," and he pronounced them all equally acceptable.

As the current slogan goes, "Love is love."

Like his predecessors, Kinsey was deeply committed to Darwinian materialism, referring to humanity in reductionist language as "the human animal." Any behavior that could be found among animals he considered normative for humans as well. For example, he claimed that certain mammals are observed to have sexual contact between males, and even across species. Therefore, he concluded that both homosexuality and bestiality are "part of the normal mammalian picture" and acceptable for humans as well.

Kinsey claimed his approach was scientific, yet his research methods clearly were not. His samples included a disproportionate percentage of sex offenders, sadomasochists, voyeurs, exhibitionists, and pedophiles. The pedophiles, in particular, were engaged in illegal behavior. Yet Kinsey took them at their word when they claimed that the children they were sexually assaulting enjoyed the experience.

Kinsey showed no concern about his unscientific research methods because ultimately he was not driven by science. According to Stanford professor

Paul Robinson, Kinsey viewed history "as a great moral drama, in which the forces of science competed with those of superstition" (by which he meant religion and morality). He even spoke as if the introduction of Bible-based sexual morality were *the* watershed in human history, a sort of "fall" from which we must be redeemed.[52] Sexual liberation would be the means for saving humans from the oppression of religion and morality.

Wilhelm Reich: New Age Sex

In the 1960s, psychologist Wilhelm Reich became a cult figure in the human potential movement. It was Reich who coined the phrase "sexual revolution" (in a book by that title). He preached a gospel of redemption through complete immersion in the sexual instincts. In his words, "The core of happiness in life is *sexual* happiness."[53] He promised that all human dysfunctions could be fixed by developing "the capacity for surrender to the flow of biological energy without any inhibition, the capacity for complete discharge of all dammed-up sexual excitation through involuntary pleasurable contractions of the body."[54]

The serpent in Reich's sexual Eden was Christian morality. He denounced it as a "murderous philosophy" that creates guilt and neurosis. A book describing his philosophy is aptly titled *Salvation through Sex*. It explains that for Reich, orgasm "is man's only salvation, leading to the Kingdom of Heaven on earth."[55]

Robert Rimmer: Sex as "Act of Worship"

Reich's ideas were widely disseminated through a 1966 novel by Robert Rimmer titled *The Harrad Experiment*, which sold three million copies and was required reading in college courses on marriage and family. The book is credited with being the main force behind the creation of coed dormitories in American universities. Rimmer's view of sex is frankly religious. One character states that intercourse "is actually an act of worship." Another says, "What lovers feel for each other in this moment [sexual intercourse] is no other than adoration in the full religious sense." Through sex we see that the beloved is "the naturally divine."[56] When I was in high school, a boy I was dating gave me a copy of *The Harrad Experiment*, obviously hoping to convert me to Rimmer's religion of sex.

In a postscript to the 1990 edition of the novel, Rimmer wrote that sex can "become the new religion—a humanistic religion, without the necessity of a god."

Foucault: Sex Is "More Important Than Our Soul"

Clearly, the architects of the sexual revolution were driven by nothing less than a vision of redemption. The philosophy of materialism claims to stay solidly in the lower story, the realm of facts and science. But like everyone else, materialists search for a sense of meaning to life, and as a result they end up climbing into the upper story—even if it means turning materialism itself into a religion.

But why do materialists choose sex as their means to salvation? Because in materialism, the core of human identity is in the biological, the natural, the instinctual—especially the sexual instincts. Sex is, after all, central to the survival of the species. Darwin's theory of evolution even elevated reproduction to the linchpin of evolutionary progress. Because the theory offers no independent criterion of success, it boils down to differential reproduction—whoever has the most viable offspring wins. Reproduction is the key to evolutionary advance.

Michel Foucault, a French postmodernist and author of a three-volume set on the history of sexuality, writes that in the past, biologists treated sex and reproduction as merely one among many functions of an organism. But in the space of a few centuries, sex went from being just one activity of life to being our core identity. In Foucault's words, geneticists now "see in the reproductive mechanism that very element which introduces the biological dimension: the matrix not only of the living, but of life itself." Sex is treated as the "master key" to knowing "who we are. . . . Sex, the explanation for everything." He goes so far as to say, "Sex is worth dying for." It is "more important than our soul."[57]

Is *My* Kid Reading That Stuff?

Why should you care what thinkers from Freud to Foucault have written? Because they function as the saints and theologians of the religion of sex. Their teachings shape today's sexual orthodoxy. Many young people say sex education programs make them feel pressured into having sex. In one study, teens reported that they felt more pressure from their sex education classes than from their girlfriends or boyfriends.[58] And no wonder: If sexual liberation is an alternative version of salvation, then sex education classes become recruitment centers.

Many families hope to protect their children from radical ideas by walling off the secular world—supervising what books they read, what movies they see, what music they listen to. But secular worldviews do not come neatly labeled so we can easily recognize them. Instead they mutate into forms that we hardly recognize, becoming part of the very air we breathe. The most powerful worldviews are the ones we absorb without knowing it. They are the ideas nobody talks about—the assumptions we pick up almost by osmosis.

The ideas we have traced from Freud to Foucault constitute the prevailing sexual orthodoxy. It informs the mindset of judges when they rule on sexual issues. It shapes the arguments of legislators when they formulate new laws. It guides the way reporters frame the news. It is the attitude portrayed in TV sitcoms, supermarket tabloids, and magazine articles. It is reflected in the lyrics of popular songs. It permeates virtually the entire entertainment industry. (How many movies have you seen that show sexual restraint as a *good* thing?)

Most importantly, it is the sexual orthodoxy that shapes the outlook of your children's teachers and the writers of your children's sex education textbooks. Virtually all of us have been influenced by these thinkers' views of sexuality—even if we have never read a word of their writings.

To have independent minds, we must learn where these theories come from and then propose a Christian worldview as a viable alternative.

History bears out what Paul says in Romans 1—that everyone bases his or her life on some definition of ultimate reality. Those who reject the transcendent God of the Bible put something else in his place. They exchange "the glory of the immortal God" for something in creation (Rom. 1:23). In short, they create idols.

Since the beginning of the modern age, many Western thinkers have been materialists. That means they put matter in the place of God as the ultimate, self-existing, uncaused cause of everything else. Matter is their idol. Logically, then, they must define humans solely as material organisms evolving by Darwinian processes. Human behavior is shaped by biological drives and instincts. Liberation of the sexual instinct becomes the path to salvation—to a sexual utopia.[59]

This explains why it is so difficult to halt the sexualizing of modern culture. Sexual liberation is not just a matter of sensual gratification or titillation. It is a complete ideology, a vision of redemption. To stand against it, we cannot simply express moral disapproval. A person's morality is always derivative. It stems from his or her worldview. To be effective, we have to engage the underlying worldview.

■ ■ ■ ■ ■

Body Language

How do we reconnect sexuality to a larger moral universe—to a vision of truth, goodness, and beauty? In a teleological worldview, all of creation declares the glory of God. The fact that humans reproduce sexually is not some evolutionary fluke. It is part of the original creation that reveals the wonder and beauty of its Creator.

The implication is that the body "speaks" its own language. We all know that a smile means friendliness while a punch in the face means hostility. Despite differences among cultures, there are broad similarities. When you hold hands with someone, does it mean anything? Does it communicate care and affection? What about a kiss? What does that communicate?

The poet John Donne wrote that the body is like a book where we read the intentions of the soul: "Love's mysteries in souls do grow / But yet the body is his book."[60]

This explains why it is possible to lie with our bodies. Have you ever kissed or held hands with someone you did not really like? Perhaps because you felt pressured into it? Or because you wanted the person to *think* you cared more than you really did? In either case, reflecting back on those situations, we can sense that we were lying—that our gestures "said" something that was not true.

That's why Judas's method of betraying Jesus was so painfully ironic: "Are you betraying [me] with a *kiss*?"—of all things (Luke 22:48, italics added).

Gestures mean something. Sexual intercourse, as the most intimate form of *physical* union, is meant to express the ultimate form of *personal* union in marriage. Common phrases for having sex indicate that it is the most you can do sexually—it is "going all the way" or "getting to home plate" or "sealing the deal." That's why it belongs only in a relationship where you "go all the way" on all other levels as well—when you commit to another person legally, economically, socially, and spiritually. You should become naked and vulnerable physically only when you are ready to become naked and vulnerable with your whole self. As C. S. Lewis put it, those who have sex outside of marriage "are trying to isolate one kind of union (the sexual) from all the other kinds of union which were intended to go along with it and make up the total union."[61]

Invariably my students ask, "Isn't it enough to be in love?" The answer is that even being in love falls short of committing one's entire self and future in biblical nakedness to another person. Biblical morality asks us to be consistent in what we say with our bodies and what we say with the rest of our lives. To tell the truth with our bodies.

Timothy Keller writes, "Sex is God's appointed way for two people to say reciprocally to one another, 'I belong completely, permanently, and exclusively to you.'"[62] When we have sex outside of marriage, we are essentially lying with our bodies. Our actions are "saying" that we are united on all levels when in reality we are not. We are contradicting ourselves. We are putting on an act. We are being dishonest.

Some people think it sounds very spiritual to say God is above caring about something so inconsequential as what we do sexually. A Catholic feminist writes, "God does not care what we do with each other's bodies, he only cares whether we treat each other as persons."[63] But can we really do *anything* to a person's body and still respect him or her as a person? Such a sharp body/person division is more Gnostic than biblical. The biblical ethic expresses a rich concept of the whole person as an embodied being. Our bodies matter.

Yada Yada

The first biblical passage that talks about sex is the Genesis account of Adam and Eve, and it speaks powerfully of the interconnection between body and person. "A man leaves his father and mother and is united to his wife, and they become one flesh" (Gen. 2:24). Does the phrase "one flesh" refer only to the bodily correspondence between the two sexes? Clearly not. The reference to *physical* unity was intended to express a joyous unity on all other levels as well—including mind, emotion, and spirit. Scripture offers a stunningly high view of physical union as a union of whole persons across all dimensions.

Genesis uses a charming euphemism for sexual relations—the verb *to know*. "Adam knew his wife Eve, and she conceived and bore Cain," her first child (4:1 ESV). The English word *know* is a translation of the Hebrew *yada*, which means to know by experience. It is the same word used in that most personal of psalms, "You have searched me, Lord, and you know [*yada*] me" (Ps. 139:1). Elsewhere the godly king Josiah is described in these words: "'He defended the cause of the poor and needy. . . . Is that not what it means to know [*yada*] me?' says the LORD" (Jer. 22:16). The term carries connotations of a deep, personal way of knowing, and when used as a sexual euphemism, it means that sex is meant to be a profound connection of two persons.

Scripture teaches that the relationship of husband and wife even has the supreme dignity of reflecting the relationship between God and his people. Through the prophet Hosea, God says to the people of Israel, "I will betroth you to me forever. I will betroth you to me in righteousness and in justice, in steadfast love and in mercy. I will betroth you to me in faithfulness. And you shall know [*yada*] the LORD" (Hos. 2:19–20 ESV). Covenant marriage is intended to be a visual image of the human-divine relationship.

In the New Testament, the same imagery of marriage is applied to Christ and to the church as his bride. Paul says, "Husbands, love your wives, just as Christ loved the church and gave himself up for her" (Eph. 5:25). And in his vision of the end of the world, John says, "I saw the Holy City, the new Jerusalem, coming down out of heaven from God, prepared as a bride beautifully dressed for her husband" (Rev. 21:2). When people witness the loving, faithful relationship between husband and wife, they are meant to see a picture of how much God loves his people.

Creation: Sex Was God's Idea

How can we gain a balanced understanding of what the Bible says about sex? The Bible teaches that all of creation participates in a great drama of three acts: creation—fall—redemption. If we are ever tempted to think that sex is corrupt or dirty, we need to remind ourselves that it was God who created it in the first place. Sex is not something introduced after the fall. It was part of the original creation of humans in God's image, which God pronounced "very good." Having created humans as male and female, God commanded them to "be fruitful and multiply." Making a culture starts with making babies.

The biblical teaching that we are created in the image of God means that even though humans are part of nature, we do not find our full identity in nature. We cannot be reduced to merely part of the natural world. Even the features we share with other organisms, such as our sexuality, cannot be fully understood in merely biological terms. Sex is not only about biological drives and needs, whether for pleasure or reproduction, but also about the communion of persons. The communion of male and female is meant to mirror the communion of divine persons within the Trinity.

The classic theological definition of the Trinity is that God is one substance in three persons. The practical meaning is that God in his ultimate being is not an impersonal force, as in Eastern religions; instead God exists as distinct persons who give themselves to one another in love. "As human beings are made in God's image," writes John Wyatt, "we reflect God's nature in our personhood; we are created to give ourselves to God and to others in love."[64]

That's why Paul calls the marriage relationship a "profound mystery" (Eph. 5:32). The Greek word for *mystery* means the revelation of something otherwise hidden.[65] Our sexuality is meant to reveal God's own character. Romans 1 says the created order gives evidence for God, and because our bodies are part of the created order, they too speak of God and give evidence of his character. We have to tune our ears to "hear" what the body says to us of the divine nature. The God who exists as a communion of Persons has created embodied persons who are ordered toward one another physically as man and woman.

The Fall: Torn Apart

Reading further in Genesis, we learn about the second great act in the drama of history—the fall into sin. The text tells us that when the first humans disobeyed God, "the eyes of both of them were opened, and they realized they were naked; so they sewed fig leaves together and made coverings for themselves" (Gen. 3:7). Throughout history, many people have concluded from this passage that the original sin was sex. Otherwise, why the reference to loincloths? But that is a misunderstanding of the text.

Genesis says that in our original created state, man and woman were "naked and without shame." This fascinating phrase means that in a state with no sin, two persons could be completely open and vulnerable to one another without fear or shame. The integration of body and soul was so complete that the body was a full, honest, genuine, undistorted expression of the person. But after the sin of our first parents, this body-person unity was torn apart. God had warned them that if they disobeyed his word, they would "certainly die" (2:17). Though they did not die immediately, they did experience a beginning of the rending of spirit from body. The body could now be used to lie and oppress and advance one's sinful goals and agendas against another person. The openness expressed by the original nakedness gave way to blame, accusations, fear, and shame. The first couple began to build walls against one another.

Adam and Eve hid not only from one another but also from God (3:8). In fact, the theme of Genesis 3 is that *all* relationships are disrupted by the fall, including our internal relationship with ourselves (our psycho-physical unity), our relationship with others, our relationship with God, and even our relationship with nature. Nature now opposes the two fundamental human vocations: the call to work (the imagery of "thorns and thistles") and the call to relationship (the warning of "pain in childbearing"). Harmony in the created order is replaced by alienation.

As a result of the fall, sex has been twisted and distorted to mean many things beside the one-flesh union that is its true purpose. Today it is increasingly difficult to persuade people that *any* form of sexual behavior is wrong or bad for us. Many Westerners think the significance of any sex act is all in our minds. We decide what sex means in any particular situation. We impose meaning on it by our own interpretation.

But paradoxically, if sex means whatever anyone wants it to mean, then objectively—in itself—it means nothing. It is literally meaningless. A drummer in Austin, Texas, told *Rolling Stone* that sex is just "a piece of body touching another piece of body." It is "existentially meaningless."[66]

This "anything goes" view of sexuality is robbing our sexual lives of their depth and significance. No wonder many people keep greedily grabbing at more sexual experiences while finding ever less genuine fulfillment.

Redemption: Good News for Bodies

After the world was broken by sin, God did not abandon it. As Adam and Eve left the garden, God promised a Redeemer who would one day set everything right again. This is act three in the drama of history. Because of the fall, "the whole creation has been groaning as in the pains of childbirth right up to the present time." But in redemption, "the creation itself will be liberated from its bondage to decay and brought into the freedom and glory of the children of God" (Rom. 8:22, 21). Not only our souls but also our bodies will be redeemed.

John Paul II wrote a massive *Theology of the Body* because he recognized that many of today's pressing moral issues involve the body. He argues that a key part of the Christian message is the healing of the alienation of body and person. He calls it "the redemption of the body," a phrase that "refers to the reintegration of bodily sexuality and personhood, that is, to the radical 'personalization' of masculinity and femininity."[67]

That process of personalization can begin even in this life. The apostle Paul ticks off a list of sinful behaviors, including sexual sins, then says, "That is what some of you *were*. But you were washed, you were sanctified, you were justified in the name of the Lord Jesus Christ and by the Spirit of our God" (1 Cor. 6:11, italics added). In other words, you have been liberated from those sinful, destructive patterns of life. The implication is that it is possible even now to begin to live the resurrected life, with a radical reunification of body and person in our sexual lives.

The Bible presents a balanced view of sex that includes the affirmation of the goodness of creation, realism about sin and the fall, and the healing message of redemption.

Churches need to make that message credible by welcoming those who need healing. A grad student of mine, Katrina, told a harrowing story of growing up in a home devastated by alcoholism and sexual abuse. When she reached adulthood, as so often happens, she replayed the same destructive pattern. But when she witnessed her own children repeating the unhealthy cycle yet again, she finally became determined to break out of it. In desperation, she started going to church and converted to Christianity. But did she talk about her painful past at church? Not on your life. She told me, "I am afraid of people finding out how sinful my past was—afraid of being treated as 'damaged' or 'used goods.'"

How tragic that people are afraid to be vulnerable in the very place where they should be finding healing. Even as churches clearly communicate the moral truths of Scripture, they must also become places of refuge for victims of the sexual revolution who have been hurt by its lies.

■ ■ ■ ■ ■

Roman Slaves and Prostitutes

In his book *Unashamed*, Lecrae Moore says he was astonished the first time he attended a Christian conference about sex: "The conference speaker said our bodies were valuable. . . . I'd never connected spirituality and sexuality before. And I had never heard someone talk about how valuable I was."[68]

Like Lecrae, many people are surprised when they first learn that the biblical sex ethic expresses a high view of the body. People often think of Christians as prudes and Puritans who hold a negative view of the body and its functions, especially sex. For example, a *Salon* article charged that the real goal of the pro-life movement is to make it harder for women "to have happy, healthy sex lives."[69] But the truth is that Christianity has a much more respectful view of our psycho-sexual identity.

It is not anti-sex, it is pro-body.

We get a clearer picture of the biblical view if we know something of the Greek language in which the New Testament was originally written. For example, in verses such as Galatians 5:21, Paul says Christians should not engage in *porneia* (which is the root of *pornography*). Older translations rendered the word "carousing" or "reveling," which made it sound like the Bible was opposed to simple fun and partying.

Recent translations use the term "fornication" or "sexual immorality." But those expressions are still far too tame. The word *porneia* comes from the word meaning "to buy," and in the polytheistic literature of the day, it meant "prostitution" or "whoring." And the practice of *porneia* was at least as dehumanizing then as it is today.

In ancient Rome and Greece, a *porne* or prostitute was normally a slave. Sex slaves were often physically abused. "Greek vase paintings show men beating them, evidently for fun," says classicist Sarah Ruden.[70] Horace, the leading Roman lyric poet in the age of Augustus, offers recommendations on how to shop for your sex slave. Comparing it to buying a horse, Horace warns that traders know how to hide flaws, so inspect your wares carefully. Herodas, a Greek writer of the third century BC, tells of a pimp who complained that one of his prostitutes had been abused—she was "shredded" and "torn" by a customer who "dragged her, beat her silly." Still the pimp immediately tries to sell her to a new customer, inviting him to "bruise your goods up any way you want."[71]

The essence of *porneia*, then, "was treating another human being as a thing," Ruden explains. What Paul's early readers would have understood is that it is no longer acceptable to treat a person as an object.[72] "Put to death" the old life, Paul says, with its *porneia* and other sins (Col. 3:5). The body is not meant for *porneia* "but for the Lord" (1 Cor. 6:13).

Bear in mind that this was an era when for a male or female slave to refuse *porneia* could mean capital punishment. Some of the early martyrs were slaves who proclaimed their freedom in Christ by refusing to sexually service their masters—and were executed for it. Potamiaena was a slave in Alexandria, Egypt, whose master was so angry when she refused his advances that he reported her as a Christian to the prefect. He, in turn, threatened to hand her over to the gladiators to be gang-raped, but she persuaded him to execute her instead by slowly immersing her in boiling pitch. The beauty of her character as she faced death inspired the conversion of several other people, including one of her guards, Basilides, who was likewise martyred.[73]

Christianity gave people the courage to say no to coercive sex and forced marriages, even if it sometimes meant arrest, imprisonment, and death. As Jones writes, "True consent was a rarity in the world in which Christianity got its start. Christianity, we might say, invented consensual sex when it developed a sex ethic that assumed that God empowers individuals with freedom."[74]

From the beginning, Christianity was not traditional; it was radically countercultural.

Sex—"As Spiritual as Preaching"

Undergirding the Bible's sexual morality is a remarkably high view of creation. When Paul argues against sexual immorality, how does he do it? By denigrating sexual pleasure? No, by elevating the body. "Do you not know that your bodies are members of Christ himself? Should I then take the members of Christ and unite them with a prostitute? Never!" (1 Cor. 6:15). Paul's rationale for sexual morality is that your body has the dignity of being a member of the body of Christ, the locus of his presence on earth.

Paul then says something truly stunning: "Your bodies are temples of the Holy Spirit" (v. 19). The temple was sacred space, where people went to meet with God. Astonishingly, this passage is saying that your body is where people will meet God. And other people's bodies are where *you* will see God.

Christians need to shake themselves free of the lethargy that settles in after hearing these phrases for years, perhaps since childhood. In their original historical context, these verses were astonishing. In the ancient world, virtually all the major "isms"—Platonism, neo-Platonism, Gnosticism, Manichaeism, Hindu pantheism—taught a low view of the material world. In these philosophies, salvation was conceived as a complete break between matter and spirit, a flight from the physical world. To make that break, adherents adopted a regimen of asceticism to suppress bodily urges and desires.

As we saw in chapter 1, to some extent even Christians were influenced by asceticism, which led to the sacred/secular split. One of the most revolutionary themes of the Reformation was its rejection of the sacred/secular split and its affirmation of the sacredness of the created world. At the dawn of the Reformation, Martin Luther left the monastery and got married. The former monk married a former nun. With that single act Luther said more than all his words could on the dignity of marriage and the value of family in a biblical worldview.

The term "puritanical" is often used to mean a mindset that is stern, severe, and otherworldly. But in reality the Puritans shared the Reformation view that all of life is sacred. The Puritan preacher William Perkins insisted that sex is as "spiritual" as preaching: "Yea, deeds of matrimony are pure and spiritual . . . and whatsoever is done within the laws of God, though it be wrought by the body . . . yet are they sanctified."[75]

Donn Welton summarizes the effects of the Reformation by saying, "Perhaps nothing sets it in contrast to medieval Christendom more than the Reformation's rejection of its denigration of the body. Within certain moral boundaries, the powers of the body were fully celebrated. Once again the old texts were allowed to sing. 'I will give thanks to Thee, for I am fearfully and wonderfully made,' says the Psalmist, who continues, 'Wonderful are thy works' (Ps. 139:14)."[76]

The new attitude applied especially to sex. Medieval theologians had typically interpreted the Song of Solomon allegorically, as speaking of love between God and the soul. Of course, all love reflects divine love on some level. But now the Song could be understood more straightforwardly as a celebration of the delights of sensuous love: "My beloved is to me a sachet of myrrh resting between my breasts." "Your lips drop sweetness as the honeycomb, my bride; milk and honey are under your tongue." "Like an apple tree among the trees of the forest is my beloved among the young men. I delight to sit in his shade, and his fruit is sweet to my taste" (Song 1:13; 4:11; 2:3).

The language is rich and poetic. As Christian ethicists Scott Rae and Paul Cox write, "The royal couple in the Song revel in each other's love, exhibiting a depth of passion that most couples would like to reproduce in their own marriage."[77]

The Hebrew language is even more explicit in its sensual descriptions than the English translation lets on. "His body [*or* member] is like shiny ivory [*or* an ivory tusk] covered with sapphires" (5:14 EXB). As Old Testament scholar Tremper Longman writes,

> The Hebrew is quite erotic, and most translators cannot bring themselves to bring out the obvious meaning. . . . There is no shy, shamed, mechanical movement under the sheets. Rather, the two stand before each other, aroused, feeling no shame, but only joy in each other's sexuality.[78]

In Proverbs, the Bible literally commands husbands to be "intoxicated" with their wives' breasts: "May her breasts satisfy you always, may you ever be intoxicated with her love" (Prov. 5:19). In a charming but realistic feature of Old Testament law, a newlywed husband was not to be drafted into the military or any other government service: "If a man has recently married, he must not be sent to war or have any other duty laid on him. For one year he is to be free to stay at home and bring happiness to the wife he has married" (Deut. 24:5). This is an astonishing departure from the low view of women in the surrounding polytheistic cultures. Ancient Jewish law was literally telling husbands their job is to "bring happiness" to their wives.

What about Paul's words that it is "better to marry than to burn with passion" (1 Cor. 7:9)? This is often interpreted negatively, as though Paul is saying you should get married only if you cannot control yourself. But "burn with passion" is a translation of the Greek word *pyrousthai*, which was a metaphor meaning to be "frustrated in love."[79] That is, it implies being passionately in love. The verse should be understood against the backdrop of Roman culture, where sexual passion was *not* thought to be important for marriage. Most marriages were arranged. Spouses were selected not for love but with an eye to status, money, and legal heirs. For sexual fulfillment, a man sought out slaves and prostitutes.[80] The remains at Pompeii reveal a sex-saturated culture full of brothels signposted with erotic frescoes tempting passersby with phrases such as "*Hic habitat felicitas*" (Here happiness resides) or "*Sum tua aere*" (I am yours for money).[81] What Paul is really saying, then, is that if you find yourself with a passionate attraction to someone, by all means, go ahead and get married. Channel your sexual energy into marriage.

Paul put the sexual genie into the bottle of marriage. By forbidding men to have sex with slaves, prostitutes, or other men, the Bible was saying that all of a man's erotic desire, affection, and sexual energy should be focused on his wife. That sparked a dramatic social transformation and had an enormous impact in elevating the status of both women and marriage.

What If You're Single?

At the same time, the Bible does not ignore the single life or treat it as having a lower status than marriage. Today the church is tragically behind the times in addressing the growing number of singles. Paul makes it clear that being single has distinct advantages. Single people can give themselves more wholeheartedly to a calling and a ministry (see 1 Cor. 7). For those with a passion to serve, the laser focus that is possible for singles can be a genuine blessing. It can answer the longing of their hearts to have a deep impact. It frees up their time and emotions to love and serve on a wider arena than married persons, who have a moral obligation to put their family first. The Bible maintains a unique balance by treating both marriage and singleness as equally valid and valuable forms of life and service.

A few years ago I met a European filmmaker whose job involved traveling around the world to produce Christian documentaries. Though he was blond and attractive, I noticed that he was not wearing a wedding ring.

"I knew from the beginning that this job requires too much travel to allow me to do justice to a wife and family," he explained. "I decided to remain single so I could pursue this unique form of ministry." The church needs to find ways to honor and support singles for the distinctive contributions they make. Would the apostle Paul have been able to take his missionary journeys if he'd had a family to take care of? No wonder he talks about the benefits of the celibate life. Singles have an opportunity to be on the front lines of ministry.

The New Testament church was impressed by Jesus's teaching that there will be no "marrying or giving in marriage" in heaven. If marriage is a symbol and sign of the union of God with his people, then in heaven we will not need the symbol because we will enjoy the reality. From the beginning, the church has borne witness to this eschatological hope by supporting a vocation to the single life.

Some of the early martyrs were women who rejected suitors or arranged marriages in favor of remaining single—an option that was not tolerated by the surrounding culture. Agatha of Syria refused several offers of marriage, especially from a Roman magistrate named Quintilian, who tried to coerce her by denouncing her as a Christian (this was during the persecution of Decius in AD 250–253). When she did not change her mind, she was tortured and eventually died in prison. Agnes of Rome repeatedly refused offers of marriage from high-ranking suitors, until one of them denounced her as a Christian. She was executed during the reign of Diocletian in AD 304. Lucy rejected an arranged marriage in order to devote her life to the Lord and to distribute her fortune to the poor. Her betrothed denounced her as a Christian and she, too, was executed during the Diocletian persecution.[82]

Those who rejected marriage were announcing that the Christian life of community and service offered a radically different path to meaning and fulfillment. Their model was Jesus himself, who lived a fully human life without sex, romance, or marriage. The lesson is that sex is good, but it should not be made an idol. Sex and marriage should not be elevated to the meaning of life.

Intentional Communities

Perhaps the most oppressive fear for single and divorced people is loneliness. But singles should not be cut off from opportunities to form deep, nourishing, intense, intimate relationships, especially in the church. Jesus himself said, "Greater love has no one than this: to lay down one's life for one's friends" (John 15:13). For whom? For one's friends.

In our sexualized culture, we tend to equate sex and intimacy. We do not think people can be fulfilled without a romantic partnership. But most other cultures have had a richer understanding of friendship.

In pre-industrial societies (which includes most of human history), when home industries produced most of the products we now buy from stores, there was always room for another adult in the home—another pair of hands to help with baking bread, churning butter, weaving cloth, planting wheat, milking cows, tending horses, and other chores. Unmarried adults did not face the prospect of coming home at night to an empty apartment. They could be an integral part of an extended household.

Even a generation ago, there was less pressure to marry and greater acceptance of alternatives, such as extended families. My great uncle remained single all his life, sharing a household with his two unmarried sisters—just like Lazarus in Jesus's day, who shared a household with his sisters Mary and Martha. In many cultures, this is still common. In my neighborhood, Christian refugees from Egypt recently moved in across the street, and the family includes an unmarried aunt living with them.

In earlier ages, the church also took the initiative to create structures for single people to live in community—namely, monasteries and convents. Protestants shut them down because they saw them as an expression of the sacred/secular split. But in the process, they lost something vital that they have not replaced. Monasteries provided recognized group-living situations where single people could experience intimate, committed relationships while practicing ministry.

The challenge today is to create new structural supports for the practice of celibacy—structures that integrate singles into our families and churches again, especially older singles who are often overlooked.[83] Some churches have fostered intentional communities (families and singles living in the same apartment complex, for example). In 2016, *Christianity Today* ran an article on "cohousing," a growing trend to share housing to overcome endemic isolation and loneliness.[84]

Finally, Christians need to start their own "Go On a Date" courses for singles who would like to get married but have lost the art of dating. I hear constantly from young adults like my students, who go out in groups but never learn how to spend one-on-one time with a person of the opposite sex. A college student named Mark observes that the church has responded to the sexual revolution "by teaching rules rather than training in social skills."[85] The church should take the lead in teaching practical relationship skills.

■ ■ ■ ■ ■

Turning Babies into Enemies

Our view of sex has repercussions for our understanding of marriage, family, children, and society. For example, Jennifer Fulwiler is a convert to Catholicism, yet for years after her conversion, she remained in favor of abortion. Why? Her answer gives an invaluable insight into the way many of our secular friends think.

Fulwiler explains that her attitude was shaped by the secular view of sexuality. The literature used in sex education courses, she says, was geared almost exclusively to questions of technique—the "how-tos" of sex and contraception. Rarely did the materials even mention words such as *love*, *marriage*, *family*, or *children*. "The message I'd heard loud and clear was that the purpose of sex was for pleasure and bonding, that its potential for creating life was purely tangential, almost to the point of being forgotten about altogether."[86]

After years of public school sex education, Fulwiler explains, "I thought of pregnancies that weren't planned as akin to being struck by lightning while walking down the street: something totally unpredictable, undeserved." She saw abortion as a humane way to protect women from something akin to a natural disaster. "I didn't want women to have to suffer with these unwanted pregnancies that were so totally out of their control. . . . Babies had become the enemy because of their tendencies to pop out of the blue and ruin everything."

Babies had become the enemy. Just as in warfare, societies tend to dehumanize the enemy in order to justify killing them.

Even materials written by Christians tend to downplay the connection between sex and babies. After her conversion, Fulwiler and her husband watched a video series on marriage by a nondenominational Christian group. "In the segment called 'Good Sex' they did not mention children or babies once. In all the talk about bonding and back rubs and intimacy and staying in shape, the closest they came to connecting sex to the creation of life was to briefly say that couples should discuss the topic of contraception. Sex could not have been more disconnected from the concept of creating life."[87]

In a culture that says we have a right to the pleasures of sex, while denying its biological function, many will end up treating babies as the enemy—intruding where they are not wanted or welcome. We cannot address abortion effectively unless we address the secular view of sex. As Fulwiler observes, "A society can respect human life only to the extent that it respects the act that creates human life."[88]

G. K. Chesterton once wrote, "Sex is an instinct that produces an institution. . . . That institution is the family; a small state or commonwealth," which includes economic interdependence, social responsibility, raising children, education, recreation, shared worship, and charity to outsiders. You might picture the institution of the family as a house, Chesterton adds: "Sex is the gate of that house. . . . But the house is very much larger than the gate. There are indeed a certain number of people who like to hang about the gate and never get any further."[89] But most of us would say there is something very shortsighted about just hanging around the gate.

Christianity is farsighted: It offers a fulfilling, multidimensional view of sexuality as the gateway to many other meaningful layers of life.

A "Happy Hookup"?

A little-known fact is that even with sex education programs that treat teen sex as a normal rite of passage, even with the glorification of casual sex in the media, more than half of teens are not having sex. A 2016 report from the Centers for Disease Control (CDC) reveals that nearly 60 percent of high school students today have not engaged in sexual activity—an increase of 28 percent since 1991.[90] It's time for public school sex education courses to start offering positive support to these teens.

Alternative programs do exist. Sexual Risk Avoidance (SRA) programs address the whole person, helping teens to set life goals and develop the skills for reaching them. SRA programs are not abstinence-only programs. They include instruction on contraception, but they "avoid turning sex education classes into condom advocacy sessions."[91] These programs unequivocally encourage teens to wait for sex. Research shows that students are no less likely to use contraception if they do become sexually active, but that they delay sex longer and have fewer partners.

Christian teens need these skills as much as anyone else. A sixteen-year-old girl who had recently lost her virginity wrote on a Christian advice site, "I don't think sex has anything to do with the fact that you're married or single. I think it's a choice each person has to make by asking themselves if they're prepared for the outcome if something goes wrong."[92] This teen may go to church, but she clearly had absorbed a secular theory of sex as nothing but a pragmatic decision, based on weighing the costs and benefits.

Even more surprising, in a ChristianMingle survey, 61 percent of self-identified Christian singles said they were willing to have casual sex without being in love. Only 23 percent said they would have to be in love. And only 11 percent said they were waiting to have sex until they are married.

On the internet, I once came across an article advising college students how to have a "happy hookup." The author recommended getting "clear consent and mutual agreement to engage in sexual acts." Then "the whole hookup experience will be more positive for everyone involved."

I glanced at the author's bio, and was surprised to discover that she was a student at a conservative Christian college.[93]

It's clear that even in Christian circles, telling young people to "just say no" is not enough. A young woman recently told me, "The main message I got growing up in church was, 'Don't get pregnant.'" But a solely negative approach often leads to hypocrisy. Years ago, our family attended a highly respected Bible church until our high school–age son confided that he was deeply unhappy in the youth group. "The kids at church are worse than the kids in my public high school," he said. "They drink more, they use more bad language, and they're constantly talking about their sexual relationships." Yet the church leaders were unaware because the teens were careful to conceal their behavior.

Young people require more than rules; they need reasons to make sense of the rules. They desperately need a worldview rationale to counter the "no big deal" view of sexuality all around them, from movies to music lyrics to sex education materials.

Imagine a child taught a "no big deal" view of food. That food is just about pleasure. That it does not matter what you eat as long as it feels good. That food is a strictly private matter and no one can judge whether any particular food is good or bad for you. That you might not like broccoli, but that's okay because what's good for me may not be good for you. It's all a matter of personal preference. If a child hears this script his entire life, he will believe it and eat a steady diet of cookies, pizza, and ice cream—and then have no idea why his body is not healthy. The child has been given no tools to understand the connection between food and the biological facts of nutrition. He needs information to understand what his body actually needs to thrive.

In the same way, young people are not being given the tools to understand the connection between sex and what the whole person needs to thrive. Sex is not merely a matter of private preference, any more than food is. Young people need information on how sex relates to an objective moral order.

A 2017 Centers for Disease Control (CDC) report found that teens who abstain from sex are also more likely to engage in a wide range of other healthy behaviors, from eating breakfast to exercising to getting enough sleep. They are also less likely to smoke, use drugs, suffer depression, or report dating violence. Why do healthy behaviors tend to cluster in this way? Researchers do not know. But in the words of Glenn Stanton of Focus on the Family, "Our children should know there's very compelling scientific evidence . . . showing how saving the precious gift of their sexuality for the safe harbor of marriage is nothing about old-time moralism or unhealthy sexual repression. Just the opposite is true."[94] It is part of an overall pattern of healthy and life-giving choices.

It is not enough for churches to teach the biblical rules of behavior as so many "dos and don'ts." They need to break out of in-house jargon and learn to speak the language that young people are absorbing from the postmodern culture around them. They need to explain why a secular worldview is ultimately dehumanizing and unfulfilling. And they must make a persuasive case that biblical morality is both rationally compelling and personally attractive—that it expresses a higher, more positive view of the human person than any competing morality.

Dear Student: A "Real Sex Week"

How can we educate people in a more wholistic and biblical view of sex? One university student took things into her own hands. Sade Patterson, president of Students for Life at the University of New Mexico, grew concerned after the school joined other universities in holding a "sex week." Workshops featured titles like "How to be a Gentleman and Still Get Laid" and "How to Have a Successful Threesome." Erotic performers were invited, with names like "Dirty Lola" and the "Pussy Posse." Organizers walked around dressed in genitalia costumes to "do away with the shame" associated with sex.

"The pattern of objectification and a lack of responsibility became evident," Patterson writes. "It was clear organizers had an agenda—teach my peers that anything goes, and there are no consequences."

Patterson decided to host what she called a "Real Sex Week." Here is her description: "We began with a workshop discussing the male and female body, the biology behind intercourse, and how the act of sex affects our minds and relationships, linking humans chemically, and contrasting the notion that one-night stands have no impact on women's psyches." The university-sponsored sex week had assured students that abortion has no lasting harmful effects, but "the women who attended our seminars were indeed in pain from their choice to abort, and received forgiveness and healing through the night filled with tears, hugs and words of encouragement."[95]

Pregnant students were connected to support groups. As Patterson explains, "When a woman becomes pregnant while still in school, the two major pressures she faces are to drop out or have an abortion. Not enough men and women are empowered and supported to continue their education and parenthood." Patterson speaks from experience, having become pregnant herself while a student. More than twenty organizations set up tables offering information on health clinics, pregnancy centers, parenting programs, child care assistance, counselors, sexual assault awareness, and more.

Radical students did not appreciate Patterson's new version of sex week. A student group promoting abortion (Alliance for Reproductive Justice) stirred up opposition, teaming with Planned Parenthood and an organization selling sex toys (Self Serve Sexuality Resource Center). They tore down Patterson's promotional posters, set up competing pro-abortion sessions, denounced the event as "homophobic," and demanded that the university president shut it down. They set up tables in front of events to dissuade students from attending. They dressed up in their genitalia costumes again and handed out condoms.[96]

But Patterson persisted, convinced of the need to offer an alternative to the culture of promiscuity on campus. Countering the body/person divide, she said, "Our biology actually points to being in a monogamous relationship."[97]

Today the sexual revolution has gone even further, not only tearing apart body from person but also separating the body from our internal sense of gender identity and sexual desire. The two-story dichotomy is at the root of theories that defend and justify homosexual practice. In the next chapter, we learn how we can become equipped to respond more effectively.

5

The Body Impolitic

How the Homosexual Narrative Demeans the Body

Sean Doherty is sexually attracted to other men. He is also a Christian ethics teacher, is happily married to a woman, and has three children. How do these things fit together?

"I became a Christian in my late teens," Doherty says.[1] "I was also exclusively attracted to men. I determined that the only course open to me was to remain celibate. I accepted the biblical teaching that God had created marriage for a man and a woman, and because I was gay, my only ethical option was to embrace a life of being single."

How did Doherty's perspective change? He explains that he began to reflect on "the sexual identity which God has given me"—namely, the "tangible fact that I am a man. . . . Thus, as a man, God's original intention for me in creation was to be able to relate sexually to a woman." In the garden of Eden, male and female were created to be one another's counterpart or complement. In the language of the King James Version, the woman is "meet" for the man—an older term meaning suitable or corresponding to him (Gen. 2:18, 20).

In short, Doherty focused on the fact that biologically, genetically, physiologically, and chromosomally he is male, oriented toward a female, no matter what his feelings and desires were. "Indeed, I came to think that in fact my feelings were what were relatively superficial, in comparison to my physical identity." He began to base his identity on his body.

Over time, Doherty began to notice a subtle shift. "Without denying or ignoring my sexual feelings, I stopped regarding them as being who I was, sexually, and started regarding my physical body as who I was." To his surprise, he found that his sexual desires began to change. "Rather than trying to change my feelings so that I could change my label, I changed my label and my feelings started to follow suit." His feelings changed enough that eventually he fell in love with a woman and got married.

Though our feelings are important, Doherty concluded, they are not what define our identity. Nor are they a reliable guide to God's purposes. Because we are fallen and sinful, our feelings fluctuate over time. The most reliable marker of who we are is our physically embodied, God-given identity as male and female.

Does that mean Doherty is free from sexual attraction to men? No; like all other fallen, sinful human beings, he is sometimes attracted to someone other than his spouse. And when that happens, typically that someone else is another man. "I would say that I am still predominantly same-sex attracted in general," he writes. But with respect to marriage, "It doesn't matter in the least whether someone is attracted to women or men in general. What matters . . . is whether someone is attracted and called to marry one person in particular."

Scripture teaches that the creational differentiation of male and female is a good thing. Our complementary nature speaks of our yearning for union, which in turn reflects the divine nature—a God who is a Trinity, differentiated Persons in relationship with one another. The question is, do we accept that created structure or do we reject it? Do we affirm the goodness of creation or deny it? Do we see the body as a reservoir of meaning, a source of moral truths? Is there a teleology of the body that we are called to respect? Or do we see the body as just a piece of matter with no moral message? These are the worldview questions at stake in the issue of homosexuality.[2]

When we make sexual decisions, we are not just deciding whether to follow a few rules. We are expressing our view of the cosmos and human nature.

We will discover that arguments supporting same-sex practice implicitly accept the same two-story worldview addressed in earlier chapters—one that denies the goodness of creation and the teleology of the body.

My purpose is not to argue for any particular theory of what causes same-sex attraction, or whether people can change. Like Doherty, some people do change, but many do not, and those who do usually move gradually along a continuum over time. Instead, my goal is to argue against the knee-jerk reaction that brands Christianity as hateful and discriminatory. The biggest barrier to even considering Christianity today is its moral standard. Many people are no longer asking: Is Christianity true? They're asking: Why are Christians such bigots? The challenge is to show that in reality biblical morality expresses a higher view of creation and the body than secular morality does. It grants greater dignity and worth to the human being, and is ultimately more fulfilling.

"Born That Way"

Most people assume that same-sex desire must have some biological basis. Certainly our sexual feelings seem to express a deep, compelling aspect of our being. It feels natural to act on those feelings. But as we saw in chapter 1 (it may be helpful to reread that section), scientists have not uncovered any clear biological cause.[3]

Many scientists consider identical-twin studies the most reliable form of evidence, and those studies do not seem to support the hypothesis of genetic causation.[4] Francis Collins, director of the Human Genome Project and America's most prominent geneticist, writes that "sexual orientation is genetically influenced but not hardwired by DNA, and that whatever genes are involved represent predispositions, not predeterminations."[5] In short, we do not have to accept genetic determinism of our feelings and desires.

Yet people on both sides of the issue may have put too much energy into arguing about genetics. Everyone recognizes that even traits that are genetically based may not be good for us. Lady Gaga may sing, "I was born this way" but even gay advocate John Corvino writes, "*It doesn't matter* whether we're born this way. The fact is that there are plenty of genetically influenced traits that are nevertheless undesirable."[6] A predisposition to things such as depression, alcoholism, drug addiction, and heart disease may be genetic (they tend to run in families). But most people would agree that we are morally responsible for how we respond to our genetic heritage. Locating a genetic link can help us be more compassionate toward people, but genetics does not tell us whether a behavior is right or wrong, good or bad for us.

Moreover, "genes are not fixed; life events can trigger biochemical messages that turn them on or off," writes psychiatrist Bessel van der Kolk.[7] This does not mean we have the ability to control our genes at will. But it does mean we should not conclude that if a trait is genetic, it is therefore fixed and unchangeable.

Some researchers respond that even if sexual desire is not genetic, it may still be rooted in biology—in prenatal hormones or in brain structure. For example, some studies find differences in the size of various regions of the brain in homosexual-identified men compared to heterosexual-identified men. But brain differences can also be influenced by experience. A *New York Times* article reports, "The part of the brain that deals with navigation is enlarged in London taxi drivers, as is the region dealing with the movement of the fingers of the left hand in right-handed violinists."[8] As a violinist, I find that fact interesting.

Other studies measure physical correlates of sexual arousal. If you wire up men to an MRI (magnetic resonance imaging) machine and show them nude photos, the brain of a man attracted to women lights up when he sees a woman, while the brain of a man attracted to men lights up when he sees a man. A similar differentiation occurs when researchers hook up men to a machine that measures genital response to photos. Many sex researchers conclude from these studies that sexual desire is biologically innate and fixed.[9]

But that conclusion does not follow. Brain patterns are not fixed. In chapter 4 we learned about neuroplasticity in relation to pornography—how it literally rechannels the brain's neural pathways. Neurobiologists have discovered that the brain can also be rewired by trauma, whether childhood abuse or military combat or an auto accident. When people relive the trauma, their brains light up like Christmas trees in a characteristic pattern (especially the amygdala, the part of the brain that registers threats). And those patterns do not remain fixed either. Brain scans taken before and after trauma therapy reveal that the pathways can be rechanneled. As van der Kolk writes, therapy can literally "change the settings of the amygdala."[10]

Even religion has physical correlates. MRIs show which areas of the brain are activated when people have religious experiences. When Catholic nuns pray or Buddhist monks meditate, they yield similar brain scans. Does that mean being a nun or monk is something fixed, innate, and genetically programmed? Of course not. So why draw that conclusion from brain scans showing sexual responses?

What the studies really show is that we are embodied beings; our thoughts and desires have physical correlates in our brains.[11] In studies on sadness, anger, happiness, and fear, says van der Klok, "brain scans showed that . . . each type of emotion produced a characteristic pattern, distinct from the others."[12] So it is hardly surprising that sexual feelings produce physical responses. Science is underscoring the fact that humans are mind-body unities—exactly as Christianity teaches. Our thoughts and feelings affect our bodies. As the book of Proverbs says, "Good news gives health to the bones," and "A cheerful heart is good medicine, but a crushed spirit dries up the bones" (Prov. 15:30; 17:22).

Interestingly, the most reliable correlate with same-sex eroticism is not any genetic or physical trait but a behavioral one: Studies find that "childhood gender nonconformity—behaving like the other sex—is a strong correlate of adult sexual orientation that has been consistently and repeatedly replicated."[13] Since this correlation is strongly supported by research, we will cover it in greater detail in chapter 6. (These two chapters should be read as a unit.)

■ ■ ■ ■ ■

Is My Body "Me"?

No matter what the causal factors prove to be, what's clear is that same-sex attraction does not align with a person's biological sex as male or female. That fact is the starting point for postmodern gender theories.

The influential philosopher Judith Butler is hailed as a founder of queer theory, defined as a theory that "focuses on mismatches between sex, gender, and desire."[14] We naturally aspire to an "internal coherence" or "unity of experience" among all three aspects of our being, Butler notes.[15] But because she identifies as a lesbian, she herself does not fit that integrated ideal. Her conclusion is that we must reject our natural aspiration to internal unity. In fact, to call it "natural" is itself an act of oppression, in her view. In queer theory, her goal is to break the link that connects biological sex to gender and desire. She promotes a theory of human nature focused on disruption and fragmentation.

Picture one of those children's toys made of three connecting blocks, with animal heads on the top block, torsos on the middle block, and legs on the bottom block. Children can rotate the blocks to create fantasy animals, like an elephant head with a giraffe body and flamingo legs. That's the image that comes to my mind when I read Butler's attempt to persuade us that the human being is a mix-and-match assemblage of physical sex, gender, and sexual desire. The idea that internal congruence is better or natural, she says, is a fiction. Rotate the blocks into any pattern you want.

Queer theory defends non-heterosexual behavior by chopping up the human being into disconnected parts that are said to have nothing to do with each other.

Queer Theory vs. the Body

We have to give queer theory credit for being logically consistent. No one really denies that on the level of biology, physiology, anatomy, and biochemistry, males and females correspond to one another. That's the way the human sexual and reproductive system is designed. Therefore, to embrace a non-heterosexual identity does cause an inner disruption. It contradicts one's biological design.

Implicitly the person is saying: Why should I care about the structure of my body? Why should I let *that* inform my identity? Why should my sexed body have anything to say about my moral choices? The body is disassociated from who we are as persons, as though it has no intrinsic dignity or purpose that we are morally obligated to respect.

This is a very low view of the body.

Think of it this way: It is widely accepted today that if a person senses a disjunction between biological sex and sexual desire, the only proper course of action is to accept their psychological state as their true, authentic self. But why? Why assume that feelings are more important than the body?

A person involved in same-sex behavior may not consciously intend to disparage the body. But our actions can have logical implications we have not clearly thought through. Our choices imply an entire metaphysic—in this case, the same two-story divided worldview addressed in earlier chapters, with its negative view of embodied existence. No wonder the New Testament says same-sex activity "dishonors" the body: "Therefore God gave them up . . . to the dishonoring of their bodies" (Rom. 1:24 ESV).

Many people denounce biblical morality as harsh and judgmental. But in reality it is based on a respect for our biology as an integral part of the person. It offers a rich, multidimensional view of what it means to be human.

The Bible Is Pro-Body

The central question is how we define our identity. It is widely assumed today that humans are driven primarily by desires, feelings, and attractions—that your sexual feelings define your identity.

By contrast, as Sean Doherty writes, the Bible has "a much more earthy, physical and bodily definition of sexuality: 'male and female he created them' (Gen. 1:27)." The Christian sex ethic is grounded in the way humans were originally created. "In the beginning" is where we learn who we are, how God made us, and what it means to be fully human.

Some forms of therapy and ministry seek to help a person change their sexual feelings. But trying to change feelings directly is rarely effective. "For me," Doherty writes, "a far more liberating and helpful discovery was that my sexual identity as a man was already fixed and secure—because sexuality (in the sense of the sexual differences between men and women) is a gift of God to humanity in creation." He concludes that instead of focusing on feelings, a better strategy "was to receive or acknowledge what I already had (a male body) as a good gift from God."[16] In short, Doherty learned to trust that the biological identity God gave him was for his good.

Christianity is often accused of being anti-sex and anti-body. But in reality it is the secular ethic that is anti-body. Gay activists downplay the body—our biological identity as male or female—and define our true selves by our feelings and desires. They assume that the body gives no reference points for our gender identity or our moral choices. In essence, the secular worldview has revived the ancient Gnostic disdain for the body. It is Christianity that honors the body as male and female, instead of subordinating biological sex to psychological feelings.[17]

Of course, many people support slogans such as "marriage equality" simply because they think it is the compassionate thing to do, or because they think other views are discriminatory. But we are not talking about people's subjective feelings or the sincerity of their motives. We are uncovering the logic of the ethic that supports same-sex practice, whether people consciously recognize it or not. In its *Obergefell* decision, the Supreme Court ruled that legal marriage has no connection to biology—that its purpose is to protect "personhood." But why set up an opposition between biology and personhood? Why accept a two-level dualism that demeans the body and alienates people from their biological sex?

Biblical morality affirms the high value of creation. In a teleological view, nature is not undifferentiated raw material with no positive character of its own. It exhibits a plan, a design, an order, and a purpose. Because of that, it gives rational grounds for our moral decisions. Our sexual identity is meant to be in harmony with our psychological identity. The goal is to overcome self-alienation and recover a sense of inner coherence.

■ ■ ■ ■ ■

We Live in "Two Worlds"

The main reason people today find it difficult to understand biblical sex ethics is that their thinking has been trained by the two-level mindset to sever the natural order from the moral order. In the academic world, a teleological view of nature as purpose-driven has been ousted by a materialist view that sees nature as devoid of spiritual and moral meaning. (See chapter 2 on the impact of a modernist view of nature.) As a result, most people no longer "hear" the body's own message—for example, how the very structure of male-female differentiation speaks of relationship, mutual love, and self-giving.

And if morality is disconnected from nature, then it becomes merely a social construction. It is whatever we decide. A *modernist* view of nature leads inevitably to a *postmodern* view of morality. Postmodern gender theory grounds your identity not in your biology but in your mind. You are what you feel.

To engage with our secular neighbors—and with our Christian neighbors who have absorbed secular ideas—we must know at least something about postmodernism. Where did it come from and how is it shaping people's ideas about sexual issues?

To locate the origin of postmodernism, we have to go back to the eighteenth-century philosopher Immanuel Kant. Though he was raised in a devout, pietistic Lutheran family and remained single his entire life, his ideas were the springboard for today's postmodern view of sexuality. Kant picked up where Descartes's two-story dualism left off (see chapter 3). Humans inhabit "two worlds," Kant said. In the lower story they are part of *nature*, by which he meant the deterministic world machine of classical physics. In the upper story humans operate in the world of *freedom* as free agents who make moral choices. Philosophers call this Kant's nature/freedom dichotomy.[18]

The reason it is a genuine dichotomy is that the "two worlds" are logically contradictory. In a materialist world where all actions are determined by the laws of nature, logically speaking, freedom is impossible. There is no logically coherent, consistent worldview that can encompass both "worlds." Kant never did find a way to resolve this contradiction—which means his philosophy never coheres into a unified whole. "Kant left a gaping abyss between his conception of knowledge and his theory of morals," writes philosopher Robert Solomon, "and so left the human mind as if cleft in two."[19]

My Mind Decides What Is Real

Kant then "cleft" the human mind in two still further. He proposed that even the lower story—the world of nature—is a creation of the mind. After all, he said, how do we *know* anything about nature? Sense impressions flood in through our eyes and ears in a jumbled chaos. How are these perceptions organized into a coherent, ordered conception of the cosmos?

By the action of the human mind. According to Kant, it is the mind that organizes our sensations by supplying the ordering principles of cause and effect, before and after, space and time, number, and so on. The human mind comprises a mental grid that injects order into the chaos of sensory data—imposing organization onto the flux of perceptions. The world *appears* to be lawful and ordered only because the human mind creates that lawful order, like pressing a lump of clay into a mold to give it shape.

The outcome is that in Kant's philosophy we do not live in a world structured by God. We live in a world structured by human consciousness. Kant wrote, "Mind is the law-giver to nature."[20] It's as though humans stood before an undifferentiated lump of raw material, a universe still waste and void, with the power to cry out, "Let there be . . . !"

Kant called this his "Copernican revolution," and it was certainly just as radical. Whereas Copernicus had set the sun at the center of the planetary system, Kant set human consciousness at the center of reality. In his words, until now, "it has been assumed that all our knowledge must conform to objects." But what if we turn that around? What "if we suppose that objects must conform to our knowledge"[21]—that is, to our minds?

Kant thus absolutized the mind, treating it as the ultimate reality to which everything else must conform.

By doing so, he sowed the seeds of postmodernism, which reduces all human knowledge to mental constructions. With Kant, "the self becomes not just the focus of attention but the entire subject-matter of philosophy," Solomon writes. "The self is not just another entity in the world, but in an important sense *it creates the world*."[22]

To grasp what a radical turnaround this was, recall that ever since the Enlightenment, many Western thinkers have been materialists, insisting that the lower story of nature is the only reality. They absolutized matter (we saw examples in earlier chapters). Kant countered by insisting that the upper story of the mind is the primary reality—and that it even creates nature as we know it.

After all, if the self is to be truly free and autonomous, it must not be confronted with an objectively ordered universe. The universe must be reduced to raw material—mere "stuff" with no inherent order. We may *think* we are perceiving an order in the world that exists independently of our minds. But that is an illusion, according to Kant. In reality the human mind is constantly imposing order on our perceptions, like a cookie cutter imposing shapes onto dough. The world as we perceive it is the construction of human consciousness.

What does that mean for ethics? For Kant, the enlightened self is completely autonomous, in the literal meaning of that word: a law unto oneself (*auto* = self, *nomos* = law). For the autonomous self, any outside source of moral law is inherently oppressive.[23]

Philosophers Rule the World

It has taken centuries for Kant's philosophy to unfold its full implications. (Plato said philosophers should rule the world, and they do—hundreds of years after they die.) Today postmodernism takes Kant's divide to its logical conclusion. It treats the material world—including the body—largely as a construction of the human mind. There is no created order that we are morally obligated to honor or respect. Consciousness determines what is real for us.

The springboard for postmodernism was Nietzsche's slogan, "Facts do not exist, only interpretations."[24] When it comes to sexuality, according to postmodernism, biological facts do not exist, only interpretations. The sexed body has no moral meaning in itself; the mind imposes its own meanings.

The postmodern body/person divide

AUTONOMOUS SELF

Free to Impose Its Own Interpretations on the Body

PHYSICAL BODY

Raw Material with No Intrinsic Identity or Purpose

A person involved in same-sex relations may not consciously accept postmodern ethics. But our actions can logically imply ideas we have not clearly thought through. Same-sex practice entails the postmodern view that our identity is defined by our feelings and desires; that we may use our bodies in ways that contradict our biological structure. As John Paul II explains, for many today, our identity as persons is equated with the freely choosing self, while the body becomes "extrinsic to the person," a subpersonal possession under our control that can be manipulated to serve our desires.[25] Camille Paglia, a self-described pagan lesbian, defends homosexuality by saying, "Fate, not God, has given us this flesh. We have absolute claim to our bodies and may do with them as we see fit."[26]

By contrast, Christianity affirms that we live in a universe structured not by blind forces but by the loving purposes of a personal Creator, and we are called to live in harmony with that structure. Critics paint the biblical ethic as negative and oppressive. But in reality a teleological worldview affirms sexuality as part of our deep design, which speaks of God and the beauty of his character.

The "Gay Script"

Secular culture presents a "gay script" that many find very compelling.[27] It is a script that says anyone who experiences same-sex desires has discovered their authentic self, and that they will be most fulfilled by openly affirming it as their true identity. This script is played out in countless films, novels, articles, songs, and TV shows. It has become a powerful narrative shaping the thinking of young people especially.

The irony is that the idea of putting sexual attraction at the core of our identity is a recent invention. Of course, throughout history, people have engaged in sexual behavior with others of the same sex. But it was seen as just that—behavior that anyone might engage in. It was not seen as an unalterable identity. In *The Invention of Heterosexuality*, historian Jonathan Ned Katz writes that from ancient times, the adjective *homosexual* was used to describe acts that anyone might perform, not an unchanging condition or an essential identity. It referred to an action, not a category of person.[28]

When was the meaning of the term changed? In the nineteenth century, as Christian moral influence waned, medical science took over the definition of sexuality. The moral terms *right* and *wrong* were changed to the supposedly objective scientific terms *healthy* and *deviant*.[29] Under this new "medico-sexual regime," says Foucault, what had been a "habitual sin" now became a "singular nature." What had been a "temporary aberration" now became "a species."[30] Science cast hetero- and homosexuality as divergent psychological types, innate and unchanging.

Lesbianism in the Gulag

But today science is changing once again. Recent studies have found that sexual desire is more fluid than most people had thought. Lisa Diamond, who identifies as a lesbian, is a researcher with the American Psychological Association and discovered (to her own great surprise) that sexual feelings are not fixed. They can be influenced by environment, culture, and context. People with exclusive, unchanging same-sex eroticism are actually the exception, not the norm.[31] The Supreme Court's *Obergefell* ruling, which declared sexuality to be "immutable," is already out of date. Diamond states bluntly, "We know it's not true. . . . Queers have to stop saying: 'Please help us, we were born this way and we can't change' as an argument for legal standing."[32]

Diamond is not claiming that everyone has the capacity for fluidity, or that we can change our sexual desires at will. Yet to say sexuality is fluid is to acknowledge that we are all susceptible to the pressures and possibilities in our environment. One of my students, Gabriela, grew up in a traditional small town, where it never occurred to her to question her sexuality. But when she left home to attend university in a large city, she made friends with women who were lesbians—and found herself being tempted. "I had no idea same-sex attraction would ever be an issue for me," Gabriela told me. "But when faced with a concrete opportunity, I was surprised to find that I was drawn in." For several years Gabriela identified as a lesbian, until she underwent a profound spiritual experience. She told me, "I came to recognize that God made me as a woman to be in relationship with a man, and I decided to trust that God's way is best for me."

Sexual fluidity may explain why situational homosexuality sometimes emerges in exclusively single-sex environments, such as prisons. In *The GULAG Archipelago*, Aleksandr Solzhenitsyn describes how lesbianism arose in the Soviet prison system after Stalin segregated the sexes: "Women suffered worse than the men from the separation. . . . Lesbian love developed swiftly."[33]

Today on college campuses it has become almost a rite of passage to experiment with same-sex relations. There are even slang terms for it, like LUG (Lesbian Until Graduation). In some places, there can be considerable pressure to conform. A young woman named Lisa, who recently graduated from a state university with a music degree, told me, "In the fine arts, if you're not gay, you're treated like you're a nobody."

In some parts of the country, parents report that their children are under immense social pressure to experiment with variant sexual identities all the way down to elementary school. A friend with an eleven-year-old daughter told me, "Schools make such a big issue of gender now, the kids are constantly asking each other, 'Are you gay? Are you trans?' My daughter has lesbian classmates asking her to be their girlfriend. I remind her that there are a lot more interesting elements to someone's personality besides gender!"

Tim Keller: Warrior or Urbanite?

Sexual fluidity means the way we interpret our sexual feelings and desires can be influenced by social forces. Timothy Keller offers this thought experiment of the Anglo-Saxon warrior versus the Manhattan urbanite:

> Imagine an Anglo-Saxon warrior in Britain in AD 800. He has two very strong inner impulses and feelings. One is aggression. He loves to smash and kill people when they show him disrespect. Living in a shame-and-honor culture with its warrior ethic, he will identify with that feeling. He will say to himself, That's me! That's who I am! I will express that. The other feeling he senses is same-sex attraction. To that he will say, That's not me. I will control and suppress that impulse.
>
> Now imagine a young man walking around Manhattan today. He has the same two inward impulses, both equally strong, both difficult to control. What will he say? He will look at the aggression and think, This is not who I want to be, and will seek deliverance in therapy and anger-management programs. He will look at his sexual desire, however, and conclude, That is who I am.

What is Keller saying with this thought experiment? That "we do not get our identity simply from within. Rather, we receive some interpretive moral grid, lay it down over our various feelings and impulses, and sift them through it. This grid helps us decide which feelings are 'me' and should be expressed—and which are not and should not be."

Humans are not self-creating, self-existent, self-defining beings. We all look to outside sources to inform us about who we are and how we should live. We look for a rule or grid to help us decide which feelings and impulses are good versus those that are unhealthy or immoral and should be rechanneled. Keller concludes, "And where do our Anglo-Saxon warrior and our modern Manhattan man get their grids? From their cultures, their communities, their heroic stories." They may think they are simply choosing to be their authentic selves. But in reality, "they are filtering their feelings, jettisoning some and embracing others. They are choosing to be the selves their cultures tell them they may be."[34]

Choosing Your Identity

The problem is that when sexual desire is seen as the defining feature of our identity, it becomes rigid and inviolable. To question someone's identity is taken as an attack on their selfhood and worth. If the person refrains from acting on their sexual feelings, they are accused of repression and self-hatred.

But why place sexual feelings at the center of our identity? The Bible offers a more compelling script that defines our identity in terms of the image of God, created to reflect his character. We are loved and redeemed children of God. When we center our lives on these truths, then our identity is secure no matter what our sexual feelings are—and whether they change or don't change.

Psychologists offer a helpful distinction between feelings, behavior, and identity. We do not choose our feelings, but we do choose our behavior and identity. Many people who experience same-sex feelings do *not* engage in same-sex behavior, and even fewer go on to adopt a homosexual identity.[35]

A 2009 report by the American Psychological Association recognized that some people with homoerotic desires are actually happier when they restrain those desires. "Acting on same-sex attractions may not be fulfilling solutions," the report said—especially for those whose religious identity is more important to them.[36] Judith Glassgold, who chaired the APA task force on the issue, said, "We have to acknowledge that, for some people, religious identity is such an important part of their lives, it may transcend everything else."[37]

In short, surprisingly, the APA has debunked the "gay script" that says anyone with same-sex feelings will be happiest affirming them openly. Instead we are happiest when we choose an identity that is congruent with our deepest convictions, living them out even when it is difficult and demanding.

Some gay activists have been highlighting the role of choice in sexual identity for a long time. In a widely circulated article from 1992, Donna Minkowitz writes,

> Remember that most of the line about homosex being one's nature, not a choice, was articulated as a response to brutal repression. "It's not our fault!" gay activists began to declaim a century ago. . . . "We didn't choose this, so don't punish us for it!" One hundred years later, it's time for us to abandon this defensive posture and walk upright on the earth. Maybe you didn't choose to be gay—that's fine. But I did.[38]

In a similar vein, Darrell Yates Rist, cofounder of the Gay and Lesbian Alliance Against Defamation, dismisses the idea that non-heterosexual persons are a genetic minority, "akin to Jews and blacks." "The ruse won't fly," Rist writes.

> In the end, science may well discover some way to describe the intricate play of genes and environment that entices any of us to make the subtle choices throughout our lives that lead us to our particular [sexual] expressions. Fine. Ultimately, though, it seems to me cowardly to abnegate our individual responsibility for the construction of sexual desires.[39]

The Changing of the Grid

How can we take "individual responsibility" for our identity and live in congruence with our deepest convictions? The biblical definition of repentance means primarily a change in mind or mental perspective. In the Greek, the term is *metanoia*, which literally means to change one's mind (*noia* is a form of *nous* = mind). Paul writes, "Be transformed by the renewing of your mind" (Rom. 12:2). Jesus connects repentance with a change of mind or belief: "Repent and believe the good news" (Mark 1:15).

We might paraphrase that as "change your interpretive grid."

As an example, take Rebecca's story. "Growing up, we lived in a rural area and my parents did not permit me to use the family car to visit my girl friends in town. The only people motivated enough to drive out to see me were boys." As a result, through her teen years Rebecca dated heavily but had no close female friends. "By the time I left home for college, I was starving for female friendship. I met another student who was a lesbian—and I was instantly hooked. There was no hesitant wondering about it. I went back to my dorm room and knew immediately that this was what I wanted."

Over the next decade, Rebecca had repeated "girl crushes," even after she became a Christian and married a man. "I finally discussed it with my husband," she said. "His response was, because you are biologically a woman, you can be certain that no matter what your feelings are right now, ultimately you will be more fulfilled by a man than by another woman." Then he added, "It goes both ways: Because I am biologically a man, no matter what my feelings might be, ultimately I will be more fulfilled by a woman than by another man. That's how God created us."

That argument seemed logical to Rebecca and it changed her interpretive grid—which proved to be a turning point in reducing her unwanted lesbian attraction. Was she completely freed from temptation? No; for example, she told me, "I still can't watch the lesbian scenes in the television series *Orange Is the New Black*." But she was gradually liberated from the intense, obsessive girl crushes that had disrupted her life and her marriage. Now that she has children, she sees sexuality as something not just for individual pleasure and romantic connection but also as part of God's larger plan to create secure and loving families, which are the basis for building just and compassionate civilizations.

Contrary to Kant, our minds do not create the world's order. We are most fulfilled when we accept a mental grid that recognizes the existence of an objective order created by God

Oliver O'Donovan writes, "Responsibility in sexual development implies a responsibility to nature—to the ordered good of the bodily form which we have been given."[40] Even when we have difficulty achieving that good, that does not mean we should change the norm or give it up. In a teleological ethic, the way to love people is by supporting their *telos*—what is genuinely good for them in light of the way God designed us to function and flourish. It's an ethic that expresses respect for the human being as an integrated psycho-physical unit. And in the end, it leads to richer, deeper sexual relationships.

A Drug Dealer Finds a Bible

It is significant that both Sean Doherty and Rebecca report that their feelings did not change completely. We tend to think in rigid categories, as though someone must be either 100 percent homosexual or 100 percent heterosexual. But as we saw above, recent research finds that many people are not exclusively one or the other. Lisa Diamond's research found that among those who identify as homosexual, 40 percent of men and 48 percent of women reported sexual attraction to the opposite sex in the previous year. Among those who identify as heterosexual, 25 percent of men and 50 percent of women reported having at least some same-sex attraction in the previous year.[41]

Both groups face the same challenges. Both are called to repentance. Both are called to change their mental grid to a biblical view of sexuality and then to live out their convictions in costly obedience.

Before Christopher Yuan became a Christian, he regularly visited gay bathhouses where he would engage in multiple drug-fueled, anonymous sexual encounters in a single day. Eventually he landed in federal prison for drug dealing, where he found a Bible in a trash can and became a Christian. In a book about his conversion, *Out of a Far Country*, he writes, "I had always thought that the opposite of homosexuality was heterosexuality. But actually the opposite of homosexuality is holiness."[42] All Christians are called to holiness, no matter what their sexual feelings. "[My] newfound identity in Christ compelled me to live in obedience to God whether my temptations changed or not," Yuan explains. "Biblical change is not the absence of struggles but the freedom to choose holiness in the midst of our struggles."[43]

No one chooses to have same-sex temptations, just as no one chooses to feel angry or jealous, or be tempted by drugs or pornography. A pastoral approach must take care not to create a sense of blame or shame in anyone just for feeling tempted. Many people spend years praying desperately to be freed from same-sex desires, fighting them and hiding them, overcome with guilt and shame. Rebecca told me, "When I realized I was attracted to women, I felt diseased—like I had broken out in leprosy. I didn't tell anyone for years."

But temptation is not sin. Scripture tells us Jesus himself was "tempted in every way, just as we are—yet he did not sin" (Heb. 4:15). Amy Riordan was involved in a lesbian relationship before becoming a Christian, and for years afterward she wrestled with an addiction to lesbian pornography. She suffered intense shame, she writes, until she realized the difference between temptation and sin: "It's not a sin to be tempted. Jesus was tempted all the time, but He never sinned. This has lifted a *huge* weight of guilt off of me that never should have been there in the first place."[44]

Where we do have a choice is in deciding how to respond to our temptations. We can choose whether to purchase drugs, or search for pornography on the computer, or engage in same-sex behavior. Everyone is called to choose holiness, whether attracted to the same sex or the opposite sex, whether married or single.

■ ■ ■ ■ ■

"God Made Me Gay"

Some Christians say God creates people with an attraction to their own sex—"God made me gay." It's true that our sexuality can feel very natural. Riordan, writing about her lesbian temptations, says, "I had dwelled on those thoughts so much that they felt so much a part of me. Thoughts of being a lesbian felt as real as my own name."[45]

Yet not everything that exists today reflects the way God originally created the world. Sam Allberry, a Christian pastor who is same-sex attracted and celibate, puts it well: "Desires for things God has forbidden are a reflection of how sin has distorted me, not how God has made me."[46]

Tim Wilkins lived for many years as a homosexual man but is now married with children. If God created some people gay, he says, then "God has played a cruel joke on them. He has engineered their minds and emotions for attraction to the same-sex and yet created their physiology to be in direct opposition to that attraction."[47] You cannot be a whole person when your emotions are at war with your physiology.

The ideal is integration—harmony between our sexual and psychological identities. This side of heaven, of course, we should not expect perfection, any more than we enjoy perfection in any other area of life. Some counseling programs have overpromised results, as though anyone who tries hard enough can overcome their same-sex attraction and become heterosexual. These programs have often led to painful disappointment and disillusionment, and as a result they have sparked intense public criticism. Therapy may well provide psychological benefits, such as emotional healing from childhood trauma. But no program is guaranteed to lead to complete freedom from temptation.[48]

As Francis Schaeffer emphasized repeatedly in books such as *True Spirituality*, the process of sanctification leads to "substantial healing," not perfect healing this side of heaven.[49] If we demand all or nothing, we often end up with nothing.

The biblical worldview has the intellectual resources to offer a balanced explanation why we cannot simply take our identity from our natural inclinations. Scripture is profoundly realistic about the destructive impact of the fall. What does it mean to say the world is fallen? We all know that when we do something the wrong way, we often damage or break something—whether just a dish, or an arm, or a relationship, or sometimes our entire life. When the first humans did something wrong, they damaged everything. They broke the entire world—including the physical structure of our bodies.[50] The fall is the Bible's answer to why there is evil and suffering, why our desires and inclinations are often skewed from the ideal.

Yet God promises to work through even the brokenness of a fallen world. When Jesus encountered a man born blind, his disciples asked, "Who sinned, this man or his parents?" Jesus refused to blame either one. Blindness is a consequence of living in a world damaged by the fall. Jesus did promise, however, that even though he was born this way, the works of God could "be displayed in him" (John 9:1–3).

The most important question is not *Where did this come from?* but rather *How can God work through it?*

Paul assures us that "in all things God works for the good of those who love him, who have been called according to his purpose" (Rom. 8:28). All things—even those that are painful or harmful or out of our control. The way we respond to those things has the potential to deepen and mature our character, so that we are better able to minister to others.

If you doubt that, read 2 Corinthians to be reminded that even incest, when repented of, has the potential to make us more holy. In his first letter, Paul had written, "It is actually reported that there is sexual immorality among you, and of a kind that even pagans do not tolerate: A man is sleeping with his father's wife" (probably his stepmother, 1 Cor. 5:1). But in his follow-up letter, Paul was able to write, "See what this godly sorrow has produced in you: what earnestness, what eagerness to clear yourselves, what indignation, what alarm, what longing, what concern, what readiness to see justice done" (2 Cor. 7:11). No matter what the situation, the way forward is to ask: How is God working for the good in this situation?

Many people who experience attraction to the same sex have prayed for years, asking God to take it away. Paul himself endured a persistent suffering that he called his "thorn in the flesh" (2 Cor. 12:7). It was not removed even though he, too, prayed repeatedly for God to take it away. God's answer was that the "thorn" created a vulnerability that drew Paul into deeper dependency on him. The thorn imagery is probably taken from Genesis, where the consequence of the fall is symbolized by the imagery of "thorns and thistles." Every one of us suffers from living in a fallen world, whether in our sexual lives, our family, our work, or our health. But by turning to God in our suffering, our "thorn" can become a means of sanctification.

The Girl in the Tuxedo

How can Christians move beyond a negative message of shame and guilt to communicate a wholistic and humane view of sexuality? Jean Lloyd, who once lived as a lesbian, explains what is *not* helpful to say to a person who is attracted to the same sex.

As a fifteen-year-old girl, Lloyd donned a tuxedo for her high school Christmas dance as a defiant symbol of her gender-bending. For several years, she lived openly as a lesbian. After that, she remained single and celibate for well over a decade. Then, she writes, "I began to trust the One who knew the truth of my identity more than I did, who wrote His image into my being and body as female, and who designed sexuality and set boundaries upon it for my good." To her own great surprise, "a flicker of heterosexual desire emerged," and today she is married with two children.[51]

Over the years, Lloyd says, many pastors have gone from "fiery sermons on homosexuality" to "declarations of love." All well and good. But some of those pastors have gone further and rejected biblical sexual morality itself as "oppressive, unreasonable, or unkind. Hence, loving homosexual persons also comes to entail affirming and encouraging them in same-sex sexual relationships and behaviors."[52]

Please realize that is *not* the loving response, Lloyd writes. What is genuinely loving is a response that helps "me honor my body by living in accord with the Creator's design. I was born this way: female. God did create me a woman. Please don't fall into the gnostic dualism that divides my spiritual life from the life I now live in my body."[53] In other words, she is saying: Don't push me into a dualism that alienates me from my body.

A loving response also holds each person to the biblical standard of chastity. Whether we have same-sex desires or opposite-sex desires, the Bible's message of the purpose of sex for bonding within marriage remains the same. "I should be credited with the same moral agency and responsibility as everyone else in the Christian community," Lloyd writes. "If unmarried heterosexuals are called to celibacy and are presumed in Christ to have the power to live out His commands, then so should I be. To treat me according to a different standard is to lower my dignity before God. I too am called to be holy."[54]

Psalm 139 says God "knits" together our bodies in the womb—which includes our masculine or feminine identity. The physiological structure of our bodies is not some evolutionary accident. It signals a divine purpose for male and female to form covenants for mutual love and the nurturing of new life. The act of giving love is the act of giving life. As O'Donovan writes, "Christians have classically believed that in the ordinance of marriage there was given . . . a teleological structure which was a fact of creation and therefore not negotiable."[55] Morality tells us how to fully participate in that fact of creation—how to be fully human.

What about "Eunuchs"?

Scripture treats marriage and celibacy as equal in dignity and value, and even teaches that some people have the "gift" of celibacy. But what about those who do not feel they have that gift—who do not feel any special calling to be single—yet have not found anyone suitable to marry or are attracted to persons of the same sex?

Paul did not choose his "thorn in the flesh," and most of us do not get to choose our area of greatest sacrifice either. When Jesus was asked about marriage and singlehood, he used the term *eunuchs*. If you google that term, you will find many authors claiming that Jesus was talking about homosexual men. But the historical evidence does not support that interpretation. In the New Testament era, explains one historian, neither Greek nor Latin had a word referring to a celibate man, so Christians used the term *eunuchs* to mean celibates.[56]

What's significant is that when Jesus talked about eunuchs, he included people who did not choose their condition: "For there are eunuchs who were born that way, and there are eunuchs who have been made eunuchs by others—and there are those who choose to live like eunuchs for the sake of the kingdom of heaven" (Matt. 19:12).

Eunuchs who were born that way may include what today we call intersex people, who are born with physical anomalies and are often infertile. God encourages them by promising that they can still reap a rich spiritual harvest: "'Sing, barren woman, you who never bore a child; burst into song, shout for joy, you who were never in labor; because more are the children of the desolate woman than of her who has a husband,' says the Lord" (Isa. 54:1).

Eunuchs who were made that way by others through castration were not uncommon in the ancient world. In affluent families, male slaves were often castrated if they worked in the women's quarters or served as sex slaves (boys were castrated to keep them young looking). In the government, high-ranking officials were often required to be eunuchs, especially if their work involved proximity to the queen or other female royalty. Old Testament examples include the account of Esther, which mentions "Hegai, the king's eunuch who was in charge of the harem" (Esther 2:15). Queen Jezebel's attendants consisted of "two or three eunuchs" (2 Kings 9:32). In the New Testament, the head of the treasury for Queen Candace of Ethiopia was a eunuch (Acts 8:27).

Eunuchs made that way by others also included captives taken in battle. (If they were of royal blood, castration would rule out any hope of founding a competing dynasty.) King Hezekiah was warned by a prophet that "some of your descendants, your own flesh and blood who will be born to you, will be taken away, and they will become eunuchs in the palace of the king of Babylon" (2 Kings. 20:18; Isa. 39:7). Those descendants may well have included Daniel and his three friends Shadrach, Meshach, and Abednego. They were high-ranking administrative officials in Babylon, and their overseer is called "master of his [the king's] eunuchs" (Dan. 1:3 KJV).[57]

When the prophet Isaiah predicts the return of the exiles to Israel, he addresses those captive eunuchs. The eunuch is assured that he is not "a dry tree." For God promises "to the eunuchs who . . . hold fast to my covenant, to them I will give within my temple and its walls a memorial and a name better than sons and daughters; I will give them an everlasting name that will endure forever" (Isa. 56:3–5). God is promising that celibacy, like marriage, can be blessed by God. Each offers unique challenges that can drive us deeper into our relationship with God, so that we ultimately have more to give in service to others.

Ed Shaw, a pastor who is exclusively attracted to the same sex and has embraced celibacy, points out that in the New Testament world, what concerned people most was not giving up sex but giving up children. Having descendants was the way people ensured that their name continued into the future. Children were also the most important form of social security in a pre-modern society. People without children had no one to support them in their old age. Nevertheless, many people in the early church chose celibacy, even though it was a huge sacrifice. Why? So the church "would have spiritual descendants," Shaw writes.[58] Celibates made a radical commitment to the church community as their family.

The challenge to today's church is to become a richly interdependent community that once again makes it possible for celibates to find their family among fellow Christians.

Freed from Freud

To support singles, we also need to recover the ideal of intense, intimate friendship.[59] We need to free ourselves from the influence of Freud, who taught that all relationships are ultimately erotic, an attitude that has made people suspicious of close friendships.

In the words of Melinda Selmys, *eros* (sexual love) and *philia* (friendship love) "are both expressions of the same primordial drive—not the biological drive to reproduce, but rather the spiritual drive to become one. *Eros* directs this drive towards physical expression, a 'one flesh' union, whereas *philia* directs it towards a union of souls." Scripture gives examples like David and Jonathan, where "Jonathan became one in spirit with David, and he loved him as himself" (1 Sam. 18:1).[60] In the church, we should nourish *philia* friendships so that singles can experience deep spiritual communion in the family of God.

Arguments for same-sex relations equate intimacy with marriage, creating the impression that if you do not marry, you are doomed to a life of isolation and misery. But ironically, some churches also elevate marriage to the point that they create the same impression, which can be very discouraging to singles. Ron Belgau should know; as a self-described gay Catholic, he is celibate. "Our culture has become very fixated on sex, but sex and romance are not the same as love," he writes. "Christ-centered chaste friendships offered a positive and fulfilling—albeit at times challenging—path to holiness."[61]

Churches should teach that marriage is one kind of intimacy, but that many other kinds of intimacy are possible and fulfilling, and can also be a means to love and serve others.

Shortly after I converted to Christianity, I attended a Lutheran Bible school where the head administrator was a strong, competent single woman who shared a home for decades with another single woman. Their mutual love and support was a vivid illustration of the beauty of long-term, committed, nurturing single relationships.

Finally, we should not rule out marriage. A book titled *Living the Truth in Love: Pastoral Approaches to Same Sex Attraction* tells the stories of people who either got married, or stayed married, even though they had homoerotic feelings.[62] These are sometimes labeled "mixed-orientation" marriages. Read Jeff Bennion's story:

> In my twenties I would have thought it was impossible that I could ever marry a woman, and even less possible that I would be happy and fulfilled in every way in that marriage. Eleven years and counting now, and I am happier than ever. . . .
>
> I don't blame people who doubt me—if I hadn't experienced it myself, I would find it dubious myself, it's so counter to the dominant cultural narrative out there.[63]

Doug Mainwaring is another example. He walked away from his marriage, engaged in sexual relationships with several other men, and even became an outspoken advocate for legalizing same-sex marriage. Then, after ten years, Doug became a Christian. He remarried his wife and they finished raising their children together. He writes, "Along the way, I learned that marriage is more than just a tradition or a religious or social construct. Monogamous, complementary, conjugal marriage is a pearl of great price worth investing one's entire life in."[64]

Marriage may not be possible for everyone with homoerotic feelings. Certainly it should not be entered into with the secret hope that it will "fix" the person. But it should be kept open as an option. Many people who have same-sex desires are quietly choosing to direct their love to their husbands or wives in order to experience marriage and parenthood.

A Christian friend of mine who calls himself "gay affirming" read these stories and responded, "I don't believe it. These men are fooling themselves." Like the Supreme Court, he thinks sexual orientation is immutable. But ironically, that objection is raised only when someone moves away from a homosexual identity, not the reverse. In the secular world, when someone who has lived as heterosexual starts living as homosexual, they are applauded for discovering their authentic self. But when someone moves in the opposite direction, they are subject to intense criticism, accused of internalized self-loathing and false consciousness.

In reality, those who choose opposite-sex marriage are saying that they are not defined by their sexual feelings but by their moral ideals. One man told Mainwaring,

> Over the years, I have had passing thoughts of giving up my family and marriage for a same-sex relationship or partner, but decided that in no way is it worth destroying my family and marriage for that. . . . I have created a family and children and I have a responsibility to them that I could never forsake. So over time, even when feeling same-sex attraction, I have chosen not to dwell on it and to remain faithful to my marriage and family. I draw immense satisfaction from that.[65]

Our feelings do not define us. Our moral commitments do. We find fulfillment when we find ways to live in congruence with our deepest commitments.

■ ■ ■ ■ ■

Love in the Cosmos

A seventy-five-year-old woman had just heard a compelling lecture by Rosaria Butterfield, a former lesbian who converted to Christianity. Afterward, she approached the speaker and recounted that she had been married to another woman for fifty years, that she and her partner had children and grandchildren.

In a voice broken with pain, she whispered, "I have heard the gospel, and I understand that I may lose everything. Why didn't anyone tell me this before? Why did people I love not tell me that I would one day have to choose like this?"[66]

Where were the Christians who should have been reaching out to her with a balanced message of love and truth?

The Bible's teaching on sexuality is summed up in the Ten Commandments: "You shall not commit adultery." The historic Christian interpretation is that sexual expression belongs within the loving bond of marriage. A sexual relationship is the means to express and refresh the one-flesh union between husband and wife—to replay their love story again and again.

Scripture even uses sexuality as a metaphor for the intimate relationship God aspires to have with his people. Throughout the Old Testament, Israel is pictured as God's unfaithful wife. Ezekiel 16 gives an especially vivid image of God as the lover of Israel, who is personified as a woman: "I gave you my solemn oath and entered into a covenant with you, declares the Sovereign Lord, and you became mine." (v. 8). In the New Testament, the church is portrayed as the bride of Christ: "I saw the Holy City, the new Jerusalem, coming down out of heaven from God, prepared as a bride beautifully dressed for her husband" (Rev. 21:2).

Our sexuality is part of the created order that is declaring the glory of God. It possesses a "language" that is ultimately meant to proclaim God's own transcendent love and faithfulness.

The theme of male-female marriage is not just a matter of a few verses here and there. The Bible is a love story from start to finish—a story about God as a Lover who seeks out his bride and rescues her. A classic hymn starts out, "The church's one foundation is Jesus Christ her Lord." It continues with this dramatic image:

> From heaven he came and sought her,
> to be his holy bride.
> With his own blood he bought her,
> and for her life, he died.[67]

Marriage is meant to reflect this cosmic love story. As O'Donovan writes, human beings are "clearly ordered at the biological level towards heterosexual union as the human mode of procreation. It is not possible to negotiate this fact about our common humanity; it can only be either welcomed or resented."[68]

When we welcome it, we affirm the goodness of creation. We affirm that our own maleness or femaleness is not a meaningless or oppressive fact of nature but a reflection of history's great storyline.

Sex and Leviticus

What are the most common objections to the biblical teaching on homosexuality? Some scholars argue that the Bible prohibits only temple prostitution as it was practiced in ancient Canaanite worship—that the text does not even address loving, committed homosexual relationships, which, they claim, were unknown at the time.

Are the biblical passages limited to temple prostitution? Jewish readers certainly did not think so. The Jews stood out from the surrounding nations for their rejection of same-sex relations of any kind.[69] For five hundred years before Christ and five hundred years after Christ, Jewish writers agreed that same-sex behavior was against the will of God.[70]

A key verse is Leviticus 20:13, "If a man has sexual relations with a man as one does with a woman, both of them have done what is detestable." The wording here is not qualified in any way that would limit the prohibition to temple prostitution. Moreover, the verse is sandwiched between prohibitions on practices that are clearly wrong for all time and all cultures: adultery, incest, and bestiality (vv. 10–17).[71]

Or take Leviticus 18:22: "Do not have sexual relations with a man as one does with a woman; that is detestable." This verse comes immediately after a verse condemning the sacrifice of children to Molech, the bloody Canaanite deity. No one argues that, because child sacrifice is mentioned in relation to the worship of Molech, therefore the text is condemning child sacrifice only in pagan worship, but that other forms of child sacrifice or infanticide are just fine.

As a result, few biblical scholars give much credence to the claim that the Levitical prohibitions of male-male intercourse were forbidding only cultic or idolatrous forms of the practice. Moreover, nothing in the New Testament suggests that Jesus or the apostles denied the unanimous Jewish conviction that same-sex behavior is sinful.

Three Types of Law

What about the fact that the Old Testament refers to practices that are clearly culture-bound, like prohibitions on blending two types of fiber in cloth? How is anyone justified in picking and choosing among Old Testament laws? In the New Testament era, the most intense controversies were over just this question. Were Christians still required to practice "Jewish customs" (Gal. 2:14), like circumcision and avoiding food sacrificed to idols? The answer was no. Moral laws still apply but ceremonial and civil laws do not.[72]

1. CEREMONIAL laws were symbolic, governing temple worship—sacrifices, feasts, foods, the priesthood, worship, circumcision, and ritual purity (the clean laws). Even in Old Testament times, these laws were not universal; they were not applied to other nations. The prophets recognized the difference between moral and ceremonial laws: "I desire mercy, not sacrifice, and the acknowledgment of God rather than burnt offerings" (Hos. 6:6). Jesus quoted the same verse to get the Pharisees to grasp the distinction (Matt. 9:13). And he explicitly rejected the clean laws. "In saying this, Jesus declared all foods clean" (Mark 7:19).[73]

   The prohibition on weaving two different fibers together was a ceremonial law, intended to symbolize purity and holiness. In fact, the history of the Old Testament is replete with symbols and foreshadowing of the Messiah.[74] But no one needs foreshadowing after the reality has arrived. Paul writes, "Do not let anyone judge you by what you eat or drink, or with regard to a religious festival, a New Moon celebration or a Sabbath day. These are a shadow of the things that were to come; the reality, however, is found in Christ" (Col. 2:16–17). The early church stopped following the sacrificial laws when they understood that Christ came as the ultimate sacrifice.

2. CIVIL laws were necessary because Israel was a nation. Even in Old Testament times, these laws were not universal; they were not applied to other nations. They ended when ancient Israel no longer existed as a political state.

   The civil law was based on the moral law, but the two were not equivalent. Jesus drew the distinction when he said divorce is *morally* wrong but it was permitted in *civil* law because people's "hearts were hard" (Matt. 19:8). Similarly, practices such as slavery and polygamy were not presented as ideal morally but were permitted legally. By contrast, same-sex relations were not permitted morally or legally.[75]

3. MORAL laws apply universally, to all people at all times. The Bible condemns all nations, not only Israel, for greed, injustice, oppression, violence, and sexual immorality. The New Testament repeats these moral principles to indicate that they continue to be valid.

   Jesus himself put his imprimatur on Old Testament sexual morality. When asked about marriage, he quoted the Genesis text as authoritative. "Haven't you read?" he asked—implying that the text should be treated as conclusive. "At the beginning, the Creator 'made them male and female'" (Matt. 19:4). Christians are meant to take their template for human nature from creation.

"Lovers of Men"

In the New Testament, a key passage is Romans 1:26–27. The text uses the phrase "contrary to nature" (ESV), which in both Hellenistic and Greco-Roman culture was a standard way of referring to homosexual practice.[76]

At the time, the term *nature* was not used the way people use it today, to mean behavior observed in the natural world. Instead it meant behavior that is normative for *human nature*—behavior that reflects the way humans were originally created, that fits the template for being human. In this sense of the term, all sin is contrary to human nature, and Paul goes on to itemize a representative sampling: "They have become filled with every kind of wickedness, evil, greed and depravity. They are full of envy, murder, strife, deceit and malice. They are gossips, slanderers, God-haters, insolent, arrogant and boastful; they invent ways of doing evil; they disobey their parents; they have no understanding, no fidelity, no love, no mercy" (vv. 29–31). All these behaviors are contrary to what it means to be fully human.[77]

Some scholars argue that in this passage Paul is prohibiting only acts that are coercive, such as sex with children or slaves, and that he did not even know about the kind of mutual, loving same-sex relationships that exist today. It is true that coercive relationships were common in ancient Rome (as we saw in chapters 3 and 4). But Paul could have used the terms for rape or prostitution, and he does not. Moreover, he places moral responsibility on both partners, which he would not have done if one was a victim. Instead he speaks of men "consumed with passion *for one another*," which implies that he was thinking of mutual relationships (v. 27 ESV).

Finally, some argue that Paul was referring only to the practice of temple prostitution connected to the worship of idols.[78] But Paul's point in this passage is that *everyone* who rejects the true Creator worships idols: They "exchanged the glory of the immortal God for images made to look like a mortal human being and birds and animals and reptiles. . . . They exchanged the truth about God for a lie, and worshiped and served created things rather than the Creator" (vv. 23, 25). Paul is saying that anyone who rejects the Creator will fasten on something in the created order and put it in the place of God as the ultimate reality, the center of their life and worship.

Louis Crompton, who himself identifies as homosexual, writes, "However well-intentioned," the interpretation that Paul's words do not apply to homosexuals in committed relationships is contrary to history. "Nowhere does Paul or any other Jewish writer of this period imply the least acceptance of same-sex relations under any circumstance. The idea that homosexuals might be redeemed by mutual devotion would have been wholly foreign to Paul or any other Jew or early Christian."[79]

Finally, it is not true that the ancient world knew nothing about committed same-sex relationships between adults. Many of the Caesars had male lovers and were quite public about it. Love poetry of the time describes men's infatuations with other men. In Plato's *Symposium*, Aristophanes says some men are "lovers of women" while others "have an affection for men and embrace them." Aristophanes adds that your character is revealed by what you love, and since men are superior to women, the conclusion is that lovers of men are *superior* to lovers of women. In his words, lovers of men are "the best of boys and youths, because they have the most manly nature. . . . They are valiant and manly, and have a manly countenance, and they embrace that which is like them"[80]—namely, other men.

It is significant that though writers like Aristophanes celebrated male-male love as superior to male-female love, nevertheless Greek and Roman law limited civil marriage to opposite-sex unions. Clearly, their marriage laws were not motivated by hatred or bigotry but rather by the recognition that societies need to give legal support and protection to the one relationship capable of creating children.

Who's on the Wrong Side of History?

Critics argue that the Christian church must change its sexual morality or risk being left behind—being "on the wrong side of history." But history proves the exact opposite. The church's sexual morality is one reason it grew so explosively in the early centuries, especially among women.

In the surrounding Roman society, wives had little status. Freeborn men married wives to obtain legal heirs, but it was accepted that they would seek sexual satisfaction with girlfriends, mistresses, prostitutes, courtesans, other men, and, most of all, household slaves—male and female, adults and minors (typically post-puberty adolescents and teens). Wives had to compete with a host of other people for their husband's love and attention.

Most infidelity took the form of sleeping with one's own slaves. For example, Horace recommends that a man vent his sexual energies on his slaves because they were readily available. If "there is a slave-girl or a home-grown slave-boy ready at hand, whom you could jump right away," why not? He adds, "I like sex that is easy and obtainable."[81]

Historical records show that wives often complained about their husband's unfaithfulness, but it did little good. A first-century poet writing in Rome even chastises wives for being jealous when their husbands have sex with slave boys. He admonishes wives to accept the fact that "intercourse is more pleasurable with boys than it is with women."[82] There is a reason the god of love, Cupid, was portrayed as a boy.

In ancient Greece and Rome (as we saw in chapter 2), male-male sex was considered morally acceptable when it involved a higher-status male dominating a lower-status male. To be the receptive partner was considered a sign of humiliation. Same-sex relationships were thus a way to prove one's virility. Women were, after all, already a lower caste. But penetration of another male was a means of subjugating him, of dishonoring his maleness by treating him as a female, thereby demonstrating one's own superiority. As a result, writes Sarah Ruden, "society pressured a man into sexual brutality toward other males." "Greek and Roman men, in public, would threaten bitter enemies with rape."

Parents had to guard their sons carefully. Ruden describes a father hovering around his son's workplace, concerned to protect him from seduction or abduction. It was also normal, she writes, "for a family of any standing to dedicate one slave to a son's protection, especially on the otherwise unsupervised walk to and from school."

Paul himself may well have experienced the same things growing up in Roman culture. "Flagrant pedophiles might have pestered him and his friends on the way to and from school, offered friendship, offered tutoring, offered athletic training, offered money or gifts," Ruden says. He would have seen prostitutes on the streets and in the doorways of brothels. He probably saw slave auctions, where youths his own age were being sold to local pimps. Though his own Jewish family would not have condoned sexual abuse of its slaves, he would know that among his non-Jewish friends, "household slaves normally were less respected as outlets for bodily functions than were the household toilets, and that a sanctioned role of slave boys was anal sex with free adults."[83]

Men in Greco-Roman culture who engaged in male-male sex were not homosexual or bisexual in the modern sense of a fixed sexual and psychological orientation. They simply did not think there were any moral limits on sexual behavior (with the exception that in Rome, but not Greece, freeborn men and women were off-limits). It was considered morally acceptable for a man to have sexual relations with men and youths just as freely as with women and girls.[84] For the dominant male in ancient Rome, virtually anyone was fair game, without regard to sex or age. Ancient culture thus gives a concrete historical example of the social chaos that results when sexuality is untethered from marriage and family.

Foucault and others have written as though the ancients had an exalted view of homoerotic love as something spiritual and sublime. We get this whitewashed picture mostly from Plato, who wrote that a man's sexual love for a beautiful youth awakens in the adult a love for the ideal beauty. But the literature of the day does not support this spiritualized interpretation. As Ruden remarks dryly, "None of the sources, objectively read, backs any of this up." It is "total hokey."[85]

In the ancient world, virtually no sexual activity was considered immoral in itself, as long as it was practiced in "moderation." The early church had to muster the courage to stand against a culture in which there were few limits on sexual behavior. From the beginning, Christians have not defended "traditional values." They have stood for truth *against* prevailing cultural norms.

The early church may have been "on the wrong side of history." But that's why it changed history.

To Each His Own

Christianity was radical because it channeled male sexual desire into marriage as the only acceptable outlet. "Marriage should be honored by all, and the marriage bed kept pure" (Heb. 13:4). As a consequence, Christianity greatly elevated the status of women while protecting everyone else from being treated as fair game for sexual seduction or predation.

The principle is enshrined in the Ten Commandments: "You shall not covet your neighbor's wife" (Exod. 20:17)—or his slaves or his children or himself.

The moral rule of monogamy essentially means "to each his own." A wife does not have to compete with others for her husband's love. No wonder women were especially attracted to Christianity. As columnist Rod Dreher writes, "Christianity, as articulated by Paul, worked a cultural revolution, restraining and channeling male eros, elevating the status of both women and of the human body, and infusing marriage—and marital sexuality—with love."[86]

We no longer realize how extensively the church fathers felt called to address questions of sexuality—especially pederasty (older men having sex with teen boys). The *Didache* condemns what it calls "corrupting boys," a common term at the time for pederasty. John Chrysostom warns that the status of women is reduced when males are seen as appropriate objects of erotic desire: "Women are in danger of being superfluous when young men take their place in every activity."[87]

Athenagoras of Athens urges Christians not to be like their pagan neighbors who "set up a market for fornication, and establish infamous resorts for the young for every kind of vile pleasure—who do not abstain even from males, males with males committing shocking abominations, outraging all the noblest and comeliest bodies in all sorts of ways, so dishonoring the fair workmanship of God."[88]

Notice the bishop's argument—that male-male relations dishonor "the fair workmanship of God." A biblical worldview honors the human body as God's workmanship. The church fathers rooted their opposition to same-sex relations in creation theology.

The irony is that the Christian sex ethic actually gives greater significance to our sexual identity than did ancient Roman hedonism. For the Romans, it made no moral difference whether the object of male sexual desire was male or female—which means *being male or female* had no moral significance. By contrast, the biblical ethic says our sexual identity has the high honor of being part of the moral structure of the universe.

These examples from ancient history illustrate how important social norms are. Once a society gives up the bright line containing sex within male-female marriage, it is difficult to draw the line anywhere else.

Ancient culture also provides a vivid image of where Western culture may well be heading. As Christian influence wanes, will Western culture revert back to a sexual free-for-all like that of the ancient world? If so, Christians will once again need to muster their courage to be radically countercultural. And they will once again need to be prepared to minister to the victims of sexual abuse and predation—those wounded by the sexual revolution. They must do the hard work of making a case for the beauty of the biblical sex ethic with both their words and their lives.

Christians must once again become known as those who honor the whole person. The reason they speak out on moral issues should not be because their beliefs are being threatened or because they feel "offended." They should erase the word *offended* from their vocabulary. After all, Christians are called to share in the offense of the cross. This is not about us.

Christians must make it clear that they are speaking out because they genuinely care about people. No matter how compelling the case for a biblical ethic, people rarely change their minds based on intellectual arguments alone. They are even less likely to change if all they hear is moral condemnation. People must be drawn in by a vision that attracts them by offering a more appealing, more life-affirming worldview. Christians must present biblical morality in a way that reveals the beauty of the biblical view of the human person so that people actually *want* it to be true. And they must back up their words with actions that treat people with genuine dignity and worth.

A Home for the Homeless

To make Christianity credible, we must create homes that reach out to those who do not have homes or families of their own—including those with sexual issues. Christians have often operated by a double standard, treating same-sex sin as though it were *more* sinful than other transgressions. Many absorbed the nineteenth-century secular view that redefined the term *homosexual* to mean an innate, deviant psychological type These attitudes are blindingly obvious to those who suffer from unwanted sexual attractions, and it makes them less likely to seek help in the church. Christians must repent of their unbiblical attitudes and find ways to communicate to those who struggle with sin of any kind that they will find a refuge in the church. Scripture says of Jesus, "a bruised reed he will not break" (Matt. 12:20). People must be able to trust that churches will protect and nurture the bruised and broken parts of their lives.

Christians must constantly remind themselves that their own character is fallen and disordered—that they have just as much capacity for sin as anyone else. Holding up a moral ideal for sexuality should have nothing to do with pride or self-righteousness. It stems from the conviction that certain acts are healthier and more fulfilling because they are in line with the way God created humanity.

The church should aspire to be a community that welcomes the outcast and the marginalized. A crushing sense of loneliness can push people into same-sex enclaves in their search for acceptance and a sense of community. As we said in chapter 4, Christians have a responsibility to create structures in which celibate singles can enjoy committed relationships and express nonsexual affection.

Those who have wrestled with sexual issues have often suffered deeply. They've had to work through their Christianity from the ground up, not simply accept it because it's what they were taught. They've made greater sacrifices than most—often giving up hopes for sexual intimacy and a family of their own. To survive they've had to dig deeply into the spiritual resources of their relationship with God. As a result, they may become "wounded healers" with deep wells of compassion, sympathy, and spiritual wisdom to offer in ministry to others. The church can benefit from their insight and experience.

How to Turn a Culture Around

Is it possible to change the public culture on these issues? Absolutely. We can take hope from the abortion issue. Millennials are now the most pro-life group in the nation (see chapter 2). There is no reason we cannot turn the culture around on sexual issues as well. We must work to educate and persuade on a worldview level. Most of all, we must sacrificially love and accept people wrestling with questions and temptations. Attitudes on abortion changed when Christians accepted young women with unexpected pregnancies and supported them both emotionally and practically with baby clothes, schooling, and job training. How can Christians offer similar support and practical help to those who have sexual issues?

Christians' greatest impact will take place when outsiders look at them and say what they said of the early church: "Behold how they love one another!"[89]

The sexual revolution has not stopped with demanding moral and legal acceptance of same-sex relations. It is barreling forward rapidly with demands to legislate protected status for transgender people and genderqueers of all varieties. How can we respond with a worldview approach that gets below the surface and addresses the key issues? How can we reveal the truth and beauty of the Christian moral vision?

6

Trans*gender*, Trans*reality*

"God Should Have Made Me a Girl"

From the time Brandon was an infant, he was quiet, sensitive, and compliant. When he was a toddler, his babysitter told his mother, "He's too good to be a boy." In preschool, while the boys roughhoused on one side of the room and the girls sat in a circle and talked, Brandon sat with the little girls. He was not interested in playing with guns or trucks. He preferred playing imaginary games with toy animals, acting out complex interpersonal relationships. From an early age, he sensed that he was different from most boys.

Today we would call him gender nonconforming.

By junior high, Brandon was experiencing painful tension. He felt sharply out of step with the prevailing John Wayne masculinity image. And he still preferred the company of girls. Boys talked about sports and video games; girls talked about emotions and relationships—the things Brandon cared about. But of course girls never shared their feelings with him as openly as with their girlfriends. So he felt he was neither really a boy nor accepted as a girl.

No matter where he went, Brandon felt agonizingly out of place. "I feel the way girls do, I am interested in things girls are," he told his parents. "God should have made me a girl."

In high school, his classmates organized a "Christian manhood" group, but it stressed stereotypical male virtues like leadership and assertiveness. What about men whose character strengths are caring and nurturing?

By age fourteen, Brandon was spending hours scouring the internet for information on sex reassignment surgery. Eventually, however, he concluded that it would not give him the results he wanted. "I realized that surgery would not turn me into a girl. It would not change my genes and chromosomes," he told me. "A person is not a computer program that you can delete and redesign from scratch."

The last time I talked to Brandon, he had graduated from university with honors and was working at his first job. At the end of our conversation, though, he tapped his chest and said with a shy smile, "But I'm still a girl on the inside."

Young people today live in a society that prompts them to question their psychosexual identity as never before.[1] Laws are being passed that treat sexual attraction and gender identity as a protected category (like race and religion) in public schools, businesses, housing, health care, prisons, and even churches.[2] These are called SOGI—Sexual Orientation and Gender Identity—laws, and when we analyze their language we find that they assume the same two-story divided worldview we diagnosed in earlier chapters. SOGI laws are based on the assumption that a person can be born in the wrong body. Thus they set up an opposition between the body and an inner sense of being male or female, between physiological facts and subjective feelings.

Christians must respond by offering a positive biblical worldview that affirms the value of the body and the unity of the human being. At the same time, Christians should be the first in line to nurture and support kids who don't "fit in" by affirming the diversity of gifts and temperaments in the body of Christ.

Your "Assigned" Sex

Many people find it easy to recognize the two-story dualism in the transgender narrative. A BBC film titled *Transgender Kids* says, "At the heart of the debate about transgender children is the idea that your brain can be at war with your body."[3] Today the accepted treatment is not to help persons change their inner feelings of gender identity to match their body but to change their body (through hormones and surgery) to match their feelings.

In other words, when a person senses a dissonance between body and mind, the mind wins. The body is dismissed as irrelevant.

This low view of the body can be detected in the language used in SOGI laws and policies. Here is a typical example from the California education code: Gender is "a person's gender identity and gender related appearance and behavior whether or not stereotypically associated with the person's assigned sex at birth."[4]

What's the operative word here? *Assigned*—as though a person's sex at birth were arbitrary instead of a biological fact. The Gay and Lesbian Alliance Against Defamation (GLAAD) says, "Transgender is a term used to describe people whose gender identity differs from the sex the doctor marked on their birth certificate."[5] A person pictures the doctor wondering, *Hmm, which sex shall we mark down for this baby?* instead of observing it as a scientific fact.

What this language implies is that *scientific facts do not matter*. SOGI laws are being used to impose a two-level worldview that disparages the physical body as inconsequential, insignificant, and irrelevant to who we are. As O'Donovan writes, the transgender narrative suggests that "the body is an accident that has befallen the real me; the real me has a true sex" *apart from* the body. "The body is an object set over against the personal subject located in the thinking-feeling mind."[6]

Consider a recent case in the Fourth Circuit Court, in which a girl who identified as a boy named G. G. demanded the right to use the boys' restroom. The judge ruled that "G. G.'s birth-assigned sex, or so-called 'biological sex,' is female, but G. G.'s gender identity is male."[7]

Her "so-called 'biological sex'"—in sneer quotes? This is a judge writing a formal ruling for a federal court, and he treats the very existence of biological sex with suspicion and disdain. Apparently he thinks the facts of physiology, anatomy, chromosomes, and DNA are less real or knowable than the girl's subjective feelings about her gender.

I ran across an internet forum discussing transgenderism, where a commenter wrote, "What does some little bit of flesh between the legs matter?"[8] Why should *that* make a difference to your sense of who you are?

This is a devastatingly reductive view of the body. Young people are absorbing the idea that the physical body is not part of the authentic self—that the authentic self is only the autonomous choosing self. This is ancient Gnosticism in a new garb. Policies imposing transgender ideology on children as early as kindergarten are teaching them to denigrate their bodies—to see their biological sex as having no relevance to who they are as whole persons. The two-story dichotomy causes people to feel estranged from their own bodies.

Biology is more than a bit of flesh between the legs. In a popular TED talk, cardiologist Paula Johnson says, "Every cell has a sex—and what that means is that men and women are different down to the cellular and molecular level. It means that we're different across all of our organs, from our brains to our hearts, our lungs, our joints."[9] In other words, no matter what your gender philosophy, when you are ill and the doctors put you on the operating table, they still need to know your original biological sex in order to give you the best possible health care.

Genderqueer, Bigender, Pangender

The term *transgender* has been expanded into an umbrella term covering several categories that used to be distinct, such as cross-dressers, transvestites, and transsexuals. Because *transgender* is more socially acceptable than most earlier terms, it has mushroomed in recent years. Today it is also used to include a host of newly minted categories such as genderqueer (people who do not consider themselves either masculine or feminine), bigender, pangender, gender fluid, and many more.

Among the public, there is a sense that there must be a genetic or hormonal basis for feelings of being in the wrong body. There is some scientific evidence to support that assumption.[10] In chapter 5 we learned that virtually all our thoughts and feelings have physical correlates. Being aware of the mind-body connection can motivate us to show compassion to people who are navigating cross-gender feelings. Yet there is no conclusive scientific evidence that transsexualism or transgenderism is caused by genes or any other biological factor.

More importantly, transgender activists themselves argue the opposite: They insist that biology is irrelevant to gender. As we saw in chapter 1 (it might be helpful to reread that section), trans activists argue that there is no connection between body and gender identity. A BBC video features a young woman who identifies as non-binary saying, "It doesn't matter what living, meat skeleton you've been born in; it's *what you feel* that defines you."[11] In the two-story worldview, all that counts is what you feel. The body is demoted to nothing but a "meat skeleton." No respect is given to the intrinsic good or *telos* (purpose) of the human body. No dignity is accorded to the unique capabilities inherent in being male or female.

The transgender narrative completely disassociates gender from biological sex.

Most SOGI laws and policies state explicitly that people claiming transgender status need no medical diagnosis, no record of hormone therapy or surgery, no change in legal documents, and no alteration in appearance. As family researcher Glenn Stanton explains, "Gender identity does not exist in any objective or quantifiable sense. There is simply no physiological, legal, medical, or physical-appearance criteria that a transgender person must meet to be properly distinguished as such. That 'reality' exists solely in the mind of the individual making the claim."[12] It is based not on biological facts but strictly on inner feelings.

■ ■ ■ ■ ■

The Lie of Queer Theory

The transgender "script" tells young people that embracing their cross-gender feelings will liberate them to be their authentic selves. But will it? Many who have tried it say no. Jonah Mix was a gender nonconforming young man who spent years immersed in queer theory. He called himself non-binary and wore tights, eyeliner, and nail polish: "It was in those queer circles that I first heard the common admonition to never define a person by their body."

Eventually, however, he realized the promise of liberation was a lie. To discover whether you identify as a man, you must first define manhood. "If we are not men by our bodies, we are men by our actions," Mix writes. Do you act stereotypically masculine? Then you are a man. Do you behave in ways that are stereotypically feminine? You must be a woman. Ironically, queer theory actually reinforces rigid gender stereotypes.

By contrast, if you take your identity from your body, Mix says, you can engage in a range of diverse behaviors without threatening the security of your identity as a man or woman. "When we are defined by our bodies, the whole width of human experience remains open. . . . There is freedom in the body."[13]

Similarly, on a trans website a commenter named Trish wrote, "As a little girl, I enjoyed both ballet lessons and playing in the mud. . . . I liked miniskirts and wanted to be an astronaut when I grew up. It looks to me like the trans movement is fighting very hard to force everyone to choose whether to live in the blue box or the pink box, and no playing mix-and-match. To me this is the opposite of freedom."[14]

When Bruce Jenner announced that he now identified as a woman and was adopting the name Caitlyn, how was the news broadcast to the world? The iconic photo spread in *Vanity Fair* "offered us a glimpse into Caitlyn Jenner's idea of a woman," says a *New York Times* article: "a cleavage-boosting corset, sultry poses, thick mascara and the prospect of regular 'girls' nights' of banter about hair and makeup. . . . That's the kind of nonsense that was used to repress women for centuries."[15] The pink box.

Contrary to what postmodern gender theory says, there is greater diversity and inclusivity when we anchor our psychosexual identity in the objective, scientifically knowable reality of our biology as male or female.

Biology Wins Out

In recent years, there has been a huge spike in the number of teens identifying as transgender and requesting hormone treatment and surgery. At some schools, entire peer groups are "coming out" as transgender at the same time.[16] Are these kids all simultaneously discovering their true, authentic selves?

Columnist Rod Dreher sometimes posts emails from readers in his columns, and this one captures the tone of many parents:

> As a parent living the nightmare of having a teen who suddenly announces she's transgender, I can tell you there are NO doctors who will do anything

> but agree. There is NO science behind this. There is NO way to medically "diagnose" her. . . . Three of her closest friends have already had full transition, paid for by their parents, so it is difficult for her to understand why we won't do the same. It is no different than having your child captured by a cult.

Why are parents going along with it? "Because they don't want to lose their kids."[17] Many schools have adopted the policy that parents may not even be informed which gender their children adopt at school.

Where did the idea come from that gender identity can be disassociated from biological sex? One of the earliest to popularize the idea was John Money at Johns Hopkins Medical School. His prime example was David Reimer, born in 1965, who, as a baby, had his penis severely damaged in a botched circumcision. Not to worry, Money told David's parents. Gender identity is completely malleable and it will be a simple task to remake this biological boy into a girl using sex reassignment surgery, along with hormonal and psychological treatments. The case was widely publicized, and when I was in graduate school, it was still being touted as irrefutable evidence that nurture (choice) is more important than nature (biology). A biological male could be induced to think he was female and to live as a girl.

It later emerged that Money was lying. He knew that David was deeply unhappy living as a girl. David refused to play with dolls, tried to seize his brother's toy guns and cars, and told his parents he felt like a boy. When David was fourteen, he grew so severely depressed that his parents finally told him what had happened. He immediately began living as a boy, and eventually married a woman.[18] The gender experiment did not work. Biology won out. Yet the myth that gender identity is independent of biological sex lives on.

Love Thy Body

Why are we not encouraging people to have a higher view of the body? Nuriddeen Knight, a black woman writing for the Witherspoon Institute, says the transgender movement reminds her of a time, not so long ago, when light-skinned black people sometimes "passed" as white. She asks, Isn't there a parallel when a man "passes" as a woman, or the reverse? In both cases, the underlying motive seems to be a form of self-hate: "A black person who wants to be white is practicing self-hate, and so is a man who wants to be a woman or a woman who wants to be a man."

Knight asks: Why won't we "encourage people to love the body they're in? We tell women to love their curves and love their age and love the skin they're in, but we won't tell them (and men) to love the sex of their bodies?"[19]

At the skating rink where my son was taking lessons, a person came on the ice with long hair, heavy eye makeup, and bright red lipstick. She was wearing a shiny ice-skating costume with a short skirt and colorful tights. But something was strange about her build. She was tall with a rugged profile, broad shoulders, and knobby knees. In short, "she" was obviously male. With her exaggerated makeup, she looked almost like someone in drag. The other skaters snickered and made derogatory comments, but I could not help but feel compassion for someone so clearly trapped in rejection of his own body.

There is a proper kind of self-love that comes from accepting God's love. A biblical worldview grants value and dignity to our identity as male or female. Gender theology is rooted in creation theology. What God has created has intrinsic value and dignity.

Blending the Binary

Because the trans narrative insists that the body does not matter—that it is not "the real you"—some transgender people do not even bother to change their bodily appearance. A friend introduced me to a local musician who identifies as genderqueer. He appears completely masculine except that he wears eyeliner and sometimes a woman's blouse or skirt. Yet he insists on being referred to as "she" and "her."

For some gender activists, refusing to change their appearance is part of a deliberate strategy to eliminate the binary categories of male and female altogether. Trans activist Rikki Wilchins, writing in *The Advocate*, says that until now, it has been relatively easy to advance transgender rights because most trans people show "at least some degree of consonance between their gender identity and usual notions of masculinity or femininity." But what happens when they refuse to change their appearance? "What happens when a genderqueer individual, who genuinely looks and sounds profoundly non-binary or masculine, declares in a binary world s/he would be most comfortable accessing the girls restroom? To say the least, the optics will no longer work." That is, a male-bodied trans woman will not *look* like a woman but will still demand access to women's spaces, such as public restrooms. At that point, Wilchins writes, we will challenge "the entire underlying hetero-binary structuring of the world."[20]

That's exactly what SOGI laws and policies are already doing. They require people to address others by their self-identified gender even when they have not had surgery or hormone treatment or anything else to change their external appearance.

Recently a friend of mine was in a restaurant bathroom when a male waiter entered. I had seen the same waiter when we arrived at the restaurant earlier that evening, and his appearance was completely masculine. (My friend noticed that he also left the seat up.) Though he had done nothing to feminize his appearance, he was claiming the right to use women's public spaces.

In 2016 the New York City Human Rights Commission released a list of thirty-one terms of gender expression—androgynous, genderqueer, non-binary, pangender, bi-gendered, gender fluid, third sex, two spirit, and so on—which employers must use or face exorbitant fines of up to $250,000. It will be all but impossible to keep track of which gender a person claims, especially if the person has not changed his or her appearance.[21] In this way, SOGI laws are doing exactly what trans activists have hoped for: They are challenging the very existence of the binary categories of male and female.

Pomosexual

Of course, New York City's list of thirty-one terms of gender expression is likely to keep expanding. Logically, there could be an infinite number of genders. Why? Because it is a concept that refers solely to inner feelings, with no reference to any physical trait.

Transgender policies are thus leading us inexorably to the postmodern view of psychosexual identity. In her influential book *Gender Trouble*, Judith Butler argues that gender is not a fixed attribute but a free-floating variable that shifts according to personal preference. Gender is a "fiction," a "fabrication," a "fantasy" that can be made and remade at will. This has been dubbed a pomosexual view (pomo is short for postmodern).[22]

What does a pomosexual view mean in practice? A psychotherapist writing in a magazine billed for "queer people" explains that people "don't want to fit into any boxes—not gay, straight, lesbian, or bisexual ones. . . . They want to be free to change their minds." The article was addressed to people who had come out of the closet and thought they had discovered their true identity, but later were attracted to heterosexual relationships. "So what *am* I?" they were asking. Not to worry, the author said. "We're seeing a challenge to the old, modernist way of thinking 'This is who I am, period' and a movement toward a postmodern version, 'This is who I am right now.'"[23]

When gender is severed from biology, it becomes something we can choose—and therefore something we can also change.

To use our two-story metaphor, gender has become a postmodern upper-story concept—indefinable, manipulable, fluid, and severed from any connection to biological facts in the lower story. Gender has nothing to do with having a male or female body. As Butler writes, when "gender is theorized as radically independent of sex, gender itself becomes a free-floating artifice, with the consequence that *man* and *masculine* might just as easily signify a female body as a male one, and *woman* and *feminine* a male body as easily as a female one."[24]

People who still hold a modernist mindset claim that sexual orientation is natural. But postmodernists claim that *nothing* is natural—that sexuality is a social construction.[25]

In the introduction we saw that the two-story body/person split stems from the same source as the fact/value split. So it is not surprising that there is a parallel: First *values* were redefined as matters of subjective personal choice, disconnected from facts, and now *gender* has been redefined the same way.

As always, young people are the first to pick up new ideas. A 2015 *Fusion* survey found that the majority of millennials believe gender is fluid.[26] A *World* magazine article says this idea "is seen as liberating, a way to take control of one's own identity, rather than accepting the one that has been culturally 'assigned.'" At some college clinics, "students no longer have to check '"male' or 'female' on their health forms. Instead they are asked to 'describe your gender identity history.'"[27]

That is, which gender identities have you embraced over your lifetime? They can change.

This is not some fringe idea. It is mainstream. Virtually all sex education curricula in America take their lead from the Sexuality Information and Education Council of the United States (SIECUS). Its pronouncements constitute the "official" view. And what does SIECUS say? "Gender identity refers to a person's internal sense of being male, female, or a combination of these," and "people's understanding of their gender identity *may change* over the course of their lifetimes."[28]

An NPR program featured students who had embraced the postmodern concept of gender identity, speaking in terms of which pronoun they preferred. At one college, the radio host said, "things were so fluid you could make up a different pronoun for a different event." You could go to lunch as a *he*, then go to class as a *she*. "We encountered high school students who said . . . I reject the gender binary as an oppressive move by the dominant culture."[29]

That postmodern view is filtering down to ever younger ages. The mother of a twelve-year-old told reporters, "Some days Annie is a girl, some days Annie is a boy, and some days she's both." When the pair went shopping for Annie's graduation outfit, they purchased both a dress and suit because they were not sure which gender the child would align with for the evening. The article helpfully explains, "Annie believes gender is more of a mental trait rather than physical."[30] Gender has become a purely mental trait with no grounding in physical reality.

Facebook: "Your True, Authentic Self"?

A few years ago, Facebook announced that its users could now choose from fifty different genders. The company explained that its goal was to give people a chance to express "your true, authentic self."[31] But there are not fifty biological sexes. So what was the assumption? That "your true, authentic self" has nothing to do with your biology. The pomosexual view represents a profound devaluation of the body.

A *Christianity Today* article featured an interview with a female United Methodist minister who underwent a sex change operation and now presents as a man. Her explanation was, "My body didn't match what I am."[32] What was her assumption? That her body was not *part* of "what I am." She treated her authentic self as completely disconnected from her physical identity.

The body has become a morally neutral piece of matter that can be manipulated for whatever purposes the self may impose on it—like pressing a mold into clay or stamping Lincoln's profile on a copper penny.

But if gender has nothing to do with biology, then what *is* it based on? No one knows. In a book titled *Omnigender*, former evangelical Virginia Mollenkott says all sexual identities are now up for grabs. A review of the book in a theology journal concluded (and this was written in all seriousness), "Arguments against women's ordination need wholesale revamping since we do not know for sure now what a woman is."

People today do not know for sure what a woman or a man is.

Christians ought to weep for people so confused about their identity—people who have absorbed a Darwinian view of nature as having no purpose or moral significance; who think their body is just a piece of matter that gives no clues about who they are as persons; who think their identity as male or female has no special dignity or meaning; who view their body negatively as a limitation on their authentic identity. By contrast, how can we present the biblical view as anything but radically positive and affirming? Christianity gives the basis for a high and humane view of the person as an integrated whole.

A defense of the body requires that we challenge the Darwinian conception of nature as purposeless and directionless. Ironically, the sheer existence of sexual dimorphism cannot be explained by any current Darwinian theories. Why did sex evolve in the first place? It is far more efficient for an organism to reproduce asexually, simply by dividing and making a copy of itself.

How did an asexual reproductive system evolve into a sexual one? What were the intervening stages? There is no universally accepted theory among scientists based on the empirical evidence. And conceptually it is difficult even to conceive any gradual step-by-step process that would lead by viable stages from asexual to sexual reproduction. Until the new structures are fully developed, they would not function and the organism would die out. John Maddox, editor of the prestigious journal *Nature*, writes, "The overriding question is when (and then how) sexual reproduction itself evolved. Despite decades of speculation, we do not know."[33] In his 2001 book *The Cooperative Gene*, Mark Ridley wrote that for evolutionary biologists, "Sex is a puzzle that has not yet been solved; no one knows why it exists."[34] It is far more plausible that sexual reproduction is a product of intelligent design—that natural processes were guided by a goal or purpose.

A teleological view of nature gives a basis for accepting the goodness of nature and affirming the value and dignity of the created order. Sexual dimorphism is not a negative limitation imposed by nature. Nor is it an oppressive move by the dominant culture. It is a positive, healthy form of interdependence that speaks of our creation as social beings designed for loving, mutual interdependence in marriage, families, and communities.

■ ■ ■ ■ ■

Evolution and Gender

Surprisingly, postmodernism is itself a product of evolutionary thinking—not biological evolution but cultural evolution. Its roots are in the thinking of Georg Wilhelm Friedrich Hegel, a nineteenth-century philosopher who taught a form of pantheistic evolution. He essentially applied Descartes's image of the ghost in the machine to the universe itself: God was redefined as the ghost in the machine of the universe, a spiritual force evolving in and through the world. In Hegel's theory, every individual consciousness is part of this cosmic consciousness. The implication is that the mental realm is constantly evolving. All ideas—law, morality, religion, art, philosophy, politics—are products of what Hegel called the "actualization of the Universal Mind"[35] through the evolution of consciousness.

The implication is that there is no eternal, universal truth. There are only partial, relative truths as each culture develops its own perspective over the course of history. This is called evolutionism or historicism, and Nietzsche sums it up neatly: "Everything evolved: there are no eternal facts as there are no absolute truths."[36]

Nearly a century before Darwin, then, Hegel was already teaching people to interpret history through an evolutionary lens. (Nietzsche even said, "without Hegel, there would have been no Darwin.")[37] Hegel's followers dropped his pantheism and secularized his philosophy. But they retained his evolutionism or historicism.[38] (They did not seem to notice that it contains a fatal self-contradiction: It says there are no universal truths—which is itself a claim to universal truth.)

What impact has evolutionism or historicism had on sexual ideology? It implies that everything is in flux; there are no firm guideposts telling us who we are or how we should act. You see, the very possibility of morality is based on the conviction that there is a human nature, created by God, and therefore there are enduring norms telling us how to fulfill our nature, how to be fully human. But if evolution is true, then there is no stable, universal human nature—and therefore no stable, universal morality.

The existentialist philosopher Jean Paul Sartre spells out the logic starkly: "There is no human nature because there is no God to have a conception of it. . . . Man is nothing else but that which he makes of himself."[39] Just as species are constantly changing and evolving, so individuals must leave behind all stable standards of behavior and immerse themselves in the ceaseless flux of life, constantly creating and re-creating themselves.

In short, the self is fluid. There is no blueprint for what it means to be human. Morality is constantly evolving through history.

This background explains why postmodern gender theorists like Foucault and Butler vigorously deny that any moral ideal (say, man-woman marriage) is rooted in human nature—because they deny there *is* any such thing as human nature. If you claim that any moral principle is congruent with nature, you are committing what they call the fallacy of "naturalizing." It is a fallacy because, in their view, *no* morality is natural. All morality is a historical construct, a product of a particular culture at a particular period of history. Postmodern theorists say their goal is to "de-naturalize" gender, which means to deny that it has any grounding in nature.

Postmodernism thus takes modernism to its next logical step. Modernism denies any purpose or teleology in nature. And if nature reveals no purpose, then it cannot inform our morality. Morality is de-naturalized.

Two forms of reductionism

POSTMODERNISM
Gender Is a Product of Social Forces

MODERNISM
Sexuality Is a Product of Material Forces

Both are forms of reductionism: Modernism reduces the human body to a product of blind, purposeless *material* forces. Postmodernism responds by reducing gender to a product of *social* forces.

Mix-and-Match Sexual Identity

Why do postmodernists want to de-naturalize gender? Because once we reduce sexual morality to merely a social construction, then we are free to *de*construct it.

And why do postmodernists want the freedom to change sexual morality? Many prominent postmodern gender theorists, including Foucault and Butler, have identified as homosexual.[40] Thus their real "enemy," in Butler's words, is "the naturalization and reification of heterosexist norms."[41] That is, their real enemy is heterosexual morality. She writes of her "dogged effort to 'de-naturalize' gender . . . and to uproot the pervasive assumptions about natural or presumptive heterosexuality." Her goal is to undermine "any and all" moral discourse that would "delegitimate minority gendered and sexual practices."[42]

In other words, she wants to legitimate her *own* minority sexual practices. She is not even trying to do objective research, despite the academic-sounding language in her books.

Reading Butler's works, one cannot help feeling compassion for her dilemma. She gives poignant expression to the difficulties she has faced in being gender nonconforming (she was subject to "strong and scarring condemnation").[43] We must always bear in mind that a real person, suffering real pain, is behind the academic-sounding theory. At the same time, it does not make sense to accept a theory of sexuality that was coined specifically to justify sexual practices that not only violate biblical morality but also demean the body and fragment the person.

Gender Unicorn—Trans Ideology for Kids

These days, even Butler is out of date. An organization called Trans Student Educational Resources has published a cartoon—the Gender Unicorn—that deconstructs sexuality into five separate factors that can all contradict one another: sex assigned at birth, gender identity, gender expression, physical attraction, and emotional attraction. The Gender Unicorn cartoon is clearly designed to appeal to young children, and it is being used in public school districts around the nation to teach students that there is no unified self.

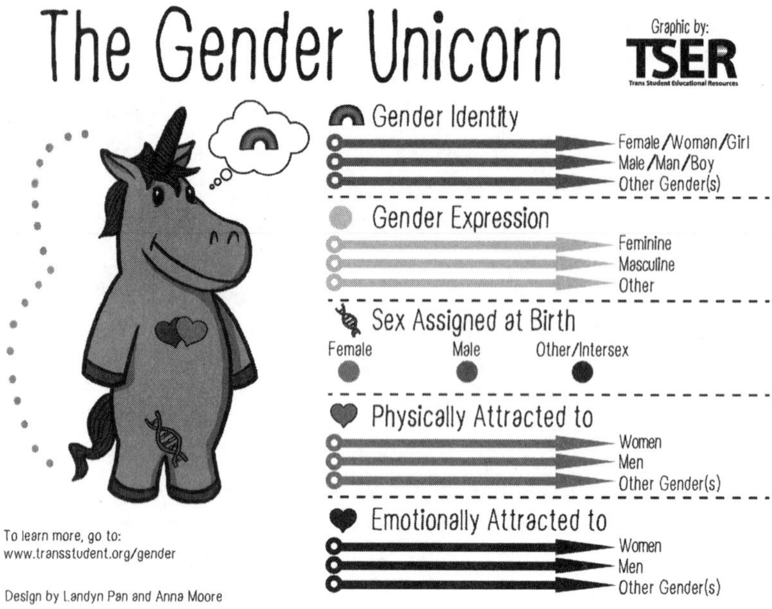

Used with permission of Trans Student Educational Resources

The message is that a human being is composed of disparate bits and pieces. Our biological sex is a relatively minor factor, with no connection to the four other factors that feed into our psychosexual identity. If Butler's view was akin to a child's toy with three blocks that can be twisted in any direction (see chapter 5), today's schools are teaching that the toy has five blocks.

Even feminists are protesting this drastic fragmentation, arguing that it alienates us from our bodies. Philosopher Carol Bigwood writes, "If we reduce the body as a whole to a purely cultural phenomenon and gender to a free-floating artifice, then we are unwittingly perpetuating the deep modern alienation of our human being from nature." Instead we should be seeking to overcome our alienation from nature, she says; we should aim at "*re*naturalizing the body."[44]

Another feminist philosopher, Maxine Sheets-Johnson, likewise protests the "disavowal of biology" in postmodernism. What we really need, she says, is a careful study of "biologically invariant structures. . . . We need to turn *toward* the body," not away from it.[45]

Of course, humans are much more than biological beings. But our biological sex is an unchanging, empirically knowable fact about ourselves, whereas our feelings can change—and often do. Therefore it makes sense to let biological facts inform our gender identity.

The Body Is a Social Construction

How do gender theorists respond? They say it is impossible to base gender on biological facts because we cannot objectively know those facts—or any other facts either. After all, we can make sense of facts only when we interpret them, and all interpretations are conditioned by our culture and history. Every definition of what it means to be biologically male and female is a product of cultural forces, which in turn are products of earlier cultural forces, which in turn . . . and so on, in an infinite regress. This is Hegel's historicism applied to the body.

The postmodern conclusion is that we have no access to what the body really is. We only know what any given culture *thinks* it is. Butler writes, "There is no recourse to a body that has not always already been interpreted by cultural meanings . . . . 'The body' is itself a construction."[46]

The body itself is a social construction? How can we make sense of such extreme reductionism? Recall that postmodernism has its roots in Hegel, who taught a kind of pantheism—that we are all part of a cosmic World Mind. The implication is that as individuals we do not really have original ideas of our own. Instead our thoughts are merely expressions of the cosmic mind. In Hegel's words, individuals "are all the time the unconscious tools of the World Mind at work within them."[47]

Hegel's pantheism was secularized by his successors—the best known being Marx, who famously said he "turned Hegel on his head." By that he meant that in his theory, humans are unconscious tools not of mental forces (a World Mind) but of material forces (economic class). What remained from Hegel in all his successors, however, was the notion that individual consciousness is part of a larger group consciousness—that our thinking is inexorably shaped by the worldview of our class, race, gender, ethnic group, and so forth. We have no access to objective scientific facts. What we think are facts are really cultural constructs—including the biological facts about sex. As Butler writes, "This construct called 'sex' is as culturally constructed as gender."[48]

A trans activist who is biologically female but identifies as a male states the claim even more bluntly: "It is a choice to refer to some bodies as male and some bodies as female, not a fact. . . . It is an ideological position—and not a scientific fact."[49]

Apparently, saying "It's a girl" is just as ideological as saying "Girls wear pink."

Postmodernists claim to liberate us from oppressive rules and roles, but is this view really liberating? Not at all. It says we are trapped within our culture's current worldview—that we have no access to truths outside what we've been taught to think by our culture.[50]

The fatal flaw in such radical skepticism is that it undercuts itself. If all humans are trapped in what their culture tells them, with no access to truth, how can postmodernists know that their *own* claims are true?

Reducing sex to a cultural construction is also hugely demeaning to the body. Lesbian feminist Sheila Jeffreys writes that postmodernism seems to be "based on the mystical principle that there is no such thing as biology."[51] Feminist philosopher Susan Bordo says postmodernism denies "the very materiality of the body." Such extreme hostility to biology should be labeled "antibiologism," she writes. It imagines "the body as malleable plastic, to be shaped to the meanings we choose." It is "a new, postmodern imagination of human freedom from bodily determination."[52]

Postmodernism is thus the latest, and most extreme, version of the body/mind dichotomy—one that treats the body itself as infinitely malleable, with no definite nature of its own.[53]

Why would anyone hold such an extreme view? What's the appeal? If the body cannot be defined, then it places no constraints on our gender identity. The goal is complete freedom to declare oneself a man or a woman or both or neither.

The sovereign self will not tolerate having its options limited by anything it did not choose—not even its own body.

By contrast, Christianity assigns the human body a much richer dignity and value. Humans do not need freedom from the body to discover their true, authentic self. Rather we can celebrate our embodied existence as a good gift from God. Instead of escaping from the body, the goal is to live in harmony with it.

■ ■ ■ ■ ■

No Women, No Rights

The irony is that postmodern gender theory undercuts women's rights. A Christian satire site called *The Babylon Bee* posted a story on International Women's Day in 2017 featuring a protester who realized that, if sex is a social construct, it makes no sense to stand up for women's rights.

> The woman suddenly stopped and thought about how her presence at the protest suggested that the concept of womanhood represented something more significant than an arbitrary social construct foisted upon females. "Wait a minute, think about what we're suggesting here," the woman said to her fellow demonstrators as she lowered her megaphone, according to witnesses. "By participating in this protest, aren't we suggesting that 'man' and 'woman' are ideals that transcend culture and subjectivity?"[54]

The *Bee* was using humor to press home a serious point: To protect women's rights, we must be able to say what a woman is. If postmodernism is correct—that the body itself is a social construct—then it becomes impossible to argue for rights based on the sheer fact of being female. We cannot legally protect a category of people if we cannot identify that category.

The postmodern view of gender is already being legally imposed through SOGI (Sexual Orientation and Gender Identity) laws. Recall that under SOGI laws, people claiming a particular gender identity need to present no evidence, no diagnosis, no medical treatment, and no change in appearance. A person is whatever gender they claim to be.

The implications are already familiar to anyone who reads the news. Male-bodied trans women are claiming the right to women's public spaces such as bathrooms, locker rooms, prisons, homeless shelters, battered women's shelters, hospital rooms, women's conferences, college dorms, elder care facilities, sports leagues, and even rape crisis centers. Most controversial are public schools, where male-bodied trans girls claim access to girls' restrooms, changing rooms, showers, and hotel rooms in overnight travel events.

Trans activists have even protested the use of terms like *man* and *woman* because some males identify as women, and vice versa. Activists have protested the practice of referring to "pregnant women" or "lactating mothers" because trans men who were born female can also get pregnant and lactate. The Midwives Alliance of North America changed their literature to delete the word "mother" and substitute "pregnant individuals" and "birthing persons."[55] A picture book titled *The Adventures of Toni the Tampon* informs young children that men as well as women are capable of menstruating. You are now deemed transphobic if you say "breastfeeding." You must say "chestfeeding" to be inclusive of trans men.

What this means is that we can no longer define women by their biological functions—which in turn means we can no longer legally protect women as a class. If we cannot name sex-based oppression, we cannot fight it.

Mary Lou Singleton of the Women's Liberation Front says, "My entire life work is fighting for the class of people who are oppressed on the basis of their biological sex," including atrocities like forced child marriage, infanticide of baby girls, and female genital mutilation, which occur across the globe. But because of the gender identity movement, Singleton says, it is now deemed transphobic even to label these victims *women* and *girls*.

"What we are seeing is the legal erasure of the material reality of sex," Singleton says.[56] Protections based on sex are being eliminated from the law.

No "Unalienable" Rights

The long-term impact of SOGI laws will be even more destructive, however, erasing legal recognition not only of women but also of the family. Stella Morabito, senior contributor to *The Federalist*, explains: "Once you basically redefine humanity as sexless you end up with a de-humanized society in which there can be no legal 'mother' or 'father' or 'son' or 'daughter' or 'husband' or 'wife' without permission from the State."

The state will then have unprecedented power to micromanage families. "If you abolish sex distinctions in law, you can abolish state recognition of biological family ties, and the state can regulate personal relationships and consolidate power as never before."[57] The state can make decisions regarding how parents educate their children, what medical treatment they use, what discipline they enforce, and so on, far beyond any current regulations.

More fundamentally, the state can decide who counts as a child's parents to begin with. Until now, it was nature (biological relationship) that defined who counts as a parent. The state saw its role as merely recognizing this natural reality. But under SOGI laws there will no longer be a presumption in favor of the child's biological parents.

When gender is de-naturalized, parenthood will also be de-naturalized.

Already federal forms are being changed to reflect the de-naturalized family. In 2011 the Obama administration's State Department announced that it was replacing "mother" and "father" on its passport applications with "Parent One" and "Parent Two."[58] The Free Application for Federal Student Aid (FAFSA), which virtually all college students fill out, uses the same gender-neutral terms.

Until now, the family was seen as natural and pre-political, with natural rights. That means it existed prior to the state, and the state merely *recognized* its rights. But if the law no longer recognizes natural sex, then it no longer recognizes natural families or natural parents, only legal parents. That means parents have no natural rights, only legal rights. You, as a mother or father, have only the rights the state chooses to grant you.

And what the state gives, the state can also take away. Human rights are no longer "unalienable."

There is a reason Aldous Huxley's classic novel *Brave New World* depicts a tyrannical world government that treats *mother* and *father* as obscene words. By making the language of family obscene, the World State ensures that its citizens form their primary loyalty to itself—rendering them easier to manipulate and control.

SOGI—So What?

SOGI laws take a huge step toward that Brave New World. Let's unpack the logic: The only way the law can treat John, a trans woman who is biologically male, the same legally as Jennifer, who is biologically female, is to deny the relevance of biology and declare gender to be a state of mind—thoughts, feelings, and desires. By sheer logic, SOGI laws *must* deny the importance of biology.

Consider the definition of gender offered by the Human Rights Campaign, a gay activist group: Gender is "one's innermost concept of self as male, female, a blend of both or neither—how individuals perceive themselves and *what they call themselves*."[59] Gender is what we call ourselves, a label we choose. We do not discover our gender identity, as though it were an objective fact. Instead we declare our identity. We speak ourselves into existence. Language takes priority over biology. It is whatever word we choose. The flesh has been made word.[60]

These legal changes do not affect only homosexual or transgender people. In the eyes of the law, *no one* has a natural or biological sex now; *all* citizens are defined not by their bodies but by their inner states and feelings. That's what the term *cisgender* means (people whose gender matches their sex). The term was coined to imply that even when your gender aligns with your biological sex, there is no natural connection. Your basic identity as male or female, husband or wife, mother or father, son or daughter, sister or brother no longer follows metaphysically from your biology but must be determined by an act of will.

But *whose* will? Ultimately, it will come down to who has the most power—which means the state. "It does not matter what you or I mean by the word 'gender'," explains Daniel Moody. "The only opinion that counts is that of the state, as the state alone has the power to impose its belief on us. In law, our gender identity is defined without reference to our body, meaning the shift from sex to gender is the shift from body to mind."[61]

By rejecting the biological basis of gender identity, SOGI laws empower the state to define everyone's identity. (We will look more deeply into these problems in chapter 7).

How Does It Hurt Anyone Else?

Every social practice is the expression of fundamental assumptions about what it means to be human. When a society accepts, endorses, and approves the practice, it implicitly commits itself to the accompanying worldview.

And all the more so if those practices are enshrined in law. The law functions as a teacher, educating people on what society considers to be morally acceptable. If America accepts abortion, euthanasia, gender-free marriage, and transgender policies, in the process it will absorb the worldview that justifies those practices—a two-story fragmentation of the human being that denigrates the body and biological bonds such as the family. And the dehumanizing consequences will reach into every aspect of our communal life.

People often ask: How does legalizing same-sex marriage hurt anyone else? The answer is that as people accept SOGI laws, in the process they will absorb the accompanying worldview—the de-naturalized definition of human personhood as a purely social construction. Human rights are based on a concept of human nature—on the recognition that there are certain nonnegotiable givens in human nature, prior to the state, which the state is obligated to respect. But if, as postmodernism claims, human nature itself is merely a social construction, something we make up as we go along, then there is nothing in the individual that is a given—and therefore there is no basis for unalienable human rights. Natural rights are reduced to legal rights, which the state can change at will.

Tragically, transgender persons will suffer just as much as the rest of us from the reduction of human rights to merely legal rights. What appears to be helping transgender people will ultimately harm them.

Terry Eagleton, a Marxist literary theorist turned Catholic, argues that you cannot have rights apart from belief in a universal human nature. "It was by virtue of our shared human nature that we have ethical and political claims upon one another." And historically, the source of the concept of equal rights was Christianity. As Eagleton notes, "The Enlightenment itself inherited concepts of universal justice and equality from a Judeo-Christian tradition, which [ironically] it frequently derided."[62]

If that Judeo-Christian tradition continues to be derided, what will be the basis for human rights?

When former pope John Paul II was a young man struggling against Marxism, he concluded that the most damaging aspect of communism (and of all atheistic ideologies) is a low view of human life. "The evil of our times" consists in a denigration of human dignity, he wrote. "This evil is even much more of the metaphysical than of the moral order."[63] To use biblical terms, there is more than one way to be lost. The Bible speaks of people being *morally* lost without Christ. But it is also true that people are *metaphysically* lost when they live according to nonbiblical worldviews.

When talking with secular people, Christians must engage with their worldview, confident that we have the power to "demolish strongholds." And what are those strongholds? They are "arguments" and "opinions" that oppose "the knowledge of God" (2 Cor. 10:4–5 ESV). Christians need to help people see that the secular view of human nature does not fit who people are. It does not match the real world. As a result, it is inevitably destructive, both personally and politically.

Christians must also show compassion to those who are pressured by a pomosexual society to despise their own bodies and reject their biological identity. Loving God means loving those who bear his image in the world, helping to liberate people who are trapped by destructive and dehumanizing ideas. Paul wrote, "Christ's love compels us," (5:14) and the same motivation should drive today's Christians as well.

■ ■ ■ ■ ■

God Should Have Made Me a Girl

What happened to Brandon, the boy we met at the start of this chapter? Young people are under heavy pressure to question their gender identity, and it's likely that today any child suffering Brandon's sense of alienation would be encouraged to identify as transgender. Instead his parents worked with him extensively to help him accept himself as a boy—just one who is unusually sensitive and emotional.

His parents urged him to take his identity from his body. Physically, anatomically, physiologically, genetically, and chromosomally, Brandon is male. Our bodies are created by God and are intended to give us clues to our gender identity.

Brandon's parents took him through personality tests like the Myers-Briggs type indicator to show him that it is perfectly acceptable for a man to be gentle and emotional. It may mean God has gifted him for one of the caring professions, such as psychologist, counselor, or healthcare worker.

Likewise, it is acceptable for a woman to be take-charge, rational, and assertive. Brandon's parents told him again and again, "It's not *you* that's wrong, it's the *stereotypes* that are wrong."

They pondered biblical examples like Esau and Jacob. Consider the contrast: Esau—the outdoorsman, the hunter, rough and hairy, the favorite of his father. Jacob—the quiet, gentle one who preferred the indoors ("content to stay at home among the tents" [Gen. 25:27]) and close to his mother. Yet Scripture never presents Jacob as any less masculine for having those traits. On the contrary, God honored him by making him a patriarch of the Hebrew nation, bestowing on him the name of Israel.

In the New Testament, the gifts of the Spirit are not divided by gender. Prophecy and teaching are not masculine. Mercy and service are not feminine. The Spirit "distributes them to each one, just as he determines" (1 Cor. 12:11).[64]

The greatest man who ever lived, Jesus Christ, described himself as "gentle and humble in heart" (Matt. 11:29).

Close friends of Brandon's family helped bring the lessons to life. One couple had spent years in frustrating marriage counseling. In the books they read and the videos they watched, the husband consistently fit the stereotypically feminine qualities, while the woman fit the stereotypically masculine qualities. After throwing books across the room, this couple literally saved their marriage when they found a counselor who used the Myers-Briggs typology. The counselor helped them to see that the entire range of human personality traits is open to both sexes—that it is okay to be different from prevailing social norms.[65] In this couple, Brandon witnessed firsthand a man who was intuitive and relational like himself, without threatening his male identity.

Princesses and Turtles

Brandon's parents also walked him through history to show that many stereotypes are arbitrary, based on historically changing social roles. (They used chapter 12 in my book *Total Truth.*)[66] In pre-industrial societies, most work was done on the family farm or in home industries, where husband and wife worked side by side. Work was not the father's job; it was the family industry. As a result, women were involved in economically productive labor, while men were far more involved in raising and educating children than most are today.

What changed all this was the Industrial Revolution. It took work out of the home—and that seemingly simple change dramatically altered gender roles. Fathers had to follow their work out of the home into offices and factories, which meant they were no longer intimately involved with their families. Women no longer had access to income-producing work that could be performed at home while raising children. The result was greatly constricted roles for both men and women—which in turn led to narrower definitions of masculinity and femininity.

Many young people today who question gender roles are chafing against the remnants of these narrow nineteenth-century stereotypes. Brandon's parents reassured him that he did not need to feel pressured to live up to whatever social roles happen to be in vogue in any particular period of history—including our own.

Every period of history has its own ways of defining gender differences. When I was a kid, my brothers and I rode the same generic tricycle. Today girls' tricycles are pink with Disney Princess stickers while boys' are green with Mutant Ninja Turtle stickers. Children can be pressed into suffocatingly narrow gender definitions. Mason, one of my students who has struggled with being gender atypical, commented, "The irony is that it is precisely those rigid stereotypes that drive gender nonconforming young people into the arms of the transgender or gay communities" in their search for a sense of belonging and acceptance.

Unfortunately, churches today often send young people contradictory messages. As Mark Yarhouse notes in *Understanding Gender Dysphoria*, on one hand, there are churches that seek so hard to be inclusive and compassionate that they mirror secular views that deconstruct sex and gender. On the other hand, there are churches that "overcorrect" by becoming stricter, narrower, and more rigid in enforcing sex roles.[67] We must take care not to add to Scripture by baptizing gender expectations that are in reality historically contingent and arbitrary.[68]

Christians should be on the forefront of creative thinking to recover richer definitions of what it means to be a man or a woman. The church should be the first place where young people can find freedom from unbiblical stereotypes—the freedom to work out what it means to be created in God's image as wholistic and redeemed people.

Because I knew Brandon personally, I witnessed firsthand the anguish and isolation he suffered because of his gender dysphoria. For many years I was one of a few people who had the opportunity to stand by him, weep with him, ache for him, and pray for him. As Yarhouse writes, "If you want a person [suffering from gender incongruence] to choose a path that seems more redemptive, you will want to be part of a redemptive community that facilitates that kind of decision making."[69] Even if it takes several years.

Battling the Binary

When talking about gender these days, one of the first questions you're likely to hear is, "What about intersex?" A very small percentage of people are born with genitals that are ambiguous or not fully formed due to genetic and hormonal abnormalities. As a result, doctors may not be sure what the newborn's sex is. (These people were formerly called hermaphrodites.) The standard treatment was to "assign" a sex and administer hormones and plastic surgery to bring the child in line with gender expectations.

In culture war rhetoric, the existence of intersex persons is being used to disrupt the male/female binary. They are often included under the umbrella of transgender to bolster the claim that there is not only male and female but also a range in between.

But that claim is self-contradictory. Intersex is a biological condition, while transgender activists insist that biology is irrelevant to gender identity.

Moreover, intersex people are not clamoring to eliminate the gender binary. According to the Intersex Society of North America, "Intersex people are perfectly comfortable adopting either a male or female gender identity and are not seeking a genderless society or to label themselves as a member of a third gender class."[70]

If you've wondered where the trans narrative got the phrase "assigned sex at birth," it is borrowed from the treatment of intersex babies. The term "assigned" may be useful in the tiny percentage of cases where a newborn's genitals are genuinely ambiguous. But it makes no sense to apply it to transgender people who were clearly biologically male or female at birth. Transgender individuals have typical sex markers (e.g., genetics, gonads, genitals) that all align with each other.[71]

The more precise medical terminology for intersex is a "disorder of sex development" (DSD) and Christians typically explain it, like other disorders, as a result of the fall. In a fallen world, we are all born with deficiencies and malfunctions in various parts of our minds and bodies—a weak heart, a proneness to depression, a tendency to high blood pressure. The world is out of joint. So it is not surprising that the effects of the fall sometimes also occur in the reproductive system.

To say that a condition is a result of the fall does not mean it is anyone's fault. As Jesus said of the man born blind, it is not a direct punishment for individual sin (see chapter 5). A great deal of human suffering is due to creation "groaning" in its "bondage to decay" (Rom. 8:22, 21). Christians are called to welcome and support intersex people and others who suffer from the brokenness of creation.

Yet even some Christians are using the existence of intersex persons to disrupt the male/female binary. Theologian Megan DeFranza argues that intersex conditions are not the effect of the fall but are part of God's original good creation. In her view, God did not create only male and female but also an entire spectrum of genetic variations in between. To insist on the male/female binary is "oppressive."[72]

It is true that a wide range of potential genetic variability was built into the original creation, leading over history to different breeds of dogs, varieties of roses, and races of humans. But there are also conditions that result from mutations, copying errors, and other breakdowns in the genetic code. It is reasonable to conclude that intersex conditions are an instance of breakdowns because most of them appear to be unhealthy.

Even DeFranza, in a book on the subject, consistently describes intersex using terms like "deficiency," "malfunction," "inability," and "lack." For example, Androgen Insensitivity Syndrome (AIS) results when individuals "are *unable* to process male hormones (androgens)" because "their cells *lack* the proper receptors." Or again, Congenital Adrenal Hyperplasia (CAH) is an "enzyme *deficiency* condition, causing a *malfunction* of the fetus's adrenal gland, which results in the *overproduction* of fetal androgen." It "represents a real medical emergency in the newborn period. CAH can cause severe dehydration leading to death within the first weeks of the infant's life."[73]

The language necessary to describe most intersex conditions suggests that they are instances of brokenness resulting from the fall.

Interest in Intersex

In recent years, intersex persons have gained media attention because they are starting to demand the right to claim their sexual identity for themselves. When doctors "assign" a sex, in rare cases, it later becomes clear that they made the wrong decision.

Take Jim Bruce.[74] Though he was born with XY male chromosomes, his genitals were not fully differentiated. Shortly after his birth in 1976, Jim's external organ and testes were surgically removed and he was raised as a girl. But Jim struggled for years, preferring "rough and tumble" play and being attracted to girls. "I knew that I wasn't a girl," he told a reporter. At puberty, he was given female hormones. Finally, when he was nineteen years old and battling depression, he tracked down his medical records and was horrified: "I was sterilized at birth—and no one ever told me."

After discovering the truth, Jim had his breasts surgically removed, took testosterone shots, and began living as a man.

Lianne Simon[75] is a Christian intersex woman with an XY/XO cell line (some of her cells are XY, while others have only one X, a condition known as Mixed Gonadal Dysgenesis). Raised as a boy, she writes, "Nobody told me I was intersex when I was a child. I'm not even sure how much my parents knew. Back then, physicians often kept such things a secret."

Yet Lianne was petite (at age nine she was the size of a six-year-old). She also suffered from micrognathia (an undersized jaw), which gave her a pixie face. She felt like a girl and was rejected by boys for her feminine mannerisms. Her body never went through puberty, and she suffered intense shame for not being the boy her parents wanted her to be. The university she attended threatened to revoke her scholarship unless she entered counseling for her obvious gender issues.

It was only after Lianne became an adult that she finally had a chromosome analysis performed. At age twenty-one, she decided to resolve her sexual ambiguity in the direction of being a woman, using hormones and surgery, and today she is married.

Intersex people like Bruce and Lianne have a genuine biological condition—and it has caused them intense suffering. When they were newborns, doctors and parents made a decision whether to raise the child as a boy or a girl, and tragically, they were mistaken. As a result, there is a push today to let the child mature for a longer period before performing surgery in order to make a more accurate assessment.[76]

People with genetic and physical anomalies should be accepted, nurtured, and protected, not used as political footballs by those who want to deconstruct the male/female binary. As Lianne told me, "How do you think it feels being a pawn in someone else's game? It hurts to be shoved into the LGBT camp by either side."[77]

Out of Alignment

In contrast to intersex people, transgender people have normal sex chromosomes and anatomy. Yet the psychological suffering caused by gender dysphoria is also real. A disjunction between one's body and one's sense of gender is, like all discordances, an effect of the fall. As Allberry writes, "Sin causes profound alienation—first and foremost from God. . . . And we're alienated from ourselves. What was meant to be whole and integrated—our mind, body, and spirit—is now deeply fractured. We don't feel aligned in ourselves."[78]

Today ever-younger children suffer a sense of being out of alignment, and Christians need to develop a pastoral approach that is sensitive and compassionate. Feelings of being the "wrong" gender are not something children choose. Some children, like Brandon, may simply be outliers in terms of gender nonconforming personality traits. In other cases, the feelings may have complex psychological roots.

"When my son was younger, he liked to dress in girl's clothes," Caroline told me. "He loved skirts you could twirl around it, and all sorts of frilly, lacey, sparkly things." When her husband saw the boy wearing girl's clothing, he was furious. "I was concerned too, especially these days when everyone jumps to the conclusion that your kid might be gay or transgender," Caroline confided. "But I also knew that my son identified more closely with me than with his father, who did not connect with him very well. I figured if I let him express that without shaming him, he was more likely to outgrow it at some point. And he did."

Roughly 80 to 90 percent of children who experience some gender incongruence lose those feelings before adulthood.[79] Children who eventually accept their sexual identity are called "desisters."

The BBC film *Transgender Kids* features a desister named Alex. As a two-year-old, she told her parents she was a boy. When they refused to treat her as a boy, she would explode in angry outbursts. "She would literally scream, 'I'm a boy! I'm a boy!'" while clenching her fists and punching herself in the genitals, her father recalls. Raising Alex "was like a battle, like a war zone." Fortunately, the family found a clinic that encouraged Alex to be less rigid in her concept of gender—to consider that "there are a lot of ways to be a girl." You can be a girl who plays with Barbie dolls, or you can be a girl who plays soccer. Both are equally acceptable.

At age eight, Alex joined a baseball team, where for the first time she met girls like herself. "I saw these other girls who were maybe *more* tomboy. They liked to do sporty things, and I never really had come across that before," Alex recalls. Though it took four more years to make a complete turn-around, that was the moment "when I started to accept myself for who I was . . . a girl that also had boy interests."[80]

Unfortunately, trans activists deny the existence of desisters, calling it a myth. In 2015, they even succeeded in closing the clinic where Alex received counseling. Trans-affirming therapists insist that even exploring "why" a person has gender dysphoria, instead of immediately accepting it as the person's authentic self, is offensive, bigoted, and transphobic.[81]

Why is it considered acceptable to carve up a person's body to match their inner sense of self but bigoted to help them change their sense of self to match their body? Feelings can change. But the body is an observable fact that does not change. It makes sense to treat it as a reliable marker of gender identity.

Putting People in Sexual Boxes

Studies find that the strongest correlate of both same-sex orientation and transgenderism—far stronger than any genetic link—is childhood gender nonconformity, kids who behave in ways that are stereotypical of the other sex.[82] A male friend who struggled for years with same-sex attraction told me, "When I was young, I liked poetry and music. My father was baffled and kept trying to 'toughen me up' by pushing me into sports and other more traditional boy activities."

In a similar vein, Christopher Yuan explores the possible roots of his homoerotic feelings: "All through grade school and into college, I was never fully accepted. I was sensitive, nerdy, and horrible at sports, and I loved music and the arts."[83]

These nonconforming children grow up feeling out of step with prevailing standards of masculinity or femininity.[84] They need support and empathy as they work through their painful feelings of alienation. Churches should encourage them to value their unique temperament and to resist pressure to interpret it as evidence they must be transgender or homosexual.

After I converted to Christianity, I attended a Bible school where a fellow student was a Girl Scout leader. Her deepest friendships were with other Scout leaders like herself—women who were outdoorsy, athletic, independent, and definitely *not* frilly or feminine. My friend felt alienated by the church's ideal of Christian womanhood. She and three other Scout leaders, all Christians, eventually embraced lesbianism.

Yet weren't these Girl Scout leaders possibly mistaking temperament for sexuality? A student of mine named Liam, who has struggled with cross-gender feelings, said, "American society is in danger of sexualizing what are really just character traits—putting people in a sexual box based on non-sexual traits and behavior."

In the body of Christ, we should celebrate a wide diversity of God-given personality types, even if they do not fit the current stereotypes. The eye is not the ear, and the hand is not the foot (see 1 Cor. 12:12–27). That diversity is a *good* thing. Each member of the body has its own unique gifts and makes its own distinctive contribution.

■ ■ ■ ■ ■

Welcoming the Stranger

The body of Christ must also become a place where casualties from the sexual revolution can find hope and restoration. The political pressure on the medical community today is to fast-track kids with gender dysphoria into transitioning. Cari is a twenty-two-year-old woman who, as a teenager, transitioned to male through hormones and a double mastectomy. A few years later, she detransitioned. Cari recalls that as soon as she had questions about her gender, she was pushed to start hormones and surgery. "If I was trans (and my therapist never gave me the impression that I might not be), my options were 'transition now, transition later, or live your life unhappy/commit suicide.'"[85]

The BBC film *Transgender Kids* features a young woman identified as Lou who likewise had a double mastectomy and later regretted it. At the gender clinic, she says, "The assumption from the outset was that if I said I was transgender, then I must be. Nobody at any point questioned my motives. . . . [I] was very much told by the community that if you don't transition, you will self-harm and you will kill yourself. I became convinced that my options were transition or die."[86]

Under the pressure of trans ideology, fewer therapists are stopping to talk to these vulnerable teens to find out what's really going on. Is *this* loving?

Walt Heyer is a former transsexual who started as a cross-dresser, then underwent sex reassignment surgery to live as a woman. After eight years, he became a Christian and eventually transitioned back to living as a man. He discovered that changing his clothing, hairstyle, Social Security card, driver's license, and even his genitals did not change who he was. In his words, he came to realize that "the restoration of my sanity would only come by reversing the gender change and going back to living as the male God had made me to be."[87] In short, by accepting his biological identity as a good gift from God.

"I was born a man, and I was still a man; my gender never changed," Heyer concludes, in spite of numerous cosmetic surgeries, hormones, makeup, long hair, nail polish, pantyhose, and high heels. "The biological fact is that no one can change from one gender to another except in appearance." Our only choice is whether we accept our biological sex as a gift from God or reject it. (The very fact that crafting a transsexual identity requires such extensive body modifications—hormonal treatment, facial feminization surgery, electrolysis to remove body hair, voice and posture training, hair transplants, top surgery, bottom surgery—tends to undermine the claim that it is natural and biologically determined.)

When Heyer was still presenting as a woman, he began attending church. Tragically, the first church he visited asked him to leave. The senior pastor actually drove to his home, knocked on the door, and said, "We don't want your kind in our church."[88] By God's grace, Walt found another congregation that accepted him and supported him through several painful, tumultuous years of emotional and spiritual healing as he went through the difficult process of detransitioning.

Is your church ready to show love and acceptance to those whose lives have been deeply damaged by postmodern sexual theories?

Many people who experience gender dysphoria or same-sex attraction have had negative encounters in the church. They have been made to feel that they pose a danger to other people in the congregation, and that they must solve their sexual issues before showing up at church. Evangelicals preach that only Christ can save us but then contradict their own words by expecting people to clean up their behavior before they are welcome in the pews. For Christians to be credible in asking others to repent, they must model repentance for their own failings that have pushed people away from the church.

Then they need to commit to giving support—even long-term support, and even to people who may never be completely changed this side of heaven. A dear friend of mine, Stephen, was a child molester. He has repented and has been in therapy and twelve-step programs for decades. He now mentors other sex offenders. I have deep respect for his spiritual maturity. He has worked through levels of spiritual and psychological healing that most Christians have no idea even exist. For years, Stephen hoped that God would heal him to the point where he could marry and have a family. But that has not happened, and he has come to realize that he may never be completely healed in this life—that his vocation may be in helping others, while never experiencing the joys of a normal family life himself. Is the church ready to stand by people like Stephen, knowing his background but also his fierce commitment to the Lord? (Applying realistic safeguards, of course. Stephen himself refuses any position working with youth or children.)

There is a wise saying that the church is not a museum for saints but a hospital for sinners. To attract potential "patients," however, it must be clear that the church is a place of care and healing.[89]

Churches must also recognize that people with gender issues are not just needy people with problems. Many have gone through intense emotional and psychological healing and have much to offer in ministry to others. As we saw in chapter 3, suffering can be an opportunity for what therapists call post-traumatic growth. Tim Otto, who is celibate, writes, "Being gay helped me by forcing me to ask deeper questions of the world that I might have otherwise, and caused me to listen carefully to Jesus because I knew I needed help."[90] A study of Christians who identify as transgender concludes, "As with most confusing and painful life experiences, gender-identity questions and concerns raise larger questions of meaning and purpose in life that can draw a person toward the sacred."[91]

Up to this point, we have discussed sex and gender primarily as they relate to the individual and personal behavior. But secular theories also affect our relationships—especially now that SOGI laws are being passed that affect marriage, parenthood, and family. This takes us into social theory, and in the next chapter we will discover that the two-level dualism is destructive not only to individuals but also to relationships. It is a major reason our relationships have grown so fragile, leaving many people today lonely and isolated.

7

The Goddess of Choice Is Dead

From Social Contract to Social Meltdown

When seminary student Philip Holck got married, his wedding ceremony included two sets of vows: the first with his bride, the second with her five-year-old son. Kneeling to face the boy, he said, "I, Philip, take you, Matthew, to be my son, to join with you, to share my life with you, to play with you, to teach and love you until death parts us."[1]

It is a touching story, but theologian Ted Peters twists it to support a new and dangerous view of the family. He argues that every parent should be required to make an explicit, articulated legal contract with each of their children—preferably with a public ceremony akin to a wedding.

The foundation of the family, he says, must shift from biology to contract.

Until recently, the standard in law and in the public mind was the biological family. Of course, there are couples who generously reach out to adopt children who are not biologically related to them. But the reason adoption works is that parents take the natural family as the norm. They strive to treat their adopted children *as if* they were biological offspring. Adoption does not deny the value of biological bonds but presupposes it.

Peters wants to turn that around. He wants to require even biological parents to make a legal contract with each child. Biological ties would no longer be the norm. Parents would treat their biological children *as if* they were adopted. The basis of the family would be transformed from biology to choice.[2]

Peters teaches at a Lutheran theological seminary, yet surprisingly he says we must jettison Christian morality as "outmoded" and "prescientific." In fact, he says we must reject "any premodern formalism based on divine dicta or traditional authority or natural law that would try to make an end run around choice."

Even "divine dicta"—God's laws? Yes. Peters writes, "Whether we like it or not, the end of the road for a disintegrating liberal society is individual choice. There is no escape." He adds sternly that it does no good to "whimper about individual choice and decry the pursuit of self-fulfillment. These are simply the cultural givens of our epoch."[3]

As we have seen in earlier chapters, the elevation of choice over biology has indeed become "the cultural givens" in regard to life and sexuality—both for secularists and for Christians who take their lead from secular thinking. In those chapters, we focused on how the two-tiered body/person dualism affects the individual. Now we turn to how the same dualism damages relationships, especially how it disparages the biological ties within the family. Peters is joined by many other prominent thinkers advocating that the basis of the family should be shifted from biology to contract. Where did that idea come from? Is it really a good idea to elevate choice to the defining feature of family relationships?

Raising the question of relationships takes us into social theory. In this chapter, we uncover the social and political philosophy that shapes many people's thinking, even if they are not consciously aware of it—both in the West and wherever Western ideas are disseminated around the globe. It is a theory that downplays natural communities like the family in favor of communities built on choice or contract. As a result, it represents yet another expression of Western society's devaluation of the body and biological bonds—with disastrous consequences.

A Totalitarian's Dream

It seems pretty obvious that if the foundation of the family were transferred to choice, children would be cut adrift, without any moral claim on their own parents. The implication is that parents are not responsible in any special way for their own children unless they choose to be. Does anyone really believe parents would be *more* committed to their children if they thought they had no natural obligation to them?

The ideology of choice also has ominous political implications. For if children must be chosen, if they do not belong to their biological parents as gifts from God, to whom *do* they belong? Answer: the state. If you read scholars like Peters carefully, you consistently find statism lurking as an underlying assumption. In one passage, Peters writes, "Society places its children in the care of rearing parents as a trust."[4]

Stop right there: *Society* gives us children? Society gives us *its* children? This view reduces both parents and children to atomistic dependents on the state.

Statism has been a recurring theme in treatments of the family since the dawn of Western culture. To an astonishing degree, Western political and social thought has been hostile to the role of the family in proposed visions of the ideal society. Secular intellectuals from Plato to Rousseau to B. F. Skinner to Hillary Clinton have been enamored with the idea of putting the child directly under the care of the state. The totalitarian regimes of the twentieth century—erected by Hitler, Mussolini, Stalin, and Mao—all sought tight state control of education, down to the earliest years, to inculcate unquestioning acceptance of the regime's ideology.

History shows clearly that when biological bonds are downplayed in favor of choice, individuals end up forfeiting choice to the state. Demanding freedom from natural relationships means losing freedom to the state.

The Abolition of Marriage

Despite the testimony of history, leading thinkers today continue to call for demolishing family bonds in favor of contracts. The internationally renowned feminist legal theorist Martha Albertson Fineman, in her book *The Autonomy Myth*, calls for "the abolition of marriage as a legal category" to be replaced by contracts. Fineman wants to replace the words *husband* and *wife* with the gender-free term "sexual affiliate" and to replace *families* with state-subsidized "caretaker-dependent relationships."[5]

In a similar vein, influential British sociologist Anthony Giddens says marriage and family should require separate contracts, with each individual parent signing a contract with each individual child.[6]

What exactly is a contract? It is a limited exchange of goods and services. Its defining feature is that in a contract, *we* define the relationship, *we* choose the terms, *we* choose the conditions under which we stay or leave, and so on. The terms and conditions are not preset by God or moral law or human nature. If the agreement no longer yields the desired benefits, it can be terminated. A contract is a deal we strike with others, which we can make or break at will.[7]

That idea resonates today because, in practical life, many of our relationships *are* contracts: our mortgages, leases, and cell phone plans. In a contract, we say, I will give you something (money) and in return you will give me a service or product. If it is defective, I can return it. It is psychologically easy for people to extend the contract model to all relationships. The economic metaphor tends to cannibalize all other relationships.

By contrast, the Bible presents our deepest relationships—with God and with our families—as covenants. In a covenant, we do not agree to perform a service but rather we acquire a status: as child of God, as husband or wife, as mother or father. We do not agree to provide a product; we pledge our very selves, for better or for worse. A covenant is not limited in duration; it is forever. And we do not set our own terms: They are already defined. We accept an array of obligations and responsibilities that are prior to our choice, defined by God, expressed in the moral law, and based on human nature as God created it.

This whole-person commitment is what we lose when we redefine all relationships as contracts. Our relationships become thin, fragile, self-interested, and easily broken.

■ ■ ■ ■ ■

Beginning with Atom

Why, then, do so many leading thinkers today urge us to redefine all relationships as contracts? Where did the idea come from that society should treat individuals as independent agents establishing contracts based on choice? That idea has a history, and we will respond more effectively if we understand that history.

From time immemorial, the most basic human relationships were regarded as intrinsic to human nature. It is natural for people of the opposite sex to be drawn to one another and raise children together. Despite the richly varied norms and rituals that surround marriage, the nuclear family has formed the core of society. In classic Christian social thought, it was God who established marriage, family, church, and state, and who defined their essential nature—their tasks, responsibilities, and moral norms.

Then, in early modern Europe, the novel idea arose that human relationships were neither natural nor intrinsic to human nature—that humans invented them, and therefore humans could change them. Where did this strange idea come from?

After the scientific revolution, people were so impressed by its astonishing success that many began to apply what they thought was a scientific worldview to every other field of knowledge—including social theory. The apex of the scientific revolution was Newtonian physics, which pictured the material world as atoms bumping around in the void under the forces of attraction and repulsion. The same metaphor was soon applied to the social world as well. Social philosophers constructed what they called a "social physics" modeled on Newtonian physics. Civil society was pictured as so many human "atoms" who come together and "bond" in various social relationships.[8]

This image gave rise to what is called social contract theory, first proposed by Thomas Hobbes, John Locke, and Jean-Jacques Rousseau. It is at the core of classical liberalism, which gave rise to *both* what Americans call liberalism and conservatism. Thus it has impact across the entire political spectrum.[9] Today most Americans absorb social contract theory with the very air they breathe. A Princeton professor says it is the unconscious assumption that students bring into the classroom: "Without ever having read a word of Locke, they could reproduce his notion of the social contract without a doubt in the world."[10]

Since this is the theory that gave rise to the contractual model of civil society, it is crucial to get a handle on what it says—and the way it is undermining marriage and family today.[11]

Mushroom Men

The goal of the social contract theorists—Hobbes, Locke, and Rousseau—was to start over from scratch and rethink civil society from the ground up. They hypothesized what human nature would be like if we strip away the accumulated centuries of morals, laws, customs, traditions, social institutions, and religions (especially religions). If we pare away all the marks of civilization as with a scalpel until we reach bare human nature itself, what is left?

The social contract theorists imagined some time in the misty past, prior to all civilization, when humans supposedly existed in an original, primordial, pre-social condition. This they called the "state of nature." As yet there was no marriage, no family, no church, no state, no civil society. All that existed were disconnected, autonomous individuals, driven purely by self-preservation. These were the "atoms" that pre-exist all social institutions.

In the beginning was the atomistic individual. Hobbes even asks us to "look at men as if they had just emerged from the earth like mushrooms and grown up without any obligation to each other."[12]

And if humans originally pop up like mushrooms, with no natural obligations, where do social relationships come from? Answer: They are created by choice. Like Newton's atoms, individuals come together and bond in various arrangements when they find that doing so advances their interest.

What are the implications of this physics-based metaphor? First, it means relationships are not part of human nature as it existed originally. Instead they are secondary, derivative, created by choice. And if they are created by choice, the implication is that they can be *re-created* by choice. We can redefine them any way we want.

Second, social duties are no longer thought to arise from moral principles such as justice or the common good. Instead they are based on utilitarian grounds—when people decide it is in their interest to contract away some of their rights. Society is merely an aggregate of individuals asserting their desires. The sole source of moral obligations is the individual will.

In this way, social contract theory reduces all relationships to, well, contracts. It has become an acid dissolving all organic or natural bonds that transcend sheer choice. Its basic tenet is that no individual can have an obligation to which they have not consented. This vision is always presented in terms of liberating the individual from the oppression of convention, tradition, class, and the dead hand of the past. That's why Rousseau's most influential work, *The Social Contract*, opens with the famous line, "Man is born free, and everywhere he is in chains." The contract was seen as the only appropriate basis for a free society because it is based on choice and thus preserves the original autonomy enjoyed in the hypothetical state of nature.

A Secular Garden of Eden

When social contract theorists first proposed the concept of a state of nature, it was clearly an alternative to the account of origins in Genesis. Political philosopher John Hallowell calls it a secularized version of "the Christian myth of the Garden of Eden."[13] Standing at the dawn of modernity, these thinkers sensed that in order to propose a new political philosophy, they had to ground it in a new creation account. Instead of recognizing social structures as ordained and defined by God, the new myth treated them as inventions of human will.

Political philosopher George Grant says the social contract theorists were "substituting the state of nature for the createdness of nature as the primal truth." They were "giving up the doctrine of creation."[14]

At first, the contract model was applied primarily to the public realm of politics and economics. As political philosopher Michael Zuckert explains, the claim "that all governments rest on consent is another way of saying that all government is a human artifact."[15] The implication is that the state is not ordained by God or rooted in human nature. It is created by the consent of isolated, autonomous individuals calculating their self-interest.

Today the contract model is bleeding into the private realm. After all, if "we the people" can create our own government through contract, then why can't "we the people" create our own definition of marriage, family, and every other social institution as well?[16] Political philosopher Michael Sandel of Harvard says the prevailing concept of the individual today is the "unencumbered self," by which he means "unencumbered by moral or civic ties they have not chosen."[17]

The same philosophy is being embedded in law. In *Rights Talk*, Catholic law professor Mary Ann Glendon of Harvard says American law is now shaped by social contract theory's depiction of "the 'natural' human person as a solitary creature." It is "based on an image of the rights-bearer as a self-determining, unencumbered individual, a being connected to others only by choice."[18]

Yet as we will see through the rest of this chapter, the contractual view of marriage and family has disastrous consequences. In particular, says Sandel, it has led to the massive abandonment of children. Shocking numbers of fathers desert their families; millions of mothers abort their children. The vast majority of child abuse cases are at the hands of a genetically unrelated male—a stepfather or the mother's boyfriend.[19] And as family bonds grow more fragile, the state takes over more of the family's functions, growing ever more powerful and oppressive.

Contractual thinking has become an acid corroding organic and natural communities.

We Are Not Robinson Crusoe

What makes social contract theory so corrosive? The central problem is that it favors acts of consent over natural or organic bonds. It is therefore yet another expression of Western society's negative view of our embodied existence—its Gnostic devaluation of the body. As Oliver O'Donovan says, liberalism "has followed the path of devaluing natural communities in favour of those created by acts of will."[20]

The social institutions of marriage and family are rooted in nature—in the natural fact that humans are embodied creatures who reproduce sexually; that mothers devote a large part of their mature life to pregnancy, lactation, and child care; that during that period, they need the economic support of the father; that children are helpless and socially needy, taking a long period of time to mature, which means they require a stable, long-term commitment of love and support from both parents. Finally, families are connected to biological networks of grandparents, aunts, and uncles because the nuclear family needs the support of a wider community. These are basic facts of nature. As Hallowell writes, "Individuals do not create society but are born into it. . . . And that fact alone imposes obligations." These obligations do not require our formal consent. They are not "a matter of choice but a matter of fact."[21]

Because these are facts of nature, people's attitude toward the family (not any particular family but the social institution itself) reflects their attitude toward nature. Do they regard nature as inherently good, a source of commitments and obligations that are beneficial and enriching? Or do they treat nature as a set of negative constraints on their independence and autonomy—limits from which they aspire to be liberated?

Social contract theory is based on the autonomous individual, apart from any natural relationships. The atomistic creature running around under the trees appears to be an independent, fully developed adult—say, a twenty-one-year-old male. But this Robinson Crusoe image is not true of anyone. Contrary to Hobbes, we do not pop up overnight like mushrooms after a rain. Each of us begins life as a dependent, helpless baby, born into a pre-existing family, clan, church, town, and nation. We grow into mature adults only because other people, especially our parents, commit to us sacrificially—to love, teach, and care for us.

Contrary to what Rousseau said, we are not "born free." Humans are intrinsically social beings who thrive on interdependence and nurturing. As philosopher Bertrand de Jouvenal noted, social contract theories "are the views of childless men who must have forgotten their childhood."[22] A realistic political theory must begin not with rational adults calculating their interests but with the helpless infant who needs a network of love and care to *become* a rational adult.[23]

Christianity teaches that nature came from the hand of God, and thus natural bonds are good. The commandment to "honor your father and your mother" (Exod. 20:12) points to the truth that societies are based on the foundation of the male/female couple and their children. Of course, humans are more than biological beings. We are also emotional, intellectual, and spiritual beings. And when the family is functioning as it ought, it provides an ideal that reaches beyond the limits of blood and kin. Jesus said, "Whoever does the will of my Father in heaven is my brother and sister and mother" (Matt. 12:50). The metaphor Jesus uses—that Christians are brothers and sisters—assumes a radically positive view of the family. Our experience of familial love is meant to "school" us in the sacrificial love that binds us to one another in the family of God. The bonds of biology train us to extend love *beyond* biology.

That's why we should be concerned that the acids of autonomy are dissolving biologically based bonds. We are losing the "school" that trains us how to function with love and responsibility beyond the family. Consider a few key issues, starting with abortion.

■ ■ ■ ■ ■

The Fetus as Alien Intruder

Many ethicists have developed arguments in favor of abortion claiming that we have no obligations to others unless we consent to them. The mother's body is not treated as naturally oriented toward her child. Instead motherhood is redefined on the model of a social contract—as though the baby in the womb were a trespasser on the mother's private property and required a formal agreement to continue living. One feminist wrote, "I own my body and I decide what I allow to grow in it."[24]

Some arguments go so far as to present the pre-born child as though it were an aggressor that must be stopped from injuring the mother. An article on the leftist *Daily Kos* blog puts it bluntly: "A fetus is a damn parasite and it invades the mother's body like one, too." On a more academic level, political scientist Eileen McDonagh writes that if the fetus "makes a woman pregnant without her consent, it severely violates her bodily integrity and liberty. . . . The fetus's imposition constitutes injuries sufficient to justify the use of deadly force to stop it."[25] Abortion is treated as an act of self-defense against an intruder.

It is not true, however, that we acquire responsibilities toward people only by consenting to them. We also acquire responsibilities to those we are biologically connected to—not only our children but also our parents, brothers, sisters, and grandparents. As philosophers Patrick Lee and Robert George sum up: "To ignore or downplay these bodily connections that generate specific responsibilities—claiming that all duties arise from acts of consent—is another manifestation of a general disregard for the significance of the bodily nature of human persons."[26] That is, it is another manifestation of the two-level body/person dualism. A low view of the body leads to a denigration of biological bonds.

Biological relationships transcend mere rational choice. Consider mother-infant bonding. During pregnancy, the mother's body produces oxytocin, the bonding hormone, which primes her to form a close attachment to her newborn.[27] "I have never been a baby person. I could take them or leave them," my friend Patricia Samuelsen told me. "But when my first child was placed in my arms, there was an explosion of emotion unlike anything I had experienced before."

I had the same experience when I gave birth to my first child. Many new mothers report being completely unprepared for the intensity of the emotional bond that overwhelms them.

Father-infant bonding can be equally intense. Studies find that holding their baby stimulates the release of oxytocin in fathers.[28] A new father wrote that when he held his newborn son for the first time, "it was as if my very brain chemistry itself changed dramatically, as I realized that the glorious creature I held in my arms would now be the most important thing in my life, a sacred responsibility."[29]

His article was titled "Fatherhood Killed the Cynic in Me."

One of my students, Will Roberts, describes a similar experience. As a college student, he got his seventeen-year-old girlfriend pregnant. Because the university was an hour's drive away from home, in his words, "I was not really involved in her pregnancy. I was at college just hanging out and having fun, putting all my time and energy into my classes." But when he accompanied his girlfriend to the hospital for the birth of their baby, he was astonished by the intensity of his emotions: "The moment my son was born, my entire mindset and love changed, and at the point I held him for the first time, it was over. I was head over heels in love with our son! He was a miracle from God and I could not explain my unconditional love for him." The intense experience bound the couple together and they decided to marry.

This depth of connection is not a product of mere rational choice. It is something far deeper. It is rooted in our nature.

Our natural bonds make moral demands on us that inspire us to grow and mature. In the classic movie *The Magnificent Seven*, a gunman played by Charles Bronson tells a group of village boys, "You think I'm brave because I carry a gun. Well, your fathers are much braver because they carry responsibility: for you, your brothers, your sisters, and your mothers. . . . They do it because they love you, and they want to. I have never had this kind of courage."[30]

When we accept the moral responsibilities that stem from our natural bonds, our character deepens. We become brave. We acquire courage.

Lines of Descent

It's true that biological ties represent a limitation on our freedom. We do not choose our parents; we do not choose our siblings; we do not choose to be born within a particular time, place, kinship group, ethnic group, or nationality; we do not choose who our children are. Yet these unchosen bonds form a significant aspect of our identity. We cannot deny them without losing a part of who we are. As Meilander puts it, we are not just "free spirits but embodied creatures. Lines of kinship and descent locate and identify us."[31]

Moreover, we are called to be thankful for these biological bonds: to honor the parents we have not chosen and to love the children we have not chosen, receiving them as gifts from the hand of God. We learn to love by first loving those who are given to us in these lines of kinship. The question is, do we accept that "givenness" or do we reject it?

My husband was adopted from a German orphanage, and when our first son was born, it was the first time he had the opportunity to see someone biologically related to himself, sharing some of his physical traits. It was life-changing for him. Yet it is an experience most of us take for granted. We rarely reflect consciously on how much our identity is shaped by being integrated biologically and genetically into an extended family. My husband is deeply grateful to his adoptive parents. Yet it was an emotionally moving experience when he sensed for the first time a biological connection to another family member.

We are not merely disembodied wills. We are biological creatures who procreate "after our kind." The family provides a rich metaphor for the kingdom of God precisely because it is the primary experience we have of an obligation that transcends mere rational choice and is constitutive of our very nature.

Sex without Strings, Relationship without Rings

In marriage, too, we see the deadly fruit of the atomistic, contractual view of society. To be sure, marriage begins in consent—but it is consent to enter into a covenant, not a contract. In a covenant, we do not merely agree to perform specified services for a limited period of time. Instead we pledge our very selves, "for better or for worse, until death do us part." We promise to sacrificially care for any children that result from the marital union.

To use modern language, marriage is a social institution. The term means that when we enter into marriage, we accept a set of rights and obligations that pre-exist our personal choices. Just as we know what behavior is acceptable in school or at work, so the institution of marriage tells us what kind of behavior is acceptable toward our spouse and children. In this way, when we marry, we submit to external expectations that help us reach our own highest ideals. Public institutions lend strength to our private commitments.

By contrast, a contractual view of marriage turns each person into an independent transacting party seeking his or her own enlightened self-interest—akin to the autonomous individual in the state of nature. Indeed, Rousseau's description of the temporary, impersonal sexual liaisons that supposedly occurred in the state of nature sounds eerily like today's hookup culture: "Males and females united fortuitously," he writes, "and they separated with the same ease."[32] When these disconnected individuals do marry, they treat marriage as a contract for meeting their own needs. (Since the rise of no-fault divorce, marriage is actually *less* than a contract: Under other contracts, at least there are legal penalties for breaking the agreement, whereas in no-fault divorce, the wronged party has no recourse.)

Judge Richard Posner, the most cited legal theorist of all time, spells out in a striking way the implications of the contractual view. The difference between marriage and prostitution is "not fundamental," he writes. In "marriage, the participants can compensate each other for services performed by performing reciprocal services, so they need not bother with pricing each service, keeping books of account, and so forth." Prostitution is simply a case of those same services being traded for ready money.[33]

People may not like this view of marriage, but many have accepted the contractual view that inevitably leads to it.

Some pundits are even starting to express outright hostility toward marriage. An article in the *New Republic* says, "The current model of lifelong, cohabiting monogamous partnership has never been such an outdated ideal. . . .

I would rather retain my single status with a few rewarding lovers to fulfill different needs at different times of my life."[34]

Because marriage is being painted in such negative hues, not surprisingly, fewer people are getting married. In 2016, census data showed that the rate of marriage has been declining steadily since 1960.[35] A study from the National Marriage Project at Rutgers University found that many of today's young adults are deciding that saying "I do" has become too risky—that it's not worth the trade-off involved in giving up their autonomy. "Today's singles mating culture is not oriented to marriage," the study says. "Instead it is best described as a low-commitment culture of 'sex without strings, relationship without rings.'"[36]

Support Science? Support the Family

Yet the data from social science shows incontrovertibly that a non-marriage culture has tragic consequences. Children of unmarried or divorced parents are far more likely to suffer emotional, behavioral, and health problems. They are at higher risk for crime, poverty, depression, suicide, school difficulties, unmarried pregnancy, and drug and alcohol abuse. One study found that the absence of fathers during childhood may even lead to brain defects: "This is the first time research findings have shown that paternal deprivation during development affects the neurobiology of the offspring."[37]

Liberals sometimes argue that children do not really need their own parents, they just need another adult in the home to provide a second paycheck and a second set of hands for caretaking—in which case, children's needs can be met by cohabitation or by remarriage after divorce. But surprisingly, studies find that neither cohabitation nor remarriage offers the same measurable benefits as marriage. One study concludes, "The advantage of marriage appears to exist primarily when the child is the *biological* offspring of both parents." Even the left-leaning research institute Child Trends had to admit, "It is not simply the presence of two parents . . . but the presence of two biological parents that seems to support children's development."[38]

Two Princeton sociologists conclude, "If we were asked to design a system for making sure that children's basic needs were met, we would probably come up with something quite similar to the two-parent ideal."[39] Those who respect science the most should also be the most pro-marriage.

Of course, there are encouraging exceptions. Adoptive parents take on daunting challenges, often overcoming the impact of trauma and neglect in a child's early years. Godly single parents can also accomplish wonders. (People like the renowned brain surgeon Ben Carson, who was raised by a single mother, give eloquent proof of that.) Nevertheless, the statistical trend is undeniable. Rabbi Jonathan Sacks says, "The collapse of marriage has created a new form of poverty, concentrated among single parent families." This trend is creating a divide in American society that is as deep as the historic racial divide, Sacks says, and "the injustice of it all cries to heaven." It will go down in history as a tragic example of the arrogance of thinking "we know better than the ages, and can defy the lessons of biology and history."[40]

In the past, most poverty had economic causes: unemployment and low wages. Today, most poverty has moral causes: family breakdown and nonmarital childbearing. The children of unmarried or divorced parents are more likely to require social services through the educational system, the healthcare system, the mental health system, the welfare system, and the criminal justice system. All these interventions are intrusive and costly. A 2008 study found that divorce and unwed childbearing cost taxpayers $112 billion each year.[41] The nanny state does not come cheap.

The upshot is that as marriage weakens, the state grows more invasive and more expensive. And as the state regulates ever more aspects of family life, citizens lose their freedoms.

Because the costs of marriage breakdown are borne by the entire society, it is reasonable for the entire society to work together to support marriage. On purely rational grounds, marriage is the least restrictive and most economical means for a society to ensure that children are well taken care of. If you care about children, and if you care about freedom, you should work to create a strong marriage culture.

Why Marriage Is "Uniquely Dangerous"

Children are not the only ones who suffer from marriage breakdown. So do adults. Statistically, those who divorce suffer higher rates of alcoholism, illness, depression, mental illness, and suicide. Though that may not be true of every individual case, the statistical trend is clear. A Yale researcher found that the effect of divorce on your health is the equivalent of smoking a pack of cigarettes a day.[42]

In developing nations, most health problems are infectious diseases. But in the First World, health problems tend to be related to behavior. Science is giving dramatic confirmation of the wisdom of the biblical view of marriage.

When asked about marriage, Jesus quoted Genesis. The early chapters of Genesis are crucial, because there we learn what was normative for human nature *before* the entrance of sin into the world. "At the beginning the Creator 'made them male and female,'" Jesus said, then added, "So they are no longer two, but one flesh" (Matt. 19:4, 6).

What does the phrase "one flesh" mean? Obviously, flesh does not mean simply *body*, because spouses do not literally become one body. Yet they do become a biological unit. The reason cultures formalize marriage with a multitude of rites, rules, rituals, ceremonies, vows, and promises is that, in marriage, two individuals who are not biologically related are *integrated into* a biological network. The couple becomes the source of new kinship lines within that network, as they and their children join an interconnected web of grandparents, aunts, uncles, cousins, nieces, and nephews.

In essence, the nonbiological relationship of marriage must begin to function *as though* it were a biological relationship—a node in a multigenerational family. In Genesis 2:23, when Adam sees Eve for the first time, he bursts into poetry. "At last! This is bone from my bones and flesh from my flesh" (ISV). Elsewhere in Scripture, phrases like this are used for family relationships: Laban tells Jacob, his cousin, "You are my own flesh and blood" (29:14). David tells his tribe, Judah, "You are my relatives, my own flesh and blood" (2 Sam. 19:12). The implication is that marriage functions as the foundation of family relationships—that husband and wife function as if they were a biological unit within the kinship network.

And in one significant sense, they are just that. A couple performs a biological function that is unique to the man-woman relationship: They have children. Most of the things required for life can be performed by individuals on their own. They can walk, eat, sleep, and work. The one thing they cannot do on their own is create children. Creating new life is unique to the male-female relationship, functioning as a biological unit.

For this reason, Eve Tushnet, a writer who identifies as "gay and Catholic," is nevertheless opposed to same-sex marriage. She points out that opposite-sex unions have serious consequences that same-sex unions do not have—they can create babies. Man-woman "relationships can be either uniquely dangerous or uniquely fruitful. Thus it makes sense to have an institution dedicated to structuring and channeling them."[43]

The state has never had a political interest in regulating romantic relationships or any other form of intense emotional relationship. You can form any sort of friendship you want, and you don't need a license from the state. But the state has always had an interest in regulating marriage. Why? Because it is uniquely generative of new life. It is the biological source of the citizens, workers, voters, teachers, and entrepreneurs without which any society cannot survive.[44]

Losing a Public Ethic

Tragically, the redefinition of civil marriage to include same-sex unions is destroying whatever is left of a marriage-supportive culture. In the Supreme Court's *Obergefell* decision, the lawyer defending Michigan's marriage law tried to explain that legal marriage did not develop to give special status to people's romantic relationships but rather, "It developed to serve purposes that, by their nature, arise from biology"—that is, to protect any children that are conceived when a man and woman engage in sex. But Justice Kennedy airily dismissed biology and declared that the purpose of legal marriage is to protect the "personhood" of same-sex couples. ("It would disparage their choices and diminish their personhood to deny them this right [to marriage].")

The Court thus enshrined into law the body/person dualism in regard to marriage.

Some argue that the Supreme Court merely expanded marriage to allow more people access to its benefits. But in reality, it de-naturalized marriage. Just like gender (see chapter 6), marriage is being treated as though it has nothing to do with the biological complementarity of the sexes or the biological relationship of parents and children.

The Court's cavalier dismissal of biology is a common theme in liberal legal reasoning. When Judge Vaughn Walker overturned California's pro-marriage

Proposition 8, he defined marriage as "the state recognition and approval of a couple's choice to live with each other, to remain committed to one another and to form a household based on their own feelings about one another."[45] There is nothing in this definition about sex. Nothing about having children. The judge did not even say that sex and procreation are *one* of the purposes of marriage. They are off his list entirely. He defined marriage as a choice based solely on feelings.

The problem with this definition is that it could apply to committed roommates or polygamous unions or multiple other combinations and permutations. It does not acknowledge anything distinctive about marriage.

On a similar note, Evan Wolfson, executive director of the gay rights group Freedom to Marry, defines marriage as a "relationship of love and dedication to another person."[46] Columnist Andrew Sullivan, who identifies as homosexual, defines marriage as "primarily a way in which two adults affirm their emotional commitment to one another."[47]

This is an unbelievably insipid definition of marriage. It does not explain what makes marriage different from other emotional commitments. Nor can it explain why marriage makes distinctive demands on us, such as faithfulness, exclusivity, and permanence. Other relationships don't make those demands. Why should marriage?

Yet this is the definition of marriage the Supreme Court wrote into the law of the land in *Obergefell*. And in the process, it has undermined marriage for everyone. After all, how strong is a contract based on a purely emotional connection, considering how our emotions fluctuate and change? We are losing a public ethic that puts backbone into people's private commitments.

"We're Lying about Marriage"

Tragically, it was only because marriage had already lost much of its distinctive character that it was possible to give same-sex unions the same legal status in the first place. Many heterosexuals have embraced a recreational view of sex, and in the process they have lost the expectation that sex belongs within a marriage relationship characterized by fidelity, exclusivity, and permanence. Katz writes, "As pleasure pursuits, heterosexuality and homosexuality have little to distinguish them. Heterosexuals are more and more like homosexuals, except for the sex of their partners."[48]

That's why political scientist and gay rights activist Dennis Altman calls the acceptance of recreational sex the "homosexualization of America" (in a book by that title). He writes, "Heterosexual ways of life no longer differ essentially from gay and lesbian life modes."[49]

In *Obergefell*, the Supreme Court made that equivalence official: It demoted marriage to nothing but an emotional attachment and pronounced it to be identical for opposite-sex and same-sex couples.

But if marriage is based merely on emotional commitment, what grounds are there for limiting it to same-sex couples? Why not give legal status to other emotional commitments? Where should we draw the line? The burden of proof is now on anyone who wants to limit marriage to *any* group.

In fact, for some people, that is precisely the purpose. They support marriage for same-sex couples *because* they regard it as the first step to transforming marriage from a public institution with shared moral expectations to a private choice where anything goes. Judith Stacey, a professor at New York University, writes, "There are few limits to the kind of marriage and kinship patterns people might wish to devise." For example, "Two friends might decide to marry without basing their bond on erotic or romantic attachment." Others might form "small-group marriages."[50]

Journalist Masha Gessen, who identifies as a lesbian, says the real goal has always been the elimination of marriage altogether. In a widely quoted conference speech, she said, "the institution of marriage should not exist."

> Fighting for gay marriage generally involves lying about what we are going to do with marriage when we get there—because we lie that the institution of marriage is not going to change, and that is a lie. The institution of marriage is going to change, and it should change. And again, I don't think it should exist.[51]

Cultural commentator Richard Pearcey (who is also my husband) summarizes: "The endgame is not to make marriage equally available to all, but to make it equally unavailable to all."[52]

Western De-Civilization

If eliminating marriage is the homosexual movement's real goal, we are well on our way to meeting it. For if marriage is not based on the biological complementarity of the sexes, there is no rationale for the other norms and obligations connected to marriage, such as permanence, faithfulness, and exclusivity.

Already the majority of same-sex couples reject those norms.[53] Most embrace "open" unions, meaning the partners agree to have sexual relations with other individuals. One study found that even same-sex couples who self-define as Christian reject the norm of exclusivity.[54]

Publications like the *New York Times* have sought to give infidelity a positive spin with articles claiming that the nonexclusivity of same-sex couples actually strengthens their emotional bond.[55] These articles claim that unions are stronger when couples essentially say, "Who cares about what you do with your body, as long as you stay committed emotionally?" It is another expression of the body/person divide.

Some people may, for religious or philosophical reasons, be able to resist this utterly deflated view of marriage. But humans are social beings; they are affected by the society around them. As a result, many may find their commitment to a more robust view of marriage being eroded. If marriage rests on a nonexclusive emotional attachment, how stable and enduring will it be?

As social institutions like marriage grow more fragile, people are becoming more isolated and disconnected—in fact, more like the atomistic individuals in the hypothetical state of nature of social contract theory, prior to the rise of civilization. We seem to be reversing social contract theory: Instead of moving *out* of the state of nature populated by lone, autonomous individuals, we are moving *into* a state where adults are isolated individuals, connecting with others temporarily and only when it meets their needs. We are regressing to a pre-civilized condition.

In the process, we are losing freedom to the state. As Hannah Arendt explains in *The Origins of Totalitarianism*, the people most vulnerable to totalitarian control are disconnected, atomistic individuals. The reason is they have no competing identities or loyalties, no social structures to protect them from the state using its power to enforce its ideology. The isolated individual is easy to manipulate and control.[56]

Secular Marriage among Christians

Sadly, even many evangelicals have lost the idea that marriage is about anything beyond romance and emotional connection. A teacher at an evangelical college, Abigail Rine, says her students are unable to recognize how civil same-sex marriage redefines the concept of marriage because *they hold the same concept* with only a thin religious veneer. As a result, "To them, the Christian argument against same-sex marriage is an appeal to the authority of a few disparate Bible verses, and therefore compelling only to those with a literalist hermeneutic."[57]

The students fail to recognize that what is at stake is not a few scattered verses but an entire worldview. Do we live in the universe described by social contract theory—an empty cosmos of atoms bumping around in the void driven by sheer self-interest? Or do we live in a cosmos shaped by a personal God who created us to be in ordered relationships directed toward the common good?

In the biblical worldview, marriage is not something humans may simply redefine at will. It comes with its own definition as the first community, reflecting the community in the Trinity. In a healthy society, young people in the throes of romantic love do not have to decide for themselves how to create a marriage from scratch. Their extended family, the church, the law, and the public ethos all help shape young couples' expectations of what marriage is and what responsibilities it involves. That's how public norms help us have healthier, happier marriages than if we functioned as isolated individuals making up our own life script as we go along.

In a wedding sermon, theologian Dietrich Bonhoeffer told a young couple, "It is not your love that sustains the marriage, but from now on, the marriage that sustains your love."[58] A commitment to marriage, with its norms and obligations, keeps husband and wife connected through the ups and downs of their emotional life.

Children of Same-Sex Couples

Redefining legal marriage also has serious consequences for children. Dawn Stefanowicz, who was raised by a homosexual father (with multiple partners coming and going), writes, "Over and over, we are told that permitting same-sex couples access to the designation of marriage will not deprive anyone of any rights. That is a lie."[59] Legal marriage for same-sex couples denies children the right to either their mother or their father or both. In effect, the state is putting its stamp of approval on the idea that children may be intentionally deprived of their biological parents.

Supporters of same-sex marriage often argue that you don't need both a mother and a father to form a family. Same-sex parents can adopt or obtain children through artificial insemination, surrogacy, or in vitro fertilization. Of course, all of these methods still require contributions from both a male and a female. It's just that one or both of those parents is denied.

And children still feel the pain of their missing parents. Speaking from her own experience, Stefanowicz writes, "Children in same-sex households will often deny their grief and pretend they don't miss a biological parent, feeling pressured to speak positively due to the politics surrounding LGBT households." Yet we all know that children feel a painful void when they lose (or never know) one of their biological parents because of death, divorce, or adoption. Stefanowicz says, "It is the same for us when our gay parent brings his or her same-sex partner(s) into our lives. Their partner(s) can never replace our missing biological parent."[60]

Heather Barwick, who was raised by her mother and a lesbian partner, reports a similar experience of loss. "Same-sex marriage and parenting withholds either a mother or father from a child while telling him or her that it doesn't matter. That it's all the same. But it's not. A lot of us . . . are hurting." Until she was in her twenties, Heather was an advocate for the LGBT movement. But now she wants people to know her secret sorrow. "My father's absence created a huge hole in me, and I ached every day for a dad. I loved my mom's partner, but another mom could never have replaced the father I lost."[61]

Children raised by same-sex parents report that when they express their feelings of sadness, they are chastised by family members, friends, teachers, and counselors for being politically incorrect.

The Universal Declaration of Human Rights states that every child has, "as far as possible, the right to know and be cared for by his or her parents."[62] Ironically, today that position is being rejected as discriminatory and insulting to same-sex parents.

Parents by Contract

The legal impact of same-sex marriage goes even further, however—in ways that will affect *all* parents. In most states, the "presumption of parentage" means the law defines parenthood by the woman who gives birth to a child, with her husband presumed to be the child's biological and legal father. Their names are put on the birth certificate, which serves as the foundation for a lifetime of parenting rights and responsibilities. But when a same-sex couple has a child, at least one of them is not a biological parent. Whose name goes on the birth certificate? Who has parenting rights?

In the past, if a biological parent had a same-sex partner, that partner was not listed on the child's birth certificate. The implication of *Obergefell*, however, is that a same-sex couple has the same presumption of parenthood as an opposite-sex couple. As law professor Douglas NeJaime explains, homosexual advocates have long sought to elaborate a new model of parenthood that is not based on either biology or gender. And that's exactly what *Obergefell* gave them: The Court "affirmed a model of parenthood based on chosen, functional bonds rather than biology alone. . . . Biology and gender took a back seat to actual family formation" based on choice.[63]

In other words, by accepting a contractual view of *marriage*, the state will now also be required to accept a contractual vision of family formation and parenthood.

The underlying reason is clear: When same-sex couples have children—whether by divorce, adoption, or third-party reproduction—those children are not biologically related to one or both parents. Therefore, if same-sex parents are to have the same legal status as heterosexual parents, logically the state must erase the assumption of natural parenthood based on biology.

The definition of parenthood must be de-naturalized.

Until now, the state has been called on to define parenthood only in cases of contested custody when an adult who is not a biological parent wants parental rights, such as a stepparent, grandparent, or a same-sex partner. The state then asks questions such as: Did the child call this adult "mother"? How much time did they spend together? and so on. The court has to decide who counts as a parent on relatively subjective grounds.

However, if parenthood is detached from biology, then the state will define parenthood for *all* children. The state will decide who counts as a parent. Instead of recognizing parenthood as pre-political reality that is logically *prior to* the state—which the state is morally obligated to respect—parenthood will be treated as something *created by* the state.

And if parenthood is created by the state, then the state has the right to define and control it. It will be much easier for state authorities to intrude into the family, make decisions about how children are raised and educated, or even take them away if state officials disagree with their parents' beliefs. Jennifer Roback Morse predicts that "natural biological relationships will be systematically and routinely overridden by socially constructed government-created relationships."[64]

Thus a de-naturalized definition of marriage leads inevitably to a de-naturalized definition of parenthood. "Civil marriage provides the entire basis for presuming the rights and responsibilities of biological parents to raise their own children," Morabito explains. "If we abolish civil marriage, these will no longer be rights by default, but rights to be distributed at the pleasure of a bureaucratic state."[65]

In this way, paradoxically, a choice-based model of the family ends up empowering the state.

In Canada it is now considered "discriminatory" for state entities (like public schools) to argue for male/female marriage or parenting. In the province of Alberta, the government has issued guidelines instructing teachers and school administrators not to use the terms "mother" and "father" when talking to students. Instead they must use only non-gendered terms such as "parents/guardians" or "partners" or "caregivers."[66]

Central planners have always wanted to bring the family under greater government control so they can inculcate their own ideology into young minds and create docile citizens. It is no accident that when government power grows overweening we refer to it as "paternalistic," or we talk about the "nanny" state. "Paternalism is what you get in a society without fathers. Nannies are what you get in a society without mothers," writes theologian Brian Mattson. That is a clue to an "important principle: that nuclear families are one of the chief means of limiting the state. They are the foundation of civil society, a buffer zone between the individual and raw power of the state."[67]

The family is the first of what political theorist Edmund Burke called the "little platoons" that stand between the individual and an overweening state. The family is a fundamental bulwark protecting the unalienable rights recognized in the Declaration of Independence.

Offspring, Inc.: Contract for a Baby

A contractual view of parenthood is also encouraged by the growing use of artificial reproduction. An article on the subject starts off dramatically: "'No sex! No sex was used to produce this child!' That was the proud proclamation made by one of the girl's two 'fathers' as she was hoisted up high and shown off" at a sexuality conference.[68] What happens to our view of children when they are separated from the act of sex between loving parents and become products created in the laboratory?

On one hand, assisted reproduction has helped many married couples have children when a biological malfunction prevented the normal process of conception from taking place. In these cases, in vitro fertilization is used in a medicinal manner—to repair or bypass a natural process that isn't working, helping it to achieve its natural purpose or teleology. Like other forms of medicine, it uses technology to overcome the effects of the fall, to repair or compensate for a deficiency or malfunctioning in nature. And like other forms of technology, it can be an expression of the biblical principle of dominion over nature.[69]

Today, however, an attitude is spreading that anyone who wants a child has the right to have a child—even if they face biological barriers such as being single, past the age of menopause, or in a same-sex relationship. In other words, even if they cannot have a child through natural means. Technology has gone from being an assist for natural reproduction to being a method to defy nature—to assert choice over natural reproduction.

If you cannot create a child, you can contract for one.

In these cases, artificial reproduction is not being used to *bolster* the natural bonds between parent and child but to *replace* them with bonds created by choice. When producing children in the lab, says a Catholic writer, "intent conquers biology, desire triumphs over nature."[70] It is another example of exalting choice while denigrating the body. The technocratic mindset celebrates unlimited dominion over the body and its functions.

When pried loose from its connection to natural parenthood, artificial reproduction can feed into the dehumanizing mindset that children are commodities to be manufactured through technological processes for paying customers. The babies that result may come to be regarded as artifacts—as depersonalized products that we plan, create, modify, and improve. In addition, the costs of high-tech reproductive services may "make procreation look more and more like business deals and consumer purchasing," warns Peters. Children become merchandise to be "evaluated according to standards of quality control." And "if the paying parents do not believe they are getting their money's worth, they may reject the product."[71]

In recent years, there have been several cases when surrogate mothers were asked to abort when the unborn baby turned out to have a disability—when the paying parents did not think they were "getting their money's worth."[72]

The technological mindset is apt to see everything, even children, as raw material subject to human control and remaking. In applying technology to reproduction, warns Meilander, "We are tempted to see ourselves as only a free spirit detached from the body. . . . What we risk here is a separation of person and body that demeans the body and makes of it a 'thing.'"[73]

Notice that the problem, again, is the two-story dichotomy—a "separation of person and body that demeans the body."

■ ■ ■ ■ ■

A "Freedom" That Dissolves Freedom

Every forward movement of the secular moral revolution is hailed as an advance for freedom from the oppressive moral rules of the past. But in reality, every step empowers the state.

As we saw in earlier chapters, a rapid expansion of state power began with abortion. In the past, the law recognized personhood as a pre-existing reality, something that followed metaphysically on being biologically human. The law merely recognized it as a prior fact. But the only way the state can legalize abortion is to deny the relevance of biology and declare that some biological humans are not persons. The state has taken on itself the authority to decide which humans qualify for the status of personhood, defined in terms of mental abilities—the capacity to think, feel, and desire. The same reasoning is being applied to euthanasia and assisted suicide as well.

What about marriage? In the past, the state recognized marriage as a pre-existing biologically based reality, something that followed naturally on the fact that humans are a sexually reproducing species. The law merely recognized it as a prior fact. But the only way the law can treat a same-sex couple the same as an opposite-sex couple is to deny the relevance of biology and declare marriage to be a state of mind—what you think, feel, and desire. In the process, the state has taken on itself the authority to define what marriage is—which emotional commitments qualify as marriage.

What about gender? In the past, the state recognized gender as a pre-existing reality, something that followed metaphysically on your biological sex. The law merely recognized it as a prior fact. But the only way the law can treat a trans woman (born male) the same as a biological woman is to deny the relevance of biology and declare gender to be a state of mind—what you think, feel, and desire. The state has taken on itself the authority to define legal gender independent of your biological sex.

Finally, what about parenthood? In the past, the state recognized parenthood as a pre-existing reality, something that followed metaphysically when a mother and a father gave birth to a child. The law merely recognized it as a prior fact. But the only way the law can treat same-sex parents the same as opposite-sex parents is to deny the relevance of biology and declare parenthood to be a state of mind toward the child—what you think, feel, and desire. The state is taking on itself the authority to define what a parent is, and who qualifies as one.

Significantly, in each case, the state has taken the postmodern approach of dismissing natural realities and substituting legal fiat. It refuses to be held in check by respect for the created world.

The concept of contract is sold to the public as a way of expanding choice. But in reality it cuts us off from natural, created relationships and hands over power to the state.

Do We Live in an Empty Cosmos?

In every decision we make, we are affirming a worldview. We may think we are just acting on our feelings of the moment, but in reality we are expressing our convictions about the cosmos. Either we are expressing a biblical worldview or we are being co-opted by a secular worldview. The secular moral revolution is built on the conviction that nature has no moral meaning, and that we are inherently disconnected, autonomous atoms connecting only by choice. As Morse writes, when we follow the dictates of the sexual revolution,

> We act as if we believe that we are alone in a meaningless and indifferent universe, as if we ourselves have no intrinsic value, that our sexual acts have no meaning apart from the meaning we assign them, that our sexual acts are simply the actions of mindless particles bumping into each other from no particular cause at all, and with no particular purpose in mind.[74]

Christianity offers a genuine alternative to an empty, pointless cosmos. It says that we are not alone, that the universe is meaningful, that we do have intrinsic value, that sexuality has its own purpose or *telos*, that human community is real, and that there is objective truth, goodness, and beauty. Most of all, we are not products of mindless chance but the creation of a loving Creator.

Each one of us was loved into existence, and we have the high calling of inviting others into the astonishingly rich experience of living in a cosmos centered in love.

■ ■ ■ ■ ■

The Primordial Community

The key to rebuilding society is to recover respect for natural communities. God did not create humans as social atoms. He created us for relationship. The picture of ultimate origins given in the Bible is not one of disconnected solitary individuals wandering under the trees in a state of nature. The picture is one of a couple, related to one another from the beginning in the social institution of marriage. The biblical doctrine of creation tells us that marriage and family is a social pattern that is original and inherent in human nature itself. Its essential nature cannot be remodeled at will. Any utopian scheme that seeks to cast the family into the dustbin of history will find itself working against human nature itself.

Yet biblical morality is not a straitjacket. Throughout history and across the globe, people have created variations on the basic structure of marriage and family—diverse social roles for husband and wife, varying conventions for raising children, contrasting ways to divide up economic functions, differences in the size and constitution of the extended family. God has granted humans a great deal of freedom in the way they shape and reshape the givens of creation.

The cornerstone of Christian social theory is the Trinity.[75] God is a tri-unity: three Persons so intimately related as to constitute one divinity. God is not "really" one deity, who only appears in three modes. Nor is God "really" three deities, which would be polytheism. In the classic theological formulation, God is one in being and three in person. Both are equally real, equally ultimate, and equally integral to God's nature.

That might sound paradoxical until you realize it is a way of saying that ultimate reality includes a perfect balance of both individuality and relationship. Or, as philosophers say, it includes both unity and diversity, both the one and the many. Each of the three persons of the Trinity is individually unique, yet they are so united they form a single deity. In the same way, writes John Wyatt, "each human person is unique, yet made for relationship with others. Personhood is not something we can have in isolation—in Christian thinking it is a relational concept."[76]

The Hebrew word for "oneness" is the same in reference to God and to marriage: "Hear, O Israel: The Lord our God, the Lord is one [*echad*]" (Deut. 6:4). And husband and wife "become one [*echad*] flesh" (Gen. 2:24). We "image" God not only as individuals but also in our relationships.

When is the first time in Scripture that God declares something "not good"? Surprisingly, it happens before the fall—before the entrance of sin and evil into the world. Having created Adam, God says, "It is not good for the man to be alone" (v. 18). The Genesis account underscores that relationships are central to what it means to be human.

The implication is that, contrary to social contract theory, humans are not originally and inherently disconnected individuals. Relationships are not the later inventions of autonomous individuals who can make or break them at will. They are part of the created order and thus "very good" (Gen. 1:31). And the moral requirements they make on us are not impositions on our freedom but expressions of our true nature. By participating in the civilizing institutions of family, church, state, and civil society, we fulfill our social nature. And we develop the moral virtues that prepare us for our ultimate purpose, which is to become citizens of the heavenly city.

Working On "the Relationship"

The biblical answer to social contract theory is that we do not *create* marriage so much as we *enter into* a pre-existing social institution with its own normative structure. As the elegant language of the older marriage ceremony says, we "enter into the holy estate of matrimony."

This language may sound abstract, but think of it this way: Everyone who has experienced a relationship knows that it is more than the sum of its parts. You will hear couples talk about "you" and "me" and "the relationship." At times they will say, "We need to work on the relationship." They sense that their relationship is a reality that goes above and beyond the two individuals involved.

Marriage is a moral entity that draws individuals into a reality beyond their own separate existences. This idea was traditionally spoken about in terms of the common good: There was a "good" for each person in the relationship (God's moral purpose for the individual). Then there was a "common good" for their lives together (God's moral purpose for the marriage). This larger common good enriches our lives in a way we cannot experience if we remain autonomous individuals.

Finally, marriage was not an end in itself. It was to be directed to the glory of God and the common good of the community. Puritan John Cotton warned couples against being "so transported with affection" for one another that they aim "at no higher end than marriage itself." Instead they should see marriage as a means "to be better fitted for God's service and bring them nearer to God."[77]

Contrary to social contract theory, Christianity teaches that the social and political order is not merely an expedient strategy devised by individuals to protect their rights. It is part of the created order, the context for developing our full human nature—for achieving our *telos*. It is not motivated by the lower instincts of self-interest and self-preservation but by higher moral ideals such as justice, mercy, duty, service, and sacrificial love.

Who Are the True Multiculturalists?

The biblical answer is not merely theoretical. Christians are called to form a model society—the local church—to demonstrate to the world a balanced interplay of individuality and relationship, of unity and diversity. The church is meant to be not just a collection of individuals but a corporate, integrated body united by a common good. Before his death, Jesus prayed for the disciples he was about to leave behind, asking the Father "that they may be one *as we are one*" (John 17:11, italics added). Jesus is saying that the communion of Persons within the Trinity is the paradigm for the communion of members within the church.

"The Church as a whole is an icon of God the Trinity, reproducing on earth the mystery of unity in diversity," writes Orthodox bishop Timothy Ware. "Human beings are called to reproduce on earth the mystery of mutual love that the Trinity lives in heaven."[78] And as we learn to practice unity in diversity within the church, we can bring that same balance to all our social relationships—our families, schools, workplaces, and governments.

This larger vision means Christianity is not reductionistic: It values the biological realm but it does not reduce us to the biological level. Relationships rooted in biology are meant to train us in a quality of love and unity that transcends biology. Christians are reborn into a redeemed community that surpasses all natural communities.

Even the family, the most basic biological community, does not determine our primary identity. Our relationship with God does. John writes that all who become Christians are "children of God—children born not of natural descent, nor of human decision or a husband's will [to have a child], but born of God" (1:12–13). This verse is especially empowering for those whose natural families are unhealthy or dysfunctional. The Bible's liberating promise is that it is possible to transcend the sin and brokenness of our natural communities because our primary identity is to be children of God.

This trinitarian view produces a wonderful balance in practice. Within our churches, differences based on biology—family, gender, ethnicity, nationality—can be celebrated with gratitude as gifts from God. Our diversity gives rise to richly textured communities. Even in heaven we will still be recognizable as coming "from every nation, tribe, people and language," each with its own cultural heritage (Rev. 7:9). Christians are the true multiculturalists.

At the same time, these biologically based traits do not ultimately define Christians or separate them into hostile, warring factions. Christians are united by the wonder and joy of their spiritual unity. "Here there is no Gentile or Jew, circumcised or uncircumcised, barbarian, Scythian, slave or free, but Christ is all, and is in all" (Col. 3:11). They are adopted into a redeemed community that transcends all human categories.

Rescue Mission, Not Culture War

As we work through controversial moral issues, it is crucial to bear in mind the main goal. It is not first of all to persuade people to change their behavior. It is to tear down barriers to becoming Christian. No matter who we are addressing, or what moral issue the person is struggling with, their first need is to hear the gospel and experience the love of God. The most important question of their life is whether they will have a relationship with the living God that lasts into eternity.

I received an email from a woman saying her eighteen-year-old niece was wrestling with whether she was transgender. The woman had heard me speak on a *Focus on the Family* radio program, and asked if she should send her niece my book *Finding Truth*. My answer was, certainly. The book is not about moral questions but it addresses the most important question facing all of us: Is Christianity true and how can we know it? How does it stack up against competing worldviews and religions? Is there a strategy we can use to test ideas and be more confident that we are finding truth?

Once a person is convinced that Christianity is true, *then* they can ask what that means for their sexuality. And only then will they have the spiritual strength and resources to find solutions to their sexual issues.

The main reason to address moral issues is that they have become a barrier to even hearing the message of salvation. People are inundated with rhetoric telling them that the Bible is hateful and hurtful, narrow and negative. While it's crucial to be clear about the biblical teaching on sin, the context must be an overall positive message: that Christianity alone gives the basis for a high view of the value and meaning of the body as a good gift from God. In our communication with people struggling with moral issues, we need to reach out with a life-giving, life-affirming message. We should work to draw people in by the beauty of the biblical vision of life.

As one Christian psychologist puts it, the goal is "more rescue mission than culture war."[79]

It is rarely effective to criticize someone else's view from within your own perspective. That just means they disagree with *you*. It is much more persuasive when you step inside the other person's perspective and critique it from within, showing how it fails on its own terms. To do that, Christians have to become familiar with secular worldviews and learn to uncover their dehumanizing and destructive implications. Only then will the other person be open to considering Christianity as a credible alternative.

■ ■ ■ ■ ■

How to Engage Globally

What are the implications for our own families and our global engagement? It was a family that helped me become a Christian. As a teenager, I had walked away from my Lutheran upbringing and had no intention of going back. Later, while attending school in Germany, I took a train to L'Abri, an evangelistic ministry founded by Francis and Edith Schaeffer in the stunningly beautiful Swiss Alps. (The name is French for "the shelter.") I did not intend to stay; I was only meeting up briefly with family members who were traveling through. But while at L'Abri, I was struck by two things. First, I heard arguments for the truth of Christianity that were more compelling than any I had heard before. And second, I witnessed a Christian community that was more loving than any I had seen before.

The Schaeffers first went to Switzerland in connection with the formation of the International Council of Christian Churches and Child Evangelism Fellowship. When their daughters reached college age, they went down the mountainside to attend the university in Lausanne. When friends raised questions about God and religion, they would respond, "You ought to talk to my dad. He's good with questions like that."

Because the Schaeffers' home was nestled in a tiny farming village high in the Alps, the students who visited would often stay for the weekend. Then they would tell their friends about it, who told *their* friends, until the Schaeffers' chalet was overflowing with students sleeping on the couches, in the hallways, and on the balconies.

In this way, L'Abri Fellowship grew organically into a residential ministry where young people could stay for several months and witness firsthand Christians living together in community. As the ministry grew, other couples and singles joined the fellowship and opened *their* homes to students. For many of the students—myself included—a major factor in converting to Christianity was seeing its truth embodied in the day-to-day activities of Christian families, fleshing out the gospel with their lives.

The biological connections that bind the members of a family together are not intended merely to meet their own needs but also to provide a matrix of loving relationships for ministry to others—to serve the common good. Before the Industrial Revolution, the home performed a host of practical functions. It was the place where people educated children, cared for the sick and elderly, ran family industries, served customers and the community, and produced a surplus to help the poor. The home reached out to the wider society. Today we are likely to think in terms of serving a larger good through our jobs or political activism or volunteer organizations. But what about through our families? Do we nurture and build up our family relationships with the goal of forming a network loving enough to draw others in? Do we think of creating a home base strong enough to serve those in need?

Scripture says, "God sets the lonely in families" (Ps. 68:6). Who is building the strong, healthy families that God can use to minister to the lonely, the wounded, and the outcast?[80]

Alysse ElHage grew up in a chaotic home. Her parents divorced when she was two years old, and afterward a string of men came and went in her home. She writes, "My mom was married several times, which meant there were always different men (and sometimes children) coming in and out of our lives. One day, I would have a stepbrother or a stepsister, and then just as suddenly, they would be gone." How could any child survive that kind of chaos without developing massive dysfunctions?

"Thankfully, I had a lifeline," ElHage writes. Her mother took her to church regularly: "Through the faith community, I was exposed to *unbroken* families, where kids had a married mom and dad who loved each other and their kids, and were raising them in generally stable, happy homes that I envied so much. I was able to see that there were men in the world who did not leave or harm their families." These men were not perfect, ElHage writes. But, "I found hope in knowing that happy and whole marriages were not just fairy tales, and that faithful fathers and husbands really existed."[81]

Are you turning your home into a place that gives hope to the lost and the lonely, the hurting and the hopeless?

This same strategy may be the church's best solution for those struggling with sexual sins. Shame and guilt leave many feeling isolated and alone. Rosaria Butterfield is a former lesbian who spent more than a decade as an English professor specializing in queer theory at Syracuse University, where she was faculty advisor to several gay and lesbian student groups. Today she is a convert to Christianity, married to a man, and a homeschooling mother of four. It is not enough, Butterfield writes, to state clearly what the Bible teaches about sexual morality. Christians must also practice radical hospitality. She calls it sharing the gospel with a house key. "If you are not sharing the gospel with a house key, especially with people for whom crushing loneliness is killing them faster—if you are not doing that, why not?"

God promises that his help is available for those who are tempted: "No temptation has overtaken you that is not common to man [and] with the temptation he will also provide the way of escape" (1 Cor. 10:13 ESV). But *how* does God provide a way? What is your responsibility? "What if *your* house is a way of escape," Butterfield asks, "but you are too busy?"[82]

People who are physically starving will eat even unhealthy food, and those who are emotionally starving will be drawn into unhealthy relationships. It is close to impossible to follow the biblical sex ethic if it is understood solely as negative chastity (don't do that, it's wrong, it's a sin). The church must provide the healthy relationships that people hunger for.[83]

The apostles commanded Christians to "offer hospitality" (1 Pet. 4:9), inviting people into their homes and treating one another as members of a common spiritual family. And not only other Christians—we are also called to "show hospitality to strangers" (Heb. 13:2), welcoming those who are different and who may make us feel uncomfortable.

In his widely read book *After Virtue*, Alasdair MacIntyre writes that as the surrounding society loses its connecting glue, the most important response is to build local, small-scale forms of community, teaching our children and our congregations how to re-establish strong, life-giving relationships in a world falling apart: "What matters at this stage is the construction of local forms of community within which civility and the intellectual and moral life can be sustained through the new dark ages which are already upon us."[84] Our families and churches must become centers of civilization that reach out beyond themselves with a model of human community.

The strongest Christian communities (families, congregations, groups of singles) are the ones driven by a larger vision—a sense of ministry. If God has given you a dependable income, a loving spouse, a strong church community, a reliable group of friends, those gifts are not just for you. They are to equip you to reach out and draw in those who are broken and searching. God is giving you the opportunity to bring hope that Christianity is real and not just words—to put flesh and bones on the message of hope and healing.

Christians must be prepared to minister to the wounded, the refugees of the secular moral revolution whose lives have been wrecked by its false promises of freedom and autonomy. When people are persuaded that they are ultimately disconnected, atomistic selves, their relationships will grow fragile and fragmented. Those around us will increasingly suffer insecurity and loneliness. The new polarization can be an opportunity for Christian communities to become safe havens where people witness the beauty of relationships reflecting God's own commitment and faithfulness.

Acknowledgments

This book received a rich wealth of feedback in the writing process. I delivered the material in lecture form at several Christian universities, schools, and apologetics conferences. In addition, I taught the entire manuscript in both undergraduate and graduate courses at Houston Baptist University. I organized two reading groups with students from the HBU Honors College. Over the summer I received feedback from a reading group of homeschool graduates organized by Kathryn Hitt Hart and Patricia Samuelsen of Schola. Another reading group was organized by David and Sue Tong, leaders of a Reasonable Faith chapter. I also led a series of classes based on the manuscript for an ethics course taught by Paul Shockley at the College of Biblical Studies.

Thanks to Barbara Challies and Maria Dunn for helpful feedback. Several members of my family read and discussed the manuscript. My husband Rick was, as always, my best editor and dialogue partner.

I am grateful to share an academic environment with colleagues who were willing to read all or parts of the manuscript. Some of them met for several weeks in a discussion group. Thanks to Agnieszka Czopik, Sara Frear, Trae Holcomb, Anthony Joseph, Jeremy Neill, Christopher Sneller, John Oliver Tyler, and Jerry Walls.

In addition, several individuals with specialized expertise or experience offered helpful comments on all or parts of the manuscript, including, Rosaria Butterfield, Alysse ElHage, Greg Jesson, Scott Masson, Darrow Miller,

Stella Morabito, Tim Otto, Jennifer Roback Morse, Melinda Selmys, Ed Shaw, Lianne Simon, Glenn Stanton, Warren Throckmorton, Eve Tushnet, and Mark Yarhouse. They would not all agree with everything I have written, but they were generous in interacting critically with the material.

As always, my agent Steve Laube was an energetic and enthusiastic supporter of the project. Finally, let me express my gratitude to the team at Baker Publishing, especially my editor Bob Hosack, project editor Lindsey Spoolstra, vice president of marketing Mark Rice, marketing manager Eileen Hanson, and art director Patti Brinks. It is a joy to work with people committed to excellence.

Study Guide

The purpose of this study guide is to help you interact more deeply with the ideas in *Love Thy Body*. As you paraphrase what you have learned, restating the concepts in your own words, you will process the material more fully. You will also connect the new ideas to the knowledge you already have, which gives the new material greater sticking power.

The key to making the best use of a study guide is not simply to give your own views and opinions. When you do that, you are merely repeating what you already know instead of learning something new. We stretch and deepen our thinking by grappling with unfamiliar ideas. The most effective strategy is to start each answer by referring to the text. First summarize what you have read in your own words. Then feel free to offer your thoughts. (Many questions specifically ask for your views.)

The goal of apologetics is to learn how to communicate your Christian convictions more clearly and persuasively. As you fill out the study guide, don't think only of getting the "right answers." Think of how you would explain the idea to someone who has questions and objections to the Christian ethic. Use the study guide as practice for real conversations you will be having. As sports coaches say, "How you practice is how you play." So practice for the real world.

Questions: For each question, write a short paragraph answer. Be sure to read all related endnotes and to include that background information in your answer. (You can skip notes that only give citations.) Some questions include multiple parts, and your answer should address all the parts.

Dialogues: Each chapter asks you to compose sample dialogues. This is the same training used by professional apologists. In a real conversation, you cannot dump an entire paragraph on someone. Instead you have to unfold your ideas bit by bit, in response to the other person's questions and objections. So strive to make your dialogues as realistic as possible to prepare yourself for real conversations with real people. Dialogues do not need to be long (about four comments by each character) but they should reflect a plausible conversation.

Each dialogue should start with a hypothetical person stating an objection based on the topic in the assignment. Then think of an answer that keeps the discussion going. Have fun by giving your characters creative names. The dialogues will help you bridge the gap between *knowing* something and knowing how to explain it to others.

■ ■ ■ ■ ■

If filling out the study guide for a class: For each chapter, choose only one dialogue to present in class, while answering the other dialogues as ordinary questions. When you come to class, print out two copies of your dialogue so you can read it aloud dramatically with a fellow student.

Introduction
A Guide to the Wasteland

1. What view of Christian morality was expressed by the Supreme Court in its 2013 *Windsor* decision? What view of religious liberty was expressed by the US Commission on Civil Rights in 2016? Have you heard the same attitudes expressed anywhere else? Give an example or two from your own experience. How would you respond?

2. Explain how a global secularism is emerging. What are the implications for missions? Sometimes people have asked me if my books on worldview apply only to American culture. I tell them what one missionary told me: that American culture is being exported around the globe! As a result, by reading *Love Thy Body* you will learn how to interact with people living anywhere in the global community.

3. Explain the divided concept of truth. In the past, atheists used to argue that Christianity is false; today they are more likely to argue that it is not even a matter of true or false but only a matter of personal feelings and experience. That is, they place it in the upper story of personal "values" (see endnote 13). How should this change the way we present Christianity to people?

4. Give a brief explanation of the two streams in Western thought—the Enlightenment tradition versus the Romantic movement. How are they related to the fact/value split? Which stream of thought is summarized by the term *modernism* and which is summarized by the term *postmodernism*?

Chapter 1
I Hate Me

1. Explain personhood theory. How is it an outworking of the fact/value split? How does it express a low view of human life and the body?

2. Define a teleological view of nature. What evidence is there for a teleological view from biology and from the physical cosmos?

3. How did Darwinism offer an alternative to a teleological view of nature? How did this affect not only scientific thought but also moral thought?

4. Explain briefly how the body/person dualism is at the heart of the most common arguments in each of these issues:

- Abortion
- Euthanasia
- Sexual hedonism
- Homosexuality
- Transsexualism or transgenderism

5. Explain how the Bible supports a high view of the body. Contrast the biblical view with the Gnostic view.

6. What are the implications of the incarnation for our view of the body? What are the implications of Christ's bodily resurrection? We often overlook the ascension. What is the meaning of the ascension?

7. Why did Jesus weep at the tomb of Lazarus? How does this event help illustrate the biblical answer to the problem of evil?

8. What does the New Testament mean when it says our citizenship is in heaven? How does the real meaning contrast with the way these verses are typically read?

9. What is asceticism? What is Paul's response to asceticism? In your own experience, do you find asceticism common today?

10. Explain the sacred/secular split. Why is it a problem? Using material in the text, how would you argue that it is not biblical?

11. Why *do* we sometimes feel estranged from our bodies? Have you had this experience?

12. Explain how to keep a balance of creation, fall, and redemption.

Dialogue

"Why are Christians so hateful and bigoted?" You are talking with a non-Christian who agrees with the Supreme Court that Christian morality is hateful and hurtful. Explain that the biblical position on abortion, homosexuality, and other issues is actually inspired by a high view of the value of the body.

Dialogue

You are talking with a Christian who thinks *this* world has little value and that our focus should be on getting to heaven. How would you defend the claim that the Bible teaches a high view of creation and of the body?

Chapter 2
The Joy of Death

1. Why do some people argue that laws legalizing abortion are neutral? Based on the text, how could you make a case that they are not neutral? (Read also page 63.)

2. Why did Descartes think his two-story dualism would function as a defense of Christianity? (Be sure to read endnote 12.) Why did his defense fail?

3. How does the two-story dualism affect people's thinking about abortion? (Reread the relevant material from chapter 1 and include it in your answer.) Why is it logically unavoidable to think in dualistic terms if you accept abortion?

4. If personhood is not grounded in being biologically human, what *is* it grounded in? What are the problems with any proposed criterion?

5. How does the same reasoning used to support abortion also support infanticide? What other practices would it support?

6. Some people argue that laws against abortion would impose a religious belief. Using material in the text, how might you answer?

7. The pro-life movement is based on scientific evidence that life begins at conception. Summarize that evidence based on the text. Do you find it persuasive? Why or why not? Add any additional evidence that you are familiar with.

8. Explain how abortion supporters have started to deny science and to rely instead on a non-scientific, non-empirical, metaphysical concept of personhood. In short, they have moved to the upper story.

9. Restate in your own words the case for saying the arguments for abortion are exclusive, while arguments for life are inclusive.

10. How does evolutionary materialism reduce the concept of human rights to a "Christian myth"? Does any worldview outside of Christianity offer a basis for human rights? Defend your answer.

11. A Christian couple faced the diagnosis of possible birth defects in their unborn child. Doctors urged them to abort the baby. The husband told his wife, "I have an opinion, but it's your choice." Do you think men have a right to express an opinion on abortion? Why or why not?

12. There are many misinterpretations of Exodus 21:22–25. Read endnote 56 and explain how the verse is often misunderstood, and how recent biblical scholarship interprets it.

13. Summarize the case that Christianity's opposition to abortion and infanticide actually expresses a high view of women. Do you agree? Why or why not?

14. What are some concrete creative ways Christians can live out the biblical teaching on the high value of human life? Give examples from your own experience.

Dialogue

"Mom, Dad, I'm pregnant. I want an abortion." Imagine this is your daughter, or that the boy involved is your son. Or imagine you are talking with a friend who wants an abortion. Using material from this chapter, practice how you might respond. Explain that abortion logically entails a dualistic view of the human being—one that inevitably devalues human life.

Dialogue

You are a college student talking with a professor who says opposition to abortion is based on religion and does not belong in the public square. In a respectful manner, interact with your professor to get him or her to see that, in reality, people who reject abortion rely on science, while those who support abortion reject science and rely on a purely metaphysical concept of personhood.

Chapter 3
Dear Valued Constituent

1. How is the two-story personhood theory at the heart of arugments for euthanasia and assisted suicide? How are even ordinary people affected, even though they are not reading academic works on bioethics? What is your own position and how do you support it?

2. Why did Darwinism lead many people to accept euthanasia? Summarize the thinking of these leading figures. What ideas do they have in common?

- Ernst Haeckel
- Jack London
- Margaret Sanger
- Oliver Wendell Holmes Jr.
- Clarence Darrow

3. "Don't impose your views on others." Based on the text, how might you respond to someone makes this statement?

4. Describe the ethical issues involved in using embryos for research. What is your own view and how do you support it?

5. Explain the reason we do not allow the sale of human beings. How does the sale of humans or their body parts denigrate personhood?

6. How does the Cartesian dualism work itself out in transhumanists' futuristic scenarios? Be sure to memorize the famous line from C. S. Lewis at the end of this section.

7. Darwin wrote a book titled *On the Origin of Species*, yet he denied the reality of species. Explain this paradox. What are the moral implications of denying the existence of species?

8. What does the text say is a biblical basis for genetic technology? Do you agree, and why?

9. What happens to human rights if they are not based simply and solely on the fact that we are human? Summarize the essence of Richard Rorty's infamous UNESCO address as an example.

10. Some people think the animal rights movement contradicts personhood theory. Explain why it does not. Then give the biblical basis for respecting nature.

11. How did the New Testament view of children differ radically from that of the surrounding Greco-Roman culture? What do you think is the likelihood that formerly Christian cultures will revert to Roman attitudes toward the child?

12. If you knew your preborn child suffered life-threatening health conditions, would you choose to abort? Explain your reasoning either way.

13. Describe the Christian vision that started the hospice movement.

Dialogue

"Kids, we called you together to let you know we've decided to pull the plug on Grandma." Imagine that you or your parents are making a decision whether to choose euthanasia for a grandparent who is disabled but not dying. Using material from the text, make a case against euthanasia.

Dialogue

A Christian man, an educated professional, recently asked me what is wrong with assisted suicide. Even though he attends church regularly, this man was so surrounded by secular thinking that he no longer understood the biblical reasons for rejecting suicide. Imagine you were the person he asked that question and write out your answer.

Chapter 4
Schizoid Sex

1. How does the hookup culture reflect the Cartesian dualism?

2. The text says, "Some may think sexual hedonism gives sex *too much* importance, but in reality it gives sex *too little* importance." Explain. Do you agree?

3. The text says, "The irony is that young people often think they are rebelling against adult culture when they experiment sexually. But in reality, they are following a script that adult culture is giving them." Explain. Do you agree that it takes courage to practice chastity today?

4. According to the text, why are some people drawn to impersonal sex, whether with another person or through pornography? How would you make a case that the Christian view of sexuality is actually more positive than the secular view?

5. Why, in your view, are many young people apathetic about pornography? List some of the negative consequences of pornography.

6. Describe how the body creates a chemical bond when we have sexual relations. What are the implications of that fact?

7. Why is porn addictive? Describe the process of addiction.

8. What was the impact of materialist philosophy on theories of sexual morality?

9. Give brief summaries of these thinkers' views: What themes do they have in common?

- Freud
- Sanger
- Kinsey
- Reich
- Foucault

10. Why do materialist thinkers turn sexual pleasure into an idol? In your answer, explain the dynamics of Romans 1. Explain how even materialist

views of sex, which tried to keep sexuality in the lower story, ended up treating it as a substitute religion.

11. How is it possible to lie with our bodies? Give a few of your own examples.

12. The text quotes Timothy Keller saying, "Sex is God's appointed way for two people to say reciprocally to one another, 'I belong completely, permanently, and exclusively to you.'" Do you agree? Why or why not?

13. Explain how the three acts of the biblical drama—creation, fall, and redemption—apply to sexuality.

14. Summarize the biblical teaching on singleness. What can churches do to better support and nurture singles?

15. How does secular sex education often communicate a sense that babies are "the enemy"? How would you explain the biblical view of sex and family to someone who holds that view?

Dialogue

"Mom, Dad, my girlfriend/boyfriend and I are in love, and I don't see what's wrong with having sex. All of my friends are doing it." Imagine this is your son or daughter. Or imagine it is a friend of yours. Using material from the text, in conversational form, practice how to make a persuasive case for a biblical view of sexuality.

Dialogue

You are talking with a Christian who says we just need to preach the Word, not study worldviews. Using the example of the thinkers who have shaped modern Western ideas about sexuality, explain how worldviews shape people's thinking—how they percolate down through entertainment, education, magazines, and movies. Explain that they are difficult to dislodge because they function as substitute religions.

Chapter 5
The Body Impolitic

1. What brought about the change in Sean Doherty's feelings from exclusive same-sex attraction to the point of marrying a woman?

2. Summarize the findings from science showing that sexual feelings have physical correlates. What is your interpretation of these findings?

3. How does engaging in same-sex behavior logically imply a body/person dualism (even if the persons involved are not conscious of it)?

4. The text claims that a Christian sexual ethic is pro-body, while a secular sexual ethic is anti-body. How does the text defend that claim? Do you agree? Why or why not?

5. Explain Kant's dualism. How did it pave the path to postmodernism? How does the quote from Camille Paglia capture the contrast between a secular and a biblical worldview regarding sexual morality?

6. The idea that sexual desire is fixed and central to one's identity is a recent invention. Explain when and how it was invented. (Read endnote 29. Refer as well to chapter 4, endnote 57.) What problems are created by placing sexuality at the core of one's identity? How has even the APA rejected the "gay script"?

7. What do scientists mean when they say that sexual desires and feelings are fluid and changeable? What are the implications of these new findings?

8. Explain the meaning of Timothy Keller's thought experiment of the Anglo-Saxon warrior and the Manhattan urbanite. Do you agree with Keller's point? Why or why not?

9. Christopher Yuan says the opposite of homosexuality is not heterosexuality but holiness. Explain what he means. What is the difference between temptation and sin?

10. "God made me gay." Imagine you have a friend who makes this statement. How would you respond?

11. Jean Lloyd, a former lesbian, advises pastors on how to give a truly loving response to people with same-sex attractions. Summarize her advice. Do you agree with it? Why or why not?

12. What does the term *eunuch* mean when used in Scripture? What are some strategies churches can pursue to help singles, whether attracted to the opposite sex or the same sex, live out a biblical sex ethic? Do you have any examples to offer from your own experience?

13. Some argue that Bible verses such as Leviticus 18:22 refer only to temple prostitution as it was practiced in ancient Canaanite worship practices and do not apply to loving, committed same-sex relationships. How would you respond? How would you support your response?

14. Explain the three types of law contained in the Old Testament. How does this distinction clarify the Bible's teaching on moral questions such as homosexuality?

15. Explain why biblical sexual morality actually increased Christianity's popularity in the time of the early church. What might be some implications for the church today?

Dialogue

"Mom, Dad, I'm gay." Imagine it is your son or daughter talking. Or imagine a friend of yours has approached you. Using material from the text, how would you respond? Write out your conversation.

Dialogue

You are talking with someone close to you, a friend or family member, who is questioning the biblical ethic on same-sex relations. Using material from the text, in a conversational form, express your best defense of the biblical ethic.

Chapter 6
Trans*gender*, Trans*reality*

1. Explain how the transgender narrative expresses the two-story body/person dualism, with its devaluation of the body.

2. The text claims that the transgender narrative actually reinforces gender stereotypes. Do you agree or disagree, and why?

3. A black woman quoted in the text suggests that a man who wants to be a woman, or vice versa, is trapped in "self-hate." Do you agree? Why or why not?

4. The text says, "Logically, there could be an infinite number of genders." Explain why.

5. Postmodernism says gender is a social construction. What does that mean? Do you agree or disagree, and why?

6. How did Hegel's historicism lead to postmodernism? Explain the steps in the progression and what postmodernists mean by "de-naturalizing" gender.

7. The text says that postmodernism (the upper story) takes modernism (the lower story) to its logical conclusion. Explain. In what sense are both postmodernism and modernism forms of reductionism?

8. Why do some feminists reject postmodern sexual theories? What do you think of their arguments?

9. Why do postmodernists say even biological facts are social constructs? What is the fatal flaw in such radical skepticism?

10. The text argues that postmodernism destroys the basis for women's rights. Why? Do you agree, and why or why not?

11. The text argues that SOGI laws will vastly increase the power of the state. Explain why.

12. Mark Yarhouse, in *Understanding Gender Dysphoria*, says on the one hand, there are churches that cave in to secular views seeking to deconstruct sex and gender. On the other hand, there are churches that "overcorrect" by becoming stricter, narrower, and more rigid in enforcing sex roles. Have you

seen either of these? What is your response to the way Brandon's parents handled his years of struggle with gender dysphoria?

13. People seeking to destabilize the male-female gender binary often invoke the existence of intersex people. How does Christianity gives resources to explain the phenomenon of intersex?

14. The strongest correlate of both homosexuality and transgenderism is gender nonconformity in childhood. How does this suggest a sensitive and compassionate strategy for responding to these children?

Dialogue

"Mom, Dad, I'm trans. Will you pay for my medical transition?" Imagine that is your son or daughter talking. Or imagine you are talking with a friend struggling with gender identity. Using material from the text, how would you respond? Write out your conversation.

Dialogue

Many people today are not asking "Is Christianity true?" They are asking, "Why are Christians such bigots?" Explain in a gentle conversational manner why the biblical ethic in regard to those with same-sex attraction or gender dysphoria is actually more loving, humane, and supportive of human rights than the secular ethic.

Chapter 7
The Goddess of Choice Is Dead

1. What is the difference between a contract and a covenant? What do you think is the appeal of a contract for many modern people? (Why might they prefer marriage, for example, to be a contract instead of a covenant?)

2. How was social contract theory modeled on Newtonian physics? Why did social thinkers take physics for their model?

3. Social contract theory is the source of classical liberalism. Describe the tenets of social contract theory.

4. Why did the early modern political thinkers propose what they called "the state of nature"? How was it meant to supplant the Garden of Eden, and how does it differ from the biblical account of the origins of human society? Summarize the impact of those differences on the resulting view of human nature and relationships.

5. Explain how social contract theory is shaping people's attitudes in relation to each of the following issues. In each case, also explain how you would critique those attitudes.

- Abortion
- Marriage
- Same-sex marriage
- Artificial reproduction

6. Summarize how the two-story worldview, with its denigration of biology, is expanding the power of the state in relation to abortion, euthanasia, marriage, gender, and parenthood.

7. What are the implications of the Trinity for Christian social theory? (Refer to discussions of the Trinity in earlier sections of the book as well.)

8. Explain how Christians can welcome our biological nature as a gift from God without reducing our identity to the biological level.

9. Many Christians think the biblical argument against homosexual practice rests on a few scattered verses. How would you make the case that what is at stake is an entire worldview? (Use material from this entire chapter, especially pages 249 and 256–60.)

10. Why are families and local churches crucial for responding constructively to what Alasdair MacIntyre calls "the new dark ages"? What are some practical ways for doing that?

Dialogue

"I own my body and I decide what I allow to grow in it." You are having a conversation about abortion with a young woman who makes this statement. Using material from the text, how will you respond? Write out your conversation.

Dialogue

"How does same-sex marriage hurt anyone else? A person's sex life is no one else's business." A friend raises this objection in a discussion with you. How do you answer? Explain how a de-naturalized view of marriage leads to a de-naturalized view of the family, and a vast increase in the power of the state. (For this dialogue, draw material from chapter 6 as well.)

Notes

Introduction

1. Chairman Martin R. Castro, "Peaceful Coexistence: Reconciling Nondiscrimination Principles with Civil Liberties," US Commission on Civil Rights, September 29, 2016.

2. For specific examples, see John Corvino and Maggie Gallagher, *Debating Same-Sex Marriage* (New York: Oxford University Press, 2012); Ryan T. Anderson, *Truth Overruled: The Future of Marriage and Religious Freedom* (Washington, DC: Regnery, 2015).

3. See Gabriele Kuby, *The Global Sexual Revolution: Destruction of Freedom in the Name of Freedom* (Kettering, OH: Angelico Press, 2015).

4. Leonardo Blair, "Nearly Two-Thirds of Christian Men Watch Pornography Monthly: They Are Watching at the Same Rate as Secular Men, Says Study," *The Christian Post*, August 27, 2014.

5. Mike Genung, "How Many Porn Addicts Are There in Your Church?" *Crosswalk*, June 17, 2005.

6. Linda Lyons, "How Many Teens Are Cool with Cohabitation?" Gallup.com, April 13, 2004.

7. Bradley R. E. Wright, *Christians Are Hate-Filled Hypocrites . . . and Other Lies You've Been Told* (Minneapolis: Bethany, 2010), 133.

8. Millennials were defined as those born between 1981 and 1996. Caryle Murphy, "Most U.S. Christian Groups Grow More Accepting of Homosexuality," Pew Research Center, October 18, 2015.

9. Samuel Smith, "70% of Women Who Get Abortions Identify as Christians, Survey Finds," *The Christian Post*, November 25, 2015.

10. Stanley Hauerwas, *Vision and Virtue* (Notre Dame: University of Notre Dame Press, 1974), 155.

11. C. S. Lewis, "Man or Rabbit?" *God in the Dock* (Grand Rapids: Eerdmans, 1970), 108–9.

12. Francis Schaeffer popularized the two-story metaphor in books like *Escape from Reason* and *The God Who Is There*, in *The Complete Works of Francis A. Schaeffer*, vol. 1 (Wheaton, IL: Crossway, 1982). He was influenced by Herman Dooyeweerd's more scholarly analysis of dualism in *Roots of Western Culture: Pagan, Secular, and Christian Options* (Toronto: Wedge, 1979; orig., Zutphen, Netherlands: J. B. van den Brink, 1959); *In the Twilight of Western Thought* (Nutley, NJ: Craig, 1972; orig., Presbyterian & Reformed, 1960); and his four-volume set *A New Critique of Theoretical Thought* (Ontario: Paideia Press, 1984; orig. published in Dutch in 1935).

13. I first recognized the connection while writing a review of Phillip E. Johnson's *The Wedge of Truth.* See Nancy Pearcey, "A New Foundation for Positive Cultural Change: Science

and God in the Public Square," *Human Events*, September 15, 2000. Historians typically trace the fact/value split to eighteenth-century philosopher David Hume. An extreme empiricist, Hume argued that because moral truths cannot be detected empirically, they are not real. What we think are moral facts are in reality only "sentiments and desires." However, it was Kant who formalized the divide (as we will see in chapter 5). And it was the logical positivists who proposed a particularly virulent form of it—that moral and theological statements are not merely false but cognitively meaningless. For greater detail, see my book *Saving Leonardo: The Secular Assault on Mind, Meaning, and Morals* (Nashville: B&H, 2010).

14. Anthony Quinton, as cited in Simon Critchley, "Introduction," *A Companion to Continental Philosophy*, ed. Simon Critchley and William R. Schroeder (Oxford, UK: Blackwell, 1998), 7; Critchley, "Introduction," 14. In the twentieth century, these two philosophical traditions were labeled analytic (lower story) and continental (upper story). One philosopher remarks, "It sometimes appears as if analytic and Continental philosophy are really two separate disciplines with nothing much in common." Michael Dummett, *Origins of Analytical Philosophy* (Cambridge, MA: Harvard University Press, 1996), 193.

15. For an analysis of why all nonbiblical worldviews must ultimately straddle the two stories, resulting in fatal internal contradictions, see my book *Finding Truth: 5 Strategies for Unmasking Atheism, Secularism & Other God Substitutes* (Colorado Springs: David C. Cook, 2015).

16. To learn how the Enlightenment/Romantic split is expressed in the arts and humanities, see my book *Saving Leonardo*.

Chapter 1 I Hate Me

1. See Jennifer Roback Morse, *The Sexual Revolution and Its Victims* (San Marcos, CA: Ruth Institute Books), 2015.

2. Miranda Sawyer, "I Knew Where I Stood on Abortion. But I Had to Rethink," *The Guardian*, April 7, 2007.

3. Ibid.

4. Schaeffer's analysis of dualism dovetails with a similar analysis by former pope John Paul II. See my essay, "*Evangelium Vitae:* John Paul Meets Francis Schaeffer," *The Legacy of John Paul II*, ed. Tim Perry (Downers Grove, IL: InterVarsity Press, 2007). I first realized that Schaeffer's analysis of dualism could be applied to abortion arguments by reading Robert George, *A Clash of Orthodoxies* (Wilmington, DE: Intercollegiate Studies Institute, 2001). See also Robert George and Christopher Tollefsen, *Embryo: A Defense of Human Life* (New York: Random House, 2008); Patrick Lee and Robert George, *Body-Self Dualism in Contemporary Ethics and Politics* (Cambridge, UK: Cambridge University Press, 2008); Gerard V. Bradley and Robert P. George, "Marriage and the Liberal Imagination" *Scholarly Works* (1995), paper 878.

Additional sources on dualism in abortion arguments are the writings of William E. May, such as "Philosophical Anthropology and *Evangelium Vitae*," http://www.christendom-awake.org/pages/may/philanthropol.htm; "What Is a Human Person and Who Counts as a Human Person?" http://www.christendom-awake.org/pages/may/humanperson.htm.

5. By contrast with dualism, monism holds that reality consists of only one substance. Materialism is monistic because it holds that there is only one substance, namely, matter. Pantheism is likewise monistic because it holds that there is only one substance, namely, spirit. See J. P. Moreland and Scott Rae, *Body and Soul* (Downers Grove, IL: InterVarsity Press, 2000). Christian philosophers who defend dualism against materialism include Alvin Plantinga and Richard Swinburne. See their essays in *Persons: Human and Divine*, ed. Peter Van Inwagen and Dean Zimmerman (New York: Oxford University Press, 2007).

6. Pearcey, *Saving Leonardo*, 85.

7. See, for example, Brian Charlesworth and Deborah Charlesworth, *Evolution: A Very Short Introduction* (Oxford, UK: Oxford University Press, 2003), chapter 5.

8. Howard A. Smith, "Does Science Suggest Humans Have a Cosmic Role? Almost in Spite of Themselves, Scientists Are Driven to a Teleological View of the Cosmos," *Nautilus*, December 2016.

To read more on information in DNA, see my treatment in *The Soul of Science* (Wheaton, IL: Crossway, 1994), ch. 10; Stephen C. Meyer, *Signature in the Cell* (New York: HarperCollins, 2099). To read more on fine-tuning, see Hugh Ross, *The Creator and the Cosmos: How the Latest Scientific Discoveries of the Century Reveal God*, third ed. (Colorado Springs: Nav Press, 2001); Guillermo Gonzalez and Jay Richards, *The Privileged Planet: How Our Place in the Cosmos Is Designed for Discovery* (New York: Routledge, 2014). To read more on teleology in nature, see William Dembski, *Being as Communion: A Metaphysics of Information* (New York: Routledge, 2014).

9. Jacques Barzun, *Darwin, Marx, Wagner* (Chicago: University of Chicago Press, 1981), 11.

10. Richard Dawkins, *The Blind Watchmaker* (New York: Norton, 1980), 5.

11. Charles Taylor, *Sources of the Self: The Making of Modern Identity* (Cambridge, MA: Harvard University Press, 1989), 148–49.

12. Philosopher David West summarizes the shift in these words: When nature was considered "a manifestation of God's will," then the goal of knowledge was "to fulfill God's design" and live in harmony with his purposes. But if nature does not reveal God's purpose, then the goal of knowledge is merely to improve "our ability to predict and control nature" to serve our own needs and preferences. *Continental Philosophy: An Introduction*, 2nd ed. (Cambridge, UK: Polity Press, 2010), 15. Similarly, Roger Lundin of Wheaton College explains, "With the loss of belief in the spiritual and ethical significance of creation and the human body," these became "essentially amoral mechanisms to be used to whatever private ends we have." *The Culture of Interpretation: Christian Faith and the Postmodern World* (Grand Rapids: Eerdmans, 1993), 102. As John Paul II explains, nature is no longer regarded as *intrinsically* good, revealing the goodness of its Creator, but only *instrumentally* good as it is used to achieve human purposes (*Veritatis Splendor*, §46).

13. "Peter Jennings Interviews Sen. John Kerry," *ABC News*, July 22, 2004.

14. Wesley J. Smith, "Personhood Theory: Why Contemporary Mainstream Bioethics is Dangerous," *National Review*, March 25, 2005.

15. See Wesley Smith, *The Culture of Death* (New York: Encounter Books, 2000), 73–78. In some cases, there may be good reasons not to prolong life by "extraordinary measures," that is, painful and invasive procedures that lead to people dying hooked up to machines in sterile hospital surroundings. See chapter 3 in this book. But food and water should not be considered "extraordinary measures."

16. Wendy Shalit, *Girls Gone Mild: Young Women Reclaim Self-Respect and Find It's Not Bad to Be Good* (New York: Random House, 2007).

17. Kathy Dobie, "Going All the Way: A Reporter Argues That Young Women Are Fooling around with Their Emotional Health," *Washington Post*, February 11, 2007; Nona Willis-Aronowitz, "The Virginity Mystique," *The Nation*, July 19, 2007.

18. "What Kids Want to Know About Sex and Growing Up," Children's Television Workshop, 1992, a "1-2-3 Contact Extra" special program. The video goes on to define homosexuality as "two people of the same gender giving each other pleasure." In other words, if sex is so disconnected from who you are as a person, why does your gender even matter? We will discuss this topic in chapter 5.

19. Benoit Denizet-Lewis, "Friends, Friends with Benefits and the Benefits of the Local Mall," *New York Times*, May 30, 2004.

20. Oliver O'Donovan, *Transsexualism and Christian Marriage* (Cambridge, UK: Grove Books, 1982, 2007), 19.

21. Jessica Savano, "I Am Not My Body," Kickstarter, https://www.kickstarter.com/projects/216830801/i-am-not-my-body.

22. Beth Felker Jones, *Marks of His Wounds* (Oxford, UK: Oxford University Press, 2007), 4, italics added.

23. Susan Bordo, *Unbearable Weight: Feminism, Western Culture, and the Body* (Berkeley: University of California Press, 1993, 2003), 301, 245. You might respond that even Paul said he "disciplined" his body and made it his "slave." But in the biblical context, it is clear that Paul is talking about fighting against *sin*, which often expresses itself in physical action. The Bible is not teaching that the body itself is the source of evil. For a fuller discussion, see the second half of this chapter.

24. Joseph Fletcher, *Morals and Medicine* (Boston: Beacon, 1954), 218.

25. "The scientific rationalism spearheaded by Descartes is above all an attack *on the body.* Its first principle is that the human body, together with all matter, shall be seen as an object of power." Michael Waldstein, "Introduction," in John Paul II, *Man and Woman He Created Them: A Theology of the Body* (Boston: Pauline Books & Media, 1997, 2006), 95.

As the Ramsey Colloquium put it, secular moral views hold "the presupposition that the body is little more than an instrument for the fulfillment of desire, and that the fulfillment of desire is the essence of the self. On biblical and philosophical grounds, we reject this radical dualism between the self and the body. Our bodies have their own dignity, bear their own truths, and are participants in our personhood in a fundamental way." The Ramsey Colloquium, "The Homosexual Movement," *First Things*, March 1994.

26. Gilbert Meilander, *Bioethics: A Primer for Christians*, 3rd ed. (Grand Rapids: Eerdmans, 1996, 2005, 2013), 6.

27. Donn Welton, "Biblical Bodies," *Body & Flesh: A Philosophical Reader*, ed. Donn Welton (Oxford, UK: Blackwell, 1998), 255.

28. Peter Brown, *The Body and Society: Men, Women, and Sexual Renunciation in Early Christianity* (New York: Columbia University Press, 1988), lix–lx.

29. Rabbi Lord Jonathan Sacks, "The Love That Brings New Life into the World," keynote speech delivered to the Vatican, November 17, 2014, http://rabbisacks.org/love-brings-new-life-world-rabbi-sacks-institution-marriage/.

30. Cited in Brown, *Body and Society*, 68.

31. The word Jesus used is "the strongest Greek word for furious indignation, referring to the fury of stallions about to charge into battle in the cavalry, rearing up on their hind legs, and snorting through their nostrils and charging. That word, to snort in spirit, the strongest Greek word for anger, is the word used of Jesus." Os Guinness, *The Dust of Death* (Downers Grove, IL: InterVarsity Press, 1973), 384–85.

32. Brown, *Body and Society*, lx.

33. John Donne (1572–1631), "Death, Be Not Proud (Holy Sonnet 10)," poets.org, https://www.poets.org/poetsorg/poem/death-be-not-proud-holy-sonnet-10.

34. C. S. Lewis, *The Great Divorce* (New York: Macmillan, 1946), 28.

35. Many people raise an objection here: Didn't Christians borrow the concept of resurrection from pagan mystery religions with their stories of dying and rising gods? No. Scholars have not found any stories that involve a resurrection prior to Jesus. Even the skeptical scholar Bart Ehrman says, "The majority of scholars agree . . . there is no unambiguous evidence that any pagans prior to Christianity believed in dying and rising gods." Bart Ehrman, *Did Jesus Exist? The Historical Argument for Jesus of Nazareth* (New York: HarperOne, 2012), 230. N. T. Wright says, the "denial of bodily resurrection is also there in Homer, Plato, and Pliny, and

it is there consistently through a thousand years of paganism, up to and through the time of Jesus." Craig A. Evans and N. T. Wright, *Jesus: The Final Days*, ed. Troy Miller (Louisville: Westminster John Knox, 2008), 77, 84.

When stories of dying and rising gods do appear, they were not intended as reports of historical events but as metaphors for the yearly cycle of the seasons. "[These] cults enacted the god's death and resurrection as a metaphor, whose concrete referent was the cycle of seed-time and harvest." N. T. Wright, *The Resurrection of the Son of God* (Minneapolis: Fortress, 2003), 80.

36. N. T. Wright, *Surprised by Hope* (New York: HarperOne, 2008), 50.

37. Ibid.

38. See N. T. Wright, *Paul for Everyone: The Prison Letters: Philippians, Colossians, and Philemon* (Louisville: Westminster John Knox, 2004), 126–27.

39. C. S. Lewis, *Mere Christianity*, rev. and amplified ed. (New York: HarperCollins, 1952, 1980), 37.

40. For an extended discussion of why the Bible does not endorse asceticism, see Ranald Macaulay and Jerram Barrs, *Being Human: The Nature of Spiritual Experience* (Downers Grove, IL: IVP Academic, 1998).

41. Lewis, *Mere Christianity*, 64. There are also liberal forms of theology that insist Jesus did not perform actual miracles in the physical world—that he did not really walk on water, heal the sick, or rise bodily from the dead—rather, those were just mythological ways of speaking that the early church came up with for expressing its faith. Liberal theology is akin to Gnosticism in its disdain for bodily life in *this* world.

42. Quoted in Felker Jones, *Marks of His Wounds*, 39.

43. Welton, "Biblical Bodies," 250.

44. Justin Martyr (attributed), "The Dignity of the Body," https://www.ewtn.com/faith/teachings/rbodb2.htm.

Chapter 2 The Joy of Death

1. Antonia Senior, "Yes, Abortion Is Killing. But It's the Lesser Evil," *The Times*, July 1, 2010.

2. To give one example, an embryology textbook says, "A zygote is the beginning of a new human being (i.e., an embryo). . . . Human development begins at fertilization when a male gamete or sperm (spermatozoon) unites with a female gamete or oocyte (ovum) to form a single cell—a zygote. This highly specialized, totipotent cell marked the beginning of each of us as a unique individual." Keith L. Moore and T. V. N. Persaud, *The Developing Human: Clinically Oriented Embryology*, 5th edition (2003), 2, 16. For additional textbook quotes, see Sarah Terzo, "41 Quotes from Medical Textbooks Prove Human Life Begins at Conception," LifeNews.com, January 8, 2015.

At some point, we have all been asked: Can't a woman do what she wants with her own body? Yes, but the fetus is not part of the mother's body. As an obstetric nurse writes,

> It's the placenta and umbilical cord which ***separate*** the mother from the baby and prove that the fetus was never part of its mother's body. . . . The placenta and umbilical cord exist precisely because the baby has a different and separate circulatory system from the mother and their blood must not intermingle. If something happens, such as a traumatic injury, that causes their blood to mix, it can cause serious complications. If the fetus were not a separate human being but were only another part of its mother's body, it would not need a placenta and umbilical cord to separate them. It could simply grow inside one of her body cavities like a tumor without any barriers between the two to protect each of them. (Cynthia Isabell, "How a Formerly Pro-Choice Nursing Instructor Discusses Abortion with her Students," *The Torch*, August 2, 2016)

3. Within hours, the newly fertilized ovum has a top-bottom axis (meaning that where the head and feet will sprout is established virtually from the beginning). "Even the earliest embryo, it seems, is more than just a featureless collection of cells; it is an integrated, self-developing organism." Meilander, *Bioethics*, 32.

Some people caricature pro-life arguments by saying if we protect embryos, then we should protect sperm and eggs. But gametes are not whole or distinct organisms. They are parts of the male or female body. If they do happen to combine, they do not survive; rather their genetic material enters into the new organism that is created. See Robert George, *Conscience and Its Enemies*, updated and exp. ed. (Wilmington, DE: Intercollegiate Studies Institute, 2016), 200–201.

4. Joseph Fletcher, *Humanhood: Essays in Biomedical Ethics* (Buffalo, NY: Prometheus Books, 1979), 11, italics added.

5. "Hans Küng Joins Abortion Debate in Mexico," *California Catholic Daily*, April 6, 2007.

6. Peter Singer, "The Sanctity of Life," *Foreign Policy*, September/October 2005.

7. *Roe v. Wade*, 410 U.S. 113 (1973).

8. For Plato, the body, through its physical demands, is constantly diverting us from what really matters—the spiritual and intellectual life. In his words the body "impede[s] us in the pursuit of truth; it fills us full of loves and lusts, and fears, and fancies of all kinds, and endless foolery." Cited in Bordo, *Unbearable Weight*, 145.

9. As Foucault points out, Descartes's proposal that nature is mechanical is not an empirical finding but a metaphysical assumption—"metaphysical because the idea that we are physically nothing more than machines was not a scientific idea, which could be verified, but one that followed from a basic, non-verifiable view of what reality consists in and is therefore 'metaphysical'" Quoted in John McCumber, *Time and Philosophy: A History of Continental Thought* (Montreal: McGill-Queen's University Press, 2011), 326.

10. The phrase is from Gilbert Ryle, "The Ghost in the Machine," *The Concept of Mind* (London: Hutchinsons, 1949).

11. Daniel Dennett, "The Origins of Selves," *Cogito* 3 (Autumn 1989): 163–73. Dennett himself disagrees with this view, but he notes that it is the way most Westerners think, whether they are aware of it or not.

12. Many other adherents to the mechanistic worldview were likewise Christians, notably Marin Mersenne and Pierre Gassendi, both members of the clergy, and the early scientists Robert Boyle and Isaac Newton. They, too, saw mechanistic philosophy as a means to defend Christianity. After all, a machine requires an inventor, a designer. If the universe is like a mechanical tool, then someone must have created it and wound it up. Besides, tools are invented for a purpose, to fulfill a function. Thus a mechanistic worldview implied that the universe was created for a purpose. As historian John Herman Randall writes, "The whole form of Newtonian science practically forced men, as a necessary scientific hypothesis, to believe in an external Creator." *The Making of the Modern Mind* (New York: Columbia University Press, 1926, 1940), 276.

Even Descartes's famous phrase "I think, therefore I am" (*Cogito, ergo sum*) was intended as a religious affirmation. Since thought is a spiritual activity, his argument served as a reply to those who denied the existence of the human spirit. And from there, Descartes built an argument for the existence of God. He argued that since God is good, he would not deceive us by creating us in such a way that we are subject to constant illusion. Thus what "I think" can be trusted. For more background on Descartes, see my book *The Soul of Science: Christian Faith and Natural Philosophy* (Wheaton, IL: Crossway, 1994).

13. T. Z. Lavine, *From Socrates to Sartre: The Philosophic Quest* (New York: Bantam Books, 1984), 128. See also Stephen Shapin, *The Scientific Revolution* (Chicago: University of Chicago Press, 1996), 30ff.

14. Jacques Maritain, *The Dream of Descartes* (New York: Philosophical Library, 1944), 179. Descartes himself may not have intended such an extreme polarization. See John W. Cooper, *Body, Soul, and Life Everlasting: Biblical Anthropology and the Monism-Dualism Debate* (Grand Rapids: Eerdmans, 2000), 14–15.

15. Of the many books on this subject, see, for example, Carolyn Merchant, *The Death of Nature* (New York: HarperCollins, 1980).

16. What about twinning? Some argue that the phenomenon of monozygotic twinning (identical twins) proves that the embryo in the first several days of its gestation is not a human individual. But twinning can be thought of as a kind of natural cloning: At an early stage, an embryo can break off a cell or group of cells that becomes a distinct organism. But this does not mean the embryo was only an undifferentiated mass of cells before that. Think of the flatworm: Parts of a flatworm can break off and become a whole flatworm. But that does not mean the original flatworm was not a whole living member of the species. Both continue to exist as full individuals, just as identical twins continue to exist and develop as full individuals. See George, *Conscience and Its Enemies*, 211–12.

17. Fletcher, *Humanhood*, 12. Similarly, Mary Anne Warren at San Francisco State University says personhood rests on the capacity for consciousness, reasoning, self-motivated activity, communication, and self-awareness in "On the Moral and Legal Status of Abortion," *The Monist* 57, no. 1 (1973): 43–61. On the inadequacy of such functional criteria for personhood, see Francis J. Beckwith, "Abortion, Bioethics, and Personhood," *The Southern Baptist Journal of Theology* 4, no. 1 (2000): 16–25.

Some have suggested that if we determine the end of life by brain death, perhaps we can determine the beginning of life by brain birth. The problem is that prenatal brain development is too gradual and continuous to allow for a clear transition point.

> Examples of the proposed milestones include the initial formation of cerebral cortex (e.g., Haring 1972) and the first detectable cortical electroencephalogram (EEG) reading (e.g., Gertler 1986). The major difficulty with this approach is that prenatal brain development is a gradual process, and lacks the kinds of punctate, qualitative transition points that would most naturally be associated with the momentous transformation from nonperson to person. Furthermore, many of the milestones that have been proposed as marking a transition depend as much on our technologies for studying fetal brain function as on the fetal brain itself. For example, if we were to measure cortical function by a more sensitive measure than EEG we might choose an earlier gestational age. If we were to measure cortical function more selectively than by EEG, that is using a method that distinguishes different types of neural activity, we might find that cortex does not begin to function as a normal human cortex until a later gestational age. As Green (e.g., 2002) has pointed out, the study of prenatal brain development has not revealed any obvious clefts separating young human nonperson tissue from young human persons or even from young human persons-to-be. (Martha J. Farah and Andrea S. Heberlein, "Personhood and Neuroscience: Naturalizing or Nihilating?" *The American Journal of Bioethics* 7, no. 1 [2007]: 37–48)

18. Scott Klusendorf, *The Case for Life* (Wheaton, IL: Crossway, 2009), 53.

19. Friedrich Nietzsche, *The Will to Power*, trans. Walter Kaufmann and R. J. Hollingdale (New York: Random House, 1967), sect. 765, italics added.

20. Sawyer, "I Knew Where I Stood on Abortion. But I Had to Rethink."

21. John Harris, "Wrongful Birth," *Philosophical Ethics in Reproductive Medicine*, ed. D. R. Bromham, M. E. Dalton, and J. C. Jackson (Manchester: Manchester University Press, 1990), 156–71.

22. James Watson, "Children from the Laboratory," *Prism: The Socioeconomic Magazine of the American Medical Association* 1, no. 2 (1973): 12–14, 33–34. Francis Crick's comment was reported by Pacific News Service, January 1978.

23. Quoted in Mark Oppenheimer, "Who Lives? Who Dies?—The Utility of Peter Singer," *Christian Century* (July 3, 2002), 24–29.

24. Lois Rogers, "Babies with Club Feet Aborted," *The Sunday Times* (May 28, 2006).

25. *Floyd v. Anders*, 444 F. Supp. 535, at 539 (1977).

26. "Abortion Doctor Kermit Gosnell Convicted of First-Degree Murder," *U.S. News*, May 13, 2013.

27. George Will, "Johns Hopkins's and Planned Parenthood's Troubling Extremism," *Washington Post*, April 5, 2013.

28. Quoted in Melanie Hunter, "Scarlett Johansson: 'Abortion is a Human Rights Issue,'" *CNS News*, October 18, 2016. See the response by J. Richard Pearcey, "Scarlett Johansson's Non-Inclusive, Blood-Stained 'Human Right,'" *CNS News*, October 19, 2016.

29. Scott Klusendorf, "How to Defend Your Pro-Life Views in 5 Minutes or Less," Life Training Institute, http://prolifetraining.com/resources/five-minute-1/.

What about the most common exceptions, like rape and incest? Think of it this way: Should a child be subject to capital punishment for the crime of the father? Moreover, research shows that 75–80 percent of women who become pregnant after rape choose to keep their babies rather than having an abortion. Why? Because abortion does not erase the trauma of rape. "It is an additional trauma for the woman, and so it compounds rather than ameliorates the trauma of rape." Isabell, "How a Formerly Pro-Choice Nursing Instructor Discusses Abortion."

Two victims of rape explain why they brought their babies to term. One gave her child up for adoption and the other kept her child. Crystal Blount, "I Became Pregnant at 14 After Rape. If You Think I Should Have Had an Abortion, Consider This," *Life News*, May 14, 2015; Jennifer Christie, "My Son Was Conceived in Rape, but His Life Has Dignity and a Purpose," *Live Action News*, April 3, 2016.

30. See the underground videos produced by the Center for Medical Progress at http://www.centerformedicalprogress.org/cmp/investigative-footage/. Planned Parenthood claims it is not selling fetal body parts for profit but only charging a "handling fee." However, the handling fee is so high that the practice has become a lucrative revenue source for the organization.

31. Leon Kass, *Life, Liberty, and the Defense of Dignity: The Challenge for Bioethics* (San Francisco: Encounter Books, 2002), 17. See also page 286.

32. Alberto Giubilini and Francesca Minerva, "After-Birth Abortion: Why Should the Baby Live?" *Journal of Medical Ethics* 39 (2013): 261–63. The authors argue that: "The moral status of an infant is equivalent to that of a fetus, that is, neither can be considered a 'person' in a morally relevant sense." Neonates "might or might not become particular persons depending on our choice," the authors argue. Until then, the newborn imposes no obligations on us "because we are not justified in taking it for granted that she will exist as a person in the future. Whether she will exist is exactly what our choice is about." The authors use the term "after-birth abortion" rather than "euthanasia" because the best interest of the one who dies is not necessarily the primary criterion for the choice.

33. Ibid.

34. See "Lives Not Worth Living: The Nazi Eugenic Dream in Our Own Time," no author listed, *Aleteia*, September 13, 2014.

35. Libby Anne, "Abortion, Heartbeats, and Souls," *Love, Joy, Feminism*, February 11, 2012, http://www.patheos.com/blogs/lovejoyfeminism/2012/02/abortion-heartbeats-and-souls.html, italics in original. Similarly, the National Abortion Action Coalition says abortion laws are "actually a means of enforcing the *religious* concept that the soul is present in the

body from the time of conception." Cited in Pamela Winnick, *A Jealous God: Science's Crusade Against Religion* (Nashville: Thomas Nelson, 2005), 18.

36. Those who do talk about abortion in terms of souls tend to embrace Eastern or New Age ideas of reincarnation—and ironically they typically accept abortion. Starhawk, a leading author on feminist neopaganism and goddess worship, writes,

> The Goddess religion has no hard and fast ruling on when a clump of fetal cells becomes a being. . . . Women are moral agents, and in the Goddess and Pagan traditions, we are each our own spiritual authority. We have a right to wrestle with these issues ourselves, not have them predetermined for us by government authorities. We have a right to determine what goes on inside our bodies. To deny that right to women is to invite government intrusion into all kinds of private and personal choices. (Starhawk and M. Macha Nightmare, *The Pagan Book of Living and Dying* [San Francisco: HarperSanFrancisco, 1997]; excerpts at https://www.onfaith.co/onfaith/2008/09/25/abortion-and-the-goddess/4187)

Similarly, Erin Pavlina claims to be a psychic "who connects with your spirit guides." She says a child is conceived when a spirit in the ether decides to reincarnate in a particular family. "Whether you lose a child through abortion, miscarriage, or early in its life . . . please rest assured there are no hard feelings, sadness, regrets, or anger on the part of the soul who goes early back to the ether. It's all part of the circle of life. And it all works out perfectly in the end." From her blog post, "Do Aborted or Miscarried Babies Come Back?" *Erin Pavlina*, http://www.erinpavlina.com/blog/2010/04/do-aborted-or-miscarried-babies-come-back/.

37. Biochemist Dianne N. Irving writes, "The question as to when a human *being* begins is strictly a scientific question, and should be answered by human embryologists—not by philosophers, bioethicists, theologians, politicians. . . . The question as to when a human *person* begins is a philosophical question." "When Do Human Beings Begin? 'Scientific' Myths and Scientific Facts," *International Journal of Sociology and Social Policy*, February 1999.

38. See Marvin Olasky, *The Tragedy of American Compassion* (Wheaton, IL: Crossway, 1992).

39. Dick Teresi, *The Undead: Organ Harvesting, the Ice-Water Test, Beating Heart Cadavers—How Medicine Is Blurring the Line between Life and Death* (New York: Vintage Books, 2012), 127, 98. Teresi is the former editor-in-chief of *Science Digest* and *Omni*.

40. "Consensus Statement on Conscientious Objection in Healthcare," *Practical Ethics*, August 29, 2016, http://blog.practicalethics.ox.ac.uk/2016/08/consensus-statement-on-conscientious-objection-in-healthcare/.

41. Paul Bloom, "The Duel between Body and Soul," *New York Times*, September 10, 2004, italics added. For a response, see Patrick Lee and Robert P. George, "Dualistic Delusions," *First Things* 150 (February 2005): 5–7.

42. Fish wrote, "A pro-life advocate sees abortion as a sin against a God who infuses life at the moment of conception; a pro-choice advocate sees abortion as a decision to be made in accordance with the best scientific opinion as to when the beginning of life, as we know it, occurs." "Why We Can't All Just Get Along," *First Things* 60 (February 1996): 18–26.

43. Quoted in Deborah Danielski, "Deconstructing the Abortion License," *Our Sunday Visitor*, October 25, 1998.

44. Sarah Knapton, "Bright Flash of Light Marks Incredible Moment Life Begins When Sperm Meets Egg," *The Telegraph*, April 26, 2016.

45. Jennie Bristow, "Abortion: Stop Hiding behind the Science," *Spiked*, October 22, 2007.

46. Alissa Tabirian, "MSNBC: Royal Baby? Parents' 'Feelings' Say When Life Begins, 'Not Science,'" *CNS News*, July 23, 2013.

47. What about the argument that if people had greater access to contraception there would be fewer abortions? No form of contraception works perfectly. Yet the false confidence created

by contraception leads people to have sex more often, with the result that there are more "contraceptive failures," thus more abortions. Jennifer Roback Morse, "The Sexual Revolution Reconsidered: The Future of Marriage," *The City* (Winter 2015), 39. See also Abby Johnson, "Sorry Folks. Contraception Access Increases Abortions. And Here's the Proof." *LifeSite News*, March 11, 2015.

48. Mary Elizabeth Williams, "So What If Abortion Ends Life?," *Salon*, January 23, 2013.

49. See Lydia Saad, "Generational Differences on Abortion Narrow," Gallup.com, March 12, 2010. "A slim majority (51%) of Millennials believe that having an abortion is morally wrong, compared to 37% who say it is morally acceptable." Daniel Cox, Robert P. Jones, Thomas Banchoff, "A Generation in Transition: Religion, Values, and Politics among College-Age Millennials," *PRRI*, April 19, 2012, http://publicreligion.org/research/2012/04/millennial-values-survey-2012/. For a summary of polls, see Kelsey Hazzard, "The Pro-Life Generation: Abortion Won't Be Around Long If Young Americans Have a Say," *Life News*, January 7, 2014.

50. Jeff Jacoby, "American Millennials Rethink Abortion, for Good Reasons," *Boston Globe*, June 9. Jacoby points out that only 24 percent of voters under the age of thirty still want to keep abortion legal in all cases: "More than any other age cohort, in fact, young adults are now the most likely to think abortion should be *illegal* in all circumstances."

51. Yuval Noah Harrari, *Sapiens: A Brief History of Humankind* (New York: HarperCollins, 2015), 108–10.

52. Ruben Navarrette Jr., "I Don't Know If I'm Pro-Choice after Planned Parenthood Videos," *The Daily Beast*, August 10, 2015.

53. Ibid.

54. Vincent M. Rue, Priscilla K. Coleman, James J. Rue, and David C. Reardon, "Induced Abortion and Traumatic Stress: A Preliminary Comparison of American and Russian Women," *Medical Science Monitor* 10, no. 10 (2004): SR5–16.

55. Timothy Keller, *Generous Justice* (New York: Penguin, 2010), 6.

56. Exodus 21:22–25 used to be a problem passage because of an earlier translation that read, "If men who are fighting hit a pregnant woman and she miscarries but there is no serious injury, the offender must be fined whatever the woman's husband demands and the court allows. But if there is serious injury, you are to take life for life, eye for eye, tooth for tooth." This wording was interpreted to mean that the life of a pre-born child was considered of less value and warranted only a fine, but that if the mother died, then the law of "an eye for an eye" applied.

However, more recent translations do not use the word *miscarries*. Instead they say "If [they] hit a pregnant woman and she gives birth prematurely but there is no serious injury, the offender must be fined whatever the woman's husband demands and the court allows" (v. 22). The Hebrew word for miscarriage is *shakal*, which is not used here. Instead the term *yasa'* is used, which is normally used in connection with a live birth. It literally means "the child comes forth." Thus biblical scholars now believe the verse is speaking about a woman who gives birth to a living baby, but the *baby* sustains no injuries from being born prematurely. See Moreland and Rae, *Body and Soul*, 235; Greg Koukl, "What Exodus 21:22 Says about Abortion," *Stand to Reason*, February 4, 2013; John Piper, "The Misuse of Exodus 21:22–25 by Pro-Choice Advocates," *Desiring God*, February 8, 1989.

57. Matt Walsh, "Wake Up, Christians. There Is No Place for You in the Democratic Party," *The Blaze*, July 28, 2016, italics in original.

58. Church father quotations are from O. M. Bakke, *When Children Became People: The Birth of Childhood in Early Christianity*, trans. Brian McNeil (Minneapolis: Fortress Press, 2005), 128, 131, 132; Rodney Stark, *The Rise of Christianity* (Princeton, NJ: Princeton University

Press, 1996), 124–35. For an overview, see Michael Gorman, *Abortion and the Early Church* (Downers Grove, IL: InterVarsity Press, 1982). Christians have sometimes disagreed about *when* life begins. For example, in a prescientific age, it was sometimes thought that life began with "quickening," which is when the mother starts to feel the baby moving. But Christians have always agreed that once human life exists, killing it is immoral.

59. Stark, *Rise of Christianity*, 117.

60. Under Roman law, it was actually forbidden to allow a deformed newborn to live. Sarah Ruden writes, "The law forbidding the Romans to let a deformed newborn of either sex live was in the Twelve Tables, which had a status somewhat like that of the U.S. Constitution today" *Paul among the People: The Apostle Reinterpreted and Reimagined in His Own Time* (New York: Image Books, 2010), 109.

61. M. R. Reese, "The Discovery of a Mass Baby Grave under Roman Bathhouse in Ashkelon, Israel," *Ancient Origins*, December 4, 2014.

62. See Jo-Ann Shelton, *As the Romans Did: A Sourcebook in Roman Social History* (Oxford, UK: Oxford University Press, 1998), 28.

63. See Mara Hvistendahl, *Unnatural Selection: Choosing Boys Over Girls, and the Consequences of a World Full of Men* (New York: PublicAffairs, 2011).

64. See the documentary *It's a Girl*, directed by Evan Gray Davis (2012), http://www.itsagirlmovie.com/.

65. Gorman, *Abortion and the Early Church*, 15.

66. For a good popular-level description of the sexual hedonism in ancient Greece and Rome, see Matthew Rueger, *Sexual Morality in a Christless World* (St. Louis: Concordia, 2016). As Louis Crompton notes, "Opportunities were ample for Roman masters" because slaves comprised about 40 percent of the population of ancient Rome. *Homosexuality and Civilization* (Cambridge, MA: Harvard University Press, 2003), 80.

67. Brown, *Body and Society*, 25.

68. "In AD 428, the Christian emperor Theodosius II enacted a law banning the use of coercion in the sex industry." Kyle Harper, *From Shame to Sin: The Christian Transformation of Sexual Morality in Late Antiquity* (Cambridge, MA: Harvard University Press, 2013), 8, 15–16.

69. Felker Jones, *Marks of His Wounds*, 90.

70. Ruden, *Paul among the People*, 107.

71. "The Epistle of Mathetes to Diognetus," Early Christian Writings, http://www.earlychristianwritings.com/text/diognetus-roberts.html.

72. Stark, *Rise of Christianity*, 105, 95.

73. Jennifer Roback Morse, "Young Women Are Gambling On a Losing Game," *The Blaze*, June 1, 2016.

74. Morse, "Sexual Revolution Reconsidered."

75. Hanna Rosin, "Boys on the Side," *The Atlantic*, September 2013.

76. C. Moreau et al., "Previous Induced Abortions and the Risk of Very Preterm Delivery: Results of the EPIPAGE Study," *BJOG: An International Journal of Obstetrics and Gynecology* 112, no. 4 (April 2005): 430–37.

77. Morse, "Young Women Are Gambling On a Losing Game."

78. Nancy Pearcey, "Why I Am Not a Feminist (Any More)," *Human Life Review*, Summer 1987. For a fuller discussion, see my book *Total Truth*, chapter 12.

79. Morse, "Young Women Are Gambling On a Losing Game."

80. A study of men in abortion waiting rooms found they reported feeling "guilty," "sad," and "afraid," even as they strove to be "supportive" of their female partners. Arthur B. Shostak, Ross Koppel, Jennifer Perkins, "Abortion Clinics and Waiting Room Men: Sociological Insights," *Men and Abortion*, 2015, http://www.menandabortion.com/articles.html#wait.

81. Quoted in Tony Reinke, "Lecrae Confesses Abortion, Invites Others into the Light," *Desiring God*, January 15, 2017. See also Christina Martin, "Grammy-Winning Rapper Lecrae: I Found a Photo of the Girlfriend I Asked to Abort My Baby and I 'Just Broke Down,'" *LifeSite News*, January 16, 2015.

82. Ibid. Lecrae describes his story in the track "Good, Bad, Ugly" from *Anomaly* (2014).

83. Danny David, "Study: Abortion Is the Leading Cause of Death in America," *Live Action News*, August 11, 2016. "Abortion is responsible for . . . 61.1% of black American deaths, and a shocking 64% of Hispanic/Latino deaths—making abortion by far the leading cause of death for blacks and Hispanics/Latinos."

84. Quoted in Reinke, "Lecrae Confesses Abortion."

85. Julie Roys, "The Secret Shame of Abortion in the Church," *Christianity Today*, February 2015.

86. Exact numbers are difficult to pin down, but even abortion advocates agree that there are roughly twice as many pregnancy centers as abortion clinics. See C. Eugene Emery Jr., "Tallies Are Too Sketchy to Say Anti-Abortion Centers Outnumber Abortion Providers 2 to 1," *PunditFact*, May 17, 2016.

87. Quoted in Ben Johnson, "Under Blackmail Threat, Pro-Life Rep's Wife Shares Moving Testimony of Regret, Healing from Past Abortion," *LifeSite News*, May 25, 2016.

88. Ibid.

89. John M. Glionna, "South Korean Pastor Tends an Unwanted Flock," *Los Angeles Times*, June 19, 2011.

90. Quoted in Fr. Mark Hodges, "Indiana Installs First 'Safe Haven' Boxes to Save Abandoned Newborns," *LifeSite News*, May 10, 2016.

Chapter 3 Dear Valued Constituent

1. Phillip K. Dick, "The Pre-Persons," available online at Pro Life New Zealand, December 29, 2012, http://prolife.org.nz/the-pre-persons-phillip-k-dick/.

2. Ibid.

3. Ibid.

4. "Sun Columnist Katie Hopkins Calls for 'Euthanasia Vans' as Britain Has 'Far Too Many Old People,'" *RT.com*, July 28, 2015.

5. Daniel Callahan, *Selling Limits: Medical Goals in an Aging Society* (New York: Simon and Schuster, 1987), cited in Philip Smith, "Personhood and the Persistent Vegetative State," *The Linacre Quarterly* 57, no. 2 (May 1990): 49.

6. A 1993 study found that 90 percent of ICU patients die because treatment has been intentionally withheld or discontinued. See Teresi, *Undead*, 242.

7. Hauerwas, *Vision and Virtue*, 176. See also Wesley Smith, *The Culture of Death*, chapter 3.

8. Singer, "The Sanctity of Life."

9. Tom L. Beauchamp, "The Failure of Theories of Personhood," *Kennedy Institute of Ethics Journal* 9, no. 4 (December 1999): 320.

10. Cited in Richard Weikart, *The Death of Humanity and the Case for Life* (Washington, DC: Regnery, 2016), 272. On the eugenics movement in America, see John West, *Darwin Day in America: How Our Politics and Culture Have Been Dehumanized in the Name of Science* (Wilmington, DE: ISI Books, 2007), especially chapter 7.

11. Ian Dowbiggin, cited in Weikart, *Death of Humanity*, 274.

12. Cynthia Eagle Russett, *Darwin in America: The Intellectual Response 1865–1912* (San Francisco: W. H. Freeman, 1976), 175.

13. Jack London, "The Law of Life," *McClure's Magazine* 16 (March 1901).

14. For a discussion of the impact of Darwinism on the arts and humanities, see my book *Saving Leonardo*.

15. Margaret Sanger, "The Wickedness of Creating Large Families," *Women and the New Race* (1920), http://www.bartleby.com/1013/5.html.

16. Cited in Albert W. Alschuler, *Law without Values: The Life, Work, and Legacy of Justice Holmes* (Chicago: Chicago University Press, 2000), 28, 27. For more on the influence of Darwinism on Holmes, see my book *Total Truth*, chapter 8.

17. Clarence Darrow, *Washington Post*, November 18, 1915.

18. John Zmirak, "We're Euthanizing Minors and Chemically Castrating 8-Year-Olds," *The Stream*, September 19, 2016.

19. Teresi, *Undead*, 89–90.

20. The Uniform Determination of Death Act, adopted in 1981, states that "the entire brain must cease to function, irreversibly." But the act fails to specify how this function is measured; hence brain death is easily misdiagnosed. In one study, 65 percent of physicians and nurses could not identify the established criteria for brain death (Teresi, *Undead*, 254).

21. Teresi, *Undead*, 252, 274.

22. Wesley Smith, "The Abandonment of Assisted Suicide," *First Things*, March 4, 2008. Other studies find that "Mental illness raises the suicide risk even more than physical illness. Nearly 95 percent of those who kill themselves have been shown to have a diagnosable psychiatric illness in the months preceding suicide. The majority suffer from depression that can be treated." Herbert Hendin, *Seduced by Death: Doctors, Patients, and Assisted Suicide* (New York: W.W. Norton, 1998), 34–35.

23. Emily Barone, "See Which States Allow Assisted Suicide," *Time*, November 3, 2014.

24. Ali Venosa, "Healthy, Retirement-Aged Woman Chooses Death by Assisted Suicide Because Old Age 'Is Awful,'" *Medical Daily*, August 4, 2015.

25. Susan Donaldson James, "Death Drugs Cause Uproar in Oregon," *ABC News*, August 6, 2008.

26. Peter Singer, *Practical Ethics*, 2nd ed. (New York: Cambridge University Press, 1993), 192.

27. Fletcher, *Morals and Medicine*, 191. He also writes, "A patient who has completely lost the power to communicate has passed into a *submoral* state, outside the forum of conscience and beyond moral being" (201).

28. Steve Reich, "Three Tales" opera (2002). Read the libretto online here: http://www.stevereich.com/threetales_lib.html.

29. Meilander, *Bioethics*, 11.

30. John Wyatt, "What Is a Person?" *Nucleus* (Spring 2004): 10–15.

31. David Hart, "The Anti-Theology of the Body," *The New Atlantis* 9 (Summer 2005): 65–73. Hart seems to be paraphrasing C. S. Lewis, who calls on Christians "to remember that the dullest and most uninteresting person you talk to may one day be a creature which, if you saw it now, you would be strongly tempted to worship." C. S. Lewis, *The Weight of Glory* (Grand Rapids: Eerdmans, 1949), 14–15.

32. Charles Krauthammer, "President Obama and Stem Cells—Science Fiction," *Washington Post*, March 13, 2009.

33. John Zmirak, "Welcome to Our Brave New World: An Interview with Wesley J. Smith," *Godspy—Faith At the Edge*, December 15, 2004.

34. As O'Donovan writes, the practice of producing embryos with the express "intention of exploiting their special status for use in research is the clearest possible demonstration of the principle that when we start *making* human beings we necessarily stop *loving* them." *Begotten or Made?* (Oxford, UK: Oxford University Press, 1984), 65.

35. Ariana Eunjung Cha, "Stanford Researchers 'Stunned' by Stem Cell Experiment That Helped Stroke Patient Walk," *Washington Post*, June 2, 2016 . Adult stem cells have also been successful in treating multiple sclerosis. See Erin Davis, "Canadian Doctors Have Successfully Reversed the Effects of MS in a Patient Using Stem Cells," *Notable*, June 10, 2016. Adult cells have even been "reprogrammed" to produce pluripotent stem cells. See "Human Pluripotent Stem Cells Without Cloning or Destroying Embryos," StemCellResearch.org, November 20, 2007.

36. "Embryonic stem cells have not yet been used for even one therapy, while adult stem cells have already been successfully used in numerous patients, including for cardiac infarction (death of some of the heart tissue)." Wolfgang Lillge, "The Case for Adult Stem Cell Research," *21st Century Science & Technology Magazine* (Winter 2001–2002).

37. Joshua Riddle, "Ben Shapiro Destroys Sarah Silverman's Planned Parenthood Tweet," *Young Conservatives*, August 4, 2015.

38. Jacob M. Appel, "Are We Ready for a Market in Fetal Organs?" *The Huffington Post*, April 17, 2009.

39. Cited in Scott Rae, "Commercial Surrogate Motherhood," *Bioethics and the Future of Medicine*, ed. John Filner, Nigel Cameron, and David Schiedermayer (Grand Rapids: Eerdmans, 1995), 234.

40. Julie Bindel, "Surrogacy and Gay Couples," *New Feminism*, June 2, 2015.

41. Adina Portaru, "Renting Wombs Is a Human Wrong, not a Human Right," *Public Discourse*, April 27, 2016.

42. Scott Rae, "Commercial Surrogate Motherhood," 234–35.

43. John Gray, *Straw Dogs* (London: Granta, 2002), 6.

44. Nick Bostrom, "Transhumanist Values," *Ethical Issues for the 21st Century*, ed. Frederick Adams (Philosophical Documentation Center Press, 2003); repr. *Review of Contemporary Philosophy* 4 (May 2005).

45. Lee Silver, *Remaking Eden: Cloning and Beyond in a Brave New World* (New York: Avon Books, 1998).

46. Mortimer J. Adler, *The Difference of Man and the Difference It Makes* (New York: Fordham University Press, 1967), 264.

47. C. S. Lewis, *The Abolition of Man* (New York: HarperCollins, 1944, 1947, 1971, 1974), 55.

48. Quoted in Gary Drevitch, "Tinkering with Morality," *Psychology Today*, March 9, 2015.

49. Quoted in Lisa Miller, "The Trans-Everything CEO," *New York Magazine*, September 8, 2014.

50. Cited in Wesley Smith, "Biohazards: Advances in Biological Science Raise Troubling Questions about What It Means to Be Human," *San Francisco Chronicle*, November 6, 2005.

51. Cited in E. O. Wilson, *The Diversity of Life* (New York: Norton, 1992, 1999), 302.

52. David King, "An Interview with Professor Brian Goodwin," *GenEthics News* 11 (March/April 1996): 6–8. Goodwin is the author of *How the Leopard Changed Its Spots* (Princeton, NJ: Princeton University Press, 1994, 2001).

53. John Paul II, *Evangelium vitae*, §19, 20.

54. I have written about this and many other ways in which Christian assumptions fostered the rise of modern science in *The Soul of Science*, especially chapter 1.

55. See my book *The Soul of Science*; also Nancy Pearcey, "Technology, History, and Worldview," *Genetic Ethics: Do the Ends Justify the Genes?* ed. John F. Kilner, Rebecca D. Pentz, and Frank E. Young (Grand Rapids: Eerdmans, 1997).

56. Adrian Woolfson, *An Intelligent Person's Guide to Genetics* (New York: Overlook Press, 2006), preface.

57. Luc Ferry, *A Brief History of Thought: A Philosophical Guide to Living* (New York: Harper Perennial, 2011), 77, italics in original.

58. Richard Rorty, "Moral Universalism and Economic Triage," presented at the Second UNESCO Philosophy Forum, Paris, 1996. Reprinted in *Diogenes* 44, no. 173 (1996).

59. Zmirak, "Welcome to Our Brave New World."

60. John H. Evans, *What Is a Human? What the Answers Mean for Human Rights* (New York: Oxford University Press, 2016). Evans also found that those who accept personhood theory are mostly professional philosophers, scientists, and ethicists. The majority of the public does not accept the theory. However, it is not clear that they have a firm basis for resisting it.

61. Singer, *Practical Ethics*, 169.

62. Bakke, *When Children Became People*, 38.

63. See Harper, *From Shame to Sin*, especially chapter 1, and Brown, *Body and Society*. Ruden says the sexual abuse of young male slaves by their masters was common, although freeborn boys were vulnerable to being raped as well. Fathers had to keep a close watch on their children to protect them from sexual predators. Among the Greeks and Romans, the active partner was praised as virile and masculine (even when they were cruel and vicious), while the passive partner (the victim) was regarded with contempt as weak and disgusting. By contrast, in the New Testament Paul treats the active partner as equally guilty and in fact condemns homosexual relations as a form of injustice (the word for "unrighteousness" in Romans 1:18 is often translated "injustice"). Because pederasty was accepted in Roman culture, and the perpetrators even admired, "Paul's Roman audience . . . would have been surprised to hear that justice applied to homosexuality, of all things" (*Paul among the People*, 71).

64. Martha Nussbaum, *Philosophical Interventions* (Oxford, UK: Oxford University Press, 2012), 73.

65. Bakke, *When Children Became People*, 285.

66. Ibid.,163.

67. Lydia Saad, "U.S. Support for Euthanasia Hinges on How It's Described," Gallup.com, May 29, 2013.

68. Anne Lamott, "At Death's Window," *Los Angeles Times*, June 25, 2006.

69. Anne Lamott, "The Rights of the Born," *Los Angeles Times*, February 10, 2006.

70. See my chapter on suffering, "Does Suffering Make Sense?" in *How Now Shall We Live?* (Carol Stream, IL: Tyndale, 1999).

71. Steve Taylor, "Can Suffering Make Us Stronger?" *Psychology Today*, November 4, 2011.

72. Cited in Taylor, "Can Suffering Make Us Stronger?" The phrase "dark night of the soul" is from St. John of the Cross, a sixteenth-century Catholic mystic.

73. Ella Frech, "Me Before You: Dear Hollywood, Why Do You Want Me Dead?," *Aleteia*, June 2, 2016.

74. Ibid.

75. Martin Pistorius with Megan Lloyd Davies, *Ghost Boy* (Nashville: Thomas Nelson, 2013), 15. See also Peter Holley, "Meet the Man Who Spent 12 Years Trapped Inside His Body Watching 'Barney' Reruns," *Washington Post*, January 13, 2015.

76. Teresi, *Undead*, 181–82, 197.

77. This tradition may also explain why Jesus waited four days before bringing Lazarus back from the dead—so no one could claim that Lazarus simply revived. See Eli Lizorkin-Eysenberg, "Resurrection of Lazarus, Jews and Jewish Tradition (John 11:1–44)," *Jewish Studies*, Israel Institute of Biblical Studies, November 28, 2013.

78. Personal interview. See also Joseph Banks, "One Heart, One Love," *Medium*, October 17, 2015, https://medium.com/@joseph3banks/one-heart-one-love-b4de709ccdb#.lltdsyp2b.

79. Nancy Flanders, "Mother of Baby Jacen, Born with Anencephaly, Refuses Abortion," *Live Action News*, April 10, 2015.

80. Marshall Shelley, "Two Minutes to Eternity," *Christianity Today*, July 2011.

81. Gwen Dewar, "The Social Abilities of Newborns," *Parenting Science*, http://www.parentingscience.com/newborns-and-the-social-world.html.

82. See Smith, *Culture of Death*, especially 23–24, 104–5.

83. Ian Haines, "I Believed That Euthanasia Was the Only Humane Solution. I No Longer Believe That," *The Age*, November 20, 2016.

84. Wesley J. Smith, "Assisted Suicide and the Corruption of Palliative Care," *First Things*, May 15, 2008.

85. Wesley J. Smith, "Doctor Sued for Saying No to Euthanasia," *National Review*, September 27, 2015; Andy Walton, "Belgian Catholic Nursing Home Has to Pay Damages for Refusing Euthanasia," *Christianity Today*, July 1, 2016.

Chapter 4 Schizoid Sex

1. Donna Freitas, *The End of Sex* (New York: Basic Books, 2013), 168–75. See also "Save the Date: Kerry Cronin on the Love Lives of College Students," *U.S. Catholic* 77, no. 9 (September 2012).

2. Freitas, *End of Sex*, 31, 177, italics added.

3. Janet Reitman, "Sex & Scandal at Duke," *Rolling Stone*, June 1, 2006.

4. Quoted in Laura Sessions Stepp, *Unhooked: How Young Women Pursue Sex, Delay Love, and Lose at Both* (New York: Penguin, 2007), 243.

5. Nancy Jo Sales, "Tinder and the Dawn of the 'Dating Apocalypse,'" *Vanity Fair*, September 2015. For a brief description of dualism from a Christian perspective, see Patrick Lee and Robert P. George, *Conjugal Union* (New York: Cambridge University Press), 74.

6. Katy Steinmetz, "Miley Cyrus: 'You Can Just Be Whatever You Want to Be,'" *Time*, June 15.

7. Sales, "Tinder and the Dawn of the 'Dating Apocalypse.'"

8. Kate Taylor, "Sex on Campus: She Can Play That Game Too," *New York Times*, July 12, 2013.

9. George Bernard Shaw, "Too True to Be Good: A Political Extravaganza," *Plays Extravagant* (London: Penguin, 1981), 93.

10. Freitas, *End of Sex*, 38. In an interview, Freitas explains how she first got interested in researching the hookup culture:

> I taught a class of undergraduates where their discussions of hookup culture and how great and liberating it was had become central to the conversation. . . . Yet then about mid-semester, the students did an about face in their attitude toward hookup culture. One student openly admitted that if she were to be honest, she kind of hated hookups and didn't know why she continued engaging in the practice—mostly because she felt she had to, she supposed. Then every other person agreed with her, and suddenly my class of juniors and seniors were reckoning with the apparent reality that, while they all knew to pretend to love hookup culture, in reality they didn't like it at all, but had been afraid they must be the only person on campus who felt this way. This surprised me deeply—and I wondered if students on other campuses felt the same way. So I set out to find out. (Amelia Evrigenis, "Author Discusses New Book, 'The End of Sex,'" *The College Fix*, July 23, 2013)

Frietas found that the only colleges that do not have a hookup culture are evangelical colleges. See Donna Freitas, *Sex and the Soul* (Oxford, UK: Oxford University Press, 2008).

11. Singer, *Practical Ethics*, 2.

12. Naomi Wolf, "Casual Sex Finds a Cool New Position," *The Sunday Times*, January 12, 2013.

13. Melinda Selmys, *Sexual Authenticity: An Intimate Reflection on Homosexuality and Catholicism* (Huntington, IN: Our Sunday Visitor, 2009), 85.

14. Meilander, *Bioethics*, 20.

15. Alice Owens, "My Rape Convinced Me That Campus Hookup Culture Is Really Messed Up," *Verily*, July 6, 2015.

16. Shalit, *Girls Gone Mild*, 85.

17. Miriam Grossman, *Unprotected: A Campus Psychiatrist Reveals How Political Correctness in Her Profession Endangers Every Student* (New York: Penguin, 2007), 3.

18. Quoted in Stepp, *Unhooked*, 220–21.

19. Selmys, *Sexual Authenticity*, 83.

20. Quoted in Stepp, *Unhooked*, 225–26.

21. Juli Slattery and Dannah Gresh, *Pulling Back the Shades* (Chicago: Moody, 2014), 46.

22. Wolf, "Casual Sex Finds a Cool New Position."

23. Gail Dines, "Is Porn Immoral? That Doesn't Matter: It's a Public Health Crisis," *Washington Post*, April 8, 2016.

24. Belinda Luscombe, "Porn and the Threat to Virility," *Time*, March 31, 2016.

25. David Schultz, "Divorce Rates Double When People Start Watching Porn," *Science*, August 26, 2016.

26. German researchers studied MRI scans of sixty-four healthy men and discovered that the more porn they viewed, the less gray matter was found in the areas of their brain associated with reward and motivation. See Simone Kühn and Jürgen Gallinat, "The Brain on Porn: Brain Structure and Functional Connectivity Associated with Pornography Consumption," *Journal of the American Medical Association*, July 2014.

27. "Teens and Young Adults Use Porn More Than Anyone Else," *Barna*, January 28, 2016.

28. Melinda Liszewski, "Sex Before Kissing: How 15-Year-Old Girls Are Dealing with Porn-Addicted Boys," originally published as "Growing Up in Pornland: Girls Have Had It with Porn Conditioned Boys," *Collective Shout*, March 8, 2016.

29. Cecilia Rodriguez, "Sex-Dolls Brothel Opens in Spain and Many Predict Sex-Robots Tourism Soon to Follow," *Forbes*, February 28, 2017.

30. Theresa Crenshaw, *The Alchemy of Love and Lust*, cited in Morse, *Sexual Revolution and Its Victims*, 150.

31. Emily Morse, "Sunday Sex Tip: How to Keep It Casual without Getting Attached (Can It Even Be Done?)," *Glamour*, July 27, 2104.

32. For an accessible discussion of these hormones, see Joe McIlhaney Jr. and Freda McKissic Bush, *Hooked: New Science on How Casual Sex Is Affecting Our Children* (Chicago: Northfield Publishing, 2008), especially chapter 2.

33. Grossman, *Unprotected*, 8.

34. Lauren F. Winner, *Real Sex* (Grand Rapids: Brazos Press, 2006), 88.

35. Peter Moore, "Young Americans Are Less Wedded to Monogamy Than Their Elders," *YouGov*, October 3, 2016.

36. See William M. Struthers, *Wired for Intimacy: How Pornography Hijacks the Male Brain* (Downers Grove, IL: InterVarsity Press, 2009).

37. Quoted in Shalit, *Girls Gone Mild*, 102.

38. Anne Maloney, "What the Hook-up Culture Has Done to Women," *Crisis*, June 14, 2016.

39. Dan and Alex are both quoted in Sales, "Tinder and the Dawn of the 'Dating Apocalypse.'"

40. Justin Petrisek, "Gentlemen Speak: Single Guys Share What They're Really Looking for in a Relationship," *Verily*, February 17, 2016.

41. Roger Libby, *The Naked Truth about Sex: A Guide to Intelligent Sexual Choices for Teenagers and Twentysomethings* (Freedom Press, 2013), 142.

42. See Slattery and Gresh, *Pulling Back the Shades*, 99–100. One study found that "in real life, the unheralded, seldom discussed world of married sex is actually the one that satisfies people the most." Another study found that "faithfully married people are the most sexually satisfied of any sexually active group." Glenn Stanton, *Why Marriage Matters* (Colorado Springs: Piñon Press, 1997), 42, 46.

43. Roy Porter, *The Creation of the Modern World* (New York: W.W. Norton, 2000), 258, 260.

44. As John Paul II explains, in materialist philosophy, the body has been "reduced to pure materiality." "It is simply a complex of organs, functions, and energies to be used according to the sole criteria of pleasure and efficiency." The result is that sexuality "is depersonalized and exploited." *Evangelium vitae*, §23.

45. Brian Leiter, "Morality Critics," *The Oxford Handbook of Continental Philosophy*, ed. Brian Leiter and Michael Rosen (Oxford, UK: Oxford University Press, 2007), chapter 20.

46. For greater detail on the architects of the sexual revolution, see my book *Total Truth*, 142–46; my article "Creating the 'New Man': The Hidden Agenda in Sex Education," *Bible-Science Newsletter*, May 1990; and my chapter "Salvation through Sex?" in *How Now Shall We Live?*

47. Jonathan Ned Katz, *The Invention of Heterosexuality* (Chicago: University of Chicago Press, 1995), 59–60, 61. Freud communicated that mechanistic view even in his choice of language, referring constantly to *impulses*, *instincts*, and *drives*.

48. Sigmund Freud, *Civilization and Its Discontents*, trans. David McLintock (London, UK: Penguin, 2004), 40. Freud even said the most common reason women are stupid is sexual repression: "I think the undoubted intellectual inferiority of so many women can be traced back to the inhibition of thought that is essential for sexual suppression." "'Civilized' Sexual Morality and Modern Nervous Illness," *Sexual-Probleme* (*Sexual Problems*), originally published in 1908; repr. Read Books Ltd., 2013, 28.

49. Margaret Sanger, *The Pivot of Civilization* (New York: Brentano's, 1922), 232. Sanger literally believed that sexual restraint caused a vast variety of physical and psychological dysfunctions, and even mental retardation. If our sexuality were given full and free expression, she promised, we would literally become geniuses.

> Modern science is teaching us that genius is not some mysterious gift of the gods. . . . Rather it is due to the removal of physiological and psychological inhibitions and constraints which makes possible the release and the channeling of the primordial inner energies of man [her euphemism for sexual energies] into full and divine expression. (Ibid., 232–33)

50. Ibid., 271.

51. Alfred Kinsey, Wardell Pomeroy, and Clyde Martin, *Sexual Behavior in the Human Male* (Philadelphia: W. B. Saunders, 1948), 263, italics added. Kinsey himself engaged in a variety of sexual encounters with students and professional associates of both sexes, experimenting with practices such as group sex and sadomasochism.

52. Paul Robinson, *The Modernization of Sex*, 2nd ed. (Ithaca, NY: Cornell University Press, 1988), 49–50, 85.

53. Wilhelm Reich, *The Sexual Revolution* (New York: Farrar, Straus & Giroux, 1974), xxiii, xxvi, italics in original.

54. Quoted in Eustace Chesser, *Salvation through Sex: The Life and Work of Wilhelm Reich* (New York: William Morrow, 1973), 44.

55. Ibid., 67.

56. Robert Rimmer, *The Harrad Experiment* (Amherst, NY: Prometheus Books, 1990), 157, 167. The second character is quoting the philosopher Alan Watts.

57. Michel Foucault, *The History of Sexuality*, vol. 1 (New York: Random House, 1976, 1978), 78, 156. Foucault is another morality critic (see Leiter and Rosen, *Oxford Handbook of Continental Philosophy*, 726–33). But he portrays both morality *and* science (especially the medical profession) as sources of oppression. In the nineteenth century, he says, moral issues were transformed into scientific rules for mental and physical health. Doctors, psychiatrists, and government health departments all got into the act. As Foucault writes, a scientifically based morality was presented as the means for extending "strength, vigor, health, and life." *History of Sexuality*, 125.

The upshot was that moral principles were no longer enforced by the church so much as by the state and medical institutions. And they were expressed not in terms of right and wrong but in the supposedly objective language of science and medicine—normalcy and perversion. Yet this scientific discourse still functioned as moral instruction—as "a great sexual sermon," Foucault says—and thus he denounces it as equally oppressive. He accuses those who accept it of being complicit in their own oppression. He calls on individuals to see through their complicity and resist all sexual norms and stereotypes.

What should we put in the place of a science-based morality? Sheer power and pleasure. One of Foucault's favorite writers was the Marquis de Sade, and he followed de Sade in adopting sadomasochistic sexual practices as a means to attain allegedly higher levels of pleasure. Foucault also reveled in the drug culture of the 1970s, using mind-altering drugs like pot, hashish, opium, LSD, and cocaine. See Weikart, *Death of Humanity*, 254.

58. "New Survey: Taxpayer Dollars Funding Programs That Pressure Teens to Have Sex," National Abstinence Education Association, September 24, 2015, http://www.thenaea.org/newsroom/taxes_funding_teen_pressuring_programs.html. The federal sex education budget currently sends 95 percent of funding to the type of programs that teens say pressure them into having sex by treating it as normal and expected.

59. For an explanation of how aspects of the created order are elevated into idols, see my book *Finding Truth*.

60. John Donne, "The Ecstasy," Poetry Foundation, https://www.poetryfoundation.org/poems-and-poets/poems/detail/44099.

61. C. S. Lewis, *Mere Christianity* (New York: Macmillan, 1960), 96.

62. Timothy Keller, *The Meaning of Marriage* (New York: Penguin, 2011), 257.

63. Quoted in John F. Crosby, "Embodiment," *Lay Witness*, October 2000.

64. Wyatt, "What Is a Person?"

65. For example: "the preaching of Jesus Christ, according to the revelation of the *mystery* that was kept secret for long ages but has now been disclosed" (Rom. 16:25–26 ESV); "to bring to light for everyone what is the plan of the *mystery* hidden for ages in God, who created all things" (Eph. 3:9 ESV).

66. Alex Morris, "Tales From the Millennials' Sexual Revolution," *Rolling Stone*, March 31, 2014.

67. As summarized in John R. Crosby, "John Paul II's Vision of Sexuality and Marriage," *The Legacy of Pope John Paul II*, ed. Geoffrey Gneuhs (New York: Crossroad, 2000), 63. What about Jesus's words that there will be no marriage in heaven? In heaven we will continue to be male and female, as we see in the example of the risen Christ, as well as Moses and Elijah. But we will express love and mutual giving in other ways, just as single persons do this side of heaven.

68. Lecrae Moore, *Unashamed* (Nashville: B&H, 2016), 80.

69. Amanda Marcotte, "Conservative Relatives Can't Let the Planned Parenthood 'Scandal' Go? Try These Talking Points," *Salon*, August 5, 2015.

70. Ruden, *Paul among the People*, 15.

71. Ibid., 16–18. Jesus used the word *porneia* in his exception for divorce: "Anyone who divorces his wife, except for sexual immorality [*porneia*], makes her the victim of adultery" (Matt. 5:32). Jesus does not say "except for adultery," which is a different word in Greek. Young's Literal Translation translates the word as "whoredom."

72. Ruden, *Paul among the People*, 17. Of course, Paul would also have in mind the Jewish use of the term: "No first-century Jew could have spoken of *porneia* (sexual immoralities) without having in mind the list of forbidden sexual offenses in Leviticus 18 and 20, particularly incest, adultery, same-sex intercourse, and bestiality." Robert A. J. Gagnon, "The Bible and Homosexual Practice," in Dan O. Via and Robert A. J. Gagnon, *Homosexuality and the Bible: Two Views* (Minneapolis: Fortress Press, 2003), 72.

73. Eusebius, *The History of the Church*, 184–85, as quoted in "Potamiaena 205 A.D.," *Women of Christianity*, May 17, 2011, http://womenofchristianity.com/potamiaena-205-a-d/.

74. Jones, *Marks of His Wounds*, 80.

75. Cited in Taylor, *Sources of the Self*, 223.

76. Welton, "Biblical Bodies."

77. Scott Rae and Paul Cox, *Bioethics: A Christian Approach in a Pluralistic Age* (Grand Rapids: Eerdmans, 1999), 104.

78. Dan Allender and Tremper Longman, *Intimate Allies: Rediscovering God's Design for Marriage and Becoming Soulmates for Life* (Wheaton, IL: Tyndale, 1999), 254.

79. Oliver O'Donovan, *Resurrection and Moral Order*, 2nd ed. (Grand Rapids: Eerdmans, 1986, 1994), 71.

80. Keller, *The Meaning of Marriage*, 241–42.

81. Stephen Hull, "Roman Prostitutes Were Forced to Kill Their Own Children and Bury Them in Mass Graves at English 'Brothel'," *Daily Mail*, August 30, 2011.

82. See, for example, Beth Felker Jones, *Faithful: A Theology of Sex* (Grand Rapids: Zondervan, 2015).

83. Julia Duin, "No One Wants to Talk About It," *Breakpoint Online*, October 7, 2002, http://www.djchuang.com/sex/singles/bpsingles.htm.

84. Liuan Huska, "Cohousing: The New American Family," *Christianity Today*, November 2016.

85. From an interview in Jenny Taylor, *A Wild Constraint: The Case for Chastity* (London, UK: Continuum, 2008), 121.

86. Jennifer Fulwiler, "How I Became Pro-Life," January 28, 2008, http://jenniferfulwiler.com/2008/01/how-i-became-pro-life/.

87. Ibid.

88. Jennifer Fulwiler, *Something Other Than God* (San Francisco: Ignatius, 2014), 210.

89. G. K. Chesterton, *G. K.'s Weekly*, January 29, 1928.

90. Susan Berry, "Pediatricians: Abstinence on the Rise," Breitbart.com, June 23, 2016.

91. "Sex Education Politics and the War on Young Women," National Abstinence Education Association, http://www.thenaea.org/docs/The_War_On_Young_Women.pdf.

92. See Tim Stafford, "What's Wrong with Sex Before Marriage?" *Christianity Today*, http://www.christianitytoday.com/iyf/advice/lovesexdating/whats-wrong-with-sex-before-marriage.html.

93. Nancy Pearcey, "Sex, Lies, and Secularism," *Christian Research Journal* 34, no. 4 (2011).

94. Glenn T. Stanton, "CDC Study Says Teen Virgins Are Healthier," *The Federalist*, November 29, 2016.

95. Sade Patterson, "Her Campus Was Teaching Students How to Have Threesomes—So She Started Her Own 'Sex Week,'" *Faithit*, May 16, 2016.

96. Ibid.

97. Rene Thompson, "Battle of the UNM Sex Weeks," *ABQ Free Press*, March 11, 2016.

Chapter 5 The Body Impolitic

1. The following section is based on Sean Doherty, "'Love Does Not Delight in Evil, but Rejoices with the Truth.' A Theological and Pastoral Reflection on My Journey Away From a Homosexual Identity," *Anvil* 30, no. 1 (March 2014).

2. Some gay rights activists have rejected the term *homosexual* as pejorative. But Andrew Sullivan, who himself identifies as homosexual, defends it as a "clinical, neutral term" that should continue to be used. "Sticks and Stones and 'Homosexual'," *The Daily Dish*, March 25, 2014, http://dish.andrewsullivan.com/2014/03/25/sticks-and-stones-and-homosexual/.

How many people in America identify as homosexual? The public tends to vastly overestimate the number. "A recent research synthesis by Gary Gates of the Williams Institute, a think tank at UCLA Law School, suggests that among adults in the United States, Canada, and Europe, 1.8 percent are bisexual men and women, 1.1 percent are gay men, and 0.6 percent are lesbians." See Stanton L. Jones, "Same-Sex Science," *First Things*, February 2012.

3. From an evolutionary perspective, same-sex attraction is clearly non-adaptive because homosexual individuals do not reproduce. Various theories have been proposed to offset the reproductive disadvantage; for example, that homosexual males contribute to the reproductive success of their sisters by being nurturing uncles. But this hypothesis is not scientifically well supported. See J. Michael Bailey et al., "Sexual Orientation, Controversy, and Science," *Psychological Science in the Public Interest* 17, no. 2 (2016).

4. Stanton L. Jones of Wheaton College reports on a large identical twin study using the Swedish Twin Registry. Among the seventy-one pairs of identical male twins of whom at least one twin identified as homosexual, in only seven cases (9.8 percent) did the second twin also identify as homosexual, which is not considered statistically significant:

> Recent studies show that familial, cultural, and other environmental factors contribute to same-sex attraction. Broken families, absent fathers, older mothers, and being born and living in urban settings all are associated with homosexual experience or attraction. Even that most despised of hypothesized causal contributors, childhood sexual abuse, has recently received significant empirical validation as a partial contributor from a sophisticated thirty-year longitudinal study published in the *Archives of Sexual Behavior*. . . . To say that psychological and environmental variables play a part in causation does not mean that biology does not, rather just not to the extent that many gay-affirming scholars claim. (Jones, "Same-Sex Science")

In a brochure, the American Psychological Association states, "Although much research has examined the possible genetic, hormonal, developmental, social, and cultural influences on sexual orientation, no findings have emerged that permit scientists to conclude that sexual orientation is determined by any particular factor or factors." "Answers to Your Questions: For a Better Understanding of Sexual Orientation & Homosexuality," 2008, http://www.apa.org/topics/lgbt/orientation.pdf. Recent research suggests that environmental factors may play a role, though at such an early stage in life that they are not matters of choice. See Sarah Knapton, "Homosexuality 'May Be Triggered by Environment after Birth'," *The Telegraph*, October 8, 2015.

5. Francis Collins, *The Language of God* (New York: Simon & Schuster, 2006), 260.

6. John Corvino, "Nature? Nurture? It Doesn't Matter," *The Gay Moralist*, August 12, 2004, http://johncorvino.com/2004/08/nature-nurture-it-doesnt-matter/, italics in original.

7. Bessel van der Kolk, *The Body Keeps the Score* (New York: Viking, 2014), 152.

8. Elinor Burkett, "What Makes a Woman?," *New York Times*, June 6, 2015.

9. J. Michael Bailey, who conducted some of these studies, concludes, "Male sexual orientation is inborn." See "Sexual Orientation: Nature or Nurture?," *What's the Story? A Multidisciplinary Discussion of Same-Sex Marriage & Religious Liberty*, symposium, December 11, 2007,

The Catholic University of America, Columbus School of Law, Interdisciplinary Program in Law & Religion, Washington, DC.

10. Van der Kolk, *Body Keeps the Score*, 297. The fact that the amygdala can be rewired is especially relevant because some studies have focused on the role of the amygdala in sexual response. For example, see Nikhil Swaminathan, "Brain Scans Provide Evidence That Sexual Orientation Is Biological," *Scientific American*, June 16, 2008.

11. Anthony Newberg and Mark Robert Waldman, *How God Changes Your Brain* (New York: Ballantine, 2009); Andrew Newberg and Eugene D'Aquill, "Why God Won't Go Away: Brain Science & the Biology of Belief," *Andrew Newberg* (blog), http://www.andrewnewberg.com/books/why-god-wont-go-away-brain-science-the-biology-of-belief.

12. Van der Kolk, *Body Keeps the Score*, 95.

13. "Children who grow up to be nonheterosexual are substantially more gender nonconforming, on average, than children who grow up to be heterosexual." J. Michael Bailey et. al, "Sexual Orientation, Controversy, and Science," *Association for Psychological Science* 17, no. 2 (2016): 45–101. Another study concludes that "childhood gender nonconforming behavior is a consistent early predictor of future nonheterosexual orientations." Gu Li, Karson T. F. Kung, and Melissa Hines, "Childhood Gender-Typed Behavior and Adolescent Sexual Orientation: A Longitudinal Population-Based Study," *Developmental Psychology*, February 20, 2017.

14. "Queer focuses on mismatches between sex, gender and desire. . . . Demonstrating the impossibility of any 'natural' sexuality, it calls into question even such unproblematic terms as 'man' and 'woman.'" Annamarie Jagose, *Queer Theory: An Introduction* (New York: New York University Press, 1996), 3.

15. Judith Butler, *Gender Trouble* (New York: Routledge, 1990), 30–31.

16. Doherty, "'Love Does Not Delight in Evil, but Rejoices with the Truth.'"

17. Ibid.

18. In Dooyeweerd's diagnosis of the nature/freedom dichotomy, he suggests that, historically, the freedom ideal arose first (during the Renaissance). It was the drive for human autonomy that motivated the development of a mechanistic conception of nature, for if nature is a machine, then we need only uncover its laws in order to master and manipulate it. Inevitably, however, the mechanistic paradigm will be applied to humans as well (through psychological conditioning, social engineering, genetic manipulation, etc.). Thus, paradoxically, the ideal of freedom will eventually lead to the loss of freedom. See Dooyeweerd, *Roots of Western Culture*, chapter 6. C. S. Lewis makes a similar point in *The Abolition of Man*.

19. Robert Solomon and Kathleen Higgins, *A Short History of Philosophy* (New York: Oxford University Press, 1996), 215. E. L. Allen writes, "Kant has given us two worlds, one of freedom and the other of nature." *From Plato to Nietzsche* (Greenwich, CT: Fawcett Publications, 1962 [1957]), 129. Dooyeweerd describes the Kantian division in these words: "Above this sensory realm of 'nature' there existed a 'suprasensory' realm of moral freedom which was not governed by mechanical laws of nature but by norms or rules of conduct which presuppose the autonomy of human personality." *Roots of Western Culture*, 171.

20. Immanuel Kant, *Critique of Pure Reason*, cited in T. Z. Lavine, *From Socrates to Sartre: The Philosophical Quest* (New York: Bantam Books, 1984), 197.

21. Immanuel Kant, "Preface to Second Edition," *Critique of Pure Reason*, rev. 2nd ed., trans. Norman Kemp Smith (New York: Palgrave Macmillan, 2007), 12. Descartes had proposed a metaphysical dualism (based on who we are). Kant proposed an epistemological dualism (based on how we know).

22. Robert Solomon, *Continental Philosophy Since 1750: The Rise and Fall of the Self* (New York: Oxford University Press, 1988), 6, italics added. Kenneth Schmitz writes, "The pivotal point in the [Kantian] shift . . . is the claim to absolutism on the part of modern human

consciousness"—i.e., that "human consciousness not only sets its own terms, it sets the terms for reality itself." *At the Center of the Human Drama: The Philosophical Anthropology of Karol Wojtyla/Pope John Paul II* (Washington, DC: Catholic University of America Press, 1993), 137, 136.

23. Kant hoped that the autonomous individual would be bound by a universal moral law based on reason—what he called the "categorical imperative." But that proved an unrealistic dream. With no transcendent source of law (no divine law), each individual makes up his own law, and morality is reduced to an arbitrary choice. Nietzsche foresaw the outcome, writing that everyone must "invent his own virtue, his own categorical imperative." Friedrich Nietzsche, "The Antichrist," *The Portable Nietzsche*, ed. and trans. Walter Kaufmann (New York: Penguin, 1982), 577 [11].

24. "Against that positivism which stops before phenomena, saying 'there are only facts,' I should say: no, it is precisely facts that do not exist, only interpretations." Nietzsche, *The Portable Nietzsche*, 458.

25. John Paul II unpacks what that means: There is an "opposition," a "dialectic, if not an absolute conflict" in modern thought between the concepts of nature and freedom. (Notice that he is using Kant's terms.) When nature is defined as "devoid of any meaning and moral values," then it is "reduced to raw material for human activity." *Veritatis Splendor*, §48, 46.

26. Camille Paglia, "Rebel Love: Homosexuality," *Vamps and Tramps* (New York: Vintage Books, 1994), 71.

27. See Mark Yarhouse, *Homosexuality and the Christian* (Bloomington, MN: Bethany, 2010); and Mark Yarhouse, *Understanding Sexuality Identity: A Resource for Youth Ministry* (Grand Rapids: Zondervan, 2013).

28. Katz, *Invention of Heterosexuality*.

29. For a historical account of how scientists took over the task of defining morality, see Julie Reuben, *The Making of the Modern University* (Chicago: University of Chicago Press, 1996). In the nineteenth century, as Christian ethics lost influence, moral issues were taken up by science. Many Westerners began to hope that the biological and social sciences would provide answers to moral problems. After all, says Reuben, "These disciplines address the nature of life and human society and therefore touched on the central moral question—What is the best way to live?" Moreover, biology reveals the negative health effects of behaviors like drunkenness and sexual licentiousness. Stated positively, then, biology seemed to encourage clean living, good habits, and public health reform. As one nineteenth-century biologist wrote, "The rules of conduct . . . formulated as religious precepts, have now been established as laws of biology." Moral issues were thus transformed into scientific rules for mental and physical health.

30. Foucault, *History of Sexuality*, 42, 43. For a Christian perspective on the relatively recent invention of the concept of both heterosexual and homosexual identity, see Jenell Williams Paris, *The End of Sexual Identity* (Downers Grove, IL: InterVarsity Press, 2011).

31. "Directly contrary to the conventional wisdom that individuals with exclusive same-sex attractions represent the prototypical 'type' of sexual-minority individual, and that those with bisexual patterns of attraction are infrequent exceptions, the opposite is true. Individuals with nonexclusive patterns of attraction are indisputably the 'norm,' and those with exclusive same-sex attractions are the exception." Deborah L. Tolman and Lisa M. Diamond, eds., *APA Handbook of Sexuality and Psychology* vols. 1 and 2 (2014): 633.

32. Lisa Diamond, "Just How Different Are Female and Male Sexual Orientation?" lecture delivered at Cornell University, October 7, 2013. See also Lisa Diamond, *Sexual Fluidity* (Cambridge, MA: Harvard University Press, 2008). Additional data supporting fluidity is the unexpected finding that "Lesbians have significantly higher pregnancy rates than their heterosexual peers. It's also true for teen gay males. They are substantially more likely to impregnate

their sexual partners than are heterosexual males." Glen Stanton, "Why Are So Many Lesbians Getting Pregnant?" *Public Discourse*, April 19, 2017.

33. Aleksandr Solzhenitsyn, *The GULAG Archipelago*, part III (New York: HarperCollins, 1974, 1985), 249.

34. Timothy Keller, *Preaching: Communicating Faith in an Age of Skepticism* (New York: Penguin, 2015), 135–36.

35. Yarhouse says those who work with teens should not assume that a teen identifies as "gay" just because he or she reports feeling same-sex attraction. In one study, "the percentage of teens who experienced same-sex attraction was almost three times as much as those who identified as gay." *Understanding Sexual Identity*, 99, 104.

36. Ibid.

37. Quoted in Stephanie Simon, "A New Therapy on Faith and Sexual Identity," *Wall Street Journal*, August 6, 2009. See also Mimi Swartz, "Living the Good Lie, *New York Times*, June 16, 2011.

38. Donna Minkowitz, "Recruit, Recruit, Recruit," *The Advocate* (December 29, 1992).

39. Darrel Yates Rist, "Sex on the Brain: Are Homosexuals Born That Way?" *The Nation* 255, no. 12 (October 19, 1992). Similarly, in an article titled "The 'Born That Way' Trap," *Ms* (May/June 1991), Lindsy Van Gelder labels the "we-can't-help-it" argument a "cop-out." She writes, "I personally don't think I was 'born this way.' She estimates that about 50 percent of lesbians choose to be that way, and calls for feminists to support "a frank, unapologetic celebration of sexual choice." Many additional quotes can be found at *Queer by Choice*, a website that describes itself as "a radical gathering place for people who have chosen to be queer." See http://www.queerbychoice.com/experiquotes.html.

40. O'Donovan, *Begotten or Made?*, 29.

41. Diamond, "Just How Different Are Female and Male Sexual Orientation?" See also Lisa Diamond, "I Was Wrong! Men's Sexuality Is Pretty Darn Fluid Too," paper presented at The Society for Personality and Social Psychology (SPSP) preconference, Austin, Texas, January 2014. Reported in Justin Lehmiller, "Women Aren't the Only Ones Who Are Sexually Fluid—Men Have a Pretty 'Flexible' Sexuality Too," *Sex & Psychology*, February 24, 2014. Diamond found that among those who had previously "come out" as homosexual, 84 percent of women and 78 percent of men reported that they had changed their sexual identity label at least once (from homosexual to bisexual, queer, unlabeled, or heterosexual).

A 2009 study of Christian therapy groups over seven years found that 23 percent of participants reported conversion from homosexual to heterosexual attraction; 30 percent reported a reduction of same-sex desire to the point of "freedom to live chaste." The rest reported either some change along a continuum or no change. The results are summarized in Yarhouse, *Homosexuality*, 88–89.

42. Christopher Yuan and Angela Yuan, *Out of a Far Country* (Colorado Springs: Waterbrook, 2011), 187.

43. Christopher Yuan, "Torn: Rescuing the Gospel from the Gays-vs.-Christians Debate," book review, *The Gospel Coalition*, January 7, 2013.

44. Amy Riordan, "My Path to Freedom" *Walking in Freedom* (blog), http://walkinginfreedom.net/my-path-to-freedom-healing-from-bi-sexuality-part-1/, italics in original.

45. Amy Riordan, "When the Enemy Attacks Your Sexual Identity (It Starts with Just a Thought)," *Walking in Freedom* (blog), http://walkinginfreedom.net/are-you-being-lied-to-about-your-sexual-identity/.

46. Sam Allberry, *Is God Anti-Gay?* rev. and expanded ed. (UK: The Good Book Company, 2015), 32. Sam Allberry, along with Sean Doherty and Ed Shaw, who are quoted in this chapter, are associated with Living Out, a British ministry to those who experience same-sex attraction.

47. Tim Wilkins, "Cruel Joke or Medical Anomaly?" Cross Ministry, http://www.crossministry.org/index.php?option=com_content&view=article&id=261:cruel-joke-or-medical-anomaly&catid=65:articles-by-tim&Itemid=278.

48. The most controversial is reparative therapy or conversion therapy. Reparative therapy for minors has been outlawed in five states and Washington, DC. In those states, it is illegal for a licensed mental health provider to help a minor change their sexual orientation or gender identity, even if the client requests it. An additional twenty states have introduced similar legislation. Despite fierce public criticism, however, studies have found that therapy is not harmful. See Yarhouse, *Homosexuality*, 90–95.

49. Francis Schaeffer, *True Spirituality*, in *The Complete Works of Francis Schaeffer* (Wheaton, IL: Crossway, 1988).

50. See Greg Koukl, *The Story of Reality* (Grand Rapids: Zondervan, 2017).

51. Jean C. Lloyd, "The Girl in the Tuxedo: Two Variations on Sexual Orientation and Gender Identity," *Public Discourse*, February 5, 2105.

52. Jean C. Lloyd, "Seven Things I Wish My Pastor Knew about My Homosexuality," *Public Discourse*, December 10, 2014.

53. Ibid.

54. Ibid.

55. O'Donovan, *Resurrection and Moral Order*, 69.

56. Harper writes, "There is no natural word for male virginity in Greek or Latin. . . . The ordinary sense of *parthenos* was 'maiden.' The continent men of the incipient Christian movement searched, awkwardly, for an expression adequate to their unusual ideal. . . . Often Christians found circumlocutions for male sexual abstinence, such as *eunouchia*." *From Shame to Sin*, 52, 104.

57. Richard M. Davidson, *Flame of Yahweh: Sexuality in the Old Testament* (Grand Rapids: Baker, 2007), 301. The first-century Jewish historian Josephus stated that Daniel, Meshach, Shadrach, and Abednego were eunuchs.

58. Ed Shaw, *Same-Sex Attraction and the Church: The Surprising Plausibility of the Celibate Life* (Downers Grove, IL: InterVarsity Press, 2015), 112. Shaw credits Stanley Hauerwas for this insight.

59. See Sam Allberry, "Why Single Is Not the Same As Lonely," *The Gospel Coalition*, July 11, 2016. See also Wesley Hill, *Spiritual Friendship* (Grand Rapids: Brazos Press, 2015); Eve Tushnet, *Gay and Catholic* (Notre Dame: Ave Maria Press, 2014).

60. Melinda Selmys, "John Paul II, Intimate Friendship, and the Fluidity of Philia and Eros," February 15, 2016, http://www.patheos.com/blogs/catholicauthenticity/2016/02/john-paul-ii-intimate-friendship-and-the-fluidity-of-philia-and-eros/?repeat=w3tc. Some have suggested that David and Jonathan had a homosexual relationship. But in the original Hebrew, the same wording is used of Jacob's love for his son Benjamin (his "soul" or "life" is "knit together" with the boy; see Gen. 44:30).

61. Ron Belgau, "Spiritual Friendship in 300 Words," August 29, 2012, https://spiritualfriendship.org/2012/08/29/spiritual-friendship-in-300-words/.

62. Doug Mainwaring, "Married and Same-Sex Attracted: Are We Hiding the Light of the Gospel under a Basket?" *Living the Truth in Love: Pastoral Approaches to Same Sex Attraction*, ed. Janet E. Smith and Father Paul Check (San Francisco: Ignatius, 2015). See also Doug Mainwaring, "I'm Gay and I Oppose Same-Sex Marriage," *Public Discourse*, March 8, 2013; Sean Doherty, "Is It Ever Responsible for People with Same-Sex Attraction to Get Married?" *Living Out*, http://www.livingout.org/is-it-ever-responsible-for-people-with-same-sex-attraction-to-get-married. See also NPR Staff, "Attracted to Men, Pastor Feels Called to Marriage with a Woman," *NPR*, January 4, 2015. Practical advice for married couples when they learn that one spouse is same-sex attracted can be found in Yarhouse, *Homosexuality*, chapter 7.

63. Doug Mainwaring, "It's Possible: Gays and Lesbians Can Have Happy Marriages," *Public Discourse*, July 11, 2016.

64. Ibid.

65. Ibid.

66. Rosaria Butterfield, "Love Your Neighbor Enough to Speak Truth," *The Gospel Coalition*, October 31, 2016.

67. S. J. Stone, "The Church's One Foundation," 1866.

68. O'Donovan, *Transsexualism and Christian Marriage*, 6. Other relationships are important to being human as well, of course, O'Donovan writes, but they "do not disclose the meaning of biological nature in this way."

69. For example, book 3 of the *Sibylline Oracles*, probably written by a Jewish author living in Egypt between 163 and 45 BC, says the Jews "are mindful of holy wedlock, and they do not engage in impious intercourse with male children, as do Phoenicians, Egyptians, and Romans, specious Greece and many nations of others, Persians and Galatians and all Asia." Quoted in David F. Greenberg, *The Construction of Homosexuality* (Chicago: University of Chicago Press, 1988), 200 n88.

70. Preston Sprinkle, *People to Be Loved* (Grand Rapids: Zondervan, 2015), 67–68.

71. If the author of Leviticus had wanted to limit the application of these verses, he could have used the term for homosexual cult prostitutes, but he did not.

> In the history of the interpretation of these Levitical prohibitions they are never construed as indicting only homosexual acts in the context of cult prostitution. On the contrary, they are taken in the broadest possible sense. For example, the first-century Jewish historian Josephus explained to Gentile readers that "the law [of Moses] recognizes only sexual intercourse that is according to nature, that which is with a woman. . . . But it abhors the intercourse of males with males" (*Against Apion* 2.199). There are no limitations placed on the prohibition as regards age, slave status, idolatrous context, or exchange of money. The only limitation is the sex of the participants. (Robert A. J. Gagnon, *The Bible and Homosexual Practice: Texts and Hermeneutics* [Nashville: Abingdon, 2001], 312–32, 130)

See also Robert Gagnon, "Does Leviticus Only Condemn Idolatrous Homosexual Practice?—An Open Letter from Robert Gagnon," guest post on Timothy Dalrymple's blog *Philosophical Fragments*, March 28, 2013, http://www.patheos.com/blogs/philosophicalfragments/2013/03/28/bible-condemn-idolatrous-homosexual-practice-gangnon-lee-torn/.

72. The distinction between these three types of law has its origin in the early church, when theologians sought to explain why Jewish civil and ceremonial laws were no longer binding on Christians, whereas the moral law still was. We find references in the church fathers as well as in Aquinas, Luther, and Calvin. See Jonathan Bayes, "The Threefold Division of the Law," first published in *Reformation Today* 177, http://www.christian.org.uk/wp-content/downloads/the-threefold-division-of-the-law.pdf.

73. Scripture makes it clear that the clean laws applied symbolically to people, not just food. Peter saw a vision of unclean foods and heard a voice from heaven saying, "Do not call anything impure that God has made clean." He rightly interpreted the vision to mean, "God has shown me that I should not call anyone impure or unclean" (Acts 10:15, 28).

74. See Richard B. Hays, *The Conversion of the Imagination* (Grand Rapids: Eerdmans, 2005).

75. In the New Testament, on the one hand, practices like slavery were radically relativized. Compared to our identity in Christ, our social, political, and economic status is far less important: "The one who was a slave when called to faith in the Lord is the Lord's freed person; similarly, the one who was free when called is Christ's slave" (1 Cor. 7:22). On the other hand, Paul also tells slaves, "But if you can become free, by all means take the opportunity"

(v. 21 HCSB). How do these two themes fit together? The New Testament is urging Christians to follow the customs of their culture whenever possible, in order to make it clear that Christianity is not primarily a program of social revolution but of inner transformation. Yet if you find ways to express that inner transformation by changing your external circumstances, "by all means take the opportunity."

And Christians did just that. As we saw in chapter 2, as soon as they had the opportunity to influence the laws of Rome, they outlawed sex slavery. In the fourth century, Gregory of Nyssa wrote "the very earliest attack on slavery" (Harper, *From Shame to Sin*, 182). Then,

> As early as the seventh century, Saint Bathilde (wife of King Clovis II) became famous for her campaign to stop slave-trading and free all slaves; in 851 Saint Anskar began his efforts to halt the Viking slave trade. That the Church willingly baptized slaves was claimed as proof that they had souls, and soon both kings and bishops—including William the Conqueror (1027–1087) and Saints Wulfstan (1009–1095) and Anselm (1033–1109)—forbade the enslavement of Christians. . . . In the thirteenth century, Saint Thomas Aquinas deduced that slavery was a sin, and a series of popes upheld his position, beginning in 1435 and culminating in three major pronouncements against slavery by Pope Paul III in 1537. (Rodney Stark, "The Truth about the Catholic Church and Slavery," *Christianity Today*, July 1, 2003)

The sad irony is that by the time Americans began to practice slavery in the New World, there was a settled conviction, reaching back for centuries, that slavery was wrong. The slaveholders were not following Christian tradition, as critics charge. They were violating a longstanding Christian moral teaching.

76. Richard B. Hays, *The Moral Vision of the New Testament: A Contemporary Introduction to New Testament Ethics* (New York: HarperOne, 1996), 387. For a good popular-level discussion of biblical verses and the Greco-Roman context, see Sprinkle, *People to Be Loved*.

77. Some scholars argue that Paul is not condemning all homosexual relationships, only those practiced by people who are "naturally" heterosexual. The phrase "contrary to nature" is interpreted to mean the nature and inclinations of the individual person. But there is no evidence that Paul, in the first century, was using the term "nature" in the individualized, psychological sense that is common in the twenty-first century. He is much more likely to be using the term in the Stoic, Hellenistic, and Jewish sense of the created order.

78. For example, Justin Lee, in *Torn: Rescuing the Gospel from the Gays-vs.-Christians Debate* (New York: Jericho Books, 2012), restricts Romans 1 to a condemnation of only a "specific group of people" who first turned to idolatry and then participated in homosexual fertility rites in pagan temples. But Paul's point is that *all* non-Christian worldviews make an idol of something in the created order. See my book *Finding Truth*.

79. Crompton, *Homosexuality and Civilization*, 114.

80. Aristophanes's speech is in Plato's *Symposium*, in *Collected Works of Plato*, 4th ed., trans. Benjamin Jowett (Oxford, UK: Oxford University Press, 1953).

81. Craig A. Williams, *Roman Homosexuality*, 2nd ed. (New York: Oxford University Press, 2010), 33.

82. Ibid., 25, 54.

83. Ruden, *Paul among the People*, 53, 51, 55, 48.

84. As Dennis Prager writes, "It is probably impossible for us, who live thousands of years [later], to perceive the extent to which undisciplined sex can dominate man's life and the life of society. Throughout the ancient world, and up to the recent past in many parts of the world, sexuality infused virtually all of society." It started with their view of the gods:

> The gods of virtually all civilizations engaged in sexual relations. In the Near East, the Babylonian god Ishtar seduced a man, Gilgamesh, the Babylonian hero. In Egyptian

religion, the god Osiris had sexual relations with his sister, the goddess Isis, and she conceived the god Horus. In Canaan, El, the chief god, had sex with Asherah. In Hindu belief, the god Krishna was sexually active, having had many wives and pursuing Radha; the god Samba, son of Krishna, seduced mortal women and men. In Greek beliefs, Zeus married Hera, chased women, abducted the beautiful young male, Ganymede, and masturbated at other times; Poseidon married Amphitrite, pursued Demeter, and raped Tantalus. In Rome, the gods sexually pursued both men and women. Given the sexual activity of the gods, it is not surprising that the religions themselves were replete with all forms of sexual activity [especially in the form of temple prostitutes, both male and female]." (Dennis Prager, "Judaism's Sexual Revolution: Why Judaism [and then Christianity] Rejected Homosexuality," *Crisis* 11, no. 8 [September 1993])

85. Ruden, *Paul among the People*, 49, 59.

86. Rod Dreher, "Sex After Christianity," *The American Conservative*, April 11, 2013.

87. Bakke, *When Children Became People*, 144. In the ancient world, men may not have needed women for sex, but they did need women for legitimate heirs. Today men only need a reproductive clinic. "For gay couples that seek to engineer children to adorn their 'marriages,' the mothers of their children are discarded as soon as the child is born. . . . Women are nothing more than breeders. When in the history of humanity have women been held in greater contempt? Never." Doug Mainwaring, "The Grand Pretension: Genderlessness and Genderless Marriage," *American Thinker*, May 20, 2016.

88. Bakke, *When Children Became People*, 141.

89. Tertullian reported that the Romans would exclaim, "See how they love one another!" "A Love without Condition," *History of the Early Church*, http://www.earlychurch.com/unconditional-love.php.

Chapter 6 Trans*gender*, Trans*reality*

1. How many people are affected by gender dysphoria? The most frequently cited estimate is about 0.2 to 0.3 percent of the population. See Tanya Lewis, "Bruce Jenner's Transition: How Many Americans Are Transgender?" *LiveScience*, April 27, 2015. For a statement by the Christian Medical and Dental Association on transgenderism, see https://cmda.org/resources/publication/transgender-identification-ethics-statement.

2. See, for example, Nelson Chan, Jeanette Hawn, and Roya Ladan, "Clearing Up the Law on Transgender Rights," *California Labor and Employment Law Review* 30, no. 4 (July 2016); Tyler O'Neil, "Massachusetts Forces LGBT 'Accommodation' Rules on Churches," *PJMedia*, September 9, 2016.

3. "Transgender Kids: Who Knows Best?" *BBC*, January 12, 2017.

4. "About SB 777," Rescue Your Child, http://rescueyourchild.com/SB_777.html.

5. "Transgender FAQ," GLAAD, http://www.glaad.org/transgender/transfaq.

6. O'Donovan, *Transsexualism and Christian Marriage*, 12.

7. *G. G. v. Gloucester County School Board*, United States Court of Appeals for the Fourth Circuit, No. 15-2056, decided: April 19, 2016.

8. "Colorado Transgender First-Grader Coy Mathis Wins Civil Rights Case," comment posted by lannister80, June 24, 2013, http://forums.macrumors.com/threads/colorado-transgender-first-grader-coy-mathis-wins-civil-rights-case.1601025/.

9. Paula Johnson, "His and Hers . . . Healthcare," TED talk, December 2013.

10. J. N. Zhou et al., "A Sex Difference in the Human Brain and Its Relation to Transsexuality," *Nature* (November 2, 1995). Some speculate that the development of a baby's brain sex can follow a different pathway from the sex of his or her body. "Sexual differentiation of the

genitals takes place in the first two months of pregnancy," writes Dick Swaab, a researcher at the Netherlands Institute for Neuroscience in Amsterdam, "and sexual differentiation of the brain starts during the second half of pregnancy." Genitals and brains are thus subjected to different environments of "hormones, nutrients, medication, and other chemical substances," several weeks apart in the womb, which may affect sexual differentiation. Cited in Robin Marantz Henig, "How Science Is Helping Us Understand Gender," *National Geographic*, January 2017.

But the truth is that, at this point, no one knows what causes transsexualism. The difficulty with genetic explanations is that the condition is so rare that the most influential studies have included only six or seven individuals. They also involved subjects who were actively involved in cross-sex–type behavior and using feminizing hormone therapy in ways that likely affected the regions of the brain being investigated. For a summary of the research, see Mark Yarhouse, *Understanding Gender Dysphoria* (Downers Grove, IL: InterVarsity Press, 2015), chapter 3.

11. "Boy or Girl?" YouTube video, 1:40, uploaded by BBC The Social, October 24, 2016, https://www.youtube.com/watch?v=udI-Go8KK2Q&feature=youtu.be, italics added.

12. Glenn Stanton, "5 Reasons Target's Trans Bathroom Policy Really Stepped In It," *The Federalist*, April 29, 2016.

13. Jonah Mix, "The Body and the Lie," *Medium*, September 25, 2016, https://medium.com/@JonahMix/the-body-and-the-lie-fc6b03c3ff9a#.rtgdjj6ek.

14. "I Didn't Like Doing All the Stereotypical Girl Things," *Transgender Reality*, December 14, 2015, comment by Trish, January 11, 2016, http://transgenderreality.com/2015/12/14/i-didnt-like-doing-all-the-stereotypical-girl-things/. See also Lindsay Leigh Bentley, "I Am Ryland—The Story of a Male-Identifying Little Girl Who Didn't Transition," *Lindsay Leigh Bentley* (blog), June 30, 2014, http://lindsayleighbentley.com/2014/06/30/i-am-ryland-the-story-of-a-male-identifying-little-girl-who-didnt-transition/.

15. Burkett, "What Makes a Woman?"

16. "About," *First, Do No Harm: Youth Gender Professionals*, https://youthtranscriticalprofessionals.org/about/.

17. Rod Dreher, "The Cult of Transgender," *The American Conservative*, August 10, 2016.

18. See Elaine Woo, "David Reimer, 38; After Botched Surgery, He Was Raised as a Girl in Gender Experiment," *Los Angeles Times*, May 13, 2004; "Who was David Reimer?," *Intersex Society of North America*, http://www.isna.org/faq/reimer; John Colapinto, "Gender Gap," *Slate*, June 23, 2004. Sadly, David continued to be tormented by his childhood ordeal, and in 2004, at the age of thirty-eight, he took his own life.

19. Nuriddeen Knight, "An African-American Woman Reflects on the Transgender Movement, *Public Discourse*, June 4, 2015.

20. Riki Wilchins, "We'll Win the Bathroom Battle When the Binary Burns," *The Advocate*, April 29, 2016.

21. Fr. Mark Hodges, "NYC Will Fine Employers up to $250,000 for Referring to 'Transsexuals' by Their Natural Gender," *LifeSite News*, December 23, 2015. On the thirty-one genders, see Robert Gehl, "NYC Just Released a List of Officially Recognized Genders," *The Federalist Papers*, n.d., http://www.thefederalistpapers.org/us/nyc-just-released-a-list-of-officially-recognized-genders.

From the perspective of transsexuals, there are genuine concerns about bathrooms and locker rooms. Diamond Dee, a former transsexual who became a Christian, says he has a problem using the men's locker room at the gym because his body is so feminized due to his sex change operation and years of using female hormones. However, the best way to balance these concerns with the privacy rights of the majority of the population is to offer single-occupancy rooms for transgender people, just as most gyms offer single-occupancy rooms for families with young children. On Diamond Dee, see "Yes! Jesus Loves Transgenders:

The Diamond Dee Interview Part 2," YouTube video, 2:07, uploaded by triplexchurch on July 15, 2015.

22. Butler, *Gender Trouble*, passim; Carol Queen and Lawrence Schimel, eds., *PoMoSexuals* (San Francisco: Cleis Press, 1997).

23. Cited in Linda Markowitz, "A Different Kind of Queer Marriage," *Utne Reader*, September/October 2000. Markowitz writes,

> For years, lesbians, gay men, and bisexuals repeated like wind-up dolls: "Love is love, no matter what body it comes in, and we deserve equal rights." But the new "fluidity" of sexual identity leaves us in a state of linguistic confusion. Should an out, gay man who turns around and marries a woman continue to call himself gay? Should an out lesbian who turns around and marries a man continue to call herself a lesbian? This new breed of queer people struggle with what to call themselves, and the gay and lesbian community has strong reactions, no matter what label they end up taking on.

24. Butler, *Gender Trouble*, 9.

25. Gay activists have been debating this question among themselves for some time under the terms *essentialism* versus *constructivism*. Sexual essentialism sees sexual identity as a natural fact, an inherent, unchanging identity rooted in biology. Constructionism sees sexual identity as a social fact, a product of culture. For a summary, see Gayle Madwin, "What Is the Difference between Essentialist and Social Constructionist Techniques for Fighting Homophobia?" http://www.queerbychoice.com/essentialism.html.

26. Jorge Rivas, "Half of Young People Believe Gender Isn't Limited to Male and Female," *Fusion*, February 3, 2015.

27. Gene Edward Veith, "Identity Crisis: College Adminstrators Encourage Some Students to Rebel against Their 'Assigned' Gender Roles," *World*, March 27, 2004.

28. SIECUS, "Guidelines for Comprehensive Sexuality Education," 3rd ed., http://www.siecus.org/_data/global/images/guidelines.pdf, italics added.

29. Margot Adler, "Young People Push Back Against Gender Categories," *NPR*, July 16, 2013.

30. Lucy Mae Beers, "'Some Days Annie Is a Girl, Some Days Annie Is a Boy and Some Days She's Both': The 12-Year-Old Whose Gender Changes on a Daily Basis Depending on How They Feel," *Daily Mail*, March 23, 2016.

31. The Facebook diversity page, posted on February 15, 2014. Facebook kept increasing the number until it finally gave up trying to track the exploding number of gender identities and began to allow users to add their own gender identity.

32. Cited in John W. Kennedy, "The Transgender Moment: Evangelicals Hope to Respond with Both Moral Authority and Biblical Compassion to Gender Identity Disorder," *Christianity Today* 52, no. 2 (February 2008).

33. John Maddox, *What Remains to be Discovered* (New York: The Free Press, 1998), 252.

34. Mark Ridley, *The Cooperative Gene* (New York: The Free Press, 2001), 111.

35. Georg Wilhelm Friedrich Hegel, *The Philosophy of Right*, paragraph 342, https://www.utm.edu/staff/jfieser/class/316/pri/2-316-hegel.htm.

36. Friedrich Nietzsche, *Human All Too Human: A Book for Free Spirits* (1878), in *The Nietzsche Reader*, ed. Keith Ansell Pearson and Duncan Large, trans. Marion Faber (Oxford, UK: Blackwell, 2006), 162 [2].

37. Friedrich Nietzsche, *The Gay Science* (1882), http://www.lexido.com/EBOOK_TEXTS/THE_GAY_SCIENCE_FIFTH_BOOK_.aspx?S=357.

38. On historicism as Hegel's main legacy, see John McCumber, *Time and Philosophy*.

39. Jean Paul Sartre, "Existentialism Is a Humanism," (1946), in *Existentialism from Dostoeyvsky to Sartre*, ed. Walter Kaufman (London: Meridian, 1989).

40. Foucault died of AIDS in 1984. Butler describes herself as a "butch" lesbian and a "dyke" in "Maria Cyber Interviews Judith Butler," http://www.scribd.com/doc/56581872/Judith-Butler-Interview#scribd. She explains that she wrote *Gender Trouble* specifically to defend butch-femme lesbian relationships. See "The Body You Want: Liz Kotz Interviews Judith Butler," *Artforum* 31, no. 3 (November 1992): 82–89.

41. Judith Butler, *Bodies That Matter* (New York: Routledge, 1993), 58.

42. Butler, *Gender Trouble*, xxi, 31, viii, xiv, and passim.

43. Ibid., xx.

44. Carol Bigwood, "Renaturalizing the Body," *Body & Flesh*, 103.

45. Maxine Sheets-Johnson, "Corporeal Archetypes and Power," *Body & Flesh*, 150, 152, italics added.

46. Butler, *Gender Trouble*, 11, 12.

47. Hegel, *Philosophy of Right*, paragraph 344, cited in Robert C. Solomon, *Continental Philosophy Since 1750: The Rise and Fall of the Self* (Oxford: Oxford University Press, 1988), 57.

48. Butler, *Gender Trouble*, 9.

49. Chase Strangio, "What Is a 'Male Body'?" *Slate*, July 19, 2016.

50. See Terry Eagleton, *Illusions of Postmodernism* (Malden, MA: Blackwell, 1996), 14, 37, 38. Eagleton comments that, ironically, postmodernism claims to be "materialist and then . . . proceeds to suppress the most obviously materialist part of human beings, their biological make-up" (58).

51. Sheila Jeffreys, *Gender Hurts: A Feminist Analysis of the Politics of Transgenderism*, (New York: Routledge, 2014), 53.

52. Susan Bordo *Unbearable Weight: Feminism, Western Culture, and the Body* (Berkeley: University of California Press, 1993, 2003), 39, 245. Elizabeth Grosz says the effect of Butler's postmodern view "is to deny a materiality or a material specificity and determinateness to bodies . . . It is to make them infinitely pliable, malleable." *Volatile Bodies: Towards a Corporeal Feminism* (Bloomington: Indiana University Press, 1994), 190. Butler herself acknowledges that the main objection raised against her theory is that it "denies the materiality of the body" (Butler, *Bodies That Matter*, preface).

Critics of Foucault raise similar objections. They say his writings almost create the impression that sexuality is purely a social construct, created by social and power relations, with no relationship to the actual body. As Foucault notes in *History of Sexuality* (151ff), his critics often ask: Aren't you ignoring "the body, anatomy, the biological, the functional?" Don't you "speak of sex as if sex did not exist?" Foucault's answer is that though sex may begin with sheer anatomy and physiology, we have no access to the *meaning* of our bodies except through cultural constructs imposed by the structures of cultural power:

> Now, it is precisely this idea of sex *in itself* that we cannot accept without examination. Is 'sex' really the anchorage point that supports the manifestations of sexuality, or is it not rather a complex idea that was formed inside the deployment of sexuality? In any case, one could show how this idea of sex took form in the different strategies of power and the definite role it played therein.

53. Bordo, *Unbearable Weight*, 275. O'Donovan sums up this dualism as a "reductionism of the body to undifferentiated matter, on which the spirit proposed to exercise unlimited freedom." *Transsexualism and Christian Marriage*, 19.

54. "International Women's Day Protester Suddenly Realizes She's Reinforcing Harmful Social Construct of Gender," *The Babylon Bee*, March 8, 2017.

55. Laura Donnelly, "Don't Call Pregnant Women 'Expectant Mothers' As It Might Offend Transgender People, BMA [British Medical Association] Says," *The Telegraph*, January 29, 2017. See also Trevor MacDonald, "Transphobia in the Midwifery Community," *Huffington Post*, September 15, 2016.

56. Quoted in Brandon Showalter, "Transgender Policies Cause 'Erasure' of Females, 'Voyeurism,' 'Eugenics' on Children, Say Women's Rights Activists," *Christian Post*, February 19, 2017.

57. Interviewed in Claire Chretien, "Bathrooms Are Just the Beginning: A Scary Look into the Trans Movement's End Goals," *LifeSite News*, May 6, 2016. See also Stella Morabito, "A De-Sexed Society Is a De-Humanized Society," *Public Discourse*, May 25, 2016.

58. Andrew Malcolm, "Obama State Department deletes 'Mother, 'Father' from forms for More Correct 'Parent One, 'Parent Two'," *Los Angeles Times*, January 7, 2011. Responding to public protest, the State Department compromised and changed the form to read "Mother or Parent One" and "Father or Parent Two." See Matthew Lee, "State Department Steps Back on Gender-Neutral Parentage, Won't Replace Terms 'Mother,' 'Father,'" *Associated Press*, January 9, 2011.

59. Human Rights Campaign, "Sexual Orientation and Gender Identity Definitions," s.v. "Gender Identity," http://www.hrc.org/resources/sexual-orientation-and-gender-identity-terminology-and-definitions.

60. See Daniel Moody, *The Flesh Made Word* (CreateSpace Independent Publishing Platform), 2016.

61. Daniel Moody, "Why You Shouldn't Use Transgender Pronouns," *The Federalist*, October 18, 2016.

62. Eagleton, *Illusions of Postmodernism*,113, 116. Ironically, even Judith Butler came to see the problem. For years she rejected the concept of a universal human nature in favor of social constructivism. But while working for the International Gay and Lesbian Human Rights Commission, she came to realize that you cannot argue for human rights without some concept of what it means to be human—some concept of universal human nature (Butler, *Gender Trouble*, xviii).

63. Cited in Avery Dulles, "John Paul II and the Mystery of the Human Person," *America* 190, no. 3 (February 4, 2004).

64. Tikva Frymer-Kensky writes,

> The Bible presents no characteristics of human behavior as "female" or "male," no division of attributes between the poles of "feminine" and "masculine," no hint of distinctions of such polarities as male aggressivity-female receptivity, male innovation-female conservation, male out-thrusting-female containing, male subjecthood-female objecthood, male rationality-female emotionality, male product-female process, male achievement-female bonding, or any of the other polarities by which we are accustomed to think of gender distinctions. (Cited in Davidson, *Flame of Yahweh*, 221)

65. The father was an INFP (gentle, sensitive, emotional, relational) while the woman was an ESTJ (no-nonsense, take-charge, rational, assertive, organized). On the Myers-Briggs type indicator, there is only one personality trait that differs between men and women: More men test as T (rational, logical, objective) while more women test as F (emotional, sensitive, relational)—about 65 percent in each case. However, as the feminist movement made it more socially acceptable for women to be in leadership, more women began testing as T, which may suggest that this difference is at least partly cultural.

66. See also Nancy Pearcey, "A Plea for Changes in the Workplace," *Pro-Life Feminism: Different Voices*, ed. Gail Grenier Sweet (Toronto: Life Cycle Books, 1985); and Nancy Pearcey, "Why I Am Not a Feminist (Any More)," *Human Life Review*, Summer 1987.

67. Yarhouse, *Understanding Gender Dysphoria*, 155. See also Vaughan Roberts, *Transgender* (UK: The Good Book Company, 2016).

68. "All of the research on gender differences . . . consistently shows that, even when there are statistically significant differences between women and men, these differences pale in magnitude beside the variations *among* women and *among* men." Heather Looy and Hessel

Bouma III, "The Nature of Gender," cited in Yarhouse, *Understanding Gender Dysphoria*, 37, italics added.

69. Yarhouse, *Understanding Gender Dysphoria*, 154.

70. April Herndon, "Why Doesn't ISNA Want to Eradicate Gender?" Intersex Society of North America, FAQ, http://www.isna.org/faq/not_eradicating_gender.

71. A report filed to the European Commission in 2011 says, "Intersex people differ from trans people as their status is not gender related but instead relates to their biological makeup (genetic, hormonal and physical features)." Cited in Emily Greenhouse, "A New Era for Intersex Rights?," *The New Yorker*, December 30, 2013.

72. Megan DeFranza, *Sex Difference in Christian Theology: Male, Female, and Intersex in the Image of God* (Grand Rapids: Eerdmans, 2015), 144.

73. Ibid., 25, 30, 31, italics added.

74. Susan Donaldson James, "Intersex Children: Boy or Girl and Who Decides?," *ABC News*, March 17, 2011.

75. Lianne Simon's story is from personal communications and various articles on her website, http://www.liannesimon.com/.

76. See Charlotte Greenfield, "Should We 'Fix' Intersex Children?," *The Atlantic*, July 8, 2014. In some cases, individuals may not even know they are intersex because their external appearance is normal. They may not discover that their genetics are mixed until they marry and find they are infertile. For example, a woman with Complete Androgen Insensitivity Syndrome (CAIS) might not know that she's XY. In Scripture, she may well be the barren woman.

77. Personal communication, April 6, 2017. LGBT means lesbian, gay, bisexual, and transgender.

78. Sam Allberry, "What Christianity Alone Offers Transgender Persons," *The Gospel Coalition*, January 10, 2017.

79. The American College of Pediatricians writes, "According to the DSM-V, as many as 98% of gender confused boys and 88% of gender confused girls eventually accept their biological sex after naturally passing through puberty." American College of Pediatricians, "Gender Ideology Harms Children," updated August 17, 2016, http://www.acpeds.org/the-college-speaks/position-statements/gender-ideology-harms-children. According to another study, when children who reported transgender feelings were tracked without medical or surgical treatment at both Vanderbilt University and London's Portman Clinic, 70–80% of them spontaneously lost those feelings. Paul McHugh, "Transgender Surgery Isn't the Solution," *The Wall Street Journal*, updated May 13, 2016, and Paul McHugh, "Surgical Sex," *First Things*, November 2004.

Tragically, many transsexuals remain severely distressed and even suicidal after undergoing a sex change operation. See David Batty, "Sex Changes Are Not Effective, Say Researchers," *The Guardian*, July 30, 2004. A Swedish study from 2003 found that post-operative mortality and suicide rates for transsexuals are many times higher than the general population. (And that's in Sweden, which has a history of being supportive of transgender individuals.) See Yarhouse, *Understanding Gender Dysphoria*, 118.

80. "Transgender Kids: Who Knows Best?" *BBC*. There has been little, if any, research on children whose *parents* are transgender. See Denise Shick, "When My Father Told Me He Wanted to Be a Woman," *Public Discourse*, March 27, 2015.

81. The gender identity clinic at the Centre for Addiction and Mental Health (CAMH), Toronto, Canada, was closed in December 2015. Many observers believe it was because the clinic supported "desisters" (helping children feel comfortable in their own bodies) instead of practicing solely an "affirmative model" (facilitating cross-gender identity), which today is considered more politically correct. See Jesse Singal, "How the Fight over Transgender Kids Got a Leading Sex Researcher Fired," *New York Magazine*, February 7, 2016.

82. "Children who grow up to be nonheterosexual are substantially more gender nonconforming, on average, than children who grow up to be heterosexual." J. Michael Bailey et. al, "Sexual Orientation, Controversy, and Science" *Psychological Science in the Public Interest* 17 no. 2 (2016): 45–101.

What about men who were highly masculine before coming out as transgender, such as Bruce Jenner? The *Diagnostic and Statistical Manual of Mental Disorders (DSM-V)* divides people with gender dysphoria into two categories. Persons with early-onset gender dysphoria are gender nonconforming from early childhood. But they are also likely to resolve their feelings by adulthood. Persons with late-onset dysphoria were typically gender conforming through their childhood. In fact, they tend to be hyper-masculine, working in professions such as the military, law enforcement, or athletics. They often marry and have children before deciding to transition, and may engage in cross-dressing first. See Yarhouse, *Understanding Gender Dysphoria*, 96–99. Bruce (Caitlin) Jenner seems to be an example of the second category. See "'He'd Wear Women's Clothes, Shoes, and Lingerie': Bruce Jenner, 'the Secret Cross-Dresser,'" *The Daily Mail*, January 11, 2002.

Some people may experience cross-dressing as sexually arousing (that is, as a fetish). It may be this group that Scripture addresses when it says, "A woman must not wear man's clothing, nor a man wear women's clothing; for the Lord your God detests anyone who does this" (Deut. 22:5).

83. Yuan and Yuan, *Out of a Far Country*, 20.

84. "Most studies report that three times more men than women seek gender realignment." Nicola Tugnet et al., "Current Management of Male-to-Female Gender Identity Disorder in the UK," *Postgraduate Medical Journal* 83, no. 984 (October 2007). Both gender dysphoria and homosexuality have historically been more common among males than females, possibly because gender standards for males are narrower and stricter. It is far more socially accepted for a girl to be a tomboy than for a boy to be a "sissy" or "effeminate." In recent years, however, the rate of girls seeking treatment at gender clinics has skyrocketed. Several studies are summarized in this post: "Why Are More Girls Than Boys Presenting to Gender Clinics?" *4thWaveNow* (blog), July 10, 2015, https://4thwavenow.com/2015/07/10/why-are-more-girls-than-boys-presenting-to-gender-clinics/.

Some have suggested that 1 Corinthians 6:9, which uses the word "effeminate," might be applicable to transgendered persons. But Harper says the meaning of the Greek term cannot be directly translated: A *malakos*, "soft one," referred to someone who indulged in excessive pleasures. As an ancient document puts it, "above all and with the least self-control" he was possessed by "a sharp and scalding madness for sex, for coition with both women and with men." *From Shame to Sin*, 97–98.

85. Interview with Cari in "In Praise of Gatekeepers: An Interview with a Former Teen Client of TransActive Gender Center," *4thWaveNow*, April 21, 2016, https://4thwavenow.com/2016/04/21/in-praise-of-gatekeepers-an-interview-with-a-former-teen-client-of-transactive-gender-center/. Cari describes her detransition in this video: "Response to Julia Serano: Detransition, Desistance, and Disinformation," YouTube video, 17:02, uploaded by Cari Stella on August 9, 2016, https://www.youtube.com/watch?v=9L2jyEDwpEw.

86. Lou adds, "I didn't understand that the degree of disconnect from and hatred of my body could be considered a mental health problem." See the BBC film "Transgender Kids: Who Knows Best?" A 2014 study that found 62.7 percent of those diagnosed with gender dysphoria suffer from psychiatric axis 1 comorbid disorders, or mental illness—which means they should receive treatment for those mental disorders and not be fast-tracked into taking hormones or submitting to surgery. See Azadeh Mazaheri Meybodi, Ahmad Hajebi, and Atefeh

Ghanbari Jolfaei, "Psychiatric Axis I Comorbidities among Patients with Gender Dysphoria," *Psychiatry Journal*, August 2014.

One highly consistent—though surprising—finding is a connection between gender dysphoria and autism:

> One finding in transgender research has been robust: a connection between gender nonconformity and autism spectrum disorder (ASD). According to John Strang, a pediatric neuropsychologist with the Center for Autism Spectrum Disorders and the Gender and Sexuality Development Program at Children's National Health System in Washington, DC, children and adolescents on the autism spectrum are seven times more likely than other young people to be gender nonconforming. Conversely, children and adolescents at gender clinics are six to 15 times more likely than other young people to have ASD. (Henig, "How Science Is Helping Us Understand Gender")

87. Walt Heyer, "Transgender Characters May Win Emmys, But Transgender People Hurt Themselves," *The Federalist*, September 22, 2015. Other examples of sex change regret can be found in Stella Morabito, "Trouble in Transtopia: Murmurs of Sex Change Regret," *The Federalist*, November 11, 2014.

88. Walt Heyer, *Perfected with Love* (Maitland, FL: Xulon Press, 2009), 15.

89. See Tim Otto, *Oriented to Faith: Transforming the Conflict over Gay Relationships* (Eugene, OR: Wipf & Stock, 2014), 89.

90. Ibid., 7.

91. Mark Yarhouse and Trista Carrs, "MTF Transgender Christians' Experiences: A Qualitative Study," *Journal of LGBT Issues in Counseling* 6, no. 1 (January 2012).

Chapter 7 The Goddess of Choice Is Dead

1. Nancy Pearcey, "I Take You . . . A Review of Ted Peters's *For the Love of Children*," *First Things*, February 1998.

2. Contrary to Peters's claim, "adoption is not a contract. No one signs an adoption 'contract,' where one party agrees to deliver the child to another, who then has rights to the child. No. Adoption confers parental status permanently onto someone." Jennifer Roback Morse, "Privatizing Marriage Is Unjust to Children," *Public Discourse*, April 4, 2012.

3. Pearcey, "I Take You . . ."

4. Ibid.

5. Martha Albertson Fineman, *The Autonomy Myth* (New York: The New Press, 2005). Fineman's motive for wanting to transform family relations into contracts is to free women from caretaking tasks. She writes:

> One focus for the dissatisfaction with the privatization of dependency is the continuing unequal and gendered division of family labor, which burdens women more than men. Within the family, there is also delegation of responsibility, for dependency-caretaking has traditionally been and largely remains gendered work, assigned to those in the family roles of wife, mother, grandmother, daughter, and daughter-in-law. . . . Of course, my goal in developing arguments is ultimately to compel the state and the market to assume more (some) responsibility for dependency. (Martha Albertson Fineman, "Contract and Care," *Chicago-Kent Law Review* 76, no. 3, 1406–7)

Interestingly, a customer review on Amazon captures Fineman's message quite succinctly: "[I] have gained much insight into caretaking relationship instead of marriage. . . . Marriage is outdated and we need to overhaul this institution!!!"

6. Anthony Giddens, *The Third Way* (Cambridge, UK: Polity, 2000). Cass Sunstein, who served as President Obama's regulatory czar from 2009 to 2012, wrote in a book coauthored

by Richard Thaler, "We have argued that states should abolish 'marriage' as such and rely on civil unions instead"—which are covered by contract law. *Nudge: Improving Decisions about Health, Wealth, and Happiness* (New York: Penguin, 2008, 2009), 212, 117–118, 224. Sunstain adds, "Under our proposal, the word marriage would no longer appear in any laws, and marriage licenses would no longer be offered or recognized by any level of government" (217).

7. See John Witte, *From Sacrament to Contract: Marriage, Religion, and Law in the Western Tradition* (Louisville: Westminster John Knox, 1997).

8. See Steven Forde, *Locke, Science, and Politics* (Cambridge, UK: Cambridge University Press, 2013). The atomistic philosophers of the scientific revolution were intentionally reviving ancient Greek atomism, especially that taught by Epicurus, who likewise applied his philosophy to social life, teaching a radical individualism in which humans are not naturally social beings but are autonomous "atoms." See David Koyzis, *Political Visions and Illusions* (Downers Grove, IL: InterVarsity Press, 2003), 48–49.

9. Locke inspired the American Revolution; Rousseau inspired the French Revolution. Today conservatives tend to follow Locke and liberals tend to follow Rousseau. See Kim Holmes, "The Great Divide: The Ideological Legacies of the American and French Revolutions," *The Heritage Foundation*, August 12, 2014, http://www.heritage.org/political-process/report/the-great-divide-the-ideological-legacies-the-american-and-french.

In much of the rest of the world, what Americans call conservatism (an emphasis on individual liberties) is still denoted by the term *liberalism*, while what Americans call liberalism (the expansion of government under the welfare state) is called *social democracy*, indicating its roots in socialism. In America, however, even the welfare state is not justified by an appeal to socialism but by an appeal to individualism—as a means for maximizing individual opportunity for those who are disadvantaged. See Koyzis, *Political Visions and Illusions*, 60.

10. Eric O. Springsted, *The Act of Faith: Christian Faith and the Moral Self* (Grand Rapids: Eerdmans, 2002), x.

11. The following section is based on my book *Total Truth*, appendix 1, "How American Politics Became Secularized." See also Nancy Pearcey, "The Creation Myth of Modern Political Philosophy," speech presented at the Sixth Annual Kuyper lecture, sponsored by the Center for Public Justice, 2000, http://www.arn.org/docs/pearcey/np_creationmyth0801.htm.

12. Thomas Hobbes, *On the Citizen*, ed. Richard Tuck and Michael Silverthorne (New York: Cambridge University Press, 1998), 102.

13. John Hallowell, *Main Currents in Modern Political Thought* (Lanham, MD: University Press of America, 1984), 102–3.

14. George Grant, *English-Speaking Justice* (Toronto, ON: House of Anansi Press, 1974, 1975), 16, 19.

15. Michael Zuckert, *The Natural Rights Republic* (Notre Dame: University of Notre Dame Press, 1996), 29.

16. In recent years, social contract theory was infused with new life when John Rawls proposed an influential modern version of it in *A Theory of Justice*, rev. ed. (Cambridge, MA: Belknap Press, 1999). Despite some new features, Rawls's version still treats humans primarily as rational calculators of their self-interest.

17. Michael Sandel, *Democracy's Discontent* (Cambridge, MA: Harvard University Press, 1996).

18. Mary Ann Glendon, *Rights Talk* (New York: Simon and Schuster, 1991), 48. Other nations, Glendon notes, have privacy laws that treat humans as having a social dimension, and thus they give greater support and protection to our social relationships. For example, many nations require a woman considering an abortion to receive counseling about alternatives that would give her services and support to continue the pregnancy and give birth.

By contrast, the US Supreme Court has struck down such requirements as a violation of women's "privacy."

19. For statistics, see W. Bradford Wilcox, "Suffer the Little Children: Cohabitation and the Abuse of America's Children," *Public Discourse*, April 22, 2011.

20. Oliver O'Donovan, *Desire of the Nations: Rediscovering the Roots of Political Theology* (Cambridge, UK: Cambridge University Press, 1996), 276.

21. John Hallowell, *The Moral Foundation of Democracy* (Chicago: University of Chicago Press, 1954), 85.

22. Bertrand de Jouvenal, as cited in Joyce Appleby, *Capitalism and a New Social Order: The Republican Vision of the 1790s* (New York: New York University Press, 1984), 36.

23. See Jennifer Roback Morse, *Love and Economics: Why the Laissez-Faire Family Doesn't Work* (Dallas: Spence Publishing, 2001). Similar critiques of social contract theory are made by feminist authors such as Virginia Held, *Feminist Morality* (Chicago: University of Chicago Press, 1993) and Christine Di Stefano, *Configurations of Masculinity: A Feminist Perspective on Modern Political Theory* (Ithaca, NY: Cornell University Press, 1991).

24. Lindy West, "I Set Up #ShoutYourAbortion Because I Am Not Sorry, and I Will Not Whisper," *The Guardian*, September 22, 2015.

25. Sasharusa, "The Fetus Is a Parasite," *Daily Kos*, April 15, 2012; Eileen McDonagh, *Breaking the Abortion Deadlock: From Choice to Consent* (New York: Oxford University Press, 1996). But Peter Baklinski counters that argument:

> Science paints a vastly different picture about the actual relationship between a baby in utero and his or her mother, showing that, far from being a parasite, the unborn child can help heal his mother for the rest of her life, as beneficial cells from the child pass into the mother's body during pregnancy. . . . One kind of fetal cells that enter into the mother's body is the baby's stem cells. Stem cells have what Pinctott calls "magical properties" in that they can "morph" into other types of cells through a process called differentiation. The baby's fetal stem cells can actually become the mother's own cells that make up her liver, heart, or brain. . . . The baby's fetal stem cells migrate to the mother's injured sites and offer themselves as a healing remedy, becoming part of the mother's very body. (Peter Baklinski, "Just a 'Parasite'? Cutting Edge Science Shows Fetal Cells Heal Mother for Life," *LifeSite News*, January 4, 2012)

26. Lee and George, *Body-Self Dualism in Contemporary Ethics and Politics*, 147, 149. As David Crawford writes, liberalism assumes "that, when it comes to public institutions and actions, the human person is *essentially* without gender or family. He can be connected to these only by an act of choice, treated as entirely arbitrary from the public standpoint." Thus liberalism "tacitly presupposes a dualistic view of man according to which the body is reduced to sub-personal matter to be privately related to the free and spiritual domain of the person by an act of choice or by a given person's innate preferences." "Recognizing the Roots of Society in the Family, the Foundation of Justice," *Communio* 34 (Fall 2007): 409.

27. M. Galbally, A. J. Lewis, M. V. Ijzendoorn, and M. Permezel, "The Role of Oxytocin in Mother-Infant Relations: A Systematic Review of Human Studies," *Harvard Review of Psychiatry* 19, no. 1 (January–February, 2011).

28. Alan Boyle, "This Is Your Brain on Fatherhood: Dads Experience Hormonal Changes Too, Research Shows," *NBC Science News*, June 15, 2013.

29. Nathan Rabin, "Fatherhood Killed the Cynic in Me," *Yahoo News*, July 4, 2015.

30. *The Magnificent Seven*, directed by John Sturges (Beverly Hills, CA: United Artists, 1960).

31. Meilander, *Bioethics*, 13–14.

32. Jean-Jacques Rousseau, *A Discourse on Inequality* (New York: Penguin, 1984), 92.

33. Richard Posner, *Sex and Reason* (Cambridge, MA: Harvard University Press, 1992), 131. In 2000, Fred Shapiro, a librarian at Yale Law School, calculated that Posner was the most cited legal scholar "of all time" by a wide margin. See Lincoln Caplan, "Rhetoric and Law, *Harvard Magazine* (January–February 2016).

34. Helen Croydon, "It's Time to Ditch Monogamy," *New Republic*, April 25, 2014.

35. United States Census Bureau, "Women's Marital Status," https://www.census.gov/content/dam/Census/library/visualizations/time-series/demo/families-and-households/ms-1b.pdf; "Men's Marital Status," https://www.census.gov/content/dam/Census/library/visualizations/time-series/demo/families-and-households/ms-1a.pdf.

36. Barbara Dafoe Whitehead and David Popenoe, "Sex without Strings, Relationships without Rings: Today's Young Singles Talk about Mating and Dating," *Report of the National Marriage Project* (New Brunswick: Rutgers University, 2000), 6.

37. Napp Nazworth, "Fatherlessness Harms the Brain, Neurobiologists Find," *Christian Post*, December 11, 2013. See also "The Consequences of Fatherlessness," The National Center for Fathering, http://www.fathers.com/statistics-and-research/the-consequences-of-fatherlessness/; David Blankenhorn, *Fatherless America: Confronting Our Most Urgent Social Problem* (New York: Basic Books, 1995); Elizabeth Marquardt, *Between Two Worlds: The Inner Lives of Children of Divorce* (New York: Crown Books, 2005); W. Bradford Wilcox, ed., *When Marriage Disappears: The Retreat from Marriage in Middle America* (Charlottesville, VA: University of Virginia, National Marriage Project; New York: Institute for American Values, 2010); Mary Eberstadt, *Adam and Eve After the Pill: Paradoxes of the Sexual Revolution* (San Francisco: Ignatius Press, 2012); Glenn Stanton, *Why Marriage Matters* (Colorado Springs: Pinon Press, 1997). A recent article sums up the findings:

> Research by Penn State sociologist Paul Amato (2005) on the long-term damage to children from divorce demonstrated that, if the United States enjoyed the same level of family stability as it did in 1960, the nation would have 70,000 fewer suicide attempts in youth every year, about 600,000 fewer kids receiving therapy and 500,000 fewer acts of teenage delinquency. . . . Adults are also vulnerable to suicidal thinking and acts after divorce. A 2010 study from Rutgers of suicide among middle-aged Americans found divorce rates have doubled for middle-aged and older adults since the 1990s, leading to social isolation. This study showed that in 2005 unmarried middle-aged men were 3.5 times more likely than married men to die from suicide and their female counterparts were as much as 2.8 times more likely to kill themselves." (Rick Fitzgibbons, "Divorce Is Killing Our Children, but We're Too Drowned in PC Nonsense to Talk about It," *LifeSite News*, May 5, 2016)

38. For more on these and related studies, see Ryan Anderson, *Truth Overruled: The Future of Marriage and Religious Freedom* (Washington, DC: Regnery, 2015), 30–31.

39. Sara McLanahan and Gary Sandafur, *Growing Up with a Single Parent: What Hurts, What Helps* (Cambridge, MA: Harvard University Press, 1994), 38.

40. Rabbi Jonathan Sacks, "The Love That Brings New Life into the World," transcript, November 17, 2014, http://www.rabbisacks.org/love-brings-new-life-world-rabbi-sacks-institution-marriage/.

41. For more on these and related studies, see Anderson, *Truth Overruled*, 32.

42. For this and related studies, see Stanton, *Why Marriage Matters*, 81, and Linda Waite and Maggie Gallagher, *The Case for Marriage: Why Married People Are Happier, Healthier, and Better Off Financially* (New York: Random House, Doubleday, 2000).

43. Cited in Mark Oppenheimer, "A Gay Catholic Voice Against Same-Sex Marriage," *New York Times*, June 5, 2010.

44. For a presentation of arguments for marriage, see Sherif Girgis, Ryan T. Anderson, and Robert P. George, *What Is Marriage? Man and Woman: A Defense* (New York: Encounter Books, 2012). A common argument is that the only difference between same-sex and opposite-sex unions is that the former are infertile—and since infertile opposite-sex couples are legally permitted to marry, it is right that same-sex couples are legally permitted to marry as well. But until the rise of the homosexual movement, no one thought the existence of infertile couples justified same-sex unions. Why not? Historically, the state has licensed the *kind* of union that leads to children. To inquire into the fertility of each couple presenting themselves for marriage would be massively intrusive and invasive of privacy. Moreover, most couples do not know if they are infertile until after they have been married for several years. And even if they intend not to have children when they get married, they often change their minds. Almost ninety percent of married couples do have children. So the rational course is what states have historically done: License the male-female union because it is the only *kind* of relationship that can lead to children, even if it does not always do so.

45. Judge Vaughn Walker, *Perry v. Schwarzenegger*, 591 F.3d 1126 (9th Cir. 2009), 67.

46. Cited in Blankenhorn, *Future of Marriage*, 122.

47. Andrew Sullivan, "Introduction," *Same-Sex Marriage: Pro and Con*, ed. Andrew Sullivan (New York: Vintage Books, 1997, 2004), xxiii.

48. Katz, *Invention of Heterosexuality*, 186–87.

49. Ibid., 187.

50. Cited in Blankenhorn, *Future of Marriage*, 133.

51. Johanna Dasteel, "Homosexual Activist Says Gay 'Marriage' Isn't about Equality, It's about Destroying Marriage," *LifeSite News*, May 1, 2013.

52. J. Richard Pearcey, "The Revolt of Intelligence Against 'Marriage Equality,'" *The Pearcey Report*, March 18, 2013. This article first appeared in *American Thinker*.

53. One study found that "82 percent of gay men had had sex with someone other than their main partner." What about marital breakups? A study from Norway and Sweden, which have sanctioned same-sex partnerships since the 1990s, found that gay male relationships are 50 percent more likely to break up than heterosexual marriages, while lesbian relationships are 167 percent more likely to break up than heterosexual marriages. (No, that is not a typo.) Stanton L. Jones, "Same-Sex Science," *First Things*, February 2012. See also Hanna Rosin, "The Dirty Little Secret: Most Gay Couples Aren't Monogamous," *Slate*, June 26, 2013.

54. For more information on this study, see Corvino and Gallagher, *Debating Same-Sex Marriage*, 136.

55. Scott James, "Many Successful Gay Marriages Share an Open Secret," *New York Times*, January 28, 2010.

56. "The masses grew out of the fragments of a highly atomized society. . . . The chief characteristic of the mass man is not brutality and backwardness, but his isolation and lack of normal social relationships." Hannah Arendt, *The Origins of Totalitarianism* (New York: Harcourt Brace, 1951), 310–11.

57. Abigail Rine, "What Is Marriage to Evangelical Millennials?" *First Things*, May 14, 2015.

58. Cited in Blankenhorn, *Future of Marriage*, 213.

59. Dawn Stefanowicz, "A Warning from Canada: Same-Sex Marriage Erodes Fundamental Rights," *Public Discourse*, April 24, 2015.

60. Ibid.

61. Heather Barwick, "Dear Gay Community: Your Kids Are Hurting," *The Federalist*, March 17, 2015. Katy Faust, another adult child of a lesbian and her partner, writes:

> I identify with the instinct of those children to be protective of their gay parent. In fact, I've done it myself. I remember how many times I repeated my speech: "I'm

> so happy that my parents got divorced so that I could know all of you wonderful women." I quaffed the praise and savored the accolades. The women in my mother's circle swooned at my maturity, my worldliness. I said it over and over, and with every refrain my performance improved. It was what all the adults in my life wanted to hear. I could have been the public service announcement for gay parenting. I cringe when I think of it now, because it was a lie. My parents' divorce has been the most traumatic event in my thirty-eight years of life. ("Dear Justice Kennedy: An Open Letter from the Child of a Loving Gay Parent," *Public Discourse*, February 2, 2015)

Morabito writes, "Whenever a parent is missing—for whatever reason—a child feels a primal wound." Same-sex parenting "requires that such children bear that burden alone and repress their primal wound in silence." "15 Reasons 'Marriage Equality' Is about Neither Marriage Nor Equality," *The Federalist*, June 26, 2015.

62. United Nations, "Universal Declaration of Human Rights" (General Assembly resolution 217 A), December 10, 1948, http://www.un.org/en/universal-declaration-human-rights/.

63. Douglas NeJaime, "With Ruling on Marriage Equality, Fight for Gay Families Is Next," *Los Angeles Times*, June 26, 2015.

64. Jennifer Roback Morse, "4 Questions about Surrogacy for Conservatives Who Support Gay Marriage," *The Daily Caller*, June 2, 2015; see also Jennifer Roback Morse, "Privatizing Marriage Will Expand the Role of the State," *Public Discourse*, April 3, 2012.

65. Stella Morabito, "Bait and Switch: How Same Sex Marriage Ends Family Autonomy," *The Federalist*, April 9, 2014.

66. Alberta Government, "Guidelines for Best Practices," 2016, https://education.alberta.ca/media/1626737/91383-attachment-1-guidelines-final.pdf. For example, "School forms, websites, letters, and other communications use non-gendered and inclusive language (e.g., parents/guardians, caregivers, families, partners, "student" or "their" instead of Mr., Ms., Mrs., mother, father, him, her, etc.)."

67. Brian Mattson, "The Family's Fair-Weather Friends, Part 2," *Dr. Brian Mattson*, June 30, 2015, http://drbrianmattson.com/journal/2015/6/30/the-familys-fair-weather-friends-part-two.

68. Jean C. Lloyd, "The Wrong Kind of Rights: Same-Sex Marriage, Third-Party Reproduction, and the Sexualization of Children," *Public Discourse*, May 5, 2015.

69. Rae and Cox, *Bioethics*, 105. See also Nancy Pearcey, "Technology, History, and Worldview," *Genetic Ethics*.

70. Rickard Newman, "Journey to Baby Gammy: How We Justify a Market in Children," *Public Discourse*, August 18, 2014.

71. Peters, *For the Love of Children*, 54, 72.

72. For example, Steven Ertelt, "Lesbian Couple Asks Surrogate to Abort Baby after Learning She Had Down Syndrome," *LifeSite News*, September 2, 2014.

73. Meilander, *Bioethics*, 19, 21.

74. Morse, "The Sexual Revolution Reconsidered," 47.

75. On the social implications of the Trinity, see my books *Total Truth*, 132–33, 138, and *Finding Truth*, 130–31, 209–12; and Stanley Grenz, *The Social God and the Relational Self: A Trinitarian Theology of the Imago Dei* (Louisville: Westminster John Knox, 2001). See also John D. Zizioulas, *Being As Communion: Studies in Personhood and the Church* (Crestwood, NY: St. Vladimir's Seminary Press, 1985); Miroslav Volf, *After Our Likeness: The Church as the Image of the Trinity* (Grand Rapids: Eerdmans, 1998), especially chapter 5, "Trinity and Church."

76. Wyatt, "What Is a Person?"

77. Cited in Taylor, *Sources of the Self*, 223, 224, 226.

78. Timothy Ware, *The Orthodox Church* (London, UK: Penguin, 1997), 240; Kallistos [Timothy] Ware, *The Orthodox Way* (Crestwood, NY: St. Vladimir's Seminary Press, 2002), 38–39.

79. Sam R. Williams, "A Christian Psychology of and Response to Homosexuality," October 2011, https://identifynetwork.org/wp-content/uploads/2015/07/A-Christian-Psychology-and-Response-to-Homosexuality.pdf.

80. One reason the modern family is fragile is that it has lost many of its former functions, such as educating children, working together in a family industry, caring for the sick and the elderly, and so on. Today all that's left is emotional connection, and that is not enough. Many homeschoolers are driven by a larger vision of renewing the family by recovering the family's traditional functions. See my book *Total Truth*, chapter 12, and my article, "Is Love Enough? Recreating the Economic Base of the Family," *The Family in America* 4, no. 1 (January 1990), http://www.arn.org/docs/pearcey/np_familyinamerica.htm.

81. Alysse ElHage, "How Could Going to Church Help My Family?" *I Believe in Love*, December 3, 2015.

82. Rosaria Butterfield, interviewed by Phillip Holmes, "A Safe Place for Sexual Sinners," *Desiring God*, January 7, 2016. See also Rosaria Butterfield, *The Secret Thoughts of an Unlikely Convert* (Pittsburg: Cross and Crown, 2012).

83. According to the Institute for Sexual Minority Studies and Services at the University of Alberta, between 20 and 40 percent of homeless youth are LGBTQ. "The number one reason for homelessness is parental rejection," said director Kris Wells. Quoted in Erika Stark, "Calgary Parents Gather to Discuss LGBTQ Guidelines," *CBC News*, March 22, 2016.

84. Alasdair MacIntyre, *After Virtue*, 3rd ed. (Notre Dame: University of Notre Dame Press, 2007), 263. For an updated and detailed vision of Christians rebuilding from the local level up, see Rod Dreher, *The Benedict Option* (New York: Penguin, 2017).

Index

About the Author

Nancy R. Pearcey is author of *Total Truth*, winner of the 2005 ECPA Gold Medallion Award for best book on Christianity and Society. She also won the 2000 ECPA Gold Medallion Award for *How Now Shall We Live?* (coauthored with Chuck Colson and novelist Harold Fickett). Her other books include *The Soul of Science* and *Saving Leonardo: A Call to Resist the Secular Assault on Mind, Morals, and Meaning*. Her most recent is *Finding Truth: 5 Principles for Unmasking Atheism, Secularism & Other God Substitutes*.

Pearcey has contributed chapters to several books and has published over one hundred articles in outlets such as the *Washington Post*, the *Washington Times*, *First Things*, *American Thinker*, *Human Events*, *Christianity Today*, *Books & Culture*, *World*, *Human Life Review*, *American Enterprise*, *The Daily Caller*, and *Regent University Law Review*. She appears frequently on radio and television, including *Fox & Friends*, NPR, and C-SPAN.

Heralded as "America's pre-eminent evangelical Protestant female intellectual" (*The Economist*), Nancy has addressed staffers on Capitol Hill and at the White House; actors and screenwriters in Hollywood; scientists at labs such as Sandia and Los Alamos; artists at the International Arts Movement; students and faculty at universities such as Princeton, Stanford, Dartmouth, USC, Ohio State, the University of Georgia, and St. John's College; and educational and activist groups including the Heritage Foundation in Washington, DC.

Pearcey is professor of apologetics and scholar in residence at Houston Baptist University; editor at large of *The Pearcey Report*; and a fellow at the Discovery Institute. Previous positions include visiting scholar at Biola University's Torrey Honors Institute, professor of worldview studies at Cairn University, and the Francis A. Schaeffer Scholar at the World Journalism Institute.

Formerly an agnostic, Nancy studied Christian worldview at L'Abri Fellowship in Switzerland under Francis Schaeffer. She earned a BA from Iowa State University, an MA from Covenant Theological Seminary, and pursued further graduate work in the history of philosophy at the Institute for Christian Studies in Toronto. In 2007 she received an honorary doctoral degree from Cairn University.

From 1977 to 1990 Pearcey wrote articles for the Bible-Science Association on the intersection of science and worldview. From 1991 to 1999 she was founding editor of the daily radio program *BreakPoint*, where she wrote over one thousand commentaries and headed up a team of writers. For seven years she coauthored a monthly column with Chuck Colson in *Christianity Today*.

Nancy and her husband, Rick, have two sons, both of whom were homeschooled.

CONNECT WITH

Nancy

To learn more about Nancy's writing and speaking, visit **NANCYPEARCEY.COM** or **PEARCEYREPORT.COM**

Nancy.Pearcey.7

NancyRPearcey